The
Jersey Lily

Also by Pierre Sichel

SUCH AS WE

THE
JERSEY LILY

The Story of the Fabulous Mrs. Langtry

PIERRE SICHEL

*"Oh, never, never, never since we joined
the human race
Saw we so exquisitely fair a face."*
—W. S. GILBERT, *Iolanthe*

Englewood Cliffs, N. J.
PRENTICE-HALL, INC.

Printed in the United States of America

50937

For my mother and father

ACKNOWLEDGMENTS

I wish to thank Theron W. Raines for his invaluable advice while I was writing this book. For important information pertaining to Mrs. Langtry, I am particularly indebted to Alfred Lunt. For their guidance and kindness in making available material, I owe thanks to Paul Myers of the Theatre Collection of the New York Public Library and Miss May Davenport Seymour, Curator of the Theatre and Music Collection of the Museum of the City of New York.

Helpful information was furnished by Mrs. Helen R. Goss, Miss May Hallatt, Miss Sybil Thorndike, Lawrence Lader, Anita Leslie, John Leslie, Jack Winsor Hansen, Arthur William Row, Emil McCabe, Kenneth Northcott, the Very Reverend M. Le Marinel (Rector of St. Helier and Dean of Jersey), Reverend J. S. Norman (Rector of St. Saviour, Isle of Jersey), Robert A. Hug, R. W. Alston, Helen Clarke, Madison C. Bates, Lt. Col. George I. Malcolm, Victor N. Malcolm, John Maas, Mary A. Benjamin, *The Illustrated London News,* The British Information Service in New York, and many others.

PIERRE SICHEL

one

Lᴵᴸᴸᴵᴱ could not pass the stationer's shop in St. Helier without looking at the photographs of the London society beauties in the window. She was particularly intrigued by the glamorous Lady Dudley, a fairy figure and part of an enchanted world. Lady Dudley wore beautiful clothes and went to parties with the Prince of Wales. She flitted about the great city, driven in a glittering carriage pulled by coal-black horses, rich, lovely, envied and acclaimed by all.

The sturdy twelve-year-old girl pushed back her long, golden-brown hair and scowled at her faint reflection in the shop window. Now she looked exactly as Quess, Jersey's best photographer, had caught her. Thinking of Lady Dudley's perfection, she groaned. Who was this wolfish creature with her mass of hair pulled back full and tight, the strained look about the eyes, the twisted line of the mouth, the harsh features? Not Lillie Le Breton, but someone Quess had frozen there with his dictatorial commands of "Hold still! *Please* hold still, Miss." She tried a smile to soften the unflattering reflection. Approaching footsteps made her start. Lillie concentrated on Lady Dudley's photograph, a flush mounting to her face as she put a hand over the eye Reggie had blackened in one of their frequent brother-sister scuffles.

The women coming back from the old glass-roofed native market, fish-net bags filled with produce, glanced knowingly at the girl staring fixedly at the display photographs. A healthy, blooming, lively girl, the sixth child and only daughter of Emilie Davis Martin Le Breton and William Corbet Le Breton,

Dean of the Isle of Jersey and Rector of St. Saviour's Parish. Born at the rectory October 13, 1853, she'd been christened Emilie Charlotte after her mother and grandmother. They'd started calling her Lillie because it was short for Emilie—or maybe it was because of her lily-white complexion; Mrs. Le Breton wasn't sure. Anyway, the nickname suited her, and the little thing thought Emilie Charlotte dreadful. Right from the beginning she'd had a mind of her own. Naturally she'd turned into an incorrigible, harum-scarum tomboy.

What else could you expect from a girl with six unruly brothers as an example? Mrs. Le Breton was much too easygoing; and the dean, no disciplinarian. Such a vague, dreamy, holy man! Madame Bisson, the family governess, had managed Lillie for a while. Now she had tutors and was taught at home. Her brothers attended Victoria College (Jersey's public school), but she ran wild just like them. Pets all over the rectory, the boys tarring and feathering the statue in Royal Square, Lillie and Reggie playing ghosts in St. Saviour's churchyard at midnight, scaring neighbors half to death. Then hadn't she and her younger brother stolen door knockers until mass complaints to the dean forced their return? And that famous rectory tea when the two set up a string by the door just the right height to knock off the men's top hats.

Exactly the sort of thing one could count on from the children of a saintly man who thought everybody was good because he was good himself. But that girl—really! Riding astride up and down the lanes, playing cricket, sailing, swimming, fighting just like a boy. And taking a dare from young Reggie and running down the rectory lane at night—like Lady Godiva without her horse! No good could come from such actions. Well might the child moon over Lady Dudley. She'd never be a lady, rich *or* beautiful.

At fourteen, Lillie's striking chestnut hair, her height, her comparatively full figure gave her a deceptive maturity. She insisted on participating in Jersey's social events—the leisurely beach picnics, the carefully chaperoned dances, the other gatherings of young people. Sensing that the boys liked her, she forgot to be the hoyden. Her brothers Frank, William, Trevor, Maurice, and Clement had left the island. Reginald, two years her junior, was still her favorite, but was neglected more and more as a companion while she became a young lady. It was good to be popular. Boys! Not one measured up to the Lochinvar she dreamed would come to the island and spirit her away. On clear days you could see the French coast to the east. England was over a hundred miles away, far out beyond St. Aubin's Bay off St. Helier, where the blue water turned to shimmering gold in the sunlight. London. There lay her destiny.

Her Lochinvar would be handsome. He would have to be rich and titled, because if you weren't of the nobility, an aristocrat or landed *seigneur,* you weren't anything in London. Lillie was drawn to Lord Suffield, Lord Ranelagh, and their families who often wintered in their great stone manor houses in Jersey. She liked to ride with their daughters. They were friends, but not good friends or even equals, for she was only Lillie Le Breton, the dean's daughter.

Nothing pleased her so much as her first real compliment, received while they sat picnicking on the beach. Lord Suffield studied her, and she blushed under his appraising eyes. "Do you know, Miss Le Breton, that you are very, very beautiful?" he said, pulling at his mustache. "You ought to have a season in London."

Mama thought so, too. Papa had been born in Jersey and had come home after being educated in England and for a short time holding St. Olave's Parish in London. London! Mama had lived in Chelsea until her marriage. When she spoke of London—the Tower, Buckingham Palace, kings and queens, lords and ladies—there was the strangest gleam in her eyes.

Lillie thought she was ready for a London season. She had a number of beaus, several of whom had proposed to her. One of them, Lieutenant Charles Longley of the military detachment, thought his chances especially good because he was the son of the Archbishop of Canterbury. How shocked he was when she smilingly confessed her age.

She was sixteen the year Mrs. Le Breton decided to combine a visit to London with acceptance of an invitation from the

3

daughters of Lord Suffield. Lillie had never been away from Jersey, never seen or traveled on a train. London dazzled her. The sights and sounds, the hustle and bustle, the traffic, crowded streets, the shops were overpowering. Never had she felt so much the crass, confused islander unable to compete with her city betters. The feeling carried over to Lord Suffield's luxurious home and the ball he gave in her honor. She felt completely eclipsed, almost dowdy in the simple gown made for her by Madame Nicolle, St. Helier's most fashionable dressmaker. She didn't know how to carry herself or what to say to the uncommunicative young men who danced with her. She was a big, repressed rustic, a peasant-costumed, *patois*-talking milkmaid to Jersey cows—and this was a nightmare without end.

As if by rebound, part rebellion, part shame, Lillie reverted to the active, outdoor life she had always enjoyed. The Le Bretons worried at the re-emergence of the tomboy, and Mr. Cooke, her tutor, scolded. Now she spent most of her time with her young brother Reggie. He was understanding, as always. For him no explanations were necessary, nor could she have confided in him. Her failure in London was too personal, hurt too much.

Her confidence shaken, Lillie spent the next years dreaming and floundering in the miasma of adolescence, quietly studying and readjusting her blurred sights on an uncertain future. At twenty, she was a lovely young woman on an island noted for its comely women. She seemed unaware of her looks, which existed as something dormant, something below the surface. Tall, limber, athletic, with a strikingly fair skin and perfect complexion, her eyes were violet-gray, her lips well formed, her chin charmingly firm, and her profile cameo-like and delicately chiseled. A classic face with beauty in the bone as well. Her figure, gracefully feminine and full-proportioned, was intensified by her challengingly erect bearing. She carried her shapely, well-poised head regally, its long bronze tresses either piled high or in a simple bun at the nape. She had changed in four years, but the memory of Lord Suffield's ball

4

still rankled. She never thought of London without a pang. She had thrilled to it and feared it, loved it and hated it. Some day she would go back, and then . . .

Dean Le Breton had an errand in St. Helier that January morning in 1874. It was cold and blustery, the driving rain intermittent, and he was glad to have Lillie accompany him. It pleased her to walk in the storm so much like her own spirit. Riding with Reggie, working with Mr. Cooke, reciting Shakespeare in the evening with her father, she appeared a happy young woman. But banked fires burned within. She wore a mask which deceived everyone, perhaps even herself.

They walked through the drenched and deserted streets to the waterfront, where flags and standards whipped crazily, gulls knifed at strange angles in the wind overhead, and crafts of all kinds tossed at their moorings. Beyond Elizabeth Castle, which stuck up like Mont-Saint-Michel on its rocky islet in St. Aubin's Bay, the water was white and turbulent. A knot of men were gathered on the quay pointing out to sea. It was inevitable that they should attract the attention of the respected dean.

Lillie squinted and strained into the wind where the men pointed. It seemed that she could see a tiny triangle of sail, but she couldn't be sure. Yes, there it was! Then it vanished and, ignoring the pelting rain, she kept her eyes fixed on the spot until it reappeared. Sheets of water crashed over the bow, the yacht bucked and rolled, and the mast shuddered as the wind bellied the sails. They hung slack for an instant, then filled out again, heeling the boat over, far over—almost perpendicular— as the wind howled in from another quarter. She was going over, she was over. . . .

Someone had handed the dean a telescope and now Lillie snatched it from his hand. She fiddled excitedly with the eyepiece. There! Three men on the deck—no, four, and the fourth appeared to be giving orders to the crew.

The rain shot down harder, the wind shrieked through the rigging of the boats at anchor. Gray clouds scudded swiftly across the low, overcast sky. Where was—she was gone! Frantically, Lillie swung the telescope back and forth. Had she really gone down? No, there was the yacht hanging on her

5

beam-ends like an overturned model in a park basin. Lillie's gaze passed over three soaked crewmen to focus on the fourth, a bare-headed, black-haired man with a white scarf streaming back over his shoulders as though he were a knight in the lists. Stalwart and unafraid, he stood at the wheel, fighting the gale. Lillie trembled and fought with him. The words popped into her head:

> Oh, young Lochinvar is come out of the west,
> Through all the wide border his steed is the best,
> And save his good broadsword, he—

"They'll get in now," said a rough voice. "Look like good sailors."

The big, white yacht was close in now, dwarfing every craft in the harbor as she loomed toward them. Lillie made out her name. *Red Gauntlet.* How appropriate! Now the rain slackened. The wind eased off, and the dirty-gray clouds parted as the sun forced its way through to illuminate the glistening sails with an unearthly sheen. Lillie felt so happy she wanted to shout. She moved off to stand apart from the cheering onlookers, her hair flowing in the wind, a secret smile on her lips.

Much later a feline biographer put words into Lillie's mouth. "One day," she was quoted, "there came into the harbor of St. Helier on the Isle of Jersey a most beautiful yacht. I met the owner and fell in love with the yacht. To become the mistress of the yacht, I married the owner, Edward Langtry." A cruel distortion of a scene that was like something out of a romantic novel to Lillie's wishful, romantic mind. Edward Langtry came ashore in the glowing mantle she had visualized for him. Behind him were his yacht captain, George Merritt, and the crew. They were congratulated by everyone.

Young Langtry stayed on to talk to Dean Le Breton and his handsome daughter, who was immediately aware of her impact on him. He explained how they had set out from Cowes on the Isle of Wight with the idea of making a southern cruise. The storm had struck without warning, and they had beaten their way to Jersey as an afterthought. He knew the island well. Yes, they'd been lucky. Good seamanship, the Dean called it, but

6

Edward Langtry hardly listened to him. All he could see was Lillie. The long, wind-whipped hair shimmering with rainy highlights, the poised head, the radiant eyes, the enchanting lips. He stared, fascinated, and Lillie, too, liked what she saw. The manly mustache, the good solid face, the cleft chin, the slight though strong torso and trunk. Lochinvar, certainly!

He asked about hotel accommodations. The dean was giving what information he had, when Lillie tugged at his sleeve. Of course! Just the thing. Why, the rectory was as big as a hotel. Plenty of room. Delighted to have him.

Lillie said little as they walked toward St. Saviour. The dean talked on in his pleasant, austere way, and Edward Langtry couldn't keep his eyes off her ravishing face. She had only one bad moment—it appeared that Edward knew her brother Willie, whom he'd met the last time he was on the island, at his marriage to a Jersey girl. Lillie stopped breathing. But poor Emmy, God rest her soul, said Edward, had died in childbirth. Lillie breathed again.

Mrs. Le Breton was the first to see what was happening. She made things easy for her daughter, soothing the dean, making excuses to Mr. Cooke about lessons, and warning Reggie away. She couldn't have been kinder to Edward, who had been felled from the instant he saw Lillie on the quay. For her own part, Lillie thought herself "desperately in love." Noting Reggie's resentment, she was convinced of it.

They rode in the hills, they walked the beaches, they went sailing on the *Red Gauntlet*. Then, as if to help matters along, Lillie's brother Willie announced his engagement and came back from India with his fiancée for a family wedding. With the exception of Clement, who was studying for the bar, she and Reggie were the only ones who had stayed permanently in Jersey. The others had all gone into Her Majesty's Service. Now they all returned for Willie's marriage.

For friendship's sake, and probably to impress Lillie, Edward gave the bridal couple a ball at the Jersey Yacht Club. One of the most elaborate affairs the island had known, to Lillie it was like an Arabian Nights' entertainment. Flags and pennants on

7

the walls, gay lanterns and flowers everywhere, and, as a crowning touch, the stairs and halls lined with sailors at attention in immaculate white uniforms. Edward was wonderful!

Two days after the departure of Willie and his wife, they broke the news to the Le Bretons. The dean thought she was too young to marry, and Mama had been counting on Lillie having a London season.

The *Red Gauntlet,* white and trim, rode proudly at anchor waiting to take her from Jersey. Nothing would shake her decision, but Lillie loved her parents and heard them out politely. After they agreed to an engagement, she did not insist on the immediate marriage she had in mind. At least she had her ring. Mr. Cooke sighed as she dreamed over her lessons.

"They think I'm too young to marry," she said, showing him the diamond, "but they are letting me wear it."

"My dear child—" he began.

"I am not a child, Mr. Cooke."

Edward Langtry was an Ulsterman, the son of Robert Langtry, a well-to-do shipping man, for many years agent and representative of the Guion Line in Belfast. Though he was not strictly of the landed gentry, the indisputable fact that the Langtry coat of arms antedated Cromwell made him upper class. Respected and a power in Belfast, he was a member of the Society of Friends and lived by a strict moral code—yet not so strict that he didn't enjoy the good things in life.

Mr. Langtry was happy to accommodate his son, whose position demanded that he enjoy the fruits of leisure, rather than be a worker. So it was at that time with all wealthy young scions in England, much more so among the envied and emulated aristocracy. He had settled a liberal amount on Edward at his majority, presenting him with a yacht when he finished at Oxford and after his study of law. Fond of pleasure, class-conscious, and moderately lazy, Edward had carried letters to members of the peerage when he set forth to uphold the honor of the Langtrys at Cowes. Outside of getting a fair education, marrying once, and becoming a fair yachtsman, he had

8

accomplished little else at twenty-six. And hardly more was expected of him.

Money had never concerned Edward, but Dean Le Breton, accustomed to the shoals of parish finances, was highly money-conscious. He called in Mr. Parents, the family lawyer, who quickly disabused Lillie of the idea that she was marrying into a fortune. According to him, Edward was living far above his means. Besides the *Red Gauntlet,* he had the *Gertrude,* an eighty-ton racing yawl; the *Bluebird,* a sixty-ton cutter specially fitted out for fishing—a sport he loved—and the *Ildegonda,* a smaller, prize-winning racing yacht. There was also Cliffe Lodge, an Elizabethan house near Southampton, a cottage outside of Belfast, a coach and four, and various other acquisitions which, on recall, startled Edward. He had already spent much of his patrimony and for income depended on some three thousand pounds a year from properties in Ireland.

It was determined that he would have to dispose of most of these luxuries and arrange some sort of financial settlement for Lillie. Mr. Langtry would have preferred his son's marrying a Quakeress. Still, he liked what he heard about Lillie as a dean's daughter. Taking funds he had set aside for Edward, he wrote that he was giving her a jointure of ten thousand pounds.

"What's a jointure?" she asked Mr. Parents.

"A legal term for property settled on a woman when she marries," the lawyer explained. "The income is designed to protect you should your husband die. A wise move under the circumstances, Miss Le Breton."

The business over the money and forcing Edward to dispose of all the things she had looked forward to enjoying chilled her. Convinced that Edward had plenty of money and that this was all put up to delay them, she now pressed for immediate marriage.

The night before the wedding, looking around the room she had occupied so long, Lillie was moved to leave behind some mark of possession. Removing her engagement ring and holding it like a pencil, she scratched her name on the window glass

9

with the diamond. Lillie Le Breton. Sprawling and spidery, but unmistakably her hand and single identity. No matter if every stitch of hers were stripped from this room, everything which had ever pertained to her, her signature would remain permanently on the glass. The thought afforded her satisfaction.

Then she blew out the lamp and slipped into bed. They were being married extraordinarily early in order to make the tide —unheard of, her father had said with his benign smile. Would sleep ever come? Lillie wondered. She remembered the friendly talk about marriage Mama had given her. Well-intended, cautious, meaningless. How would she feel tomorrow night at this time? Sexual education was unknown in the eighteen-seventies, when sex was never discussed. The wedding night was an ordeal every woman had to face unprepared, if she were decent. Suffering, both mental and physical, awaited her. Sexual union was something to be enjoyed by men and supinely submitted to by women; if a woman gave any hint of finding pleasure in the marriage bed, she was clearly a depraved hussy.

Lillie had a calm, practical turn of mind. Convinced that she loved Edward Langtry, she decided to do as other wives did. So much for that. Much pleasanter to dwell on her prerogatives as Mrs. Edward Langtry, mistress of Cliffe Lodge, free to live as she pleased, buy what she wanted, incline to her own tastes. No more skimping, asking Mama and Papa for things, and doing without. The jointure would last forever . . . Edward was rich and handsome . . . they would be happy . . .

"Four o'clock, dear," said Mrs. Le Breton, shaking her arm.

Lillie jumped out of bed immediately. But it was black outdoors and she was so drugged with sleep she had to ask herself why Mama could possibly have awakened her at such an hour. Her wedding day! March 9, 1874. Six weeks since Edward had arrived in the storm. She washed her face with soap and cold water, put up her hair, and slipped into her traveling dress. In the flickering lamplight, her mirror showed a cool, contained, terribly serious image—someone she didn't know.

Mrs. Le Breton was still fussing over her daughter as a carriage came into the yard. In a few minutes a maid brought up Edward's bridal bouquet. He had gone ahead to St. Saviour's

Church across the way to join the dean. Lillie sniffed the flowers and listened blankly to Mama's blurted admonitions. Before leaving the room, still a little dazed, she touched the cold window glass where she had scratched her name.

The church was dark and glacial; the figures of Edward, her father, and the few witnesses were ghostly in the wan candlelight reaching the front pews. She saw her brother Clement, the watchful Mr. Parents, Captain George Merritt and the rest of the yacht's crew. Reggie was missing. Surely Reggie would come; surely he wouldn't fail her.

The service was short and hushed. Dean Le Breton's voice had never been more resonant in his empty church. Straight and solemn in a dark suit, Edward made his responses with an impassiveness matched by Lillie. (Oh, where was Reggie?) She felt removed from the ceremony, observing something that had little direct concern with her. Then Edward slid the gold band on her finger, and they kissed briefly. (How cold and dry his lips!) A few minutes of small talk, felicitations (*Reggie, where are you?*), and laughter in the cold, rosy-dark promise of morning. A festive carriage awaited them, with self-conscious and shivering postilions trying to keep eyes front. The extra bit of style tickled Lillie. She held Edward's hand on the drive to St. Helier, hardly conscious of what he was saying or the pressure of his hand as she kept looking for Reggie.

Later she remembered the red carpet on the steps of the Royal Yacht Hotel, the hilarity of the wedding breakfast echoing around her, toasts and cheers, kissing Mama, Papa, and Clement good-bye, and a peculiar empty feeling.

They cast off with the sun low over the water and the air chill. Lillie stood looking back until every face had merged into the background of town and harbor. Slowly, the *Red Gauntlet,* with Captain George Merritt at the wheel, moved across St. Aubin's Bay in a good following wind.

Something on a promontory high on one of the land arms encircling the bay caught her eye. Lillie borrowed Edward's telescope and adjusted it. She saw a figure on horseback looking out at the yacht. Unmistakably Reggie, and she waved excitedly. The figure gave no sign. She wanted to cry, but when

Edward called to her she turned her back on Jersey and walked forward where the waves were blue and dancing.

> *So faithful in love, and so dauntless in war*
> *There never was knight like the young Lochinvar . . .*

Lillie did her duty as a wife, looking on "the act" merely as part of the marriage contract. Edward seemed to get much out of it—that was correct for a man—but then, really, what was the fuss about? Her curiosity was satisfied. Compliant and submissive, she found their union not unpleasant. It made her husband happy, and she was pleased to give such happiness. She had no idea whether her response was adequate; she had no basis for comparison, just as she had none for Edward's love-making. He was tentative and solicitous. Considering her own inexperience, she ought to be grateful he was not like some husbands. Still, deep down a few kernels of doubt lingered, little gnawings of disappointment.

Cliffe Lodge was big and comfortable. Many rooms, tasteful appointments, a butler, cook, maid, and a coachman, all of whom knew what to do without instructions from the new, twenty-year-old mistress of the house. Lillie hardly had time to assert herself before Edward took her on a filial visit to Belfast. She was put off by the Quaker severity of her father-in-law, but her shy beauty and robust country-girl charm won him over easily. He decided she was just what his son needed: a good, strong woman who would bear him a lot of children—not a shrinking violet like poor Emmy, his first wife.

Edward's sister, Agnes, was immediately attracted to Lillie. Her father was master in his home, her mother a passive nonentity (in contrast to Emilie Le Breton), and she envied Edward's freedom. Before they sailed away, Mr. Langtry assured them he could always find a place for his son in the shipping firm, if Edward chose. Plainly the thought was abhorrent to Edward, who feared his father's authority, and Lillie approved his independence. To live in London was still her dream. She rarely mentioned it because, by nature and disposition, her husband had all the country-gentleman attributes—yachting, fishing, open-air leisure, and reading. But perhaps, if handled tactfully, he could be made into a city gentleman. Edward was irritable when crossed. She had yet to learn how to impose her will without mild argument. He had an arbitrary conception of feminine behavior. He would have to learn that she was no Emmy.

Between trips back to Cliffe Lodge, the remainder of the spring, all that long, golden summer and well into the fall, they were aboard the eighty-ton yawl *Gertrude,* cruising, racing, and following the sun. Edward never said so, but his attitude betrayed that he blamed her for Mr. Parents' economic strictures. The *Gertrude* was the only yacht they kept, and they reveled in her and the glorious present, never, never planning or discussing the future.

Lillie thrived on the tilting deck. The sun was kind to her fair skin. She loved the hazards, the sense of danger, the excitement of sea water boiling over the bow as competitors fell behind in the *Gertrude*'s wake. They went from regatta to regatta, winning among other important events the International Yacht Race at Le Havre, being natty and nautical, and frequenting this yacht club or that. Lillie recognized the power of money, the prestige and acceptance it brought. It was really too bad they had only one yacht left.

As winter came on, they were confined to Cliffe Lodge. The glow of the honeymoon, the magic of being together had not worn off, but the romantic mists were clearing. She no longer saw Edward as Lochinvar, and she had other doubts. Neither of them was quite what he or she had seemed in the rarefied atmosphere of Jersey. There were times when they were uneasy with each other; conversation came hard. Lillie was ill prepared for domesticity and not conditioned to it. She had not been trained to keep house. Her supervision of Cliffe Lodge and the servants was a farce she assumed, for Edward's sake, as a conscientious young bride.

To keep her satisfied, he set about diligently introducing her to his Southampton friends, most of them respectable middle-aged people or very proper young couples. Here Lillie's shyness and uncertainty were evident. The women were patronizing, seeing her as an innocent rustic fresh from Jersey's pastures and with a good thing in uxorious Edward Langtry. They invited her to their tea and whist parties and chatty sewing circles. Lillie detested them. She had been brought up with six brothers and had lived as a seventh. She had had few friends of her own sex, and her personality was not oriented toward women, their gentle ways—and their sheathed claws.

In self-defense, she exalted her father's position so that the Dean of Jersey seemed next in line to the Archbishop of Canterbury. Her father's warnings on the perils of the wine cup, card playing, and dancing had always amused her. Now she became more censorious than her friends. She approved of few of their pastimes and of none on Sundays. The last vestiges of the tomboy were gone. Lillie was increasingly bored. Her days were interminable. She lived in a vacuum of dull, well-bred, well-meaning people, among whom she regrettably had to include her indolent Edward. Ever afterward, she looked back on these empty years with loathing. More than fifty years later, in her autobiography, she wrote: "I need dwell no further on my life at this period. It was uneventful. . . ." An understatement to describe a deadly time that finally wore her down.

"Why don't we live in London?" she suggested more than once. "It's so gay there, and there's so much to do."

"No gayer than Southampton if you put your mind to it. You have a lovely home, Lillie. A devoted husband, good friends, everything. I can't understand why you—"

"Couldn't we try it for a while?" she pleaded. "It would be new and exciting."

"Perhaps some day," said Edward. "But I don't look for excitement, nor does it interest me. I'm not a city man. And you wouldn't like London after the quiet of Jersey."

Oh, wouldn't I! she thought.

In time she was taken ill, and Edward jumped to a conventional conclusion as he sat by her bed. They had rarely discussed children, but the idea of fatherhood pleased him. It was just the kind of effortless achievement he could best appreciate. The doctor, however, diagnosed typhoid fever. Her convalescence was long, and, while she continued to languish, Edward fretted.

14

It was then that Lillie had her little talk with the doctor. She had observed that Edward usually gave ground before official authority, as he had done with Mr. Parents, the Le Bretons' lawyer, and the doctor was sympathetic.

"A complete cure is sometimes beyond a doctor's power, Mr. Langtry," he pontificated. "Your wife is inherently a healthy young woman with a strong constitution, but there are other aspects worthy of consideration." He twirled his rusty walrus mustache and smoothed the lapels of his frock coat. "A change can work wonders, you know. A different locale, new faces, an environment that offers, say, the interests of the arts, the theater, great music—the salutary diversions that only a big city can provide. It might be well to consult a specialist in London, too. I can give you a name."

In the next room, Lillie lay back on her pillows, smiled, and thought about London.

two

Because there was something shatteringly final in dismissing the servants, selling the lodge and their last yacht, and severing himself from everything he owned, Edward managed it with fumbling distaste. Helpless outrage mingled with his apprehension as they traveled to London. Whereas Lillie was shy mostly from inexperience, her husband was morbidly so. He feared London and everything it represented.

"I hope it's for the best," he said darkly, looking out the streaked window of the railway carriage. "I feel lost. I don't know why the doctor suggested London. It's never been known as a health resort. Jersey would do you much more good, and I could fish and sail there."

They were silent when the train arrived at Waterloo Station. They had been married two years, and there were times now when they were as cautious with each other as Alpine climbers crossing a snow field. The surface was inviting enough, but just beneath lurked mushy spots and crevasses. Walking down the platform that January day, Lillie smiled up at the murky, overcast London sky. Edward scowled. They stood outside the station looking at the grimy, soot-coated buildings and the traffic, both pedestrian and vehicular, surging around them. Their being uprooted weighed heavily on them in different ways. Then a carriage came up, their baggage was piled on, and Edward hesitantly gave the name of an unpretentious first-class hotel a friend had recommended.

Because she was technically an invalid and Edward seemed

to have run out of momentum, they scarcely stirred from the hotel for a few days. Then, at Lillie's urging, they set about finding an apartment and becoming Londoners. They chose quarters in Eaton Place, an area which had once been part of a footpad-infested swamp district known as Five Fields. It was a modest place, but Lillie liked it, while Edward's lack of enthusiasm was as evident as a rash. He did appreciate the fact that the previous owners of the building had been forced to leave their furnishings behind. He was a poor man now, he reminded Lillie.

Despite her previous impressions, Lillie felt with Samuel Johnson that "When a man is tired of London, he is tired of life; for there is in London all that life affords." The city still overwhelmed her with its bigness, turmoil, and indifference, but it was full of good things too. She had merely to find them; she suspected that when she did, she would find herself.

The commercial and financial capital of Europe for centuries past, London in Queen Victoria's reign was indubitably the capital of the world. In 1876, its population was about 4,000,000 and, to Lillie's provincial eyes, the endless rows of buildings, the streets stretching to infinity, the thoroughfares seething with humanity were awesome proof that this metropolis was, indeed, the hub of the universe.

The Langtrys did all the things that tourists do. They visited museums, the Tower of London, St. Paul's Cathedral, Westminster Abbey, the Houses of Parliament, the picture galleries, the opera, the theater. They saw the changing of the guard at Buckingham Palace; they saw Hyde Park, Rotten Row, the fashionable shops along Regent Street, Savile Row, Bond Street, and the attractions of Piccadilly Circus, where life revolved dizzily to clopping hoofs, jingling harnesses, shouts, and nerve-tingling confusion. They made a pilgrimage to St. Olave's Church in Southwark, where her father had been curate before his call to Jersey. Located in Hart Street and Seething Lane, a slum area, it disappointed Lillie. The gloomy, squalid neighborhood sickened her because she was unused to poverty. Edward led her home, complaining that his feet hurt. Arm in

17

arm they went up the steps at Eaton Place—Edward heavily, Lillie lightly. Mrs. Walsh, their landlady, met them at the door, a piece of paper in her trembling hand.

"I've been waiting for you," she announced, excitement and curiosity crossing her amiable, broad-featured face. "A telegram came for Mrs. Langtry."

Lillie was wretched when she reached Jersey. The train ride, the overnight Channel trip in rough weather were unbearably long under the stress of her tormenting grief. She had gone sleepless since receiving the telegram. Coming into St. Helier Harbor, she let her eyes turn involuntarily to the promontory on which she had seen the horse and rider silhouetted against the sky. Reggie hadn't come to the wedding, and she hadn't written him a line since she had left. Now he was dead. The youngest, the bravest, the best of her brothers.

She dried her eyes and made a special effort to compose herself before the boat docked. Her parents were not there, but Marshal the coachman, white-haired and red-eyed, was waiting with a carriage. The dean had become rector of St. Helier, so she missed the ride to St. Saviour.

"He was so brave, Miss," said Marshal mournfully, quite forgetting she was married. "He laughed when we carried him into the house, his body all bent and twisted. He blamed himself, not the horse for falling on him." The hunched old coachman wiped his streaming eyes with the sleeve of his black coat. "She was going to win the Queen's Cup for him sure at the Gorey race meeting in July, and he had to hurry to get well."

Long after the dean went to bed, Lillie and Mrs. Le Breton sat up talking about Reggie. The poignant memories came back unbidden: climbing trees together, riding their horse Flirt, collecting door knockers in their nightly raids, torturing Old Man Wilkins in Deanery Lane by hitching a cord to his doorbell so that it jingled at every passing, that wonderful afternoon they'd gone swimming in the nude . . .

"I'm glad you're living in London," said Mrs. Le Breton. "Does Edward like it there and are you happy?"

"Yes," Lillie lied. Mama had enough troubles.

18

"Your clothes—you'll be making friends and going out soon. Do you have an evening dress? No? We must stop at Madame Nicolle's before you take the boat. She has all your measurements and can send it on."

It was no use telling her mother that they had no London friends and that she would never have the occasion to wear an evening dress.

"I don't feel like going anywhere now. It wouldn't be right."

"You have to live, child. For yourself as well as your husband. We'll pick out something pretty in black that will be fitting."

With every mile Lillie's spirits sank, and the sight of London and Edward did nothing to relieve her depression. He was a man she happened to be married to, London a city she happened to live in. She had no interest in either, and she wouldn't have stirred from Eaton Place if it hadn't been for Edward. Entertainer was a new role for Edward, who did his best. She rarely smiled now, her animation was gone, and the cold-fish slap of reality had left her in shock.

"You can't grieve forever, dearest. Reggie wouldn't want it."

"Reggie never liked you," she snapped. "In fact, he didn't want me to marry you."

Edward winced. He was so vulnerable, so easy to hurt she felt sorry for him and ashamed of herself.

"I'm sorry," she added. "Let's not talk about it."

Because she couldn't bear his anxiety—hadn't she herself maneuvered the move to London?—she submitted to the things she had previously been fond of doing. They roamed about London, but Lillie was sunk so far into herself that she barely looked up as Edward pointed out the Prince of Wales passing on a handsome horse in Rotten Row. Nor was she less apathetic seeing Ellen Terry as Portia in *The Merchant of Venice* at the Prince of Wales's Theater, or Henry Irving, the talk of London, as Hamlet at the Lyceum.

After the sunshine and mild air of Jersey, English winters were a trial. London was an icebox, the chill penetrated to the marrow, and the grimy fogs which settled on the city were oppressive because of her mood. The Eaton Place apartment was glacial and always sooty. Curtains, rugs, draperies, and furniture in somber colors concealed the dirt but intensified the gloom.

Edward was often insufferable in his infinite patience and understanding, so Lillie liked to steal off by herself to the park. Here she walked, stared at the smartly dressed ladies and gentlemen, the nicely-turned-out equipage of aristocrats, and thought sad thoughts. A lonely Jersey girl lost in the big city, she thought there was nothing unusual about her—and yet she was observed by William Graham Robertson, a sensitive young artist and actor, who had no idea who she was. He was crossing the road at Hyde Park Corner and saw her making her way past Apsley House toward the Park. She made such an impression that he could still record it vividly in his reminiscences fifty-five years afterward:

> At first glance it seemed a very young and slender girl, dowdily dressed in black and wearing a small, close-fitting black bonnet; she might have been a milliner's assistant waiting upon a customer for all her gown said to the contrary, or a poorly paid governess hurrying to her pupils. As I drew near the pavement the girl looked up—and I all but sat flat on the road.
>
> For the first and only time in my life I beheld perfect beauty.
>
> The face was that of the lost Venus of Praxiteles, and of all the copies handed down to us must have been incomparably the best, yet nature had not been satisfied and thrown in two or three subtle improvements. The small head was not reared on the white column of the throat as a capital crowns a pillar, but drooped slightly forward like a violet or a snowdrop, the perfect nose was made less perfect and a thousand times more beautiful by a slight tilt at the tip. The wonderful face was pale with the glow of absolute health behind the pallor, the eyes grey beneath dark lashes, the hair brown with hints of gold in it, the figure in its poise and motion conveyed an impression of something wild, eternally young, nymph-like. . . .[1]

It seemed a hallucination to Robertson. "No human being could look like that," he was convinced, "and if she appeared

[1] *Life Was Worth Living*, by William Graham Robertson. New York: Harper & Brothers.

to me again I should certainly consult the family doctor about her."

Unaware of her upsetting influence on anyone or of her beauty, Lillie revived slowly as spring came on because she was young and it was necessary to resist Edward. He wanted to leave London and spoke of trying Belfast, as his father had suggested. The cold lessened, the fogs lifted, she continued to brood over Reggie's death, but London resumed its fascination. She talked Edward into visiting the new Royal Aquarium at Westminster.

"Good heavens!" said a clipped voice from the throng. "It's Lillie Le Breton, isn't it? Whatever are you doing so far from Jersey?" Before she could answer, a familiar face studied hers. "And what a beauty you've grown into!"

"I didn't know you knew anyone in London," said Edward afterward.

"I'd forgotten the Ranelaghs—the Suffields and Rendleshams, too. But wasn't it lucky to meet like that? How kind of Lord Ranelagh to ask us to stay with him in Fulham. It'll be such a pleasant change from Eaton Place."

"Do you really think he meant a few days?" Edward asked worriedly.

"That's what he said. His daughters told me everybody comes to their Sunday afternoon garden parties."

The rest of the week went slowly, until they arrived at Lord Ranelagh's handsome home with its lovely grounds, great trees, and green lawns sloping down to the Thames. Lillie timidly enjoyed every moment, particularly Sunday afternoon with the gardens filled with guests. Everyone was gay and well dressed, the conversation scintillating to her innocent ears. This seemed London at its best. Near a trellis a gallant whispered to a well-groomed girl, who threw her head back in laughter. Lillie watched enviously. They belonged. She was only a guest, someone the Ranelaghs had known in Jersey, still the dean's daughter. Perhaps, if Edward were a different kind of man . . .

"Are you glad you came?" Lillie asked him.

"It's a beautiful spot," he granted. "But the people—they're so many. I must say it's a little overwhelming." They turned to take some cakes from a silver serving tray held by a liveried footman. "But if you're enjoying yourself, Lillie, I'm very glad. It may help you forget about your brother."

She felt a spur of guilt at the reminder. She hadn't thought of Reggie since they'd come to Fulham. When they were ready to leave, Lord Ranelagh kissed her paternally.

"It's been marvelous having both of you," he said, looking only at Lillie. "I heard a great deal of favorable comment about your wife, Mr. Langtry. People asked me who she was, where she'd been hiding. Londoners aren't used to healthy beauty, you know. She has an unspoiled freshness none of these women can match."

Driving back in their hired carriage, they said little. A taste of society wasn't enough, but that was apparently all she would ever get. How could she dream of taking part, of having a season in London, when she was a nonentity? And those empty compliments of Lord Ranelagh's! No, better resign herself to her dull, backwater life. At least it was better than settling in Belfast.

The first important invitation came a week later when they were out listening to an open-air concert. They walked in, dusty and tired, and Mrs. Walsh greeted them with an envelope addressed to Mr. and Mrs. Langtry. Because it had been delivered by a footman in a handsome carriage, at first she had thought it a mistake.

Lillie opened it calmly. "It's from a Lady Sebright. A card for a Sunday evening at home."

"Don't know her," said Edward, taking off his shoes.

"I remember Lord Ranelagh introduced me. She's a patron of the arts who's done some amateur acting, and she always has writers and artists about her. It should be amusing."

"Sounds like a fancy affair." He rubbed his feet. "What about clothes? You're still in mourning."

"I have that black dress of Madame Nicolle's."

"But all the women will have expensive gowns. We'll be out of place. We're not society people or—need I point out?—patrons of the arts. We can't compete with that crowd." He put on his slippers with a sigh. "You'll be disappointed if we go."

"I'll be more disappointed if we don't."

"We're country cousins, dear. At least in their eyes."

She wasn't going to argue or get angry. He could say whatever he pleased, but they were going. Few people got such invitations. They owed this one to Lord Ranelagh, and nothing was going to prevent Lillie from attending Lady Sebright's at home.

three

CLOTHES had never meant much to Lillie. She had emulated her brothers in her youth and now fussing over petticoats, dresses, coiffures, and other feminine accouterments seemed an affectation and a waste of time. She didn't care what the other ladies wore at Lady Sebright's; she'd wear Madame Nicolle's black silk dress and the devil take them.

Savoring her defiance like a connoisseur of rare-vintage wine, she studied her mirrored reflection dispassionately. That black dress with its high neck. Hmm! Snorting, she got up so suddenly she knocked over her chair, and reached for the scissors. Snip, snip. There, it was done! Much better cut square and exposing her neck and shoulders.

Impatiently, she seized her hair, which was gathered in a single, heavy chestnut plait, wound it into a loose coil, and pinned it halfway down her neck in a thick, figure-eight twist. She brushed the top and sides smooth, fingered the shortened and curled bangs into position on her forehead. It never occurred to her to use make-up of any kind. And, besides, her superb complexion and perfect skin didn't need it. She had no jewels and, in her present temper, wouldn't have worn them if she had. She gave herself a final inspection, made a moue, put her Jersey cape over her arm, then joined Edward who was pacing the parlor. He wore conventional evening clothes without distinction. From his mien he might have been going to a funeral or an execution.

From their rented four-wheeler they looked expectantly at the dignified buildings in Lowndes Square and the carriages drawn up outside of one of them. Here the windows seemed dazzling rectangles of color, and from inside came the sound of music, the babble of voices, peals of laughter. Lillie took her husband's arm, breathed deeply. Feeling her heart thump against her ribs, she went up the red-carpeted steps to the glass door, where a footman in regal red livery was waiting. They went inside, up some more stairs, past another footman, and on to an anteroom where still another footman attended to the gentlemen's hats and coats and a white-uniformed maid took the ladies'.

Edward led her to the ornate double doors of the living room. A butler, the final barrier to high society, asked their names. His eyebrows shot up and down, either in amazement or disapproval, and his jowls worked as if gathering saliva.

"Mr. and Mrs. Edward Langtry!" he bawled.

And there was their hostess, a dressmaker's dummy on wheels, bright and bejeweled, a toothy welcoming grin on her florid features as she held her left hand out to Edward and her right to Lillie.

"How nice of you to come!" she simpered. "And you're from Jersey, aren't you?" she said to Lillie. "Isn't that simply *too* wonderful? I have a very distinguished person here from your island. You *must* meet him. Now come along, both of you."

The Langtrys followed her. Just inside the door, the butler fluttered up, jowls trembling, and whispered in her ear. She rolled away, leaving them bereft and uncertain.

"What'll we do?" Edward said anxiously. "We can't stay here."

"The far corner," Lillie said. "There's an empty chair."

Set apart from the convivial scene in her corner chair, Lillie contrasted the severity of her gown with the other women's and felt dowdier and more rustic than ever. It had been cruel of Lady Sebright to abandon them without an introduction. Edward moved restlessly behind her chair, and she gave him an encouraging smile which he did not notice in his embarrassment. Everything blurred suddenly. Lillie sensed her eyes were filling with tears, and she dabbed delicately with her handkerchief while pretending to blow her nose.

Self-conscious and crucified, she was unaware of being anything but ignored, though the eyes of all the men in the room were on her. They had lost interest in the chattering of their feminine *vis-à-vis* and were answering mechanically now. Soon the women were shooting keen stares at Lillie in her remote corner. Because she was unknown to the company, it had taken time for her presence to register. Next to the elaborate satin and brocade dresses embellished with gilt and froufrou, the gloves, the plumes, the combs, the upswept coiffures, the stomachers and earrings and pendants, the stark simplicity of Lillie's black dress and her lack of any adornment was as striking as it was captivating. Her own classic twenty-two-year-old beauty was even more eloquent.

Lovely and composed as she appeared, Lillie's mind was churning, and she was looking blankly ahead without seeing. Then Edward behind her gave a start, and she saw her beaming hostess confronting her with a solid, stocky, distinguished-looking man.

"Mrs. Langtry, I regret leaving you, but Blackwell reported a culinary emergency." She tittered. "Everyone is dying to meet you. First, I want to present the Jersey friend I mentioned— John Everett Millais, a member of the Royal Academy and one of England's most eminent painters."

The introductions over, Lady Sebright bubbled on. "Mrs. Langtry, I must tell you what John said about you. It's so consummately utter that I must. He dashed up to me and exclaimed, 'Ah, madam, you have a goddess among your guests!' Isn't that precious?" She giggled.

"She's blushing!" said Millais. "My word, how intense. How refreshing in the jaded atmosphere of London. But you are a goddess, you know. A Greek goddess with that perfect head, that neck, those shoulders of alabaster." He stood back to admire her. "The Greek line from the top of the head to the tip of the ankle." He gestured, his hands forming a frame. "Perfect! I can't wait to do a portrait of you, Mrs. Langtry. There will be many others, but I must be the first."

Lillie agreed. It was all she was capable of doing. Just then a tall, foppish man tugged at Lady Sebright's elbow and begged to be introduced.

"This is Lord Frederick Leighton, head of the Royal Academy, a great artist and sculptor, and a dear, dear friend of mine."

Dramatically Leighton held up a finger and squinted along it, as artists do to measure proportions, moved forward, back, circled Lillie, forcing Edward against the wall, and came back to face her. "Millais, you may have seen her first, but I discovered her neck—and what a neck! Never have I seen such a neck and shoulders, and I shall so tell the world." His eyes thanked heaven. "And that face, beauty incarnate. Venus de Milo, Venus de Medici. I can't find the words."

"Why don't you compromise with 'too all-but'," a piercing, high-pitched voice put in. "That's one of society's current favorites, and we all know how Royal Academicians adore keeping pace with the *haut monde,* eh, what?"

Millais and Leighton backed away with an air of patient resignation. Lillie looked at the dandyish little man teetering on his toes before her. He wore a dinner jacket, a black tie on a frilly white shirt—and white-duck trousers. His hair was glossy black and thick, clustered in ringlets on his neck, and, most curious, he had a trained white lock above his right eye that made a distinctive slash in the writhing blackness. A cocky bantam with bushy eyebrows, a monocle clamped in one of his gray-blue eyes, the nose and mouth of an artist, the jutting chin of a fighter, the sensitive fingers of a violinist, and long, talonlike nails. How could she have missed him before?

"Mrs. Langtry, may I present myself?" He bowed. "I am James Abbott McNeill Whistler, better known as Jimmy, which I advise you to call me. I am not a dear, dear friend of Lady Sebright's. I am *not* a dear, dear friend of anybody's, d'ye know?" He raised an eyebrow, his monocle popped out, flashing light, and he retrieved it with a satanic smile and screwed it into his eye. "But, ha-ha—" The barked expletive made Lillie jump—"I am henceforth your ever-willing slave." He grimaced comically. "What do you think of that, Mrs. Langtry, eh?"

27

"I don't know what to think, Mr. Whistler. Y-y-you came from nowhere like the genie from Aladdin's lantern."

"A good touch, indeed! I shall disappear to nowhere presently, but think of me as just that. Rub when you need me, what?" His elastic features crinkled ludicrously. "Jimmy, the genie. Oh! Oh!" Again Lillie was startled by his burst of mad laughter. "I suppose Millais and Leighton want to paint you. Tarnish your beauty with Academy paint? Never! Let Whistler paint you, madam, and posterity will cherish your memory. Yellow will be the color. 'An Arrangement in Yellow' I'll call it."

After that she had a receiving line of her own—Lillie the gracious queen receiving homage, Edward her squirming, constrained consort. She was overwhelmed—it was incredible that she should be meeting these famous people! Yet she was and had the good sense to be true to herself. She continued to be natural, she responded to her admirers simply and winningly, and she took care to include her husband in the conversation whenever she could. Henry Irving, whom she had seen as Hamlet; William Yardley, an amateur actor and expert cricket player who was delighted to hear that she had played the game with her brothers; Lord Wharncliffe who owed his fortune to the discovery of coal on his land in Sheffield and was using his money to collect art. Abraham Hayward, who called himself an essayist, delivered a monologue on beauty.

There were many others, middle-aged and older. She was attracted to Frank Miles, an intense young artist close to her own age. He had a streak of recklessness about him, as if he would have thought nothing of jerking the chairs out from under some of the pompous older people or shocking them in some other fashion. A spirit of camaraderie flickered between them.

"I'm no Millais or Whistler, Mrs. Langtry. Just a popular artist who works for newspapers, magazines like *Life,* and people who want pretty pictures of themselves. Nothing Royal Academy about it since I do it for money. Mostly pencil and pen-and-ink drawings—and always of beautiful women. That's why I must do you, make London aware of the supreme beauty hiding in its midst."

28

"I haven't been hiding, Mr. Miles."

"Then where have you been until now? You'll have to meet a friend of mine who's still at Oxford. He'll go mad over you. The most warmhearted and amusing person I've ever known. He writes poetry, and he's extraordinary in every way. A genius."

"Even more extraordinary than Mr. Whistler?"

"My God, yes! Just wait till you meet Oscar. Remember the name, Oscar Wilde. And please accept this as a souvenir of the night your beauty burst on London like a bombshell."

It was an envelope which had once contained a bill from a men's clothing store on Savile Row. On the front was a quick pencil sketch of Lillie in profile with her hair in a twist at the neck, boldly executed in slashing strokes.

"I had to do it when I saw you sitting in the corner like an elegant empress in exile. That's one thing I've never done before, draw at a party. I hate parlor tricks, Mrs. Langtry, and I never, never work out of my studio."

"Thank you, Mr. Miles. I'm terribly flattered. Look, Edward."

A breathless Lady Sebright, her tiara askew on her gray hair, was dashing up with still another celebrity. This was a crazy game fate had set in motion, and Lillie was meeting all comers. The cause, the circumstances confounded her, but what was the point of analysis? It was happening: she was the center of attraction, and she was going down the line with fickle fortune, making the most of an opportunity that might never come again. And she didn't have to pinch herself. She was burning alive, radiant, blooming.

There was a scramble to escort her to the table, but Millais won by claiming that he had priority as fellow countryman. Lillie acknowledged the friendly smiles and nods of the other men and women. The transformation amazed her the more. There had been no spell, no magic, nothing that could account for the change save Madame Nicolle's black dress, which she had snipped so arbitrarily. If they thought her beautiful, then she must be beautiful. And she felt beautiful in spite of the wonder and uncertainty in her heart.

Lillie listened to Millais, turned now and then to Hayward who had managed to take the seat on her left. She said just enough to impress them with her charm and good sense. Edward was too far down the table for her to see. Whistler's strident voice, raucous laughter, and mannerisms dominated the room.

"I do so love real art," a woman was gushing next to him. "Why, only yesterday I was riding down by the Thames with a friend, and we both commented on the exquisite haze in the atmosphere. It was a perfect series of Whistlers."

"Yes, madam, nature is creeping up."

The laughter washing around the lady did not disturb her. "I draw a little myself, as did my father before me—oh, nothing to compare with your masterpieces, Mr. Whistler!—but, tell me, do you think genius is hereditary?"

"I cannot say, madam." He speared a piece of meat, chewed and swallowed it quickly, then fixed his gimlet monocle on her. "Heaven has granted me no offspring. You'll just have to be patient."

"Well," said the lady, ignoring the laughter again, "some people can't make up their mind about artists, but I know what I like. With all due respect for others, there are only two painters in the world—Whistler and Velasquez."

"Oh, why drag in Velasquez?" Enjoying the effect of his response on the others, Whistler winked at Lillie. "Everyone knows how deep-rooted the Royal Academy is in the dry rot of the classical tradition. They're imitators, not original, never creators. Paint a woman with a cryptic smile and what do they have to call it? 'The New Mona Lisa.'" He gave a seal-like bark. "What would Raphael have to say about the Pre-Raphaelites, eh?"

Millais was used to Whistler's outbursts, but thin-skinned Lord Leighton could not let these ravings of an alien upstart pass. "As an American," he said sarcastically, "how can you forbear to keep your credo so far from your mother country? Surely it's unfair to deny them your pearls of artistic wisdom?"

"You're right, Leighton. One cannot continually disappoint a continent. It's been suggested many times that I visit the home of my ancestors, but, you see, I find art so absolutely irritating that, really, I hesitate before exasperating another nation."

"I've never known you to hesitate at anything," Leighton went on in the same labored vein. "But granting that the English are stupid, would you say the Americans are as dense?"

Glancing at Lillie, Whistler screwed his face into one of his weird grimaces. "Heaven forbid that the Englishman's one undeniable superiority be challenged, but he is so honest in his stupidity that one must love him for the—uh—virtue. Whereas the American is a 'smart aleck' in his ignorance, and therefore intolerable."

"You have said it," Leighton replied smugly. He addressed the table. "Isn't it a good thing we can't see ourselves as others see us?"

"Ha-ha, isn't it!" chirped Whistler. "I know in my case I should grow intolerably conceited."

The men stayed behind in the dining room for brandy and cigars, while the ladies congregated in the parlor. This was a trial for Lillie. Her extreme shyness concealed her uneasiness before the pitiless feminine judges. She stayed close to Mrs. Millais, spoke softly in answer to questions about herself, and omitted any airs because she had none to put on. Outclassed and outshone by a nobody, and thus disposed to find fault, the women found themselves disarmed by Lillie's honest simplicity.

Lillie noticed nothing further until she and Edward were in the carriage and trotting away. She must have floated down the steps, for certainly she was in the clouds and suspended in space. Overhead the stars flashed, the moon shone, and London stretched away on every side in endless enchantment. It was wonderful. She smiled. Simply too all-but. Dream or not, nothing could take away the memory of that bewitching night.

The room was bright with sunshine. Edward was not in his bed. It seemed like any other morning until the recollection of Lady Sebright's at-home came to her like a posthypnotic suggestion. She jumped from her bed and looked at herself in the dressing-table mirror. She was in a long, white nightgown; her

31

golden-brown hair hung in a tangle below her shoulders, framing her lovely oval face. To her sleepy eyes she looked a wraith. Then she saw the envelope with its Savile Row address and Frank Miles's sketch. It was no dream! Here was something as tangible as Cinderella's glass slipper dropped at the palace.

Everything came back to her. Pushing back her hair, she ran to the window with a happy cry. London was miraculously fair in spring sunshine, her heart was swollen with happiness, and she wanted to call down to the little girl skipping rope on the sidewalk. Like Ebenezer Scrooge after his last, eye-opening expedition with the Spirit of Christmas Yet to Come, she felt the same ecstatic relief, the same overwhelming joy. Gone was the dingy barrenness of the house on Eaton Place; gone the apathy of the people in the streets, the dirt, the grime, the obliviousness of London. It was a great shining city and she was part of it.

She dressed hurriedly, eager to be out and about. Edward's solemn appearance could not dampen her spirits. He said the weather was just right for fishing; the events at Lady Sebright's couldn't have been further from his mind. After plaiting her hair and fastening it in a twist at the nape, she tweaked his mustache and kissed him playfully on the nose.

"Do you feel well?" he asked.

"If I felt better, I'd explode! Come on, Edward, let's set a record and do London in one day."

"It's after eleven o'clock. You ought to have some breakfast."

"Oh, bother breakfast! I want to get out in the sun."

After a tremendous late lunch, which Lillie put away with ease, Edward suggested going home. She wouldn't hear of it. There was too much to do, too much to see; they must never rest. She never stopped talking, pointing out the sights, or darting to examine a fascinating window display. Afraid she was feverish or delirious, he persuaded her to take a cab and gave the driver their address. Bloated with happiness, Lillie fell asleep against her husband.

Shouting, cursing, and the crack of a whip. Lillie yawned. There was a bitter taste in her mouth. It was cold now, the sun hidden behind the buildings. She shivered. London had its unfriendly mask on again. She hated it. She hated everything and everyone, including Edward and herself. She was *so* tired.

At Eaton Place, she let Edward help her down, waited slumped and unseeing as he paid the driver. A door flew open as they entered. Mrs. Walsh came toward them, flushed and important, envelopes fluttering in her hand. Lillie had visions of another telegram—Mama or Papa dead or dying this time —and felt faint.

"Ever since you left—the most extraordinary thing! They never stopped coming. I just couldn't get over it."

"Who?" said Edward. "What?"

"Visitors, footmen, carriages, messages, invitations. The table's heaped with them in the hall, and these just came a few minutes ago." She favored Lillie with a motherly smile. "You said you knew nobody in London, Mrs. Langtry. All of a sudden you have hundreds of friends."

Lillie went up, pressing the letters lovingly to her breast. Then, spying the snowstorm of envelopes on the hall table, she fell on them, murmuring inarticulately. Balls, dinners, dances, teas, receptions, at homes. Staggering! Embossed cards, crested enclosures, engraved missives, ducal messages, social summoneses in pink, white, pale blue, and apple green. "The Duke and Duchess of Strantheam request the company of Mr. and Mrs. Langtry at . . . ," "Sir Robert and Lady Moncrief take great pleasure in asking Mr. and Mrs. Langtry to . . . ," "Lord and Lady Wharncliffe request . . ."

"Edward! Isn't it—isn't it fantastic?"

"I wouldn't believe it if I didn't see our names. We don't know any of these people."

"But they want to know us."

"No," he said bleakly, "just you."

"You're exaggerating," she said, knowing he wasn't.

"What are we going to do with all these invitations?" he demanded.

Lillie burrowed under the scattered letters, lifted her arms; and her eyes sparkled as the envelopes fell like bright autumn leaves.

"Do? We're going to accept every single one of them!"

33

Lillie decided first on the Wharncliffes. They were the only people she knew among the dozens who had extended invitations, and she was apprehensive enough without risking everything on the basis of one incredible success. To date, Lady Sebright's at-home had been the high point of her life, far too unprecedented for her to hope for a repetition. Yet she had made a splash. The deluge of invitations meant something; she couldn't disappoint these people—or herself. She could no more ignore this challenge than she had been able to resist the taunts of her brothers in the rectory long ago. Still, it was terribly difficult to know what to do, how to proceed—Edward was no help—and, to tell the truth, she was afraid.

The gnat-like doubts vanished immediately in the acclamation that greeted her. Lady Wharncliffe knew she had a prize. Lillie was presented to everyone as Exhibit A, with Edward trailing as an appendage. She didn't have to do or say anything; merely be the beautiful Mrs. Langtry, and she was. Again the impact of her presence, which prior to this week had never attracted attention, astonished her. The company clamored about her, impressed by her endearing shyness, dazzled by her smiles, overwhelmed by her looks, and greeting every simple sally as brilliant wit.

She was escorted to dinner by an impressive man, some lord whose name she didn't quite catch. He was round-faced, snub-nosed, and his prominent eyes had an ironic glint. His full mustache had an elegant twist Edward's could never match. He had a strong chin, receding hair parted in the middle and brushed back over his ears, and his charm was a subtle, commanding thing. He said he'd just come down from Ireland.

When the meal was over, the women left the men behind, and Edward threw his wife a drowning look as she went. Lillie said little, feeling conspicuous among the women. She found herself staring at Lady Wharncliffe who was snubbing out one cigarette to light another.

"Don't look so shocked, Mrs. Langtry," said Lady Sebright, sitting next to her. "She's been smoking for years. It's quite the thing in London now. And how did you like having Lord

Randolph Churchill next to you at supper? Charming, isn't he?"

"Very," said Lillie, looking round-eyed.

"Did you know that he infuriated the Prince of Wales and was exiled to Ireland?" Lady Sebright brought her powdery-red face close. "His father, the Duke of Marlborough, was forced to become viceroy because of the scandal. Randolph went along as his secretary. It had to do with his elder brother, Lord Blandford, who had an affair with Lord Aylesford's wife, Edith." She tittered. "Well, the Prince was furious and said so, and Lord Churchill, bold man that he is, somehow got hold of some love letters the Prince had written to Edith. He threatened to publish them if the Prince didn't stop blackening his brother's reputation.

"And then do you know what happened?" Lady Sebright's eyes shone in maniacal enjoyment. "The Prince was so livid at his impudence that he challenged Lord Randolph to a duel. Wasn't that just too consummately utter? Of course, the whole thing was hushed up, but the Churchills have naturally remained *persona non grata* to the Prince. That's why Lord Randolph was packed off to Ireland with his darling American wife, Jennie Jerome—a dear, dear friend of mine—and their sweet baby, Winston. I don't know *what* Randolph is doing in London. A good thing the Prince isn't here."

"Does the Prince go to parties like this?" Lillie asked.

The naïveté of the question made Lady Sebright clutch at her string of pearls. "My dear child, he goes everywhere. I mean *everywhere*," she repeated meaningfully, "and he does *everything*. You'll learn soon enough when he hears of you."

four

ALTHOUGH Lillie had heard about a season in London ever since she could remember; and Mama had always wanted her to have one, the true meaning of it had always escaped her.

The best people knew the rules by instinct, having no need to consult the calendar. Many stayed away from London from October through February; though some would return for Christmas and the "Little Season." Parliament opened its six-weeks' session in February, so members and their families returned to London at that time; others waited till the city was gayer. Then Belgravia was set for the season which, as Lady Randolph Churchill put it, "was looked upon as a very serious matter which no self-respecting persons who considered themselves 'in society' would forego, nor of which a votary of fashion would willingly miss a week or a day."

Things began with the Boat Race, as it was called, between Oxford and Cambridge on the Thames before thousands of spectators—common, ordinary folk predominating. Dense cheering crowds lined the riverbanks, while boats of all descriptions loaded to capacity followed the sweating crews from Putney to Mortlake. This was early in April. It was just the kind of spectacle Edward Langtry enjoyed—much more than he enjoyed the opening of the Royal Academy at Burlington House, which kicked off the official ten-week season in early May.

After that came a parade of events: the Chelsea and Botanical Garden Flower Shows; the smart charity bazaars with fashionable beauties starring in *tableaux vivants*; pigeon shooting at Hurlingham; the Easter Monday Military Review; the Epsom Spring Meeting; the Annual Islington Horse Show; Derby Day; the Cambridge-Oxford Cricket Match; the Eton-Harrow Cricket Match; soldiers from England, Scotland, and Ireland shooting it out at Wimbledon for the Elcho Challenge Shield; Trooping the Color; the Royal Courts; Newmarket; Ascot; the International Horse Show.

The Goodwood race meeting marked the official end of the season, with time off only for the Whitsuntide recess. Then, after a little recuperation, came Cowes Week for the yacht races off the Isle of Wight, and London was socially quiet until the following year; although for the shotgun set, there was still grouse shooting in August, partridge shooting in September, and pheasant shooting in October.

While the days called for attendance at picture galleries, bazaars, walking or riding in Hyde Park at stated hours, royal pageantry, horse racing, cricket matches, picnicking, and sailing, the nights were filled with the ballet, the theater, the opera, musicales, dinner parties, balls, at homes, receptions, and entertainments of every conceivable nature lasting far into the night. And Lillie, the new discovery, the great find of the season, was invited to everything everywhere. She was buried under an avalanche of invitations that caused an upheaval in her life. A never-ending stream of visitors descended on the modest Langtry apartment. Mrs. Walsh, torn between admiration and indignation, was compelled to hire an assistant merely to answer the door and accept invitations from one footman after the other.

With the help of her devoted maid, Dominique, Lillie listed every invitation, wrote her acceptance, and budgeted every hour like a doctor with his appointment book. Sometimes she attended two or three parties the same night, flying from one engagement to the next, acknowledging introductions, dispensing smiles like favors, eating a bit here, dancing a few measures there, and then rushing off again, breathless and glowing, to another stop on her timetable. Edward followed faithfully. No longer was there any question of Lillie's listen-

37

ing to or heeding his advice. He could say or think anything he wished; nothing would deter her.

The word was out on Lillie Langtry, Frank Miles helping to spread it even as his drawings of her appeared in *Life,* and fanciful stories of her discovery tried to antedate Lady Sebright's at home. Lord Suffield was said to have come on her as a wild beauty, her hair rippling to the waist in the Jersey sands; Captain Allen Young, a frustrated polar explorer, claimed to have found her on one of his romantic voyages. Whatever the story, anyone named her discoverer was immediately a man of mark. The gay blades were fascinated after Lord Rosslyn confirmed the reports of her beauty. He gave a dinner for her, after asking a dozen competent critics to be on hand at his upper Grosvenor Street house to pass judgment. Lillie arrived with a terrible cold.

"I have the sniffles so badly I can hardly see," she confessed. "But I didn't want to disappoint you."

Lord Rosslyn fretted. This would hardly do before the gallants invited to appraise her.

"My dear," he told her grandly, "go home and turn the corner of your cold. I would not for all the world show that face with a doubtful nose and red eyes."

He sent her and Edward home hungry in a carriage one of his friends had just arrived in. Edward grumbled that this showed bad taste. In spite of not having wanted Lillie to go out at all with her cold, he was glad to find things to object to.

Another time, he asked, "Must we endure these dripping flowers?" as they drove away from Devonshire House in a hired brougham. "I never felt so conspicuous in all my life!"

Festooned and garlanded with water lilies, their carriage was so much like a decorated float that Lillie broke into helpless laughter, recalling the bearded, dignified Lord Hartington as he had plucked them from the water. It had been a combined social and political reception because their host—Harty-Tarty to his friends—held some high government job in spite of his scandalous private life. He had left his place in the receiving line to meet her at the top of the great marble staircase and had led her into the gardens past platoons of footmen in gold livery.

"I can understand all I've heard about you, Mrs. Langtry. My friend the Prince of Wales will want to meet you. He has an eye for beauty, you know."

Lillie gave her usual disarming reply, then exclaimed at the marble pools filled to choking with water lilies.

"If you like them, you shall have them!"

Stooping in his impeccable morning clothes, Harty-Tarty knelt by the sculptured pool, plunged both arms to the elbow into the water, and stood up with an armful of slimy blossoms. He walked her back up the manicured paths leisurely, not at all disturbed by his muddy, oozing burden. Startled eyes turned to them as they joined the throng, but Lord Hartington was oblivious. He turned the soggy flowers over to some footmen, ordering them to decorate her carriage.

"Wretched things!" Edward cried on the way home. "What a stench!"

Poor Edward. So many things bothered, worried, nagged, plagued, and upset him, yet faithfully he squired Lillie to the opera, the regatta, and the ball.

She wondered about the latest photographs she had posed for that morning. Of course, the sessions with Mr. Millais were continuing; Frank Miles wanted endless sittings; then there were those other artists she had agreed to pose for: Poynter, Watts—such a dear old man and that business of his marrying Ellen Terry when she was only a child!—Burne-Jones, and . . . she couldn't remember the rest. Oh, those photographers with their peculiar ideas and artificial poses. Edward had objected, saying nice people had their pictures taken only for personal use. But the thought of her photograph being exhibited in the stationer's shop in St. Helier amused her.

"They're dripping all over the seat on my trousers. Oh, damn!"

He began pushing the lilies out through the window, the muddy roots clutching at his sleeves octopus-like. As they streamed to the road, people ran toward them shouting.

"There she is—in there! Hurry!"

"With the flowers. That's Mrs. Langtry!"

"Blasted fools!" Edward snapped as Lillie peeped out.

"She's throwing us flowers. Come on!"

"Whip up your horses, driver!" Edward snatched at a garland around his ankle. "Driver, whip up your horses! Take us away."

Lillie looked out through the rear round window as they sped off. Men, women, and children were picking up the battered lilies, fighting over choice lengths.

"What's the world coming to?" Edward grumbled, wiping a dagger of green slime from his trouser leg. "Do you like being worshiped by a pack of beggars?"

"I don't understand it either, Edward."

It was not something one ever got used to. Perhaps those photographs had something to do with it. Still, it was amazing the way news filtered through the social grapevine of London, from society's inner sanctum outward. Lord Hartington had been talking about Millais' portrait which was to be called "The Jersey Lily." She had thought that was to be kept secret until the painting was finished, but people had already heard, and they invariably passed rumors on.

Because the artist had eulogized her as a Grecian beauty in the classic tradition, Lillie expected Millais to paint her draped in a flowing white robe, laurel on her brow, hair flowing down her back. He chose, however, to paint her without contrivance—in a close-fitting black dress fastened with little black bows, a white lace collar at the throat, plus a special touch that was to give her a new name destined to be her trademark.

Millais was by now a highly successful painter, the hit of many shows at the Royal Academy; and his knack of painting in the popular commercial idiom was later to be rewarded with knighthood. He lived in a mansion at Palace Gate, Kensington Gardens, with great halls and staircases of Italian marble. Near his first-floor studio a fountain squirted in a great, marble oval.

40

Millais was always waiting when Lillie arrived. He first sent her into another room, where Mrs. Millais helped her dress, and then immediately set to work. He painted frantically for twenty minutes, sucking at his pipe, never saying a word. Then he stared at her fixedly for so long a time that she felt pinned to her chair.

"Do you always paint by fits and starts?" she asked.

"You are the most exasperating subject I have ever painted, Mrs. Langtry," he said, squinting at her. "You look simply beautiful for about fifty-five out of sixty minutes in the hour, but for five minutes along in there you're absolutely amazing. It's enough to make any artist despair." He grunted and sucked at his pipe. "By the way, isn't there a lily grown on our island called the Jersey lily?"

"I think so, but it isn't really ours. Mama told me it dates from long ago when a ship coming from Africa went on the rocks off the north coast of Jersey and was pounded to pieces. There were a lot of bulbs on her, and the next spring they popped out of the sand. They looked so pretty the islanders transplanted them."

"That's native enough. Send for a few, will you?"

Mrs. Le Breton with her love of flowers was delighted to fulfill her daughter's request, but Millais was disappointed at the small, delicate crimson blossom.

"I had hoped for something more decorative and imposing. But 'The Jersey Lily' it shall be."

These sittings extended for months. There were always people hanging around at Millais' studio when she arrived or when she left, but the artist dismissed all visitors when he stood before his easel. One morning as she took her chair she noticed an older man lingering in the studio. A cold-eyed frosty man with a wide-winged collar, crude bow tie, a mouth clamped in so tight a line it seemed lipless. He looked like the old, hated, tyrannical headmaster of a boys' school.

"Mrs. Langtry, Mr. Gladstone." Millais smiled. "I'm sure you've heard of the distinguished gentleman I am presently immortalizing on canvas like yourself."

"Oh, yes. The news even gets to Jersey—after a time."

41

"Jersey, Jersey?" Gladstone mused. "Let me see, when did we take Jersey?"

"Take Jersey, eh?" Millais laughed. "You mean when did we Normans conquer Engand? And I say, Mrs. Langtry, when did *we* subjugate London?"

"Well put," said Gladstone. "Mrs. Gladstone and I rarely find time to go out socially even during the season—the stress of parliamentary work, you know—but I've certainly heard much about you, Mrs. Langtry. And seen your photographs."

Millais shuddered. "That obscene art is supposed to be making great strides these days, but all to the bad. How can a little black box capture such beauty?" He flung a hand at Lillie. "It's an insult to art, but that's the way with fads."

"Ah, even politics has its fads. Good day to you, sir, and Mrs. Langtry. It's been a great pleasure. I would gladly have welcomed you to 10 Downing Street before my recent attack of dizziness." He smiled thinly at his joke on Disraeli. "I hope to see you again."

"You undoubtedly will," Millais boomed. "She's been unanimously elected prime ministress of London."

"Couldn't think of a better choice. Thank heavens beauty is not another of Disraeli's gifts."

Edward was impressed by his wife's meeting with Gladstone and asked all sorts of questions about the statesman. She was glad for his interest because he had returned from a solitary walk highly disturbed by the photographs of her displayed in shop windows and hawked on the streets by disreputable vendors.

"There was even one fellow with a sort of trick post card that hid your face. 'The Jersey Lily!' he was shouting. 'The puzzle is to find her.' Where in the name of heaven did he get *that name* for you?"

She told him about Millais and the flower.

"Oh, yes," he recalled in disgust. "The portrait not finished and already the talk of London. You know how I feel about notoriety, Lillie. It just isn't decent to be talked about like this. I don't like it at all."

42

"I'm afraid it can't be helped."

Lillie had learned how to be composed and at ease. She knew the delights of mild flirtation and smoothly keeping a dozen men entranced just listening to her, vivacious, witty, and self-possessed. Simplicity was her secret, some said. Certainly she was getting a lot of mileage out of Madame Nicolle's black dress. It set her apart from women dressed more elaborately; her headgear did the same.

Once when she was dressing to go to the races with Edward in Sandown Park, she improvised a hat out of an odd piece of black velvet, shaping it into a neat toque and sticking a feather through it into her hair. Two days later her spontaneous creation was in milliners' shops all over London billed as "The Langtry Hat." Her coiffure also was being imitated. Hairdressers were busily turning out customers with "The Langtry Knot," but like the toque it worked its magic only on Lillie.

She and Edward were followed and pointed out in the street, trailed by groups of people arguing whether or not she was *the* Mrs. Langtry. They couldn't even shop without having her recognized. People pressed noses against the glass store fronts, business halted inside, and so many fought to get near her that the management had to escort them to safety out the back door.

What most impressed Lillie in London was the exciting spectacle of Rotten Row between twelve and two, the brilliant, animated, and fascinating scene as fashionable society congregated there to ride, drive, walk, see, and be seen. Everyone was smartly dressed, gay, and at his best—the women in the latest mode, the men in frock coats, pearl-gray trousers, varnished boots, and, of course, top hat. For two hours the crowd pushed and jostled slowly up and down each side of the Row, bowing and smiling, watching the four-in-hand coaches, pony carriages, tilburies, broughams, and the dignified barouches with their handsome, high-stepping grays, blacks, or whites, the coachmen and footmen rigid in flashing livery. Rotten Row (a bastardized version of *Route du Roi*) was also a

43

showcase for outstanding horsemanship, and again Lillie wished she had a horse as she watched the women on their thoroughbreds in close-fitting braided riding habits, all parading with that insouciance so indispensable to a woman of style in the public gaze.

William Graham Robertson, the artist-actor, wrote of walking in Hyde Park on a Sunday around noon and noticing a commotion among the solemn promenaders. A crowd collected, women got up on chairs for a better view, and people converged from all directions. A total stranger gripped his arm excitedly and shouted, "Mrs. Langtry—run!" He ran—and saw a young lady in pale cream color, "her head in its close bonnet drooped forward like a violet or snowdrop. It was my dowdy divinity of Hyde Park Corner, my pathetic governess—the now world-famous Jersey Lily, Venus Annodomini." Not since the Gunning sisters of a hundred years before had such universal worship been paid to beauty. "Yet she was simple in dress and manner, her gray eyes looked gravely at the city prostrate at her feet; she made no parade of her beauty, and none was required."

Frank Miles lived in an old corner house on Salisbury Street, just off the Strand and bordering on the Thames, and Oscar Wilde had rooms below him. No better place could have been found for the exotic pair. The building was a ghostly antique of winding staircases, blind passages, dusty niches, and piles of decrepit furniture. Still the two managed to make their quarters as brightly distinctive as their own personalities, particularly Frank, who had pots and jars of flowers all over his studio.

Lillie was his greatest discovery. While she posed for him, he stopped sketching just long enough to introduce her to all the people who congregated there. Jimmy Whistler dropped in, jaunty and biting as ever; lovely Ellen Terry, Irving's co-star and England's greatest actress; Graham Forbes-Robertson, a promising matinee idol; modern poets such as the brooding Dante Gabriel Rossetti, the studiedly romantic Charles Algernon Swinburne, the many-gifted William Morris, and Vio-

44

let Fane, a heretic poetess who raised Victorian hackles with her flaming love epics.

Walter Pater was a visitor, looking as critical as benefited him. At teatime there were always representatives of the nobility who professed to relish art—or was it the unusual? The Duchess of Argyle, the Duchess of Westminster, the Duchess of Beaufort, Lord and Lady Rosslyn, Lord and Lady Dorchester—all these Lillie came to know well as she smiled down from her dais above Frank Miles. With them were numerous rich young men-about-town making the rounds, and Oxford students come to see the incredible Wilde.

Royalty, too, made the pilgrimage to Bohemia. Her Royal Highness Princess Louise was often present, as well as His Royal Highness Prince Leopold, tall, intelligent, and sickly. Lillie and Edward had met him at the Marchioness of Ely's party, again at Alick York's, and he had stopped by at Eaton Place a few times. For a shy person he could be surprisingly direct. One afternoon he bought a sketch of Lillie outright the minute Miles put his pencil down. Then he had it mounted in a silver frame and placed it over his bed in Buckingham Palace. When he was sick, Queen Victoria went to his room, saw the picture, and asked who it was. "Mrs. Langtry, Mama," he answered. "The most beautiful woman in England." Gossip had it that the queen pushed a chair to the wall, got up on her own little royal feet, and removed the offending picture.

Of all the people she met that first season none other was so arresting as Oscar Wilde, fresh out of Oxford, belaureled with university honors, his genius already burning brightly as London blinked. A bulky six-footer of twenty-two, he carried himself with brazen self-assurance in a flamboyant checkerboard suit which went well with his generous, bubbling nature. His thick dark-brown hair was brushed straight back from his fine forehead and worn conspicuously long. His large flabby face was pale, his nose prominent, his mouth well shaped, his full lips sensuous, and his bad teeth had a greenish tinge. His features were plain, rather horsy, but they borrowed vitality from his magnificent all-seeing eyes, which seemed to change color, and from his ebullience.

45

He had tapering, artistic fingers with nails seldom as clean as they might be, and his large expressive hands were always in motion. Never fastidious, he dressed for shock value. Lillie always thought him on the grotesque side, but his enthusiasm and magnetism fascinated her. Laughter surrounded him, and his speaking voice enthralled—soft, flexible, roundly mellow, and capable of the intonation of a trained actor. Whatever he said was wittier or cleverer because of his presentation.

The impudent Wilde was a rising threat to the established iconoclast Whistler, and since their personalities were so much akin, sparks flew as they dueled in conversation. They admired each other, but they were temperamentally and competitively incompatible, and Lillie soon sensed a cleavage growing between them.

"Don't you think the development of art in a country is a sign of decadence?" inquired a youthful patrician voice.

"I don't know," said Whistler in his piercing nasal voice. "A good many countries manage to go to the dogs without it."

Whistler slipped into his cape and turned to Lillie. "Sunday breakfast," he said peremptorily. "Don't forget." He tilted his wide-brimmed hat at a rakish angle over his glossy ringlets, raised his long bamboo cane at the company in a fencer's salute, and swaggered out of the room.

"A royal command from the miniature Mephistopheles," said Wilde. "But you must go, Lil. Jimmy's breakfasts are priceless." He reached for another biscuit. "You don't know how starved and exhausted I am because of you. I'm dedicating poem after poem to the new Helen. I worked on them all morning and took out a comma." He sighed. "This afternoon I put it in again."

"Don't jest, Oscar!" Miles held his arms out to Lillie. "It's a crusade, and she's the Holy Grail. I with my pencil, you with your pen, will make her the Gioconda and Laura of this century."

"I'm not sure I want my future planned along those lines," said Lillie. "What about your own future, Oscar? What do you want to do?"

46

"Amuse the mob, infuriate the middle class, and fascinate the aristocrats."

"That won't do," Miles smirked. "Lillie means your ambition in life."

"What a dreadful word, ambition. But God knows. I won't be a dried-up Oxford don, anyhow. I'll be a poet, a writer, a dramatist. Somehow or other I'll be famous, and if I'm not famous, I'll be notorious." He smiled to himself. "Or perhaps I'll rest and do nothing. These things are on the knees of the gods. What will be, will be."

"No! You must burst forth in a blaze of glory like Lillie."

Oscar puffed out his cheeks like a bullfrog. "I spend all my time bursting, Frank. The blaze of glory is more difficult. After all, there is only one Lillie." Miles agreed vehemently, and Wilde gave a prodigious sigh. "But the Lily is so tiresome. She *won't* do what I tell her. I assure her she owes it to herself to drive daily through the park dressed entirely in black in a black victoria drawn by black horses with 'Venus Annodomini' emblazoned on her black bonnet in dull sapphires. But she won't."

"Too much, too much. Our Lily doesn't need gilding."

"All of us need gilding. Nothing succeeds like excess, you know. Just give me the luxuries, and I can dispense with the necessities."

"Don't let his words deceive you, Lillie. He's a fighter, too. I remember the fuss at Oxford when he had to fill out a census paper. He gave his age as nineteen, his profession as genius, and his infirmity as talent. The story spread, and Oscar was deliberately assaulted by some ruffians to prove his masculinity."

"A tedious business," sniffed Wilde.

"Our mountainous genius nearly killed them," said Miles proudly. "Oscar is no sportsman, but he would make an amazing pugilist."

"Sweat may be honest, but the word offends to the core. The only possible form of exercise is talk. Coming, Lil?"

They walked slowly, Oscar keeping up a scintillating flood of conversation, stopping only to fish out a cigarette. He never took one from the same pocket but carried six cases: leather, enamel, silver, and gold.

She asked, "Why so many?"

"I like them, and I couldn't bear being without. A cigarette is the perfect type of perfect pleasure. It is exquisite and leaves one unsatisfied. What more can one want?"

"Oh, Oscar, there's no one quite like you!"

"Naturally, Lil, but sometimes a dull sheen must do for brilliance. Have you noticed that in modern life nothing produces such an effect as a good platitude? It makes the whole world kin."

"Surely you don't want to be kin to the whole world?" she teased.

Oscar shuddered. "I am the only person in the world I should like to know thoroughly, but I don't see any chance of it just at present."

"But you go everywhere, I notice. You must like society."

"To be in it is a bore, Lil, but to be out of it is a tragedy. Your entrée is your sublime beauty, mine— To get into the best society nowadays, one has either to feed people, amuse people, or shock people. That is all. I take the path of least resistance, while you are simply your gloriously beautiful self and manage all three."

"Don't flatter me. This thing that's happened to me doesn't seem real at all. I can't believe any of it."

"One's real life is so often the life that one does not lead. But you are the key. No man has any real success in this world unless he has got women to back him, and women rule society."

"Then you're just using me—is that it?" She looked away from a group of men who were devouring her with their eyes. "They're talking about me and I hate to think about what they're saying."

"What do you care, so long as they don't stop talking about you? It is better to be beautiful than to be good, but it is better to be good than to be ugly. Some women face a terrible prospect."

He stopped abruptly and led Lillie to a florist's window.

48

"Please don't buy me flowers, Oscar," she said, knowing his penchant for gifts he couldn't afford.

"It's very sad. Very sad. I must go in for a minute."

She accompanied him, and the proprietor's face lighted up at the sight of Mrs. Langtry in his store. Obviously he envisaged a big sale. The other customers moved back to give the incongruous couple staring room.

"Would you remove those right-hand bunches of flowers from your window?" Oscar requested in his melodious voice.

"With pleasure!" said the little man eagerly. "How many will you have?"

"Oh, I don't want any, thank you," Oscar replied casually. "I only asked to have them removed from the window because they look tired."

Then he nodded and went out with Lillie, leaving the florist bewildered. She was dying to say something, but Oscar rambled on with his usual imperturbable good humor as they headed for Eaton Place, just as if he'd come from the hospital after inquiring for a sick friend. At a street corner Lillie noticed a man who had been in the florist's shop pointing out Oscar to his woman companion.

"There goes that bloody fool Oscar Wilde," he said loudly.

Oscar beamed and tipped his hat. "It's extraordinary how soon one gets known in London."

"You don't mind that sort of thing?" Lillie asked.

"Mind it? Praise makes me humble, but when I am abused I know I have touched the stars."

Oscar idealized Lillie, and he wanted her to be as wise as she was beautiful. He took her to King's College to attend the learned Professor Charles Thomas Newton's lectures on Greek art. Her presence delighted the students, filled the hall, and fired the archeologist to fresh eloquence as she sat in the front row where Oscar had ostentatiously led her.

"There was a consummate appropriateness to that scene which I found rapturous," he said afterward. "With your perfect Grecian profile and that exquisite column of a throat with its three *plis de Vénus,* you were a living exponent of the very classical type he was describing."

49

Sometimes Lillie had too much of Oscar. He was always around the apartment, waiting for her, pursuing her as she kept her round of engagements. His excuse was the poem he was writing about her—it obsessed him and he had to be near her, her house, her possessions until his thoughts crystallized. She told him she needed a little peace and that he ought to stay away for a while. His big eyes throbbed with hurt, and he let her know he felt crushed. Lillie thought nothing of it until she went to the theater that night to see Irving and Terry.

"Isn't that Wilde down there?" said Edward, pointing from their box to the stalls before curtain time.

She stared. Oscar looked up at her, and there was some sort of a disturbance below.

"Good heavens!" Edward exclaimed. "Now what is the man doing?"

People were craning their necks as Frank Miles led Oscar slowly out of the theater—a hunched-over, sobbing Oscar in black frock coat, red-and-yellow flowered vest, a flowing white-silk necktie fastened with a huge amethyst stickpin, fawn-colored trousers, and drooping lavender gloves.

"Why, the idiot's crying!"

"I'm afraid it's my fault." And she told Edward of her slight.

"The gall of the man! Do you know, I found him sleeping on your doorstep a few nights ago. He was curled up like a great disorderly black bear, and I tripped over him in the darkness. He told me I had shattered his poetic dreams, and he was prepared to resume his hard couch until I ordered him to leave. The audacity of the fellow!"

Naturally the story spread, as Oscar had hoped, but Lillie was not deceived and chided him.

"Ah, Lil, don't malign my Spartan sacrifices in your holy name."

"Who said 'Give me the luxuries and I can dispense with the necessities'? Oscar Wilde would never lie on a bed of nails by choice."

"You probe too deep, Lil. The day may come when I have no choice."

"The New Helen" finally appeared in Edmund Yates's *The*

50

World, a newspaper dedicated to art, society, and reform. It consisted of ten ten-line stanzas of Grecian eulogy, frustration, and despair. Oscar had read the poem to Lillie in manuscript, his musical voice tasting each word like some succulent fruit before it fell from his lips.

> Lily of love, pure and inviolate!
> Tower of ivory! Red rose of fire!
> Thou hast come down our darkness to illume.
> For we, close caught in the wide nets of Fate,
> Wearied with waiting for the World's Desire,
> Aimlessly wandered in the House of Gloom,
> Aimlessly sought some slumberous anodyne
> For wasted lives, for lingering wretchedness,
> Till we beheld thy re-arisen shrine,
> And the white glory of thy loveliness.

It was sound for the sake of sound, beauty for beauty. Lillie felt honored and flattered, even though she thought the poem a bit ridiculous as applied to her.

"I love it," she said as he waited for her reaction.

"It's sublime," he agreed modestly. "An intensely sublime tribute to a sublime woman."

Later on, the poem was printed in a collection, and Oscar presented her with a slim, vellum-bound copy inscribed, "To Helen, formerly of Troy, now of London."

"You know I favored a small edition, but my publisher outvoted me. My first idea was to print only four copies: one for you, one for myself, one for the British Museum, and one for heaven." He paused. "I had some doubt about the British Museum."

"I shall always cherish this," she promised.

"You must always keep it on a shelf of its own beyond compare. And now your usual homage." He went to where he had dropped his coat and returned with a single amaryllis lily. "Why buy more when this great blossom personifies all of your exquisite beauty?"

Oscar's funds were low, but he always bought her a flower from the Covent Garden flower market. Then he wandered down Piccadilly with his one bloom, certain to attract maximum attention as he made his acolyte's way to Eaton Place. Eyebrows were raised, another Wilde story passed into history, and a lyric writer called William S. Gilbert took note.

"You are a true Apostle of the Lily, Oscar," Lillie said, thanking him.

"Am I not!" he said cheerfully. "I worship at my favorite national shrine. Lil, you must divorce this Langtry fellow and marry me. With your beauty and my genius, we simply couldn't find enough worlds to conquer. We'd have to create more worlds, as I am constantly doing."

Oscar was the first to dedicate a poem to Lillie. Next Frederick Locker-Lampson met her just as she was "sailing with supreme dominion on the buoyant wings of her beauty," and felt compelled to honor her with delicate verses. But the oddest poetic tribute she inspired was a spur-of-the-moment stanza from Joaquin Miller, a man as purposefully unique and implausible as Wilde himself.

Lillie and Edward were attending a party at the Arlington Street home of Lord Houghton, an elderly widower, considered one of London's most charming hosts, when they met this "Byron of Oregon, the great interpreter of America." In languid literary London Joaquin Miller was a sensation because he dressed like a road-company Buffalo Bill. Lillie stared at his haggard face, short beard, and yellow-blond hair that hung in stringy curls below his shoulders. He wore a buckskin shirt, a blue polka-dot bandanna around his neck, studded-leather wristlets, fringed-buckskin trousers, polished hip boots, and carried a sombrero as though it were a broad-plumed helmet.

"*You* are poetry," he declaimed. "You, you, you. As you look, as you stand, as you smile, as you speak. Those blue eyes! Where did you get those blue eyes?"

Lord Houghton vouched for her as an inspiration to all poets, though he confessed he himself was too old to do her justice. Thereupon Lillie said jokingly that Miller should write a poem for her.

52

"Mrs. Langtry," he announced, "*is* a poem, complete and perfect as she is."

Lillie looked for him later, but Miller had disappeared. Then Lord Houghton brought up a stocky, stiffly erect man in a poorly fitting black suit. He had a stern appearance and gray, grizzled mustache and beard clipped short.

"Mrs. Langtry, this is our guest of honor, General Grant, the victorious leader of the Northern armies in the war against the Southern rebels some years ago. This is quite fitting, this meeting of Mars and Venus."

General Grant smiled benignly as he escorted Lillie to dinner. She tried hard to make him talk, but he was curt and ill at ease. He kept glancing down the table at a stout woman with big, round arms who, he said, was Mrs. Grant.

"What did you do after the war, General?" Lillie asked innocently.

"Served two terms as President of the United States, madam."

Toward the end of the evening Joaquin Miller reappeared. "I've done it," he broke in importantly, holding up a torn envelope. "Would you like to hear it?"

His strange appearance, plus his dramatic announcement, had the effect of a waiter dropping a loaded tray in a crowded restaurant. He cleared his throat and pulled at his beard in the expectant hush.

"To the Jersey Lily," he read, bowing to her.

> "If all God's world a garden were,
>   And women were but flowers,
> If men were bees that busied there
>   Through endless summer hours,
> O! I would hum God's garden through
>   For honey till I came to you."

His harsh voice did not drop but gave the impression that more was to come. Naturally the audience remained silent. Then he raised his shaggy head and held out his arm to Lillie in salute.

"Let this verse stand! It's the only one I ever wrote to a living woman." He gave her the torn envelope. "For you, lovely lady."

Several nights later Joaquin Miller eclipsed himself at Lady Brassey's musicale. He stood part way up the white marble staircase leading into the house. The door was open behind him to the entrance hall where Lord and Lady Brassey were greeting their guests. Recognizing Lillie as she approached, he moved back from the carved railing, holding his high-crowned, broad-brimmed sombrero in his hands. He dipped a horny hand into the hat and, backing awkwardly up the steps before her, scattered rose petals at her feet. At her side Edward reacted as he might have to hot coals.

"Thus be your path in life!" Joaquin Miller intoned fervently, scuttling backward and strewing petals. "Thus be your path in life, oh Queen of Beauty!"

The poet tripped on the top step, the butler steadying him with the same aplomb he would have used for teetering champagne glasses. Miller made a sweeping motion with his sombrero so that the last of the rose petals wafted over Lillie's head. They clung to her dress and hair as Lord and Lady Brassey welcomed her, everyone behaving as if a rose-petal shower were a commonplace salute.

Edward declined to escort Lillie to Whistler's celebrated Sunday breakfasts in Tite Street, Chelsea, where he lived in dynamic artistic confusion, and therefore she went alone.

About twenty guests, most of them painters, disciples, or pretty women, milled about as Whistler darted in and out of the kitchen preparing the meal and discharging waspish remarks. Outside of a few straight-back chairs, there was nothing to sit on except crates and packing boxes, and Whistler was quick to criticize complaints.

"Are you a sultan that you have to loll on pillows? Do you have a spine made of jelly, eh? You should have trained at West Point as I did. Make a man out of you. If you want to be comfortable, go to bed."

The table was set with a white cloth on which blue and white china glistened. There were two centerpieces, a bowl of goldfish and, for Lillie's benefit, an exotic Japanese vase containing a solitary Madonna lily. Whistler scurried about bringing in buckwheat cakes, popovers, corn muffins, oatmeal, and sausages; all the while hooting, laughing, filling up wine glasses, darting back to the kitchen, mocking the Royal Academy, and explaining just how his American delicacies should be consumed. Because the butter was too yellow, he tinted it a harmonizing green, and he made the rice pudding a delicate pink to overcome its pebbly white look.

The food was good, hot, and unusual, but Jimmy's performance, his wrigglings, grimaces, running back and forth, and pungent conversation gave it a virtuoso fascination. Sometimes his creditors provided interruptions, Jimmy identifying them by their knock—the big ones tapping discreetly, the small ones loudly—before he disposed of them with his ruthless charm.

"How long must we wait for a Whistler landscape?" asked a disciple.

"There are too many trees in the country. Nature plans things so badly, d'ye know? Where no tree should stand, you see a hundred; where a wood is called for, none stands. An intolerable situation!"

"I heard you shot a dog a few weeks ago," said Lillie.

"The West Point in me compels that I take gun in hand every few years, but the dog—I had to pepper the beast. He was a canine without artistic habits and had placed himself badly in relation to the landscape. I did both a favor."

Jimmy manipulated his effects carefully. He insisted that Lillie remain where he had seated her—the firelight playing on her lovely face to give her complexion a delicate brilliance in the darkened room, softness and strength contrasting in the flowing line of her curved figure. The total picture was glowing with vigor and vitality when the critic, George W. Smalley, walked into the room and had the exact impression Whistler had stage-managed.

"Of course, you and Mrs. Langtry know each other?" Whistler said grandly.

Smalley bowed. "Until now I have never seen her."

"Then you have never seen the loveliest thing that ever was! Don't tell me that you don't think her perfect. It doesn't matter what you think. She *is* perfect! Her beauty is simply exquisite, but her manner is more exquisite still. She is kindness itself." His stance challenged Smalley. "You agree, eh, what?"

The critic smiled. "How can I help it before a charming beauty and a genius of the brush?"

five

BEAUTY had always been a desirable asset and an object of public worship, but perhaps never so much as in the late 1870's and early 1880's, when the cult of the professional beauty raged in London, with each charmer having her own fervent adherents even after the newest arrival, Mrs. Langtry, had clearly lapped the field.

As a special attraction at a party the presence of one or more professional beauties was essential. Titled hostesses took to adding an important P.S. to their invitations: "Do come! Some P.B.'s will be there." Often this meant that guests would see Lady Dudley, Mrs. Luke Wheeler, Mrs. William Cornwallis-West, the Duchess of Leinster, Lady Helen Vincent, Miss Violet Lindsay, Lady de Grey, Lady Ormonde, Lady Gerard, Ida, Lady Dalhousie, Lady Mary Mills, Lady Randolph Churchill, or the also-ran seasonal flashes, certain invading foreign beauties. To the general public, the Professional Beauties were the glamour girls of their day. Gawking at their photographs in shop windows was a form of peepshow entertainment. The term was a puzzling one and its notoriety carried with it a taint of the risqué—yet these were all well-bred, often aristocratic women.

Lillie's photographs were all over London and spreading to the provinces and beyond. Besides the craze for the Langtry toque and the Langtry knot, enterprising shops were *au courant* with Langtry shoes and gloves.

Lillie herself felt like a museum piece, and her life, heretofore dull and mole-like, now seemed fantastically unreal. Every

57

hostess felt it was imperative to her self-esteem to entertain Mrs. Langtry, and Lillie had to satisfy all the demands on her. She was the toast of Belgravia. She ruled society's world which extended north to Bayswater, south to South Kensington, with Piccadilly the center of activity and Mayfair the heart of the élite's domain. Before long she had passed the line from social phenomenon to public figure worthy of preservation. In 1878, when Cleopatra's Needle was erected on the Victoria Embankment, which stretched along the Thames from Black-friars to Westminster Bridge, the Jersey Lily was properly time-capsuled for posterity. Into the foundation of the Egyptian obelisk—sixty-eight feet high and weighing one hundred eighty tons—was set "an iron box containing photographs of Mrs. Langtry, current coins, and other trifles of the time."

Royalty was always sought after, and the gay, party-seeking, woman-loving Prince of Wales was *the* social catch. The prospect of being the first to bring together the popular Bertie and the beauty queen was enough to make any hostess' head reel. The Prince was known to be in the habit of annexing each beauty at the height of her popularity; it was inevitable that he should reach the Jersey Lily sooner or later. Society expected its king to claim its new queen, and breathlessly awaited developments. Lillie was willing to wait, although the idea of being courted by a future King of England was exciting. Meanwhile, there was so much to do, so much to see, so much of everything.

The time came when she had to do something about her single black evening dress. Besides being a trademark, it was also a symbol of good luck, but it was wearing thin. Her maid, Dominique, urged her to throw it away. Lillie clung to it because she liked being different. Her husband was supposed to be poor, and she hated the endless trying-on sessions at dress-makers'. Mary Cornwallis-West settled the issue for her. A friend of the Prince, the mother of three handsome children, small, brown-haired, brown-eyed, and vivaciously lovely, Mary begged the loan of the famous black dress for an evening at Covent Garden, where Adelina Patti was singing. Lillie was tired that night and agreed reluctantly. The dress was re-

58

turned in shreds—for Mary had gone on to a ball after the opera and had danced until dawn. She said she was very sorry.

Since black was her magic color, Lillie ordered a smiliar model from Madame Nicolle, this time of stronger black satin. This turned out to be on the rigid, unyielding side and lacked the simplicity of its predecessor. Still, Lillie might have continued with black if it hadn't been for Lord Dudley, who was giving a great ball for King Leopold of the Belgians at Dudley House. Lady Dudley dropped in to tell Lillie that her husband loathed black and forbade her wearing it. Would Lillie please spare him pain and wear something else?

Mrs. Stratton, then the smartest dressmaker in London, was enchanted to be of service to Mrs. Langtry. Fitters clustered around, and Lillie explained that she wanted something simple. She chafed at the succession of fittings, the tuckings-in, pullings-out, stitching and restitching, but the result was worth while. Turning before the glass the night of the ball, she recognized that Mrs. Stratton had seen her as a Grecian beauty, modeling her creation on flowing, traditional lines, studding the white velvet with pearls and yet keeping all the flattering simplicity she had loved in the black dress.

"Is that the new dress?" said Edward. "Why, it's stunning. White does wonders for you. Much better than black. Couldn't understand why you wore black so long."

"This was very expensive."

"Oh, we're not quite paupers, my dear. You deserve the best in your position."

"But the black was something I could wear every night. I can't do that with white."

"Then buy all you need," he said grandly. "Clothes mean a lot in London, and it's important that you keep up."

This was a new tack for Edward. It puzzled her. She had never had a clear picture of their finances. There were many things she wanted, and she had always felt she had to hold back.

"But can we afford it?"

"Certainly. We have to afford it, don't we? Oh, by the by, I met a most interesting man through Sir George Chetwynd

59

this afternoon—Charles Freake, who began as a common laborer and is now worth millions. He's a building contractor, very impressive in spite of his background, and he wants to meet you."

"He sounds interesting. Edward, I would love to entertain and give a few small dinner parties. But we can't do it here. Don't you think we ought to move to a larger apartment?"

"Whatever you say, dear," he said, eying her admiringly. "You better hurry. The four-wheeler is waiting."

This business of hiring carriages—that was another thing they'd have to remedy, thought Lillie. A new house, transportation of their own. It bore thinking—too much thinking—and she was relieved as they pulled up before Dudley House on the corner of Park Lane and Upper Brook Street. Her dress caused immediate comment. Lord and Lady Dudley usually received at the top of the imposing staircase, but Lillie's arrival was duly semaphored. Lord Dudley descended to greet her, a gesture observed by all present. Everyone stopped talking as Lillie entered the ballroom, a glowing goddess in shimmering white. Monocles were readjusted, mustaches twirled, trains straightened.

"How wonderful!" Lady Dudley laughed with pleasure. "It would appear that in appeasing my husband you have achieved another triumph."

Leopold, King of the Belgians, was a short, bearded man, undistinguished in his black tail coat to which numerous decorations were haphazardly pinned. She curtsied to him and in a burst of accented English he said, "Please, please, it is I who should kiss your feet, madame. You rule here."

As they danced later, his eyes devoured her with a prurient gleam which Lillie preferred to take for admiration.

"Ah, you are beautiful as a queen should be, except that they never are. I have learned from sad experience. It is not what people think, to be a king." He laughed breathily. "We can no longer chop off people's heads when we want." He stroked her forearm above her gloves. "So lovely. You must be a good friend of the Prince of Wales, eh, Madame Langtry?"

60

"I have met his brothers, Your Majesty, but I have never had the pleasure of meeting the Prince."

Leopold stared incredulously. "I do not understand it. Perhaps it is just that he is getting older, or the old mama-queen frightens him." He chuckled. "No, Bertie is too much like myself. In some things we never grow too old. That you will learn, Madame Langtry."

Lillie was too absorbed to question the motives back of Edward's change of heart. He no longer nagged about expenses; he encouraged her to spend; he liked their new home at 17 Norfolk Street. Mrs. Walsh was glad to see them go; and Lillie was pleased to have larger quarters to decorate and furnish to her own taste. Dominique came with them. They added another maid to care for Lillie's extensive wardrobe, as well as a butler, a cook, and a coachman, for now they had their own smart brougham and a horse to pull it.

She spent hours decorating the place and choosing furniture, but she was dissatisfied with the living room, which she had made gloomier with the deep purple hangings she had chosen. She mentioned this to Jimmy Whistler one night at Her Majesty's Theater during an opera in which Christine Nilsson sang the lead. He promised to find a remedy, so it was no surprise when he turned up on her doorstep, his white forelock a doughty plume, a Mephistophelian smile on his face. He held out a bundle of palm-leaf fans, a can of gold paint, and some brushes.

"You always look so elegant, Jimmy. Surely you don't propose to paint in those clothes?"

"Naturally. D'ye know, if I had only an old rag to cover me, I should wear it with such neatness and propriety—with the utmost distinction. The secret is flair. I have it; you have it. But now to work." He examined the room. "The plum-colored draperies have made you miss the effect, but no matter. We'll salvage it with the bit of garishness this mausoleum demands."

Lillie helped him gild the fans and place them on the walls, working with such enthusiasm that she took no notice of the gold paint with which they splattered themselves. After the fans were in position, he asked for a stepladder. He scooted up it and while talking animatedly began painting on the ceiling—blue sky with drifting white clouds against which some bright-yellow birds spread their wings in full flight.

He put down his brushes. "Pretty, eh? Perfect, what? A gem, ha?"

She praised it highly and Whistler was delighted.

"My word, your hair, your dress—you're spotted with gold paint. Even your eyelashes glitter. The Langtry gold polka dot! Have tea with me at the Café Royal or Silferino's. We'll show London your newest style."

Minutes later, the beautiful Mrs. Langtry was walking down the street with the startling Jimmy Whistler, who wore a specially designed short blue coat, white waistcoat, a peculiar scoop-shaped collar with stringy black tie, the habitual white-duck trousers, and his favorite thin dancing pumps sporting pink bows on patent leather. A stranger coming toward them smiled expectantly.

"Damn!" Whistler scowled, and his overlong bamboo cane twitched in his hand. "He's seen us."

"We can turn around," Lillie suggested helpfully.

"I don't know him well enough to avoid him."

"How do you do?" said the man, now even with them.

"I don't." Whistler ignored his hand and kept going.

"Oh, Mr. Whistler, how are you getting on?"

"I'm not," he snapped. "I'm getting off."

"Really, Jimmy!" said Lillie. "How could you be so rude?"

"My dear, I will tell you a secret. Early in life I made the discovery that I was charming, and if one is delightful one has to thrust the world away to keep from being bored to death." He pointed with his cane. "Look at that newsboy, will you? That filthy urchin, that enchanting ragamuffin." His face softened as they stopped before the grimy-faced boy with his newspapers. "How old are you, laddie?"

"Seven, sir."

"Oh, come now, you must be more than that." He turned to

Lillie. "I don't think he could get that dirty in seven years, do you?" He put some coins in the boy's black hand. "Don't let anyone make you wash, d'you hear, laddie? You're perfect just as you are."

"Jimmy," said Lillie further along, "you surprise me. You're really a kind man and a thoughtful one."

"Don't ever tell a soul! You'll destroy my reputation utterly."

Poems, works of art, flowers and such gifts could be accepted without obligation. Nevertheless, Lillie had plenty of admirers who dangled jewelry and other expensive things in front of her, ostensibly with no strings attached but with a strong hint that an exchange of favors would be appropriate. Some were coy about it, others callous where Edward was concerned, but Lillie was blessed with good judgment. The Le Bretons had all been religious people. Her comparative naïveté was good protection, and she clung to it. She knew how to let down ardent, sensual men without letting them feel less bewitched.

Ralph Moran and Monty Guest were among these, but Moreton Frewen was cleverer. Listening to Lillie's talk about riding in Jersey, watching her eyeing the horses yearningly in Rotten Row, he sought to ingratiate himself with an irresistible gift—his handsome, thoroughbred chestnut Redskin. This was no ordinary horse, but so splendid an animal that he had attracted attention every time he was ridden in the "Ladies Mile" in the Park. The eccentric, romantic novelist Ouida (Louise de la Ramée), admiring Redskin's color, action, symmetry, and manners, had fed him caramels just to meet his owner.

Moreton Frewen was a typical rich young member of the landed gentry. He lived in Melton Mowbray, Leicestershire, and his life consisted of "November to April Melton, then a month's salmon fishing in Ireland; May, June, July London; then Goodwood and Cowes, then grouse-shooting somewhere, and Doncaster; next a broken week or two at Newmarket and a little schooling of young Irish horses." He was in love with Lillie, a persistent suitor, and shrewd enough to guess she couldn't refuse Redskin.

Edward took a little persuading. But they had a stable now and Lillie had been dying for a horse. Thereafter, after meeting Frewen, he agreed.

Lillie rode every day, a striking figure in her riding habit. Mounting Redskin and reaching the Park, however, was an ordeal, for a throng always gathered in Norfolk Street, awaiting her exit. It became necessary to shut the stable yard gates so that she could mount in privacy. A cheer went up as the gates were opened. She had to spur Redskin on before the crowd closed in, Frewen following on another horse. Her arrival in the Park was awaited by a troop of distinguished horsemen who accompanied her on the daily canter. Moreton Frewen was annoyed that his gift gave him no special privileges. He had simply made equestrians of Moran, Guest, and all the others.

"No man objects to decent competition," he said glumly, "but what can I do against your personal cavalry?"

Her own house, her own horse, her own rounds! Life was much more orderly now. She continued to transform her Norfolk Street home, which was one of many red-brick dwellings in what once had been a fashionable neighborhood. She filled the nine drab rooms with Elizabethan and Chippendale pieces, bright draperies, exotic pictures, striking rugs, and other effects which expressed her personality. She knew she had been hoodwinked by supposedly reputable antique dealers in many cases, but Edward approved of everything, including the touches she borrowed from her friends in the much-reviled aesthetic movement.

Oscar Wilde came with John Ruskin, Slade Professor of Art at Oxford and an art critic whose opinions were the arbitrary last word. Oscar deferred to Ruskin in everything, showing such awe and humbleness that he seemed unrecognizable. At her mention of Whistler, Ruskin smiled sneeringly. Lillie thought of him as a malevolent shaggy lion with long, floppy hair, thick eyebrows, craggy nose, bushy sidewhiskers, and tufty beard. An incredibly humorless, opinionated man.

"Ah, yes, poor Whistler, who can appreciate nothing but his own crude daubs and knows nothing of Greek art upon which

64

all beauty is based." Ruskin glanced at a table on which a single white lily floated in a wide, shallow blue-glass bowl. "That is lovely, Mrs. Langtry. Blue has been everlastingly appointed by the Deity to be a source of delight. Whistler's yellow—bah! I associate yellow with disgust—if emotions can have a color, and I believe they can—and also with poltroons."

Oscar nodded as if great truth had been spoken, but Lillie was offended. She decided that Ruskin was a monster with tyrannical ideas, and she was glad Jimmy had won his recent libel suit against him. (It dated from Ruskin's remark: "I have seen much and heard much of cockney impudence, but never expected to have a coxcomb ask two hundred guineas for flinging a pot of paint in the public's face." The court sessions had been like a side show, with Jimmy testifying in his best histrionic fashion. His lawyer hadn't helped by displaying the disputed picture upside down to the jury. Whistler was finally awarded a farthing's damages and proceeded to mount the coin on his watch chain as a victory symbol. But Ruskin's disciples considered the victory theirs and the artist permanently discredited. As if anyone could discredit Jimmy!)

"Ruskin!" Whistler had snorted later, showing her the farthing on his chain. "Did you ever hear of a critic who didn't insist on making five out of two and two? A thoroughly decadent, incompetent idiot!"

Lillie met the Prince of Wales unexpectedly. She and Edward had been asked by Sir Allen Young to a late supper after the opera. There was an interminable wait before they sat down. Lillie was ravenous, Edward uneasy and impatient as always. Alleno, as his intimates called him, had plenty of time to talk about his explorations. She thought him a likable man, if rather silly.

Rich and unmarried, he had tried to go to either the North or South Pole—she wasn't sure which—and to find a Northwest Passage or something. Yet he was the kind of man who had trouble just opening a door or lighting a cigar. A restless, fumbling man with a lost, abstract manner who mumbled on about the icy regions. The expeditions were "difficult," the

Arctic "cold," the Eskimos "curious," polar bears "ferocious." Lillie yawned.

Then came the sounds of someone arriving. The ladies smoothed their hair and dresses hurriedly, the men straightened their ties. Sir Allen rushed out precipitately, stumbling in his haste. Edward glanced at Lillie, and she raised her eyebrows.

"I'm afraid I'm a little late, Alleno," said a hearty, guttural voice. "These official functions always take longer than one anticipates."

Lillie couldn't catch their host's reply, but he sounded humble, obsequious. This was somebody important. The guests were all standing, quiet and respectful, and she had a sudden panicky flash of intuition. Oh, no! It couldn't be. Then the Prince of Wales stood in the doorway, looking very much as in his pictures. Lillie's hand went to her fluttering heart; Edward looked as if he wanted to hide under the table. The Prince wore well-tailored evening dress, blazing with medals and decorations, a glittering, regal presence that was dazzling in the small room. He greeted the company genially, apologized for his tardiness, and circled the room receiving curtsies from the women, bows and handshakes from the men.

Lillie managed a shaky bending of the knee as she spread her skirts. She took the firm hand offered her and met the look of the deeply inset eyes on the smiling bearded face. She had met kings and princes before, but now she felt inexplicably frightened and shy. If the Prince had heard of her or been anxious to meet her, he gave no sign. After he passed on, she found pleasure in Edward's stammered replies to royal questions.

There was talk of horses and horse racing, Cowes and yachting, and the London season. The Prince was relaxed, tried to make everyone feel at ease with his gracious good cheer. He worked at it effortlessly and, as she listened, Lillie felt that here was a man one would take for a king at first sight. Whatever the nature of his private life, his interest in the theater, the peculiarities of his fast friends, and his supposedly scandalous sojourns in Paris, he took his royal calling seriously. A man

66

of the world and *bon vivant* who liked to laugh, he never lost his dignity or encouraged familiarity even among his intimates. His friends could do or say as they pleased—so long as they never forgot his position. Unlike King Leopold, he had a sovereign manner and aspect; he wore his royal heritage like an invisible mantle; yet he was human, fun-loving, and real.

She sensed a directness in the Prince's hooded eyes as he looked her way, but then didn't all pretty women find favor with him? She asked herself how Mary Cornwallis-West and the other beauties had achieved royal-favorite status. Most of them were married women as she was. She blushed, touching her cheek to hide the telltale flush. Probably a good deal of the gossip was exaggerated, jealous maliciousness. He had a lovely wife in Princess Alexandra and was a devoted father. How—?

"You are warm, Mrs. Langtry? Your cheeks are so red."

"Yes, your Ma— Yes, Sir. It is close in here."

Oh, God, she was burning up. She must be crimson, flaming. Be calm, she told herself. Show your teeth. Smile. Look at Edward.

"I have seen your photographs all over London. I must say they hardly attest to your beauty."

"Thank you, Sir." She made a supreme effort to escape monosyllabic replies. I must show him I can talk, she thought frantically. To beauty must be added wit, *anything* to make him remember me. "I am not so handsome as my father," she blurted. "He was the finest man in England. I shall always love the dear old church where he preached."

"Jersey, isn't it? That lovely isle off Normandy."

To titillate the Prince of Wales, to provide some fresh novelty to amuse him, as well as triumphantly to establish her position as a party giver, was the object of every London hostess with any claim as a leader of society. The emergence of Mrs. Langtry as the top professional beauty had been welcomed as a chance to please Albert Edward, and the trick had been to get them together. Edward Langtry himself unwittingly brought this about.

Since he continued to express his admiration for C. J.

Freake, the self-made millionaire, Lillie gave a small dinner party for Mr. and Mrs. Freake and Sir George and Lady Chetwynd. Sir George was a member of her cavalry in the Park. He had also gone out of his way to be nice to Edward, inviting him frequently to his club and otherwise disarming him. Sir George had confessed that Lillie had only to snap her fingers to make him her slave. He had made advances several times when he had invited the Langtrys to stay at Grendon Hall in Warwickshire. She was more impressed by the estate than by the man. Deer in the park, swans on the lakes, great expanses of lawns, flowerbeds, shrubs, rooms filled with priceless furniture, thick rugs, liveried servants! Never before had she been so aware of the smallness and shabbiness of Norfolk Street. Yet here were the Chetwynds and Freakes having a perfectly wonderful time at her house.

C. J. Freake was a heavy-set man in his sixties with a large head, a bulldog face, and huge workingman's hands. Right away she knew he had something on his mind, something he wanted to communicate to her. After ascertaining that she had met the Prince, he spoke of his own friendship with him and of how he had learned of His Highness' interest in music. Determined to honor his future king, he had put up all the money for a building to be known as the Royal Academy of Music. He explained that he liked being of service to the Prince and therefore wanted to know if Lillie would like to have the Prince as her friend. She looked at him.

"Please don't misunderstand me, Mrs. Langtry. These matters must be handled delicately through—uh—intimates. Lord —I can't tell you his name—is close to the Prince in spite of his poor financial standing. I was told that the Prince is much interested in forming a possible friendship with you."

"What do you hope to say through this impoverished lord, whose financial standing should improve now?"

Freake reddened. "That his Royal Highness may pay his respects to the lovely lady in the privacy of the Freake mansion," he said bluntly. "I am a businessman first and always, Mrs. Langtry."

"Why are you doing this, Mr. Freake?"

68

"Why?" He mopped his face with a silk handkerchief. "I am rich and ugly, you are not-so-rich and beautiful. We move in society, and yet you are *Missus* Langtry and I am *Mister* Freake. Frankly, I want my wife and me to have the social position we deserve."

"I should think the Royal Academy of Music should suffice."

"Not quite enough to achieve the necessary results."

She did not like Freake or his methods of doing business. If he could arrange a friendship between her and the Prince, that would climax his career as master builder and millionaire. No one would sneer at him with "Sir" before his name; he would no longer have to depend on money sufferance alone. He was shrewd, so shrewd that he must have guessed her reaction to his suggestion. Had Cinderella refused to try on the glass slipper?

"I'm so glad you had a nice talk with Freake, dear," said Edward, as they were going to bed. "I told you he was an interesting man."

"Very interesting."

If such a man could be rewarded with a baronetcy, she thought, brushing her long hair vigorously before the mirror, why not Sir Edward and Lady Langtry? But then what could she offer comparable to the Royal Academy of Music? Yourself, said her conscience cynically, but they don't give titles for bodies, not in England. Troubled by her thoughts, she glanced at a pleased Edward absently caressing his mustache. Favors begat favors and—oh, who and what was she, anyway? She was so alone with Edward, so confused when she had time to think. Queens of beauty had no cabinets or advisers. Life was so much easier when she was enjoying herself. But Edward was waiting with that predictable light in his eyes.

"I'm so tired," she said, letting him kiss her. "And I've got *such* a headache."

Edward's instantaneous solicitude annoyed her. Before she fell asleep she decided to suggest separate rooms since she liked sleeping late in the mornings. She liked children and some day she wanted a family, but not now. Not now.

69

Deceit did not prove to be as disagreeable as she had thought it would. Edward worried about her because he was at such loose ends himself, and she had to account for every minute away from him. So the story that she was going to pay an afternoon call on Mrs. Freake went down very well. She spent a long time getting ready with Dominique's help, and she was confident except that she didn't quite know what was expected of her—and she didn't want to know.

The Freake mansion was exactly the kind of place one would expect from a man who had risen from bricklayer to millionaire contractor. A butler escorted her to a little room where a worried Freake was waiting.

"You're punctual, Mrs. Langtry. He's waiting for you in the drawing room."

He led her to the door and disappeared. It would have seemed more fitting for the Prince to come to her, but this was royalty. She thought of HIM in capital letters just as Freake did, entirely subscribing to the mystique of monarchy.

"Good afternoon, Mrs. Langtry."

She curtsied. "Your Highness."

"So good to see you like this. I'm very glad Freake arranged it so we can talk quietly. A good sort. You are lovely, much lovelier than I realized at Alleno's the other night. I hope we can be good friends."

"I have many friends, Sir."

"So have I, but I do not seek friendship, nor give it lightly." He looked at an ornately carved table on which Lillie noticed crystal goblets and a silver ice bucket with champagne. "Will you join me in a toast to our friendship, Mrs. Langtry?"

While Albert Edward was entranced by what he saw, Lillie's feelings were mixed. In his black frock coat, white shirt, wing collar, conservatively patterned necktie, and gray trousers, he was more impressive as a future king than as an ordinary man. Thirty-eight years old, married for fifteen years to the delicately lovely Princess Alexandra, and the father of five children, he had a high, balding forehead, deep-set hooded blue eyes, an aristocratic aquiline nose, and a thick black beard cut short and full so that his mouth and chin were concealed. He had the

Guelph look and a brusque geniality that Lillie imagined concealed a violent temper.

"You have conquered London in one season, Mrs. Langtry. Quite an accomplishment. Your photographs and portraits are everywhere, the ladies copy your coiffure, and your hat, gloves, and shoes are for sale in all the shops. I shall expect your statue in the public squares yet."

"I find imitation tedious, Sir," she said, borrowing Oscar Wilde's favorite word.

"No doubt, no doubt, but someone must set the pace. I find everyone going to Mr. Poole since he is my tailor, and merely leaving open the lowest button on my waistcoat made the oversight a new fashion. And I can tell you that a slight disability of Her Highness has brought about what, I am told, is 'the Alexandra Limp.' It is amusing what society will do when it looks up to people."

The time passed quickly as they chatted. Champagne in the afternoon left her deliciously lightheaded. She wondered what it would be liked if he kissed her with that strong cigar smell about him. In moments of intimacy with a prince and monarch-to-be, did one keep on saying dutifully, "Yes, Sir," or "Please don't, Your Highness"?

She was still in a glow when he left, after expressing a wish to see her often in the future. She seemed to drift to her carriage with only strength enough to tell the coachman to drive by Rotten Row on the way home. The Park was green and lovely with flowers, trees, and lawns. Well-dressed ladies and gentlemen stared at her, but she looked at them unseeingly, a thoughtful smile on her face. She asked to be driven past the Royal Academy of Music. It was natural for the structure to be a Freake-style mass of pretentious red brick with elaborate stone facings. Well, the contractor's mission was accomplished. She had met the Prince officially and unofficially, and every hostess in London could breathe easily. The name Lady Langtry had such a lovely liquid sound. Lillie smiled as the brougham moved on toward Norfolk Street.

At parties, henceforth, it was always the Prince and Mrs.

71

Langtry. He was Number One, the beauty of the season was his prize. He rode next to Redskin at the head of her cavalry in the Park, and they were paired off everywhere. Yet much as he monopolized her company, he did nothing to impose on their friendship; she lost none of her other admirers, although they did hang back when the Prince was around. Since they had acknowledged the direction of their friendship privately, for the present it suited Albert Edward to lead her devoted train. The *status quo* satisfied Lillie. If there had to be a rein—and she wasn't prepared to admit one existed—she preferred a loose one. She was gratified at the manner in which the Prince always sought out her husband, overlooking Edward's wooden confusion to draw him into conversation about yachting, a good safe middle ground.

Since she had achieved her eminence on beauty alone, irrespective of background, wealth, or breeding, some aristocrats frowned on her as an upstart. After all, who *was* this Mrs. Langtry? When the Prince of Wales put in his claim, their disapproval increased. A real lady was not sought after, ogled, and publicized. It was in execrably bad taste, what? And Edward, who had to be mollified constantly, agreed with the duchess who said that a lady's name appeared in the newspapers once when she was married, once when she died, and that was twice too often. If more than that, she was notorious, a ghastly business. But the Jersey Lily was being chronicled all the more as she became an established feature.

Lillie had adjusted to her unlooked-for, implausible success. As an insignificant person thrown into a position of tremendous military or political responsibility grows suddenly in stature, so Lillie accepted her leadership with a grace and good will that endeared her to all except those who considered her notorious. Her husband could do no more than follow grudgingly, objecting when he could, observing her many admirers with a jaundiced eye, and barely holding onto his own dignity and pride. He was not a city or party man, but he loved his wife and trusted her.

Lillie encouraged him to seek the company of his own friends, go to Sir George Chetwynd's club, sail and fish when he could, but if she was aware that he had begun to drink heavily she gave no sign. They had separate bedrooms now. She had a special closet built for her clothes, and Dominique was always with her, it seemed—even late at night. He was gambling, too —sometimes looking glum when he came in; sometimes beaming and jingling coins in his pocket. A foolish, deceptive vice, but then she was in no position to criticize.

six

LILLIE was now one of the privileged few—queen of fashion, beauty, and society—and the heights agreed with her. She associated with kings and princes, duchesses and dukes, knights and ladies, and the world of people stopped there.

She looked on the past with bemused horror. How could she ever have been the nothing she was? How had she stood it? That was not living. Now she did what fashionable women were expected to do: attended Parliament in the purdah-like confines of the cloistered Ladies' Gallery of the House of Commons, had tea on the broad terrace of the Palace of Westminster, and went to the Foreign Office receptions that followed the State Opening session. Here she met Disraeli.

Lord Hartington was about to make the introduction, just as Lady Sebright darted forward and tapped Disraeli archly on the shoulder with her fan. "You're about to have a great privilege," she said, giggling.

"Who is that little monkey?" said Disraeli in a loud voice, as Lady Sebright scampered off. Lord Hartington explained, and Dizzy grunted, "See-dull would suit her better." He fastened his monocle in his lined face and stared at Lillie comically. "So *this* is the Jersey Lily, eh? What can I do for you, madam?"

"I need four new gowns for the Ascot races," she said lightly.

Disraeli laughed appreciatively. "That's the first sensible request I've heard all day! Many a woman in your position would have asked to be made a duchess in her own right. You are as witty as you are beautiful, Mrs. Langtry. Millais has not done you justice."

74

"Do you think he did Mr. Gladstone justice in his portrait?"

"Ha! That is too much to ask of anyone."

His good humor made her bolder. "Mr. Gladstone complained to me of dizzy spells. Is there any known cure?"

Again Disraeli laughed. "None whatever, and long may he suffer them."

Lillie was tireless, her stamina dismaying Edward as much as it captivated both her old and young followers, especially the Prince of Wales, who set the example by being the most tireless of all. In the full swing of the season, the parties were never ending, one succeeding the other so that there was no letdown —an orgy of good times that were to Lillie "a dream, a delight, and a wild excitement." She dedicated every fleeting minute to enjoying herself. Edward tagged along, always the vigilant mentor, but he couldn't keep pace.

Many times after dancing from dusk to dawn, Lillie was so wound up she was ready to go around the clock. The sun was up as they drove home in the brougham. Edward began to undress sleepily, glaring as she changed from evening dress to riding habit.

"You're not going out into the Row *now?*"

"It's the best time to ride, dear. In the brilliant early-morning sunlight with the grass wet with dew, the flowers nodding freshly, not a soul about, and the birds singing just for me."

"Stop talking like Oscar Wilde! Lillie, must you keep going on and on till you drop?"

"I won't drop, Edward. I'm just not sleepy. You go to bed."

Often the Prince would be waiting for her on his great horse, or other cavaliers of the *cinq à sept* set, hoping for a solitary morning ride with the Jersey Lily but content to tag along with her party.

Sometimes rain sent her straight to bed. One morning she was awakened by the butler knocking on her bedroom door. It was barely nine o'clock, she noted fuzzily. With the rain thudding against the window like that, surely no one in his right mind . . .

"His Majesty, the King of Belgium is calling, madam."

Leopold was infatuated like the others, and formality de-

75

manded her appearance. Dominique helped her dress hurriedly. She went downstairs and found Edward painfully exchanging banalities with the king, whose black frock coat and trousers were bedraggled, his umbrella a limp scepter dripping water on the carpet. Courtesy required that they give audience to their royal visitor until he chose to retire—a dreary business for Lillie, dazed with sleep as she was. Leopold repeated his unannounced early-morning calls until finally Lillie decided to send word she was not available. For once Edward was on her side.

"One forgets what ordinary mortals kings are until one meets them. I find it incredible that royalty can make the most unreasonable demands and be so utterly free of responsibility. Besides, Leopold has a most dissolute private life. I'm told he is an immoral—"

"Really, Edward! Next you'll believe all the gossip about the Prince."

"More often than not gossip has foundation in fact, my dear," Edward said mildly. "I have great admiration for the Prince, but you must admit he's not at all like his father."

"Thank heaven for that! I'm going back to bed."

Many attended parties only in order to meet Lillie. Riding Redskin in the Park one day, she let drop that she probably wouldn't be present at Lady Basquette's ball that night because she was feeling poorly. Late that afternoon, her butler made six trips to the door, in each case admitting a doctor dispatched by a solicitous admirer. The first of the six had been sent by the Prince, another by Sir George Chetwynd, others being the personal physicians of Moreton Frewen, Lord Hartington, Lord Lonsdale, and Sir Edmund Glovere. She refused their services, but the tribute revived her so that she was able to attend the ball and give joy all around.

Whitsuntide, the seventh Sunday after Easter, a traditional holiday, was a welcome break in the seasonal activity. Lillie, startled at the beauty of the English countryside and the magnificence of the big estates, decided that few compared with Heron Court in Hampshire, the hereditary country seat of old Lord Malmesbury, a retired diplomat. The entrance was marked with great sculptured herons mounted on the towering gateposts. The tremendous house had stone floors with deer-skins as scatter rugs, pieces of armor in every nook, and walls covered with hunting trophies, swords and spears, tapestries and heraldic banners.

The grounds were particularly beautiful, especially the three-mile drive lined with blooming rhododendron. The guests fed the swans floating gracefully in mirrored ponds, admired the peacocks strolling as disdainfully as some professional beauties, and snooped about the gardens which were ablaze with color. Lord Malmesbury entertained in the royal manner, and when Lillie went riding with Lord Manners, he dispatched a groom to chaperon them—but Lillie sent the man back to the stables.

"You have disobeyed my orders!" Lord Malmesbury stormed on her return. "No woman rides unchaperoned at Heron Court. You may have both been sniffing the rhododendron or chasing my deer, but there must be witnesses to good intentions."

"My lord," said Lillie. "You exaggerate the dangers that beset youth."

"My diplomatic experience has made me distrustful of human nature, and rightly so. People have vicious tongues, and I mean to keep them silenced."

Lillie apologized, and by dinner time Lord Malmesbury was again enchanted with her. He was a widower, and the house lacked a woman's touch. She filled the place with flowers over the earl's insistence that their fragrance spoiled the flavor of meat. He was a gourmet and prided himself on his master chef. Tonight they were having a *spécialité de la maison*.

"A great delicacy," he told Lillie. *"Gratin à la Grammont* —named after my relative *la duchesse*. You will like it."

The first to be served, Lillie tried a little of the concoction, which seemed to be a compound of minced chicken and chopped cauliflower. Tasty enough, it burned her tongue, and she hastily swallowed some water.

"Well?" he demanded. "Superb, isn't it?"

Nursing her tongue, Lillie looked from his anxious face to the others around the table who were eagerly awaiting her verdict. She wanted to get back at him over that ridiculous

77

chaperon affair. Here was an opportunity the latent tomboy in her could not resist.

"Excellent," she said flatly, "if it were not so cold."

"Cold, eh?" He looked affronted. "Impossible! Henri would never dare—here!"

He plucked at the footman's arm, served himself a steaming plateful, dug his fork into the gratin, and shoveled it into his mouth. The shock was instantaneous. Lord Malmesbury's eyes protruded. His cheeks turned brick red, his scalded mouth gaped, and he cried out hoarsely. He fumbled for his water glass, knocking it over, and Lillie was ashamed. It was a poor joke at best. The others hid their amusement at their host's distress, and she regretted her impulse.

"Forgive me, my lord," she pleaded.

"If you were a man, I'd run you through with that pike up there." Water gurgled down his throat. "Cold, eh?" He slapped the tablecloth and guffawed, all the guests happily giving in to pent-up laughter.

The next morning Edward ventured out early for his constitutional. Lillie breakfasted leisurely, then went to her room to write letters, since it was the accepted routine for women on country visits to set aside time to scribble notes. The amenities called for a barrage of ceremonious letters and cards accepting one invitation, giving thanks for another, and filling in family and friends with the latest day-to-day happenings. A desk and crested letter paper were provided in every room for this purpose.

The sun shone warmly through the window at Lillie's back, birds singing under the eaves to the scratch of her pen as she jotted down her impressions of Heron Court. She saved an important letter for last, blotted it carefully on the luxurious, leather-tipped desk blotter, and stuffed it into an envelope just as Edward came in from his walk. He washed up while Lillie left to give her letters to an upstairs maid to post.

A trip to the banks of the Avon River, which cut through the estate, was on the agenda, for Lord Malmesbury had planned a picnic by the water's edge with fishing for those interested in the sport. A squadron of servants had assembled, and the guests

78

were expected to gather punctually at the blast of a hunting horn.

Lillie was looking out the window as Edward called angrily. When she turned she saw him holding up the desk blotter before the dressing-table mirror.

"Do you take me for a fool? I'd know your handwriting anywhere! This is a love letter!" His eyes blazed accusingly. "How dare you write to the Prince like this?"

"I was thanking him for the brooch he gave me," she said casually. Lillie showed him the small circle of diamonds pinned to her dress. "It's his habit to present gifts to all his friends. You know that."

"You have no business accepting anything from him or from any man. You're *my* wife!"

"You let me accept Redskin."

"A horse is a different thing, and Frewen, at least, is forthright." He held up the pad and squinted into the glass. " 'Wearing your lovely brooch reminds me of all the happy times we've had together,' " he read, " 'and I must admit that I do think of you constantly in spite of myself. I hope you will be a guest the next time we visit in the country and that—' " He squinted hard. "I can't make it out!" He flung the pad on the floor. "My God, what am I to think?"

He cut such a pitiably contemptible figure standing there that she was tempted to blurt the truth: that she didn't care what he thought, that she hadn't cared for a long time. But then she had already refused to face the truth for too long a time. Edward wasn't at all the man she had thought him when she married. Looking back, she understood what a baby she had been back in those Lochinvar-smitten days at St. Saviour's. She had never loved him; she had only thought she loved him, had wilfully and blindly convinced herself of it. There were no Lochinvars, there never had been. She had only wanted someone virile, strong, and commanding. She couldn't blame Edward for being himself.

"I've told you the truth, Edward," she said calmly. "It's a harmless letter. Indiscreet perhaps, but harmless."

"Not harmless! You haven't been the same since we moved

to London—and this madness that's come over you. You've re-fused to be a wife to me, bear my children. You've done noth-ing but put me off with empty promises. Look at Mary Corn-wallis-West. She's a professional beauty, a friend of the Prince. That hasn't kept her from having three children and being a good wife."

"Our positions aren't quite the same. Mary has always—"

"Don't lie to me! Do you love me, or don't you?"

It was useless trying to make him understand something that he should have realized long before. From outside came the sound of a hunting horn, the chatter of guests, the imperious voice of their host, and laughter. She had changed, her life had changed, and Edward was still inadequate as husband, lover, everything. The knowledge was bitter, but she had no cause to be. Edward had always been a spoiled boy who never grew up.

"Of course I love you," she lied.

"Then show me!" he implored.

The hunting horn blared again. Edward stood palpitating for an answer, something tangible and demonstrable, and she felt only revulsion and pity.

"You heard the horn," she said, fighting back tears. "Go on down and tell them that I'm not going. Some feminine weak-ness. Anything."

"But you can't stay here when—"

"I can! You go with them. Fish to your heart's content, and leave me alone. I'm sick, do you hear!"

Frightened, craving her forgiveness, he came forward as if to take her in his arms. Lillie turned away angrily. He hes-itated and then went out. She looked out the window and saw him, flushed and embarrassed, mumbling excuses to Lord Malmesbury. Then the party went off and, mercifully, Edward with them. Lillie fell on her bed and wept most of the day. She saw only more disillusion and conflict ahead. She roused herself before everyone returned, had a bath and changed, but she could not conceal the redness around her eyes. No one chose to recognize it except her host, a sensitive, sympathetic man in his seventies who could get away with asking a lovely woman the cause for her tears.

"A letter," she murmured. "I wrote one that I shouldn't have, I suppose, and—and—Mr. Langtry saw it."

"These *contretemps* happen," he said soothingly. "But how is it your husband saw it?"

"He held up the desk blotter to the mirror," she explained, her lips trembling. "It was nearly all there."

"The blotter, eh?" His jowls quivered with indignation. "Blast and damn those servants anyway! They have strict orders to change all the desk blotters in every single room every single day, just to prevent this kind of thing. I'll have them all sacked!"

His apoplectic fury made her feel much better. "Has this happened before, my lord?"

"Things happen only when the opportunity arises. One must prevent it from arising. When I was Foreign Secretary, I had every blotter and scrap of paper burned daily. Who knows what traitors lurk in the woodwork?"

The next week the Prince had tea at the Langtrys' house in Norfolk Street with Edward sullenly quiet as he and Lillie chatted. A day later a royal messenger called with a note for Mr. Langtry and a box containing a pair of cuff links initialed "E. L." Edward was puzzled until Lillie explained that the gift was merely an appreciation of a host and friend. The note took more explaining; Edward could see no point in his attending a levee and being presented to the Queen.

"You've got to go," she told him. "To refuse would be an insult. Besides, it's an honor that the Prince should want to present you."

Edward survived the ordeal and came back thrilled. Victoria was an amazing woman, the Prince had been more than decent. He'd been all wrong about the Prince. He'd never mention the subject again, and he was terribly sorry about their quarrel at Heron Court. Lillie said nothing. Her mind was on her own forthcoming presentation in Court. Curtseying before the Queen at one of her famous "drawing rooms" in Buckingham Palace terrified her, as it had Edward, but hardly for the same reasons. She was known throughout England, marked as the Prince's

81

favorite, and it was imperative that she carry off the occasion successfully. She knew that the traditional ceremony, the social high point of any Englishwoman's life, was a trial for even the most sophisticated.

"I'm excited," she confessed to the Prince beforehand, "and a little afraid."

"Who isn't?" he said, smiling. "I'm not at ease with Her Majesty myself. A holdover from her strictness in my childhood. But you'll have no trouble. It may be that the Princess of Wales will receive you in her place. The Queen rarely stays to the end of the drawing room—it's dreadfully fatiguing in all that crush."

Lillie's "presenter" was to be the Marchioness of Conyngham and her companion at court Lady Romney, but all the same she wanted her mother there. Mrs. Le Breton came gladly. Characteristically she took her daughter's beauty and fame quite as a matter of course. Lillie's dress was of ivory brocade, low-necked and short-sleeved, with a long Empire-style train hanging from the shoulders to complicate walking and curtseying. Both were decorated with pale yellow Maréchal Niel roses, as was her white tulle veil, and represented much fitting, hand-sewing, and expense. She was coached repeatedly on her royal curtsey and on how to catch her train after rising from her knees when the pages would throw it to her—a procedure which had baffled many a woman.

"How proud the dean would be to see you," said Mama, her blue eyes glittering fondly. "I remember when the Queen and Prince Albert came to Jersey and attended some official function at Victoria College. The dean handed her a pen to sign some document, an old quill and utterly useless. She let it fall from her hand and waited imperiously for another as the crowd held its breath. An agonizing moment for the dean, I can assure you."

All women had to wear feathers on presentation. The large ones were awkward adornments, and the Queen disapproved of the small ones that were so popular. The Lord Chamberlain had just issued an edict that feathers had to be at least visible. Lillie decided to wear the three largest ones she could find.

Queen Victoria would be satisfied—and the Prince would have no doubts about her *"Ich dien"* (or "I serve," the Prince of Wales's motto under his three-feathered coat of arms). Dominique brought in a huge, distinctively wrapped package containing an immense bouquet of pale yellow Maréchal Niel roses. Lillie pocketed the card signed "Albert Edward."

"You look lovely, Lillie. Do you know what General Sir John Pennefather said when the dean attended one of Queen Victoria's levees?" Mama asked. "He stared at the dean for a long time and said, 'Do you know, sir, that when you joined the church the army lost a deuced fine sergeant-major!' You're like your father in the proud way you stand. It's the Le Breton heritage."

"It is time," Lady Romney announced ominously.

Inside the palace, she had a blurred impression of great paintings, lush carpets, massive chandeliers, high ceilings. It was like a museum, and the steamy ready-room was a sheepfold jammed with worried women fussed over by companions and presenters. The sun beat against the windows, and fans flapped weakly in limp hands. Friends were too upset to recognize each other, and Lillie, who would have attracted attention at any other time, was only another distracted female. Her tulle veil was smothering her, the long ostrich plumes were uprooting her hair, and her bouquet of roses made her dizzy with its cloying fragrance.

From inside only silence, except when a door opened and the Lord Chamberlain spoke a name. Rustling and mumbling in a stifling atmosphere. So-and-so had fainted, so-and-so had tripped and failed to catch her train. The Queen had left, she hadn't left. Then it was Lillie's turn, and her knees buckled. She took a deep breath, brought the heavy bouquet in front of her as a shield, and glided forward. She gave a waiting page her train without looking at him and moved on, Lady Romney fluttering at her side with the card bearing Lillie's name. The hushed room was packed.

"Mrs. Edward Langtry," the Lord Chamberlain boomed.

She saw a short, dumpy woman with graying hair parted in the middle and topped by a small diamond crown. She was dressed in low-necked black ringed with pearl necklaces, the short sleeves revealing fat jeweled arms, the bulging front crossed by the blue of the Order of the Garter and other decorations. A wrinkled face, sharp nose, thin tight lips, small receding chin. (So that kind of chin was what Albert Edward's beard concealed!) Black feathers behind her head, a tulle veil, and a sallow complexion. Undistinguished, but a woman who somehow managed a dignified majesty in spite of her physical lack.

Unmoving and bullfrog-like, the Queen looked directly ahead until Lillie had reached the presentation point. No welcoming smile crossed her face, not a glimmer of interest. Her expression was severity itself, her eyes dull with fatigue, and she brusquely shot out a pudgy, ringed hand as Lillie curtseyed. Only a matter of a few seconds, but the two queens had taken each other's measure. Lillie still had to genuflect to a long line of royalty. These were familiar faces, and she smiled as she made her second curtsey to the Prince of Wales.

"Well done," he whispered. "I'm proud of you, my beauty."

Then Lillie was before Alexandra, Princess of Wales, delicately lovely, her smile forced as Lillie bent before her. The Duke of York, the Duke of Edinburgh, Leopold, Clarence, and the others. It was easy now, all smiles and handclasps, and her curtseys slacked off to knee dips. She was near the end of the line, every eye following her as she approached the tricky rear-exit leave-taking. One final curtsey. Timing, Lady Romney had said. The page was watching and alert. He had the train, she started her retreat—flip!—the train was over her outstretched left arm, and that was it.

"You did beautifully, Mrs. Langtry," said Lady Romney.

Lillie laughed. "Didn't I though!"

"You were by far the loveliest woman there," said the Prince, as they danced in Marlborough House that night. "And those big plumes you wore." He chuckled. "I didn't fail to notice the symbol, Lillie."

"Did Her Majesty?"

"It's hard to know what Her Majesty thinks, but she wanted to see you very much—that I know."

84

"So Her Majesty was curious about me?"

"Very much so."

If she had to be classified as a professional beauty, then the Prince fitted just as aptly into the professional-lover category. He was a connoisseur. He tracked lovely women like an avid hobbyist, taking plenty of time to enjoy each trophy until he went on to the next rare item and the next and the next. It was in the royal blood, a royal prerogative, the natural result, some claimed, of his monastic, restricted upbringing. Loving him, Princess Alexandra forgave his indulgences and bore with him like a fanatic hobbyist's wife. His promiscuity was nothing new. It had been going on for years, would go on till his death, and Lillie did not deceive herself: she was only one of many.

"With Milton I say, 'They also serve who only stand and wait,' " she murmured.

"I'm no damned intellect, Lillie. I don't try to understand people; I adapt myself to them."

"As you have to me?"

"There I am not fully adapted. It is a thing you must permit." He was breathing hard from dancing. "We need champagne. Come."

Never had Lillie been so carefree and at ease as tonight dancing in the Royal Quadrille with the Prince. This was the summit with no place else to go. Bertie made the rules, and beauty had to conform. She could not delay or prevent the finale, the foregone conclusion of being added to the royal collection. It was rather sad, but the champagne was delicious.

"You've been so kind, Bertie. So very kind to me. May I be bold?"

"My pleasure being kind to you, Lillie. And do be bold."

"Edward—my husband. It would mean so much if he could have something, a title. I don't know how to put it, but if you could arrange for a knighthood, it would change his whole life."

"One can't confer them just like that," he said stiffly. "The recipient must be worthy by accomplishment."

"Edward isn't wealthy enough to donate an Academy of Music."

85

"I don't know what you mean."

But he did, and he was angry and she should never have risked it. Foolish to ask a boon, more foolish to incite his wrath. Every advance required some sort of sacrifice, an immolation that was the price of prestige.

One of the enthusiasms she and the Prince shared was horses. Lillie never missed any of the races, appearing in a different dress every day of the meeting, and always sitting near the Prince. She and Edward were in the Royal Enclosure at Ascot to watch the traditional procession, the grand entrance of the Prince in a handsome coach and four. Surrounded by a dazzling royal retinue, he rode the Straight Mile up the course to his box as the crowd exploded with cheers. Excitement! Fever in the air! A pulse-quickening atmosphere, and rhythmic beauty of horses beating round the track. And Derby Day at Epsom Downs was practically a national holiday with a crush of half a million people, high, low, and in-between, all shrieking as the horses swept by Tattenham Corner.

For Cowes week Queen Victoria was in residence at Osborne House. The Prince and Princess of Wales and their family lived on the royal yacht *Osborne,* and the Langtrys were guests of Sir Allen Young on his schooner *Helen.* Life was more informal than in London, but nightly parties and entertainments continued at the same tempo. During the day sailboats competed in every class, leading to the big King's Cup and Queen's Cup features. The Prince competed in many races and, as usual, events revolved around him. But with the Queen perched high on Osborne House he had to be discreet.

Cowes was a haven for royalty. The Langtrys met them all, and attended all the parties given by the Prince and Princess of Wales aboard the *Osborne* for the King and Queen of Denmark, Empress Eugénie, German and Austrian princes and princesses, and a maharajah and shah or two. Edward took the King and Queen of Denmark rowing, entered races in a borrowed yacht, and could hardly contain himself at Bertie's suggestion that they use his schooner *Hildegarde* for a cruise.

The offer was as irresistible to him as Redskin had been to

Lillie. The arrival of the big schooner manned by royal sailors was a state occasion.

Lillie was treated like a native heroine as she stepped ashore in St. Helier. Never had two parents been so untouched by their daughter's success as hers were now. They approved of their famous daughter's triumphs but made little of them. Jersey was as lovely and peaceful as ever and Lillie's true home, but to be back on the island with Edward was disillusioning. He had arrived as Lochinvar in a storm, and she could remember, oh, so clearly, how he and she had been then. She no longer resembled that Lillie in any particular, while Edward was unchanged, a man who let life drift him about just as the gale had driven him to Jersey. Passive, unambitious, unresourceful.

Another fire-breathing suitor joined the lists with the arrival in London of Crown Prince Rudolph of Austria. A young man, tall, slender, and insolently imperious, he took a possessive interest in Lillie on introduction. He came unannounced to Norfolk Street and took no notice that she was supposed to be the Prince of Wales's favorite.

Baron Ferdinand de Rothschild arranged a sumptuous ball in Rudolph's honor at his palatial Piccadilly house, and naturally Ferdy intended it to be one of London's most-talked-about occasions. The professional beauties were to be on display and at their scintillating best, and he offered to buy them all ball dresses at Doucet, ravishing creations to go with the décor of his great white ballroom. Lillie chose an expensively fringed dress of thin silk in pale pink with a suitable petticoat. She passed before Ferdy on her arrival, and was congratulated on her choice, although months later Doucet billed her for the petticoat since the baron had specified dresses only.

Rudolph monopolized her on the dance floor. He took Alice Rothschild in to supper under protest, left her flat at the table, and made a scene until Lillie agreed to sit beside him. The Prince of Wales was present and, possibly to avoid international misunderstandings, ignored the proceedings while Ferdy played diplomat. Later on Rudolph claimed Lillie for the cotillion and made her conspicuous by grabbing all the favors for the different figures and presenting them to her, as the ever-watchful Edward looked on in amazement. The night was warm. Rudolph danced uninhibitedly, smugly insolent at having captured the belle of the ball, and taking no thought of her delicate crepe-de-chine gown.

"There are marks on your dress," whispered Mary Cornwallis-West, a fetching sight in light blue. "Make him put on his gloves before he ruins it."

As they whirled into another figure, Rudolph's hands gripped her waist unnecessarily tight, and she asked him to put on his gloves.

"Ce n'est rien," he said, smirking. *"C'est vous qui suez, madame."* ("It is you who are sweating, madam.")

Crown Prince or not, the precocious royal cub was insufferable. Like a debutante imploring the stag line for rescue, she looked around the ballroom until she saw Bertie. He recognized the signal, put down his champagne, and came forward as Lillie pretended a sudden dizziness.

"Of course, he's a boor," he said later, "but I can understand the boy. He's never free from supervision at the Austrian court. This represents emancipation. I went through the same sort of thing myself." He smiled reminiscently. "You have to give youth its head early."

"Did you always do as you pleased, Bertie?" she asked teasingly.

"I did—and I do. You're going down to Goodwood Park for the racing, aren't you? Ferdy mentioned that you and Edward were to be his guests."

"He's asked us every year, but Edward would rather go fishing."

"So he's told me, and it's been arranged. I introduced him to Sir Humphrey Coyne, who has a splendid salmon fishing lodge of his own. No reason why Edward shouldn't enjoy himself while you're at Goodwood, eh?"

The Prince looked into her eyes, and Lillie did not flinch.

"None," she said.

"Ferdy has kindly asked me to be his guest. It will be good to be with you."

88

For the remainder of his stay in London, Prince Rudolph continued to haunt Lillie at her apartment in Norfolk Street. He refused to take "No," "*Non,*" or "*Nein*" for an answer; he was pleased when he succeeded in forcing an expensive ring on her. He assumed this gave him certain automatic rights. In protest, Lillie threw his ring into the fire and looked on in disgust as he cried out and pawed about in the ashes for it.

Her suitors were thinning out because their chances were so remote. One of the first to give up was Moreton Frewen, who was sailing to America for fortune and adventure. He wrote that he had stopped going to Norfolk Street because of Rudolph, an "inconveniently frequent visitor in whose favour *les convenances* obliged me to give place." He added that it was "quite impossible to compete with Prince Rudolph, much less the Prince of Wales, but I had the joy of seeing her riding my horse when out exercising with H.R.H. Anyway, lillies can be dreadfully boring when not planted in bed."

Hostesses took it for granted now that the Prince of Wales must be sent the guest list in advance when he was asked for a ball, reception, or weekend visit. Mrs. Langtry had to be on the roster, or Bertie would not come. He rode with her in the Row daily now, equerries and other companions trailing the pair discreetly, and convention demanded that she accompany him until he called a halt, a practice that incensed Edward. They rode so late in the evening that hostesses were often compelled to schedule dinner for nine o'clock or later.

It was ten o'clock as their brougham arrived at the Clark-Thornhills in Eaton Square. Edward, a bear for punctuality, scowled in angry silence. Lillie went up the steps prepared to apologize, but, miraculously, there was no need.

"Ah, Mrs. Langtry, we've been expecting you," said their hostess amiably. "Lady Warringford saw you riding in the Park on her way here and, as we knew you couldn't get away, we postponed dinner indefinitely. No trouble at all."

"Thank you, Mrs. Clark-Thornhill." Her lips twitched. "We were so worried at the thought of inconveniencing you and your guests, weren't we, Edward?"

They said little as they prepared for bed that night.

"I'm sorry I spoke crossly to you, Lillie. It was most discourteous of me, and I failed to realize the allowances people are prepared to make for you."

"Royal etiquette can be troublesome," she said vaguely.

"You don't mind if I don't go to Goodwood with you? Coyne's asked me to go after salmon."

"Please yourself, Edward."

"Awfully good of you, dear."

He came near her, his cheeks flushed, his eyes glittering. He kissed her cheek, and the scratch of his mustache and the dryness of his lips were repugnantly familiar. She had smelled whiskey on his breath before, but never so strongly. She wondered if he were drunk. Edward smiled, caressed her shoulder, and Lillie eased away.

"Good night," she said briskly, going to her room.

"Good night."

He waited till her door was shut, sighed deeply, padded over to his dresser, and dug a bottle out of the drawer.

seven

How odd to be off without Edward, thought Lillie, as she looked at the wide lawns and great shade trees of Goodwood Park. With other guests she was seated on a crested folding chair watching twelve footmen and assorted cooks and chefs clustered around the huge hampers, preparing to serve the royal picnic. It was a gigantic operation with Bertie expecting ten to fourteen courses exactly as at Marlborough House.

A big woman with a well-developed figure, Lillie usually had a good appetite. Not today, however. She had no stomach for the banquet. The little wine she sipped made her dizzy in the buzzing July heat, and she hoped no one would notice what she left on her plate.

"A perfect day for fishing," said the Prince, as they strolled under the grand old trees. "Mr. Langtry and Coyne should do well."

The thought made her gag. The Downs shimmered before her. Waves of heat made the turf undulate, and branches spun like windmill arms. The heat did not seem to affect Bertie, who had wined and dined well. He was crisply natty in black frock coat, gray trousers, black Ascot tie with pearl stickpin, high stiff collar, shiny black boots, black topper in hand, and leather binocular case over his left shoulder. A film of sweat on the high forehead, thinning hair parted in the middle, black beard and clipped mustache bristling, the hooded eyes twinkling as he surveyed Lillie's beauty. A future king . . . a present lover.

"You are the loveliest woman in the entire world."

"Thank you," she said simply. "Bertie, tell me a little about

Ireland. We have property there, and they say the situation is bad since the famine. What is the government going to do about it?"

"Many things, my beauty, but I told you before that in my position I may not express political opinions. Let us go back. My valet is waiting, and I must change for the afternoon's activities."

"How many times a day do you change, Bertie?" she asked curiously.

"Six or seven. Not that I keep count, but that's what clothes are for, isn't it? So many people fail to realize the primary importance of the proper clothes for each occasion—clean linen, and all that goes with it. A remarkable thing about you is your exquisite taste, your clothes. Pink and white becomes you—and that gay parasol." He looked into her eyes. "I'll see you at Ferdy's."

When Bertie and Alexandra were being helped into the royal carriage, from his elevation he sought out Lillie and their eyes held. He waved to the company, but the gesture was for her. Her eyes misty, she watched him leave with his wife. She too wanted to go. Plead sick, hide somewhere, spite Bertie deliberately by throwing herself into another man's arms— she had plenty to choose from, princes, too, but not *the* Prince.

"Alone?" said a bright mocking voice. "I can't believe it, Mrs. Langtry."

"It happens, Lord Lonsdale. Infrequently, but it happens."

"Well, at least Chetwynd isn't about. But that complexion of yours. I never cease to marvel at it! Surely that Jersey bloom isn't skin deep. Shall I try to rub it off?"

"It's been tried before." Lillie did not conceal her boredom.

"Ah, but not by me." He brought out a silk handkerchief. "It's a challenge I cannot resist." Lord Lonsdale bent over her. "I'm mad about you, Lillie. I'm staying at Ferdy's, too, and I must see you there—*alone*. We have much to say to each other."

"Don't tell me Mrs. Langtry has a cinder in her eye," said a

92

laughing voice. "That's *one* pose the photographers have missed."

Lord Lonsdale backed away hurriedly. "Ferdy's tonight," he whispered, arching his eyebrows significantly. "I shall be there."

Tonight!

It was so easily done that she wondered later why she had worried. House parties called for a practiced host and hostess with an intimate knowledge of their guests, their affairs past, present, and hoped-for. They had to be alert for the faintest change in the climate of love in order to avoid embarrassment and effect a quick re-assignment of rooms. Hospitality demanded that one accommodate one's guests; they couldn't be tracking all over the mansion, blundering into the wrong rooms, bumping into a rival— Horrors! Tactics, strategy, and the right maneuver at all costs. Anything to prevent a *contretemps*.

They dined late, talked, played cards, and had a midnight snack. Then one by one people drifted off to bed. Lillie did the same. Actually she was lonely in her room without Edward's pacing, criticizing, and abrasively reassuring presence. She bathed, powdered and perfumed herself, and brushed her golden-brown hair before the mirror as always. She put on her newest and prettiest nightgown with an ermine-trimmed peignoir, and sat around waiting, wondering with a smile whether she was expected to welcome His Royal Highness like a gracious hostess. Certainly she wasn't going to curtsy, dressed as she was, but what was royal protocol in the bedroom?

The house was quiet now. Looking out the windows she saw that most of the rooms were dark, and she forced herself to take out her presentation copy of Oscar Wilde's poems. But she could not keep her mind on her reading. She stared for a long time at the blurred print in a near doze and then decided to go to bed. Perhaps Bertie wasn't coming. She turned off the lamp, listened at the door, and then slipped in between the sheets, throwing back the blanket because the night was warm. Footsteps in the corridor. Her breath caught, her heart pounded, but they went past her door. Someone else on the prowl. The footsteps came back. Lord Lonsdale! Suppose he and Bertie collided in the hall? The footsteps faded away. She lay back, her muscles let go. She thought of Edward snug in bed and dreaming fishy dreams, of her parents, of Jersey, of her brother Reggie. . . .

Then there was a click. The door opened and shut quickly, and a bulky man was in her room.

"Lillie?"

The familiar guttural voice, the smell of cigars, and the fear Bertie could inspire in her. He always got what he wanted.

"Yes," she said tightly. "I'm almost asleep."

"It's a lovely night, so warm and still except for those bugs fiddling and chirping like things possessed."

She laughed. (How calm she was suddenly!) "They're serenading their lady loves."

"Sensible little creatures. That's what nights are for."

In the dim light streaming in the window, she could see his short, squat figure. She was tempted to laugh, but resisted. This was one time when Bertie did not summon a person into his royal presence; it was he who had sought her—Mrs. Langtry, Lillie Le Breton that was. A prince, a king-to-be, ruler of England. A little titter escaped her.

"Always gay and laughing. That's another thing I like so much about you, my beauty."

His arms swept her into his bear-like embrace, his beard and mustache tickled her cheeks and chin as his mouth closed over hers. She gave a shiver and a sigh.

Light was breaking as he left, and the insects had long ceased their serenading. A few birds were tuning up their pitch pipes as if they'd never sung before, and the earth reposed in a heavy, drugged weariness. It had hardly been the ordeal she had envisioned and, truthfully, had meant little emotionally or physically to her. Judging from his reaction, the experience had been highly satisfactory to Bertie, just as it had always been to Edward. One was much like the other, royalty and commoner.

"Did you have a good time?" Edward asked.

94

"Did you catch any fish?" she countered.

Lillie did not show the handsome diamond bracelet which had been given her.

Besides the usual parties, Bertie often took her on moonlight sails in the *Hildegarde*. An unseen crew handled the yacht while they enjoyed the sea air and watched the moon etch silvery streaks on the water. They did not stay on deck long after snacking on champagne and caviar.

For Cowes week Sir Humphrey Coyne asked Edward to assist his yacht crew in the races. Edward was flattered by Coyne's friendship and thought it a coincidence that he and Coyne had similar sporting interests. He groaned over bills but did not curtail Lillie's spending.

Since he no longer insisted on accompanying her everywhere, Lillie's problem was considerably simplified as she visited country houses all over England with the Prince of Wales always the honored guest. Sometimes Princess Alexandra came with her husband, but mostly she was occupied with the royal nursery and did not share his passion for gallivanting. When he wasn't in London for the season, he was visiting country seats, shooting grouse here and pheasant there, cruising on the Mediterranean, sojourning in Paris, taking the waters at Marienbad, or soaking up the sun at Biarritz or on the French Riviera.

At country estates it was taken for granted that Lillie's room must be close enough to save Bertie from drafts in his roaming up and down the carpeted hallway. Of course the Prince's stay always caused considerable upheaval, since he was accompanied by his own staff: two valets to tend to his personal needs, a platoon of footmen to attend him at meals, two loaders for shooting, grooms and stablemen to care for the royal horses, plus a gentleman-in-waiting, a secretary, and various equerries. Besides, it was imperative that Bertie be kept amused. Every hostess provided a schedule of sporting events, games, dances, and entertainment. Meals were huge and lengthy. Much time was taken up resting and still more in changing clothes hour after hour throughout the tedious day. Bertie's mood was a barometer, and his preoccupation with Lillie—his desire to be with her constantly—was a god-send to nail-biting hostesses.

In places like Glen Tanar Lodge in Aberdeenshire, Scotland, where it rained for days on end, Lillie's tomboy background made it possible for her to improvise amusement. One idea hit her the instant she saw the steep pitch of the thickly padded staircase. Soon all the company had joined her sliding down it seated on big silver serving trays. At night, there was dancing in the ballroom—waltzes, schottisches, polkas, a Highland reel, and often solo sword dances by young lords in kilts.

The Prince also organized large-scale house parties at Sandringham, his great, rambling country home surrounded by stables, model dairies, nurseries, chicken runs, piggeries, and pheasant preserves. Bertie, who delighted in slapstick practical jokes in which he was never the butt, was ringmaster at his lavish birthday celebration on November 11. Champagne dousings, battles with seltzer bottles, lather passed off as whipped cream, pratfalls—almost everything but bladder bouts by jesters convulsed him, as it did all the Marlborough Set.

Lillie was no longer in awe of society, nobility, or royalty. She had broken all rules by surviving successive seasons as queen of beauty, and she seemed assured of an enduring reign with Bertie's backing. She had her own court; and the grand ball at Buckingham Palace fulfilled her dreams of a prince-and-princess fairyland. All the women wore their most elegant dresses, the men the prescribed court costume complete with honors, medals, knee breeches, silk stockings, and black pumps. It was *the* social occasion of the year. Only those who were somebody were invited, and under one roof were gathered the most glittering array of lords and ladies in all of Europe.

Lillie admitted afterward that her dazzling social success went to her head. What could be more natural? Her face was more familiar to country people than Queen Victoria's. Thousands of reproductions of her paintings and photographs were in circulation, her name was daily in every newspaper, she was the heroine of many fashionable novels, women scrambled to wear the Langtry bun, toque, glove, and shoe. Waiters gawked and trembled when they served her. Her fame was so widespread that in Cairo one of the donkeys used by tourists was called the Jersey Lily, and her portrait was nailed up in a railroad snowshed on Marshall Pass, Colorado. Roy Bean, the Law west of the Pecos, hung her photograph on the wall of his dingy Jersey Lilly *(sic)* saloon in Texas.

When the Comédie Française was the talk of London, Oscar Wilde was overcome by Sarah Bernhardt's genius and her "divinely symmetrical Latin features." He dragged her to the British Museum to compare her profile with likenesses on old Roman coins. He made her a friend of Lillie's, and the Divine Sarah, like Lillie, was news when it was vulgar to be news. Henry James, then writing dramatic criticism in London, coolly dismissed both in a manner that was to become familiar: "Indeed, there came a time when the Comédie Française threatened to rank with the weather, or with Mrs. Langtry, as a subject available only for persons who had resigned themselves to lack of originality."

Dressmakers vied with each other in creating for the Jersey Lily, the Prince's favorite, the rage of London. Madame had unlimited credit, and money was something one did not talk about. Lillie's originality in clothes became as distinctive as the Langtry knot and her bangs. Whatever other women wore, Lillie outdid them. She was proudest of a tulle gown in Whistler yellow, covered with clouds of gold fishnet enclosing big and small artificial butterflies in various colors, which she wore to a Marlborough House ball.

When Bertie called at Norfolk Street the next day, he said, "You were never lovelier, my Jersey butterfly. But you lost a lot of the insects. I picked up a dozen this morning. They seemed so sad and neglected lying there that I had to bring them back to you." He looked about for Edward. "Have you ever been to Paris, Lillie? No? How you would love it—with your French background—and how I would love to show it to you!"

"I can't possibly go."

"Nothing's impossible. There are no prying eyes in Paris. We can be ourselves there. Think about it, Lillie—oh, how is your husband?"

"Worried about our finances. I've been extravagant, and he's in Ireland to see about his estates there. The revenues have fallen off."

"A troublesome business, Ireland. And how long will he be gone?"

Lillie stopped with her parents in Jersey just long enough to have an excuse when she faced Edward again, then went on to meet Bertie, who was traveling incognito. She loved Paris. Bertie was an enthusiastic Francophile and, free from the shackles of his homeland, behaved like a lover—the carefree boulevardier and man-about-town. They held hands at Maxim's, attended the races at Auteuil, the theater, opera, and ballet, and of course were entertained appropriately by Sarah Bernhardt and other prominent Parisians. It was a whirlwind frolic. Lillie acquired some smart gowns and another diamond bracelet, and then they had to go home.

Gossip might place them on the same floor of Paris' Hotel Bristol, but gossip was notoriously unreliable. She doubted whether Edward would hear it, any more than he had heard of the flat at 20 Wellington Road where she often waited for Bertie of an afternoon. (That was one rent Edward didn't have to pay.) The newspapers would publish nothing about their escapade because of the libel laws, especially since Lillie had successfully won earlier suits. (On October 29, 1879, in Old Bailey, one Adolphus Rosenberg had been convicted of libels on Mrs. Langtry and Mrs. Cornwallis-West. On January 2 of that year, 1880, the editor of *Town Talk* had been jailed for the same offense. In the Central Criminal Court Mr. Justice Hawkins had levied a four-pound fine on the printers, plus one hundred pounds toward the cost of prosecution.)

Still, when Edward returned, he seemed to be in a desperate, driven mood. He swallowed her lie about her trip to Jersey, but he was incensed at the additional expenditure and went pacing the room, rustling a sheaf of bills.

98

"One hundred pounds for one dress, and the number of dresses you've bought! It's fantastic."

"You never complained before. In fact, you used to encourage me."

"Things have changed radically. We've got to retrench."

"How can we, at this stage? If we do, the Prince will cut us, and so will your friend Sir Humphrey Coyne. Everybody will follow suit, and our credit will vanish. We'll be worse off than ever." Dominique peeped into the room, and Lillie signaled for her to stay away. "Besides, what good are the properties when our income has dwindled so? Why not dispose of them, take your principal? I'm sure everything will come out all right before that's gone."

"I can't. They're starving, Lillie, and the properties are so run-down I couldn't sell them to anyone. I had to lower the rents just so the tenants might survive."

"Lower the rents, when we—?"

"I had to! Their pigs and other animals have died. Roofs have fallen in. Floods and famine have all but ruined Parkgate."

"You saw your father, I suppose?"

"Yes, I thought he might give me a loan or let me represent the Guion Line in London, but he made all sorts of impossible conditions. Even Agnes was shocked," he added ruefully.

"What conditions?"

Edward reddened. "I'm ashamed to tell you. I appealed to him as strongly as I could, but he wouldn't—" He gave a short, ugly laugh. "Father's dead set against you, Lillie. We're a proud family and a conservative one. Your photographs and your friendship with the Prince have brought notoriety to the Langtry name—a cloud of scandal."

"Why, I thought your father liked me!"

"As an unknown wife, not a public figure." He crossed to a table and poured himself whiskey from a decanter. He stared at his glass for a few seconds and drank it neat. "He'll take me into the company, pay my bills, and reinstate me if—if I divorce you. My God, what an insult! I'd never divorce you, not if I were starving. I love you too much."

"He's so harsh, so unfair." But her lie about her trip to France and Mr. Langtry's judgment were bile to her. "What are you going to do?"

"Look around for work. We have plenty of influential friends, and I'm an Oxford man with legal training. There must be something I can do. It's just a question of finding the right thing, isn't it?"

"Of course," she said, unconvinced. "I'll help all I can."

For a week he kept at it, and the clumsy refusals were bitterly humiliating. He had been a country gentleman too long, he had little ability, he didn't know how to sell himself— he had nothing to sell. Coyne was evasive, their titled friends all but unapproachable on the subject.

"Not one situation," he lamented. "It's come down to taking anything that'll keep body and soul together, but they won't talk to me—not about anything as shoddy as money." He groaned and started off.

"Where are you going, Edward?"

"Coyne's asked me fishing." Lillie's glance made him uncomfortable, and he flushed. "Damn it, I've got my end to hold up, too."

She thought of taking her troubles to Bertie. She had told him something of them and was ashamed to confess their increasing seriousness. At any rate, her royal-favorite status was too precarious for that. She was much to blame and willing to admit it, but Edward was—admit that, too—such a fool. Continuing to live with him was impossible. There was just about as much future in it as her relationship with Bertie. The second conclusion, impinging on the first, was frightening. Corroding self-doubts, held back by more than three years of undreamed of, unprecedented triumphs, flooded her conscience. Everyone she knew had some obligation. The aristocrats had the money to live up to their titles; the artists and writers were devoted to their muse, the others to making money, to protecting a reputation, to serving the Queen, or *something*.

The Jersey Lily was an idler obligated only to herself. Never had there been an emptier title than queen of beauty. It was a sham. Yet she had to keep on spending money she didn't have, blinding herself to the reality of poverty. All the while the curious lined up respectfully in Norfolk Street, people clambered on chairs in the Park to see her ride by, and with William S. Gilbert the people of England sang about her:

"Oh never, never, never since we joined the human race
Saw we so exquisitely fair a face."

She had the power and glory, yet the bills kept coming marked "past due." Tradesmen knocked at the door asking for money pleasantly enough, with just a hint of iron in their tone, and Edward was always off somewhere fishing, leaving her to cope with the situation. Oh, if only she could laugh! It was funny, only it was tragic too. Had Cinderella been asked for money? Had Lochinvar been dunned?

Dominique put out her Pierrette costume for the masked ball at Marlborough House. Lillie hated the sight of the frilly, expensive thing. She had no spirit for party gaiety, but she had to go, for six doctors and one of Bertie's nervous equerries would rush to her if she pleaded illness. She felt listless and low. She had ridden Redskin in the Park as usual, but today there had been no zest in the outing. And where was Edward? Probably fishing, drinking, or gambling. It hardly mattered; he would never attend masked balls anyway.

The maid helped her dress, tried to chat as usual, and looked hurt at Lillie's sharpness. She had to remind Lillie to take her mask.

"Thanks, Dominique," Lillie said heavily. "But it looks as if I'm unmasked for good."

"Madame is sick perhaps?"

"Not sick, just empty. I'm sorry I was so cross."

"That is all right. And the bad feeling will pass with the gaiety and the ball."

"Nothing will pass tonight, Dominique."

She heard a snore as she passed Edward's room and looked in. He was lying fully clothed on his bed, unshaven, dirty, rumpled. He reeked of whiskey.

"I lie to you, madame," said Dominique hurriedly, behind her. "I have to do it, then I forget to shut the door. He come in, say he have to speak to you right away. I say no, sleep first."

"Thank you," she said softly, feeling neither hate, nor love, nor anything for her husband. "Let him sleep."

All joy was drained out of her as she entered Marlborough House. It had nothing to do with either Edward or Bertie. The usual fuss was made over her, the expected exclamations uttered over her daring Pierrette costume. Tonight she found the coy byplay before unmasking tiresome, a deadly weary frolic altogether. She could hardly respond to Bertie's high spirits and felt like telling him that he looked ridiculous in Pierrot whiteface, particularly with his beard and mustache. But she went through the familiar motions, forcing her gaiety, and the effort passed unnoticed in the general hilarity animating the cavernous room.

She had never cared for alcohol. Tonight it went down more easily than ever before, and her champagne glass kept being refilled. She was hardly conscious of how much she consumed but reveled in the tonic-like recklessness that was the perfect antidote for her melancholy.

"You're not yourself tonight," said the Prince, breathing heavily as they danced.

"No, Bertie, for once I'm really myself. May I stay with you here tonight? I don't want to go home to Edward. He's drunk."

"You know you can't do that!"

"What *can* I do then? I know! More champagne. That's what I need."

Frowning, he led her to the tables.

"To Bertie-Wertie," she said, toasting him.

"I don't understand you tonight," he said stiffly.

"*Pauvre* Pierrot," she murmured, straightening suddenly as something pricked her. A pin, but Dominique was never careless . . . Ouch! *Again*. She glanced into her bodice, saw something, and plucked it out deftly. What a darling little flea! Composed and smiling, she dropped it into Bertie's glass, laughing as his eyes rolled in his foolish, whitened clown's face. "I dare you to drink a toast to the Jersey Lily."

102

"What is that thing?"

"A flea that hopped off Redskin seeking my fair white body. It ought to be precious to you, Bertie."

The couples in masquerade costume, who had moved back to let them reach the refreshment table, were watching, listening closely. Bertie's ears reddened under his pomponned Pierrot hat. His eyes sparked anger.

"Go on, Bertie-Wertie," Lillie taunted. "It won't bite."

Bertie raised his glass and drained it in one gulp.

"Bravo!" Lillie clapped her hands. "That's my prince. Drowned in champagne in the royal tummy. What a noble end for a poor flea."

"You forget yourself, Lillie," he snapped.

"Oh, I wish I could!" She stumbled through a curtsy and put the back of her wrist to her forehead in mock humiliation. "Why don't you say, 'We are not amused,' like your mother? I hear she's been sick," she went on loudly. "How *is* your mother, Bertie-Wertie?"

Somehow, Pierrot costume and whiteface notwithstanding, the Prince of Wales managed to portray outraged regality. "Her Majesty the Queen is better, Mrs. Langtry."

"Isn't that nice?" He was glaring, the red showing through the white cream on his face. "Don't be angry over a civil question."

The music had stopped a few minutes before. More couples had come for champagne, and now they joined the others staring in amazement.

"Oh, you're burning up, aren't you? What a shame," Lillie cooed solicitously. "This'll cool you off nicely."

As neatly as she had extracted the flea, she snatched a piece of ice from a champagne cooler. In a swift movement, she plunged it down the Prince's collar. Bertie wriggled as the ice slithered down his back, stared at Lillie as if he couldn't believe the indignity she had perpetrated, and spun on his heel. Overcome with horror, the crowd gave way silently, and Lillie's laughter echoed through the room.

The Prince's heels clacked as he stalked majestically across the oak floor of the big room. Princess Alexandra, a pretty

Dresden shepherdess, detaching herself from a group, crossed the room hurriedly and went up the stairs.

People looked at one another questioningly. The orchestra leader stood poised, his violin under his chin, awaiting a signal, and the footmen moved about confusedly. Lillie sipped her champagne, laughing to herself, sublimely unaware of the enormity of what had happened. The guests shrank away from her, congregated in excited knots, and discussed the shocking incident. Her back to the room, she stood alone. Two by two people drifted off, looking her way and shaking their heads, exchanging gossip, savoring and distorting what they had witnessed, and hardly able to contain themselves before spreading the news all over London.

The musicians asked questions; their leader shrugged. Now they began putting away their instruments in their corner of the huge hushed drawing room still bright with lights.

"Is the party over?" Lillie asked a footman.

"I can't say, madam," he said, bewildered.

"Well, give me more champagne. To the brim, please. This will have to last for a long, long time."

She held the glass up, toasting she knew not what, and drank it down like water. Then she retrieved her cape from the empty cloakroom. Pall Mall was empty except for her broughham. The streets were dark and deserted. There was no sound except for the turning of wheels, the clop-clop of her horse.

All in one night the world had come to an end, and she was the last survivor.

Lillie awoke with a headache that clamped down on her skull like a steel trap, its claws punching into her brain. Her eyes were lead balls depressing the sockets, her throat raw and rancid. She stirred restlessly and finally dared open her eyes. She shrank from the sunlight as from a blow.

"You are sick, madame?" Lillie groaned, and Dominique clucked and stroked her burning head. "A little cool ice on the head perhaps?"

Lillie shuddered. "No ice." She groaned again. "Just let me sleep."

By noon, she had revived to the point where she could take a little nourishment. Dominique propped her on the pillows and served her anxiously. Lillie's eyes were heavy and painful. Her joints seem to fit badly, her brain floated painfully each time she moved her head, she ached dully from top to toe.

"You are better, madame?"

"No. Where is Mr. Langtry?"

"Out. Fishing maybe."

"Naturally. Have there been any calls today?"

"Only shopkeepers and tradesmen, madame. They wanted—"

"Don't tell me!" She grimaced. "I mean invitations, you know." Dominique said no. Lillie's scowl deepened, and memories of the night before began to take ominous shape in her consciousness. "I have dug my grave wide and deep. There will be no mourners."

"What do you mean, madame?"

"Champagne. Fleas. Ice."

Dominique looked all the more puzzled.

Lillie nerved herself to a late ride in the Park, looking deceptively lovely and serene to her admirers lining the curb in front of her Norfolk Street home. Still London's premier attraction, it seemed. Someone called her name and she raised her hand weakly. Reassuring, business as usual, but she was not deceived. Premonition weighed her down as she rode. From a shop window banked with them, her photographs stared mockingly in a variety of poses. Further along she looked away, passing three stores to which the Langtrys were deeply in debt. In Hyde Park, heads turned as usual at the sight of her. French governesses rushed across the road, black veils streaming, for a glimpse of her. But it wasn't the same. A familiar carriage over there, Lady Wharncliffe's. Staring eyes, but no recognition; the chin going up, the nose high. Further along, a barouche. Lady Sebright chatting with Lady Roosebury. Silence suddenly and long cold looks. Then Lord and Lady Stanwood, Lady Mawlebrooke, the Duke of Marrwaithe, all her friends, people she knew. No smile, no welcome, no acknowledgment.

No doubt about it—the cut direct. The word had gone out and she was dead. *Persona non grata* everywhere. Brought down from the heights by a lowly flea and a lump of ice. Her head ached. The air was cold. She swung Redskin around and started back. Should she go to Wellington Road and wait? No. Bertie's wrathful disfavor had excommunicated her from the Marlborough Set, the inner circle—all circles.

I don't care, she said to herself, I don't care at all. But it was a lie. Her stinging eyes and sinking heart told her so.

Edward was still out, and she was just as glad. She had tea, then asked Dominique to draw a bath.

"Get out the green satin. I'll wear that to Lady Greenwood's reception tonight." What else was there to do except keep going? Dominique was looking at her. "Well?"

"Lady Greenwood's footman called while you were out. His lady is indisposed, and the ball has been canceled. He gave me this." Dominique was abashed. "More came, too." She gulped, holding out half a dozen more envelopes. "The affairs you planned to attend later this week have all been changed. The people are sick, or something has happened."

"Something *has* happened." Lillie tore open the embossed notes one after the other. "Anything else?"

"I was at the door all the time. When it wasn't a footman, it was someone with a bill. The shopkeepers were not nice, madame."

"Why didn't you let the butler answer the door? It's his duty."

"Belcher refused. He was insolent. The cook, the downstairs maid, the coachman, too."

"They want their money, is that it?" Lillie slapped the envelopes against her palm. "And you, too, I suppose. Right now, this minute."

"I want nothing." Dominique began to blubber. "Nothing, madame."

This touching devotion seemed to stiffen Lillie. She felt

clear-headed, resigned. She had no one to depend on except herself. No tears, no eleventh-hour appeals would get her out of this mess. There might be one way of getting money, she mused, remembering the fervent proposals made in the past by various infatuated gentlemen. But these were as repugnant in extremity as they had been on the pinnacle, that dubious summit she should never, never have taken for granted.

"We'll survive somehow, Dominique. Let's dry those tears and think."

Not that there was much to think about; only a little consolation in having to rely on one's self. She was young, thought beautiful and intelligent. Anyone could be strong in success. Disaster was the test. But how nastily and persistently urgent were the creditors, now that she was no longer Jersey Lily "by special appointment to His Royal Highness, the Prince of Wales," now that she was shorn of royal esteem, held in disgrace by society compelled to follow their leader's example. And the bills! Dressmakers, milliners, musicians, florists, caterers, grocers, butchers, plus what they owed the landlord and their servants.

Edward was rarely home now, entering only by the back door when he came. Sober, he was loving, spineless, and without recrimination against her. Everybody had lied to him. He had never trusted the Prince and his friends. Their ruin proved he had been right about city people and city living. London society breathed poisoned air, which had had to infect them. Drunk, he was capable of saying vicious things which he regretted, later growing maudlin and confessing his great faith in and love for his beautiful, maligned wife. Then he would collapse.

"We'll probably have to sell everything, Edward. They won't wait much longer without bringing suit."

"Damn the leeches, then! I refuse to lower myself to bargaining with knaves."

"We have no choice."

"I'll get something, Lillie! I'll get the money and throw it in their faces, even if I have to go back to Belfast and fight with Father! You'll see."

Her ostracism was a restful, troubling phenomenon that took getting used to after her ceaseless round. She stayed at home all day now. The invitations that had rained in heretofore had stopped short. She looked at her unaccustomed four walls and fretted, wondering if her photographs had been taken down from shop windows. No callers, no admirers besieging her door, no crowd waiting in the street, nothing. She knew that not all her friends were faithless, but she thought less of them for fearing to risk royal disfavor either by seeing or communicating with her. Bertie's edicts were tyrannical; he threw a mighty, obliterating blackball.

The ice story was in all the society journals in veiled, garbled form, and there was thinly concealed malice at her passing. (My dear, they say Wellington Road has lost a lovely tenant.) After all, who *was* this Mrs. Langtry? She had no real social background, no aristocratic family, no standing whatsoever with her royal prop removed. A dean's daughter, a peasant from Jersey who just happened to catch the Prince's eye for a time—and he was no man to discriminate when he chose a mistress. Three years had been much too long for such as Mrs. Langtry to rule the magic circle. The woman was like the bills she and her uninteresting husband couldn't pay—long past due. And gossip had it that Bertie had tired of her. He had long sought for a way to thrust her aside, and now (what a capital joke!), the Jersey Lily had withered and died on the vine, had resolved everything with her own mad, inexcusable prank. She'd gone up like a blazing sky-rocket and come down just as fast, once her brilliance was dampened by a piece of ice.

Who had taken her place, Lillie asked herself? Where her presence had once been so vital for a successful occasion, what was used to fill the void? Some new figure, perhaps? Society was so fickle, and society seemed to be the world.

eight

For two weeks Lillie continued to delay the inevitable by pleading sickness. She remained more or less incommunicado, with Dominique keeping away the curious, the choplicking trade jackals, and the bill collectors. With the shining exception of the incomparable Dominique, the servants deserted her one after the other, openly showing their contempt now that wages were owed them and she had fallen from grace. The brougham and its horse were taken away to be sold, but Lillie refused to part with Redskin just yet. All the money that Edward could scrape together, plus the amount realized from the jointure his father had settled on her, was used to hold off their creditors. Still the bailiffs came to Norfolk Street with a writ prescribing immediate payment of all outstanding debts.

With Edward off brooding and drinking, it was up to Lillie to charm the authorities into postponing the final liquidation. Though languishing under royal opprobrium, she was still able to captivate under siege. She made light of her position, thought about the future, and mulled plans for a remunerative career of some kind. She was more fitted for work than Edward, and she was open to suggestion. Frank Miles, Oscar Wilde, Jimmy Whistler, none of whom cared a damn for society's strictures, had the positive ideas one might have expected of them.

"Gardening is the thing for you," said Miles. "Flowers and the Jersey Lily go together. Besides, florists need things to sell and a market garden would give them a steady source of supply. Why, you could develop a whole new industry!"

"The stage is for her," Oscar insisted. "Only the stage."

"But flowers are nature's poems, the loveliest things in the world. How fitting that Lillie should grow them!"

"You're a romanticist, Frank. Picture those lovely hands digging in the muck, handling grimy bulbs, shoveling fertilizer like a peasant." Oscar shuddered. "The horror of the divine Lily tramping the fields in muddy boots. The stage, Lil, the stage. Think on it!"

"I have no talent for acting."

"You have great beauty and charm. Everything." He smiled expansively. "I love acting. It is so much more real than life."

"My life is quite real enough now, thank you."

"Yes, but, as I've told you, one's real life is so often the life one does not lead."

Their visit cheered her as did Whistler's. Debts, creditors, and bailiffs were familiar to him.

"Just keep them hopping and hoping, most beautiful Lillie. And why not become an artist? Those little caricatures you did while posing for me have merit. A little training, and the Royal Academy will be outraged. Then you'll equal my success."

Mary Cornwallis-West thought she ought to be a dressmaker; Lady Lonsdale a milliner, because of the good taste she had always shown in clothes. Maggie Wheeler suggested interior design because of her knack for "tricking up" rooms with fans, screens, and draperies. It was rather a game, this dreaming up a career for a scapegrace beauty. All these things had possibilities, but none appealed strongly enough.

Then came a reprieve which helped her ignore her financial despond for a while.

Maggie Wheeler brought the official word. "You shouldn't have done it," she chided.

"I know, but we always got along famously until I put that piece of ice down his neck. We were good friends, and he's always been keen on practical jokes. What about poor, funny

110

what's-his-name who lets brandy be poured over him just so he can say 'As Your Royal Highness pleases.' I'm sure Bertie would have taken it as just a bit of a lark if there hadn't been such a lot of people there."

"It was a big company and, being a prince and all that, he had to snub you after it happened. It's the precedent."

"Yes. Princes can't go around having people put ice down their necks. I was wrong."

"You must so acknowledge for his dignity and your neck. Bertie likes you, Lillie, he really does. He misses you, too. He's going to the Duchess of Westminster's ball at Grosvenor House tonight, and you're invited. Here's your invitation in her inimitable hand."

"How will I get there? I can't go on Redskin, and I'm not sure I have the money to hire a carriage." She gave a weary exhalation. "I'm not sure I like facing all those people, knowing what they know."

"You must, and Bertie expects you. You're reinstated, and everyone's been told to pretend it never happened." Lillie said that was impossible, and Mrs. Wheeler agreed. "But you're famous for your composure, dear, and what is that saying of your father's?"

"Bien faire et laisser dire."

"Just so! Tonight at eight, then. I'll call for you." She started out. "Your Dominique is priceless. She gave me some jewelry of yours to smuggle out. She wants to keep your baubles out of the bailiff's hands." They kissed. "Trust your friends, Lillie. You have a lot more than you think."

Lillie might just have returned from Elba that night at the Duchess of Westminster's. Her welcome was warm and vociferous. She was back from exile and as popular as ever—except for a subtle difference which she was quick to note. All eyes were on her as she curtseyed before the Prince of Wales and Princess Alexandra. From their smiles and handshakes no one would have known she had ever been in limbo. The ubiquitous Lady Sebright, who had cut her publicly and disowned her, joined all the others at the shrine of the Jersey Lily now that it was permitted to worship there once more. Everyone behaved as if her ostracism had been a trivial incident. The hypocrisy both amused and enlightened Lillie.

For once she saw the gathering in a cold, undiluted light. She felt detached and in transition, the future looming over the present with remorseless questions demanding undeviating answers. Nonetheless, she laughed, sparkled, charmed, danced with admirers that flocked back to her. She was unmoved by the gaiety, brilliance, and fun. It was all meaningless; all that mattered was "Where do I go from here?"

"You're more beautiful than ever," said Bertie, as they left the dance floor arm in arm. "No one can touch you. That's why your troubles grieve me."

"Oh, Edward will rescue us somehow," she said lightly, not believing it any more than the Prince did. "We'll bounce back from adversity. But I must say it. I am ashamed of what I did. I have no excuse, and I regret everything."

"It never happened," he said magnanimously. "Things are just as they always were between us, as they will remain."

His eyes did not waver, and she met them with refreshing candor, knowing as he surely did that his words could not be true in the nature of things. In spite of words said, nothing could ever change things done.

"I am delighted to know that, Your Highness."

The endearing manner in which her voice dropped, pronouncing his title, made him smile.

"We are all cast in different molds," he said. "Mine is particularly difficult in that I can never forget it for a moment. It pains me when custom directs that I remind others of my position. How much more fitting it would be if someone as lovely as you had divine rights—and you have, of course."

Lillie bobbed a quick curtsey.

> " 'There's such divinity doth hedge a king,
> That treason can but peep to what it would.' "

"Good heavens!"

"That's from *Hamlet*," she said quickly. "Henry Irving quoted it to me one night. I don't know why I remembered it."

"Everything about you surprises me, Lillie. Everything!"

Later in the evening she refused invitations to dance—something she had never done before—and wandered into the library. The sound of music, laughter, and muted conversation coming from the other room seemed an intrusion as she was drawn to a vivid painting of the superb actress Sarah Siddons. Here was a woman who had done something with her life, been more than just a pretty face, worked and achieved greatness. It was time for Lillie to cut the strings attaching her to this sickly, artificial social-butterfly life. But how could she become a worker, too?

Edmund Yates, novelist and editor of the society paper, the London *World,* had once talked to her about using her God-given beauty to some purpose. "Don't be just another member of the insidious 'Do-Nothing Brigade,'" he told her contemptuously. "Life can't be just one long party:" When he hinted to Henry Irving that the Jersey Lily was thinking of the stage, the gallant actor (about to present *The Lyons Mail* at the Lyceum) offered her a leading role in the melodrama. "You'll make a grand entrance in a stagecoach," he had promised. "Every eye will be on you as it clatters on the stage." The scene had entranced her, for she saw it in the glowingly romantic terms that always colored her life. But perhaps Irving was just being nice. Besides, she wasn't serious about the stage anyway. Her eyes dropped reluctantly from the portrait. She hated her uselessness.

Maggie Wheeler was supposed to drive her home, but the ball was far from over. Lillie couldn't bear taking part in it again. She got her wrap, slipped through the front door, and walked home. It was raining. Mud soon stained her thin white satin slippers, but conviction moved her, and the night air was refreshing.

Her reinstatement sat well with tradesmen and creditors. She was given additional grace, and the bailiffs agreed not to act just yet. Edward came home from Ireland, flushed and angry, spoke briefly to her without making much sense, and dashed off again. She had as many invitations as always and now found herself faced with the necessity of attending them all, with both interest and desire gone, in order not to offend Bertie.

For several days now Lillie had been feeling poorly. She tired easily and her meals nauseated her. She was restless, irritable. She had never been ill except for the bout of typhoid fever, which had resulted in their move to London. At first she attributed the malaise to her mental state over money, but it continued. Dominique had a question on her lips, but Lillie wouldn't let her put it. She herself guessed the truth, and it terrified her. This was one thing that must *not* happen, must not be allowed to happen.

All that week she rode Redskin daily in the Park, extending her rides, galloping hard, outlasting her companions on the bridle paths. On Sunday night she went to Marlborough House for one of the Prince's small, intimate dinners, and fought nausea all through the meal. While she was sitting in the drawing room afterward, beads of sweat came to her brow. Her cheeks went as white as her lace handkerchief, her lips had a bluish tinge, and she had to support her head as she slumped in her chair. Miss Charlotte Knollys, Princess Alexandra's secretary, noticed her distress and asked Her Royal Highness if Mrs. Langtry might be excused. Alexandra suggested that she go home to bed instantly. Lillie left without paying her respects to the Prince, who was deep in conversation at the far end of the big room.

"Back so soon?" said Dominique in astonishment, as she staggered in. "I knew it, madame. So beautiful, so stubborn, so foolish."

Lillie was violently sick before the maid got her to bed. Dominique bathed and changed her, and as she lay there giddy and weak, the doorbell made them jump.

"I can't see anyone. Tell them to go away, even it if is my husband, Dominique."

The maid hurried off. Lillie heard her chirping, excited voice, then a deeper one. My God, not Bertie! Heavy footsteps came up to her room.

"You are in bed. Good!" The well dressed, distinguished-looking man smiled. "I am Francis Laking, Royal Household

114

Physician. I have been sent by command of the Princess of Wales to see you and report to Her Royal Highness on your condition."

"It is most kind of Her Royal Highness, but it is nothing. Only indigestion and a chill."

"We will know after we examine you."

"Please, doctor, I beg of you! I am exhausted. My schedule is a taxing one, and it has been too much for me, that is all. No examination! That is the truth."

"Well," he said, "a few powders perhaps . . ."

"Give them and the instructions to my maid. I *must* sleep. And thank you, doctor, and thank Her Royal Highness, too, please."

Dominique showed him out and came back with a cup of tea for Lillie, who gagged and shook her head. Then Dominique sat staring darkly at her mistress, a gargoyle in judgment.

"Stupid doctor!" she spat. "He believes what women tell him —like all men. Stupid! Stupid! But we are women, madame. We know these things, do we not?" Lillie pretended not to hear. "Indigestion, eh, doctor?" Dominique's hands were on her hips. "It is that special indigestion that men give to the ladies for a present."

"Dominique!" Lillie's hands went to her mouth.

"So! So! Just now I see it, but you know for a week now, no?" She glared. "And every day you go riding the big horse in the Park like a—like a— What you do that for, eh? For why, tell me!"

Lillie turned her head against the wall.

"Your husband must be told immediately, madame. That will bring him around."

Lillie sat up abruptly, tried to speak, and then slumped down. "He certainly must not be told. No!"

A pause. "I see." Dominique nodded to herself. "I see."

"Perhaps you do." Lillie softened. "Forgive my anger. You've been so good to me."

"You are my lady."

"Oh, Dominique, I am so frightened!"

"Everybody is frightened, but the lion only jump on the deer because he stand still and shake. You must move, go, run while there is still time."

"Where? If I go, I can never come back. I am finished in London."

"London!" Dominique spat. "It will be nothing. You are still beautiful, still the Jersey Lily. Everybody loves you."

"I won't be beautiful much longer."

"Bah! Like a Madonna you will be."

"What a Madonna!"

The next day Lillie was astonished to have Princess Alexandra call on her, accompanied by Miss Knollys. Dominique's face was a startling red under her cap of white hair as she announced Her Royal Highness. Lillie automatically got out of bed to curtsey, but the Princess graciously waved her back.

"Do get back under your blankets, Mrs. Langtry. We've all been so worried about you."

"I'm much better." Lillie lay back, tense and uneasy.

The drawing room was filled with the Princess of Wales's refreshing violet perfume and, for want of something to say, Lillie said she liked it.

"I have it specially made for me, you know. I do hope it isn't too strong for you in your condition."

What could she possibly mean? *Could she know?* Not the Princess. She went on chatting, and Lillie relaxed before her kindness. How different she was from Bertie, yet the perfect wife for him. So pretty, so regal, above gossip and scandal, superior to his Marlborough Set just as a princess should be. And Lillie thought of her own presumptuousness in having aspired to Alexandra's position in her most willfully romantic dreams. A sweet, thoughtful woman removed from pettiness. Now she was describing a bout of indigestion that had crippled her at one time. Lillie wondered what the Princess would say if she knew the cause and nature of her illness.

"Your princess is a very great lady, madame," said Dominique, after Alexandra had gone. "She has never visited you before?" Never, said Lillie. "And so now she sends her doctor and comes herself." Dominique clucked. "Life is full of surprises, *n'est-ce pas?*"

"Too full. Bring me pen and paper please, Dominique. I have some important letters to write."

"You write later. Now you eat. That is more important for the health."

Lillie smiled at the maid's orders. Dominique was a remarkably indomitable and resourceful woman. Without a penny in the house, it was a mystery how Dominique managed to feed her. They had been besieged that morning both by tradesmen and bailiffs. Dominique had rallied to the attack in her fierce Latin way, and she had let them take Redskin off, apologizing to Lillie afterward.

"They need the beast, madame," she said. "You have no need of him any more."

She saw to it that her mistress had her favorite quail for meals, that she took red wine to prevent anemia, that she slept undisturbed. Lillie's dresses had to go in batches—and what a lot there were!—to hold off creditors. Still Dominique had food in the larder. Lillie imagined that she was stealing from the market, but she dared not say anything.

Mary Cornwallis-West came to Norfolk Street after Dominique had delivered the first letter. Long considered bitter rivals, Mary and Lillie had always liked and admired each other. Now she did not fail Lillie in her need. They cried in each other's arms like sisters. Lillie's second caller arrived late in the evening, a black cloak hiding the medals and decorations blazing on the lapels of his tail coat. He had come from the opera and was to go on to a ball. From his jaunty air, Lillie guessed that the secret rendezvous appealed to him. He was reliving his youthful London escapades, but then the trysting spirit had never left him, as he had often proved at 20 Wellington Road.

"I was delighted that the Princess called and found you better. Indigestion's always a miserable thing."

"Thank you for coming, Bertie. Would you like a drink?"

"Scotch whiskey is always welcome." He started for the side-

117

board. "I shall help myself, but we must watch out for the ice, hey?"

He gave a grunting laugh, and Lillie forced a smile.

"I'm leaving London, Bertie. I'll be gone quite a while."

"Your creditors, I presume?"

"I have to vacate the house immediately. Then up goes the 'carpet flag' courtesy of the bailiff. Everything's to be sold."

He sipped his Scotch. "Pity. Very sorry to hear it."

"That's not why I wanted to see you," she said quietly. "I haven't got indigestion. I never did have." Bertie started to raise his glass. "I'm going to have a baby."

The glass stopped just before it touched his lips. He stared at her intently for a few seconds, then drank slowly.

"I'm leaving with Mary Cornwallis-West tomorrow. You know her Ruthyn Castle in Wales? I'll be staying near there where I'm not known. After the child is born, I shall go to Jersey for a while. Then I don't know. I may come back to London. I may not."

He went over and poured himself more whiskey. "I hope you do, Lillie. Your friend Wilde thinks you would make an ideal actress. Others have said the same, and I believe it. I'm prepared to do all I can to see you safely launched."

"I have no dramatic talent, Bertie. No talent of any kind."

"Nonsense! You have every talent. There's never been anyone quite like you." He drank. "Has your husband abandoned you?"

"I don't know where Edward is or what he's doing. He knows nothing of what I've told you. I hope he never does know."

"You're wise. Not a bad sort, but I never could understand the fellow." He took an envelope from an inside pocket. "This is for you, dear. Odd, I meant to give it to you the night of the—uh—ice business."

"I can't take any gifts from you, Bertie. You're sweet, but no."

"It's not exactly from me, but you must take it. You'll need it more than ever now." He put the envelope in her hand.

Lillie went over to the light and tore it open. A check for

two thousand pounds signed by Sir Allen Young. "But why—?"

"I would have preferred giving it to you directly, but in my position I can't very well. There's enough in the press about us, as it is. Take it, use it, and say no more. It's for your needs, remember, *not* your husband's. And I've told Alleno you'll pay him back when you can. No hurry about it, of course." He gathered his cloak about his shoulders. "Take care of yourself for my sake. You're not alone, you know. I hope it's a girl and she looks like you. She couldn't ask for more."

"That's the nicest compliment you ever paid me."

He looked at her. "I could say more. I could say so much! I—" He swathed his impulse with dignity, biting his mustache as he checked himself. "But one thing, this sudden departure. There's going to be talk. Have you thought of that?"

"I've talked to Mary Cornwallis-West and Maggie Wheeler. They're going to drop a few hints to the society writers concerning my retirement." She smiled wanly. "That's rather a good term for it, don't you think?"

"As good as any." He sounded tired now. "Ah, well. Write to me, Lillie. Tell me where you are, what you're doing, and whether you need anything. I shall always be interested in you —and the child. Count on that." His arms went around her. He looked into her brimming eyes, then his mustache and beard scratched her cheeks as he kissed her tenderly. "This isn't an end, but a beginning. Things never really end, you know. They go on and we go on, difficult as it may be. Goodby, my dear. You'll make a lovely mother. I should like to see that."

"A beginning of what, Bertie?"

They walked to the door holding hands. Then he withdrew his hand and touched her hair briefly. He might be my father, she thought.

"That's what we'll have to wait to find out, isn't it? And now smile for me. Be the Jersey Lily once more." She smiled, and he took her hand and kissed it. "I shall always remember you like this. Beautiful, beautiful."

119

She watched through the window as he entered his carriage without looking back; then she went upstairs where Dominique was packing feverishly.

"Clothes. There are not many now. Just what you need. But books, there are too many and they are heavy. You want these?"

Lillie discarded several of them, then picked up Oscar's thin volume of poems with its dedication, "To Helen, formerly of Troy, now of London." And of Wales and Jersey, she thought wryly. She opened the book to his "The New Helen."

> O Helen! Helen! Helen! yet a while,
> Yet for a little while, O tarry here,
> Till the dawn cometh and the shadows flee!
> For in the gladsome sunlight of thy smile
> Of heaven or hell I have no thought of fear
> Seeing I know no other God but thee . . .

"I shall keep this one, Dominique."

The maid shrugged. "You are sure Mr. Langtry will find your letter?"

"He'll find it."

One of her major creditors was at the door early the next morning. Dominique spoke to him, but he was so abusive that Lillie came down herself. She showed him Sir Allen Young's check and implied that his establishment would be reimbursed immediately. It was humiliating, but it worked, and she was relieved when Mrs. Cornwallis-West arrived in a closed carriage. She left Edward's letter with the landlord. She could not escape a sneaky, cowardly twinge as they drove away. Typically, the day was bleak and rainy, the streets deserted. For once, no spectators breathlessly awaited the appearance of the Jersey Lily.

Such was the fame of Mrs. Langtry that the New York *Times* of October 4, 1880, reprinted in full on its front page an article from the London *Figaro* with the heading "Retirement of Mrs. Langtry from Society." Things were apparently going according to plan. On November 6, 1880, the *Times*'s London correspondent had further news.

Mr. and Mrs. Langtry have given up their London residence and for the present Mrs. Langtry remains in Jersey. Is beauty deposed or has beauty abdicated? The result on London society will be the same. Public pets may be objectionable, but few could so well have survived the ordeal of universal admiration and preserved so much of the natural good-hearted woman as Mrs. Langtry.

The auction took place at Number 17 Norfolk Street the week after Lillie's departure. Everything was disposed of, and the big curious crowd paid high even for trifles, among them Whistler's gilded fans. There would have been bids on the artist's ceiling if that could have been put on the block. Lady Lonsdale wrote, "Everything went for immense prices—your little tea-table with your initials on, down to your skates—so I hope your horrid creditors are satisfied." Lillie's friend was especially proud she had bought a stuffed peacock, shot for the Jersey Lily by Lord Brooke at his Warwick Castle. Whistler had made the bird high-style with the stunning decor of his "Peacock Room," and Lillie had mounted it as a screen. But she had never liked her peacock and had suspected it of bringing bad luck.

The auction was covered by reporters, who were amazed at the taste which had changed a thoroughly unfashionable old house into "a bower of beauty." One wrote:

The woman who could manage the metamorphose that was made in that house should not be permitted to live in idleness. . . . She should be induced to teach aesthetic art to common minds and show the unimaginative how to cover dingy walls and tapestries with green draperies and convert cheap windows into bowers of flowers. . . . The art she possesses is one of the very rarest. . . . With a few handsome rugs and easy chairs, plenty of draperies and not many articles of virtue she transformed an old London house into a charming house, where guests were sure to enjoy their surroundings and note its restful beauty. Mrs. Langtry is, therefore, more than a professional beauty.

The barrage of misinformation, half truths, and wild im-

121

probabilities surrounding Lillie's retirement or abdication admirably suited her purpose. So deftly was her disappearance managed that few people ever knew where or when the child was born. No Extract of Birth is available from authorities either in England or the Island of Jersey, nor is a Certificate of Baptism. It may be that the birth was not registered. In any case, Jeanne Marie Langtry appears to have been born in March, 1881, very likely in Jersey.

Because Dean Le Breton was old and in poor health, he had asked for a less taxing position and in early autumn of 1880 was given Marylebone Parish Church in London. Lillie learned of his move only after she had gone to Wales, and friends communicated with Mrs. Le Breton, who immediately went to her daughter. It was decided that both of them would return to Jersey. Of course Edward complained to his in-laws, greatly troubling the dean, but Mrs. Le Breton automatically sided with Lillie. Edward had become both a drinker and gambler. He had wasted his fortune and failed to provide for Lillie, and their daughter was sick and unhappy. There was no thought of divorce. Edward had proved unfit as a husband by leaving her at Norfolk Street to square the debts; he was just as unfit to be a father. No point, then, in telling him about the expected baby. He would only make a difficult situation more difficult.

Of course Lillie knew that the facts were cruelly distorted and her husband's character unfairly blackened. However, she felt she had no choice but deception under the circumstances. In her farewell letter she had told Edward something she had long known: their marriage was at an end; life would be better for both of them apart. He had reacted like a timid pheasant crashing to earth at the sound of the shot when no pellets had hit it. Although the dean was baffled, Mrs. Le Breton was utterly persuasive where Lillie was concerned. He went along through force of habit, with Edward Langtry doing nothing to help his cause by his inability to stand up to his father-in-law. He collapsed along with his pride and finances.

Sheltered in an isolated Jersey cottage, Lillie devoted herself to nursing and caring for her baby with the help of Mama and Dominique. The feelings that Jeanne Marie aroused in her were a revelation. This was hers, something real she had helped create out of herself. Never had she loved anything so much, never had she felt herself capable of possessing so much love for anyone or anything. This love came from her as naturally as breathing, exhilarating in its newness, overwhelming in its strength. She had always loved her parents and brothers deeply, but what she felt for the baby was hardly comparable.

This rather shocked her for—at the beginning, anyway—she had assumed she loved Edward more or less as most wives loved their husbands. Now she realized she had never loved him. Why, I've *never* been in love, she thought—not with Edward, Bertie, nor any man. What must it be like to love a man? And, looking down at her sleeping baby, it occurred to Lillie that she had failed herself quite as much as Edward. To love, to love. The thought of her husband off alone somewhere, brooding on the injustice done him and drinking heavily, depressed her. But all she could feel was a mixture of pity and contempt.

"Have you ever been in love?" she once asked Dominique.

"I am a woman," Dominique answered simply. "I have had many men."

"You loved them all?"

"Yes—no." She shrugged. "What is love? For it to be good, the man must give, the woman, too. It is not possible for either sometimes, and one suffers."

"Do you still like men?"

Dominique gestured in her inimitable Latin way. "Men are slaves, madame. The most foolish thing a woman can do is to permit herself to care even a little bit for them." She gave a roguish, coquettish laugh. "But we women must be slaves to our slaves to be happy a little bit."

Lillie loved the peacefulness of Jersey, the freedom from gimlet eyes and cutting tongues. While the island would always be her home sanctuary, the place she would always come back to, she belonged in London, even though she ruled there no more. She was impatient to return. Sir Allen Young's check had paid for the cottage and would see to Jeanne Marie's care for a time. Bertie would come to the rescue again if she appealed to him, but she didn't want to be dependent on him or anyone except herself. There was life to live and money to earn. Somehow she had to do both and graft the Jersey Lily on a new and firmer stem. The professional-beauty phase of her life was over. She was passé on that score, and she had no regrets. All that remained outside of her debts was the name she had made for herself, the fame she had acquired (slightly tarnished now), and her many friendships (curdled perhaps).

She left the baby with Mrs. Le Breton and a governess, her mother planning to join the dean in London later. The impression in Jersey was that Jeanne Marie was an ailing niece either on her husband's or brothers' side. In London, Lillie took rooms in Ely Place. Dominique, glad to be in sole charge again, bustled happily about, making a new home. Lillie let her tend to everything because resettling was such an effort. She felt so let down and unsure of herself that at first she wished she had remained in Jersey, where there were no decisions to make and life was cut and dried. She was like someone who had been very ill, had passed an uneasy convalescence, and was struggling to find a place on an old and yet unfamiliar road.

She had privacy now. No one waited for the Jersey Lily outside the door. Those who recognized her on the street stared at her with the same bemused pity they might have given an ex-champion or an old general whose exploits were long past. No one followed her or pointed her out; her photographs gathered dust in shop windows; she might never have been famous. It was restful and a little sad.

Then came a letter telling of another family tragedy: her brother, Maurice, was dead in India. He had been in civil service, and the villagers had sought his help in killing a marauding tiger. The animal had clawed Maurice, and he had died of blood poisoning. Coming at such a time, this was a great blow to Lillie. How ironic to be at loose ends in London and in mourning again! Her wardrobe was the same as it had been during her mourning for Reggie, and two dresses sufficed. She went out very little, and she had no inclination to wear lovely dresses or do much of anything.

124

She did call at Frank Miles' studio and found Oscar Wilde there. Both men greeted her enthusiastically, gay and high-spirited as always. Oscar's clothes were more flamboyant than she remembered. His hair was longer, his nails dirtier, but the old bounce, the sparkle, and his alluring voice struck a familiarly warm responsive note.

"Of course, you're going on the stage," said Oscar.

"Well, Henry Irving did offer me a part, but I couldn't do it."

"Those mannerisms of his and that walk," said Miles. "His stage shuffle spoils all his effects."

"Look on him with an artist's eye, then," said Oscar. "Both Irving's legs are delicately intellectual, but his *left* leg is a poem."

They laughed and talked for a while. Miles prepared to make tea and was interrupted by a knock on the door. He looked at Oscar and withdrew. The poet answered, showed no surprise at the policeman there nor at his request for information as to the whereabouts of Mr. Frank Miles, against whom a charge had been made. Oscar lied with charming assurance. The policeman went off, all apologies. Then Oscar began to pour boiling water, singing in an oddly musical voice:

> "Though the Philistines may jostle
> You will rank as an apostle
> In the high aesthetic band
> As you walk down Piccadilly
> With a poppy or a lily
> In your mediaeval hand."

Humming, he handed Lillie a cup of tea. "Isn't that delightful? I've been satirized in plays as an aesthete—whatever that is—a fraud, a swindler, an effeminate man, but it's so much better in operetta, isn't it? 'High diddle diddle will rank as an idyll if I pronounce it chaste!' Gilbert and Sullivan are *so* clever. Ah, to be immortalized at my tender age! Caricature is the tribute mediocrity pays to genius, so why shouldn't I feel flattered?"

Lillie laughed and asked about Frank and the policeman.

"Oh, that. You see, Frank likes beauty, very often in the shape of pretty little girls. He seems to have the fanciful habit of exposing a portion of his anatomy that is startling to these toddlers, more so perhaps to their dear parents."

"An exhibitionist?"

"Must we label him? Frank takes understanding, like all of us. I like persons better than principles, and I like persons with no principles better than anything else in the world. Frank is Frank, Oscar is Oscar, and Lil is—devastatingly lovely." He laughed boisterously. "And I've an idea. Why not ask Ellen Terry about your chances on the stage? Nell should know how to advise you."

While a reigning celebrity, Lillie had of course met Sarah Bernhardt, Helena Modjeska, and Ellen Terry, the finest actresses of their time and considered by some the best the stage had ever produced. Bernhardt was a special case—daring, esoteric, putting on make-up publicly, and flaunting her lovers. Ellen Terry described her as "transparent as an azalea, only more so; like a cloud, only not so thick. Smoke from a burning paper describes her more nearly! She was hollow-eyed, thin, almost consumptive-looking. Her body was not the prison of her soul, but its shadow." She was "more a symbol, an ideal, an epitome, than a *woman*."

Modjeska was a more solid, practical woman. She first met Lillie at a party given by Hamilton Aide for the Prince of Wales. Aide put on a play in which Modjeska and Genevieve Ward both had parts. At supper afterward Modjeska sat next to Bertie, with Lillie and Mary Cornwallis-West *vis-à-vis*, and frankly admired the Jersey Lily's neck and shoulders. At another time, visiting backstage at *Romeo and Juliet*, Lillie placed on her own head the wreath of small roses which Modjeska wore in the tomb scene and also the skull cap she had introduced for Juliet. Modjeska, insisting that Lillie looked bewitching in both, asked, "Lillie, have you any inclination toward the stage?" and Lillie, smiling, said noncommittally, "Oh, yes, it would be nice to be an actress!" but nobody took her seriously.

Nell, as her friends called Ellen Terry, was five years older than Lillie; Bernhardt and Modjeska, nine. The three actresses

126

had one thing in common: they had been on the stage since childhood and had served a long, difficult apprenticeship on the way to stardom. Lillie had neither the background, time, nor desire to dedicate herself to a profession. Therefore, when Oscar Wilde took her to call on Ellen Terry she was not surprised at Nell's discouraging words.

"Beauty is always an advantage to an actress, Lillie. You might satisfy public curiosity by displaying yourself on the stage for a time, even with no talent. But like painting or writing, acting demands long training. You would start at the top and be judged on that basis. I can see no greater disadvantage. The stage is a hard, demanding life, full of difficulties and bitter disappointments. You can't imagine the sacrifices, the drudgery."

"I know," said Lillie softly.

"I hate giving advice, hate receiving it. But they'll expect a lot from you, Lillie, then damn you as an amateur. As a beauty, you've been petted, spoiled, and you've never worked hard. As an actress, you'll labor and be brutally criticized. The stage doesn't take part of your life; it takes all. It devours you. And you must be a good actress. You must! Who would want anything else?"

"Well, I've learned something, anyway, Nell."

"Have you? Never listen to other people. They always insist they're being objective, but are they? Ask yourself that always."

Two days later at a big party at Millais' home, Lillie met Lester Wallack, the American producer. He surprised her by asking if she had ever thought of going on the stage. She wondered if he were a mind reader or had been listening to gossip.

"Mr. Wallack, would you give me an engagement, inexperienced as I am?"

"I would jump at the chance. I'll give you two hundred and fifty dollars a week to come to Wallack's Theatre right now. That comes to about one thousand two hundred and fifty pounds your money." She looked startled. "I assure you I couldn't be more in earnest, Mrs. Langtry. You could make a very good thing out of it."

"Whether or not I am a good actress?"

"Whether or not. It's Mrs. Langtry the public wants to see."

He gave her his card, and Lillie told him she would advise him of her decision. She recalled Ellen Terry's pride in her profession, the years and effort she had put into it. Lester Wallack would only exhibit the Jersey Lily as a freak, the social butterfly and the queen of beauty on a shoddy pedestal. Her career would be short. The idea was degrading, yet the large salary was devilishly tempting.

Bertie called on her at Ely Place, kissing her on the lips like a lover greeting a long-absent sweetheart. An old forty-one, he was shorter than she by several inches, portlier than before. His hair was receding fast, and his mustache and beard were streaked with gray.

"Marienbad is good for me," he announced, tapping his stomach. "I've lost several inches here. A struggle."

"It would look much better if you had your waistcoat taken in."

"I suggested it, but my valet says I shall soon fill it out again." He laughed. "Very forward of him, eh? But tell me about the child. A girl, isn't it?"

"Yes. Jeanne Marie is a fine healthy baby."

"Wonderful! And a pretty thing, I take it. Your husband's been seen around Southampton, Coyne tells me. You'll divorce him, won't you?"

"Edward would never consent. There must be grounds and —Bertie, he could make things very unpleasant."

"You're right. I suppose a reconciliation would be the best thing."

"You know that's impossible."

Bertie later asked her to a dinner attended by John Hollingshead and Arthur Cecil, producers and actor-managers. They were not helpful. Both were conscious of her being under royal patronage and were prompted to reflect the Prince of Wales's opinions rather than their own. Hollingshead was guarded, but Cecil asked her "to take the step of going on the stage." She had beauty, which was most desirable, he said, and,

128

lacking experience, the only way to gain it was in the theater. Simple as that.

"The decision seems clear-cut to me," said Bertie afterward.

"I'm less sure than ever," she confessed. "But thank you."

"I'm here to help, Lillie. Depend on me."

The invitation to spend a week with Lady Lonsdale at Lowther Castle was fortuitous, since her mind was in such ferment. Her friend met her at the Carlisle Station in her trim pony cart and stopped at the estate entrance to point out a long-legged creature parading on the lawn.

"An emu, my dear. All the way from Australia. Isn't it fascinating? I don't believe there's another one in all England."

Lady Lonsdale had great wealth, position, security. Now she had an emu to set her apart from the rest of the aristocrats. A costly, exotic novelty to add spice to a dull, ordered life. Lillie's spirit rebelled at the idea of seeking out exotic trifles just to put one's friends' noses out of joint. Desperately, she decided she *must* come to some decision about her future. The luxuries of Lowther Castle seemed terribly artificial to her. She had once been a novelty like the emu and now she felt sorry for the silly, flightless bird.

Back in London, she continued to evade the issue and gladly accepted the next weekend invitation that came her way. The Duke of Fife's home at Sheen was filled with titled guests. She enjoyed watching the races at Sandown, but now the routine seemed weary, stale, flat, and unprofitable.

The contrast of these luxurious houses with her drab Ely Place rooms was overwhelming. She felt empty, frustrated, and furious with herself. She needed money badly, time was passing, she was doing nothing. This can't go on! she kept telling herself. I must do something. *I must!* But it did go on and, to her disgust, she would let it go on. As she sat there bemoaning her tendency to let things drift and chewing what she liked to call "her mutton chop of adversity," Dominique brought up the card of a Mrs. Henry Labouchère. Lillie knew no one by that name and asked Dominique what the woman wanted.

The maid shrugged. "It is a personal matter like anybody."

Lillie went down after a suitable interval. A small, stoutish woman leaped to her feet and came forward with her hand out. She was about forty, her curly hair splashed with gray, and her vivacious good-natured smile softened her square-jawed, belligerent features.

"I am very glad to see you, Mrs. Langtry," she said in a strong voice. "You don't know me, but I was seized with an idea and I simply had to see you myself. You may have heard of my husband, Henry Labouchère, the editor of *Truth* and an active Member of Parliament. Very active." Lillie said she knew of him. "I'm perhaps better known by my stage name, Henrietta Hodson. I've been retired some years now, but I still love the theater, and still act on occasion." She gargled a little laugh. "And that's what I wanted to talk to you about. I understand you want to be an actress."

"For once it would seem rumor has lied," said Lillie instinctively. The woman was domineering, offensive, and presumptuous. "I have never thought of going on the stage."

"That fits in perfectly with my plans," Mrs. Labouchère went on, appearing not to have heard. "We have a home in Twickenham, and I am organizing a benefit performance for one of our charities there. It'll be an amateur affair, a simple playlet or two. Just the sort of thing in which you ought to get your stage wetting. How does that sound?"

"I have no talent, nor do I have the capacity for working or learning, Mrs. Labouchère."

"You have beauty, presence, poise, and brains. With my experience I can make an actress out of you. I know I can."

"I'm afraid you're optimistic."

"On the contrary, I'm realistic. I simply see what is there and I know how to use it. So you'll come to Twickenham and live with us at Pope's Villa until the performance. We'll work together."

"But, Mrs. Labouchère, I can't—"

"Call me Henrietta, and of course you can! I'll expect you tomorrow then. Tell your carriage driver Pope's Villa, Twickenham. Everybody knows where it is." She started for the door.

"Wait! How can I possibly decide immediately?"

"That's the only way *to* decide. Take the plunge head first. Once in, one swims about because one has to, and the water is delightful. You'll see!"

She shot off like the Red Queen, leaving Lillie speechless and prickling with anger at the impulsiveness with which she had been committed to Twickenham willy-nilly. I won't do it, she told herself. I'm not going to let myself be coerced into making a fool of myself by that outrageous woman! Lillie could see herself stumbling about the stage, forgetting her lines, struck dumb while her friends in the audience shook with derisive laughter. Oh, God, the humiliation of it! She had fallen from esteem, as it was, but a failure such as this . . .

"I like the lady," said Dominique, grinning from the doorway. "She knows what she wants, and she says it."

"Have you been listening at the door again? I've told you before—"

"Do not rage at me, madame. I know you are miserable and do not know what to do. But it is interesting what this lady proposes, and you will do it, I think."

nine

NEVER before had Lillie seen a house so grotesque as Pope's Villa, Twickenham, which sheltered Henrietta Hodson and Henry Labouchère, a couple apparently mismatched yet strangely compatible. A sprawling turret-and-gingerbread pile set on a bank of the Thames, it had supposedly been the home of Alexander Pope, and Labby (as Henry was called) took pleasure in keeping the myth alive. It is true that the poet had lived on this site, but the present monstrosity was the creation of an imaginative Swiss.

Lillie had had the idea that acting was merely a matter of memorizing and speaking lines. The naïveté of this conception quickly betrayed itself in her lack of expression and inflection. Her words came out flat as a schoolgirl's recitation. Henrietta criticized, interrupted, corrected, and criticized again. Lillie had never worked so hard or spent so much time on a project, and she was discouraged in spite of her coach's praise. She worried and fretted, forcing herself into the character of Lady Clara, whose motivation seemed shallow and artificial. Henrietta spent hours with her, going over the lines again and again, making every step of progress appear a monumental achievement. Sometimes Labby looked in on them owlishly, amused as if they were rehearsing a charade.

It was dogged, exacting labor for Lillie. Without Henrietta's constant prodding, she would have abandoned the whole thing but, because she had agreed in a moment of weakness, she went through with it. They trooped back and forth over the lawn facing the river, the Roman-numeraled tower clock striking the hours, Lillie's voice cracking, her throat parched, her eyes blurring in the sun, and Henrietta cajoling, lashing, urging. Lillie saw no improvement. She wondered over and over why she had ever been fool enough to conceive of herself as an actress, and she began to hate Henrietta.

As the day of the performance drew close, Lillie became even more anxious and fretful, while Henrietta, thrilling at the chance to be on stage again, chortled with excitement. The benefit performance was scheduled for the evening of Saturday, November 19, 1881. Lillie had to appear with Henrietta in a simple little comedy called *A Fair Encounter,* a curtain raiser to Tom Taylor's melodrama, *Plot and Passion,* which featured Lady Monckton, a perennial amateur actress. Theirs was a twenty-minute duologue, a battle of wits between two women, and Henrietta cleverly assured Lillie she had no cause to worry since everyone was coming to see the renowned Lady Monckton, anyway. They would open the program, giving the spectators the chance to take their seats at leisure before the main attraction. No one would judge a minor *divertissement* harshly.

Lillie was neither reassured nor deceived. She tried to believe the disclaimer, and Lady Monckton's superior attitude was helpful. Granting a certain public interest in Mrs. Langtry, Lady Monckton knew she herself was still the star of the occasion.

Calm and composed as Lillie had always managed to seem in times of stress, she experienced the neophyte's usual trepidation as Henrietta applied the make-up in the small dressing room of Twickenham Town Hall. She was sensible enough to know that, because of her reputation, more would be expected of her than of a rank amateur. Many in the audience would be only too happy if she flopped right on her lovely face. "My dear, it was too, too ghastly. You can't imagine!" There would be gossip for weeks to come: the Jersey Lily's débâcle. She didn't have to go on. This was only a curtain raiser. She could plead sick and leave the boards to Lady Monckton.

"I don't feel well," she blurted. "I can't do it today."

Henrietta smiled. "There's no escape now, Lillie. You'll hate yourself worse if you don't go on."

Dressed in delicate pink, Lillie trembled in the wings, awaiting her entrance. Every fault Henrietta had found, every doubt she herself had felt plagued her. She peeped through the curtain. The hall was crowded. Many of the people she knew, and she broke into a cold sweat that congealed on her. Swallowing at the dryness in her throat, she stared numbly as Henrietta dumped into her shaking arms the bundle of roses she was to carry as Lady Clara, and whispered heated encouragement much as a mother robin before kicking her fledging out of the nest. The curtains parted, a veil torn on hideous reality. Henrietta urged her, "Smile! Smile!" and shoved her forward.

There she stood, gazing woodenly into a maelstrom of hard eyes, twinkly opera glasses, and vacuous faces, smiling fit to crack her lips, and every single word of her opening speech was gone from her mind. Her brain whirled, her eyes burned, her mouth ached, her stomach was a tight knot. She wanted to faint. Then Henrietta's voice, low and piercing, came through the flimsy door through which she too was next to make her entrance. She had been listening for her cue from Lillie, and she was calm and steady as she prompted. Once she hissed the first words of Lillie's soliloquy, a second time with more bite —and then Lillie had it. Instantly her brain was a model of order, the controlled part rising above the panic it had dissolved.

Lillie felt her beauty projecting, the light of her charm glowing full, her smile encompassing the audience. *A Fair Encounter* went on more or less as it had been rehearsed.

"You did well," said Henrietta, after the curtain.

"Aside from forgetting my lines," said Lillie, conscious of her dress clinging to her back. "I almost died before you—"

"Perfectly natural. No one noticed it, so don't mention it. Say you loved every minute of it."

The applause was heavy. They returned for a curtain call, shared the audience's approval hand in hand, then Henrietta gave Lillie the stage. The applause redoubled—a rather pleasant shattering, rushing noise, thought Lillie—and there was Henrietta back to present her with a great bouquet of white roses. More bursts of applause—and they drifted off stage to make way for *Plot and Passion*.

"Your protégée did beautifully," said Lady Monckton as they passed her in the wings. "For a beginner, that is."

Applause, loud and sustained, broke out again, and Henrietta rushed Lillie back on stage.

"Some beginner!" Henrietta crowed. *"She* has no claque."

As they undressed, Lillie plucked an envelope from the huge bouquet, tore it open, and scanned the familiar handwriting. "I know you're going to be a tremendous success, and I wish I were there to congratulate you properly." It was signed "Albert Edward."

Henrietta smiled archly. Lillie shrugged and tore the message to shreds.

"Well, that's over! I'll be glad to get back to Ely Place."

"Whatever gave you that idea? I'm going to make a real actress out of you."

Though she felt bullied and put upon, Lillie was a willing pupil. Her reception and the favorable reviews had helped change her mind, as had a talk with George Lewis, her lawyer. He told her that Edward was eager for a reconciliation and refused to consider a divorce. Lewis felt that her secret daughter complicated her already difficult situation. It was imperative that she become self-sustaining in order to free herself from any of Edward's claims.

Lillie saw now, particularly after the Twickenham experience, that the stage was her only answer.

"You have a shrewd manager in Mrs. Labouchère," said Lewis. "She is bringing you along nicely, and you'll no doubt get many professional offers. In fact, I have a good one already. I was going to Brighton by train with Edmund Yates of *The World* and John Hollingshead, who manages the Gaiety. You have met them, I believe?" Lillie nodded. "Yates asked me if you were going on the stage. I let the cat out of the bag and asked Hollingshead if he would take you up. He replied with pleasure and offered a hundred a night for three months."

135

"Pounds?"

"Certainly, pounds!" he said, laughing at her astonishment. "What shall I tell him?"

"Nothing yet." She caught his arm. "Mr. Lewis, can you do something about Edward? I went to my rooms in London last week, and he was there. He had been drinking, and we had an unpleasant scene. He could make my London appearance a disaster."

"What do you suggest then, Mrs. Langtry?"

"I'd like Edward out of the way for a time. Some task that would take him out of London."

"I see. Well, I can't promise anything, but I'll speak to him."

Although the thought of Henrietta's new project gave her palpitations, it was a great coup. Supported by professionals, Lillie was to play Kate Hardcastle in a matinée of *She Stoops to Conquer* for the benefit of the Royal General Theatrical Fund.

"You'll start as a professional after the matinée," Henrietta said, "and you couldn't ask for better managers than the Bancrofts. They're giving you eighty pounds a week."

Edward Langtry called at Pope's Villa the day before Lillie left to begin rehearsals at the Haymarket. He looked sallow-faced, flabby, middle-aged.

"I behaved abominably last time we met, Lillie. I can never forgive myself, but I'm going to change. I'm going on a business trip, and I had to see you before leaving."

"Where are you going?" she asked, although she knew.

"It has to do with the theater, strangely enough. George Lewis told me about it and made the arrangements. You remember that young Shakespearean actress, Adelaide Neilson, who died recently? Drank iced milk on a hot day at the Pré Catalan in Paris. Well, I have to look after her property in America to settle the estate. Business and legal matters. It shouldn't take long."

"That's wonderful, Edward. I should love to visit America."

"Not at all like England, I'm told. Tell me, are you determined to go on the stage?"

"I need money. I need it desperately."

"But this is exactly the thing to turn Father against you forever. I begged and pleaded with him to help us, and I'm sure he'd relent if—"

"Edward, I'm not going to beg and plead with anyone."

"It's no profession for a lady. You know what actors and actresses are—their reputation. How *can* you do it?"

"Because I have to."

"Lillie, I've had a bad time." His bowler hat slipped from his hand, making a clonking sound as it struck the carpet. He stooped for it awkwardly. "Will you take me back?"

"We've separated permanently. I made that clear in my letter."

"Remember how good it was in Jersey—Southampton——yachting? It can be again. I know it."

That he should really believe such an appeal would move her at this point startled Lillie. How little he understood her and the emptiness of their married life!

"No, Edward," she said firmly. "No."

"A wife can't throw her husband out of his home."

"We have no home," she reminded him. "And you left me."

"You'll have to take me back, and you can't divorce me because—because you'll never untie the knot your father tied at the altar! I know all the things they said about you and the Prince and the others. I didn't choose to believe them, but maybe they *were* true." He smiled in weak triumph. "Do you dare deny them again?"

"I admit nothing, I deny nothing," she said wearily.

He slumped down in a chair, his face in his hands. "This is a terrible thing, Lillie. I don't know which way to turn any more." He pulled himself to his feet with an effort, looking ashamed. "I'll go, then, and do my best for Lewis. When I get back—don't shut me out, Lillie, please." His plea was part sob, part whine. "We'll talk about this again."

"We'll see," she said, not wanting to hurt him more.

Apart from her parents, who were always for her, and people like Bertie, Oscar, and Jimmy Whistler, most people decried Lillie's stage ambitions and shared Edward's feelings about the

137

low character of the profession. No one wanted her to lower herself. Some friends wrote that since she was bound to be an actress, they wished her luck, even though they could not applaud her plan. This was ironic, since it was only Henrietta who was determined; Lillie was the tail of the kite.

Public curiosity was intense—the Jersey Lily appearing with the finest actors in England!—and the rush overwhelmed the box office. All the more expensive seats were sold far in advance. Crowds jostled in front of the pit and gallery doors early on the day of the performance, December 15, 1881, prepared to wait for hours with sandwiches and box lunches, squatting on the curb and on camp stools, cursing anyone who tried to push ahead in the line.

"Never, perhaps," wrote the Bancrofts, "was a theatre more besieged for seats. All sections of society fought for places."

The Prince and Princess of Wales occupied the Royal Box, the Duchess of Manchester sat in another with a coterie of titled guests, the aristocracy was heavily in evidence, as well as first-rank actors, actresses, playwrights, authors, poets, artists, representatives of fashion, and critics. The house buzzed with anticipation. Lillie's friends and admirers sat in front, licking their chops at this new sensation of which they were part because, y' know, they *knew* the Jersey Lily. They were Society, the *haut monde,* and she was their late, great, acknowledged queen. They could hardly accept the incredible fact that one of their retired members could take acting seriously.

This was different from Twickenham. She did not blow any lines, nor did she feel even a twinge of stage fright. The first rows of the Haymarket was a solid phalanx of opera glasses and lorgnettes. There had been a brisk hire in glasses, and one enthusiast in the gallery sported a telescope. Things went just as Henrietta had hoped. Lillie, two months past her twenty-eighth birthday, never faltered. A roaring ocean of applause washed over her as her supporting actors stepped back to let her take her bows alone. Bouquet after bouquet was thrown at her until her arms could hold no more. She stood numb before the footlights, bowing and smiling at the shouts of "Bravo!" and the tireless clapping of hands. She was happy for Henrietta and for herself. It was over now, like a dream, and she moved in a daze at the party that followed.

"Wonderful!" said Princess Alexandra. "You were superb."

"Wonderful!" said Bertie. "But I knew you would be, my beauty."

"Wonderful!" said Whistler. "More divine than Sarah, do y' know?"

"Wonderful!" said Oscar. "I shall write play after play for you when I get back from America. Did you know I was going to lecture to the savages there? They want to see Bunthorne in the flesh."

"Wonderful!" said Lord Lonsdale. "May I see you alone later?"

"Wonderful!" said Henry Irving. "A great beginning."

"Wonderful!" said Ellen Terry. "Never listen to anyone."

"Too, too wonderful!" said Lady Sebright. "And you can thank me."

Apart from either the ecstatic or damning reviews, discerning critics saw the truth between the two extremes: Mrs. Langtry could not be judged as a professional because she was yet untried and had much to learn.

From the start, Lillie read everything written about her, pleased with praise, anxious to learn from just criticism, wincing at barbs. Those who had always resented her society success were hoping for her failure on the stage. And there were just as many who were indifferent, now that she had damned herself by embracing an impossible career. Lady Randolph Churchill had already started a movement to have ladies of quality withdraw their photographs from shop windows, leaving the field exclusively to Mrs. Langtry. And she was gratified now because "the more Mrs. Langtry becomes an actress, the less she will be a lady."

Lillie spent Christmas with her parents, glad to be free of Henrietta for a few days. They were delighted with her success. The dean joked about the Le Breton family guild of the incompatibles—the church and the stage. He liked Marylebone Parish and the chance to be near his daughter, but Mama said he missed Jersey. She told Lillie that the baby was thriving on the island, and wondered if they could bring her to London. Lillie said no. She would try to visit Jeanne Marie after the Haymarket engagement, but the child must stay there. She might be able to pass her off as her niece, but Edward could make trouble if he popped in unexpectedly—thank heavens, he was in America—then there was the nosy press. She must think of someone else, too.

She was rushed before the opening on January 19, 1882, at the Haymarket in Tom Robertson's *Ours*. Squire Bancroft and his wife, Marie Wilton, went out of their way to guide her through the drudgery of rehearsals in the cold dim theater, the endless repetition, the prolonged arguments over details which seemed to have little to do with *Ours* at all. Lillie presented them with a gift during rehearsals, attaching a note reading, "With real affection from your pupil (*dull*, but grateful for the pains taken with her)." It wouldn't have done to say so, but she thought *Ours* a ridiculous play: melodramatic, crudely artificial, and tedious, one implausible situation following the next.

The reviews followed the same pattern as before, with a slightly different twist. "Mrs. Langtry is captivating as Blanche Haye," said *The Penny Illustrated Paper*, "though as an artiste she cannot be said to possess a tithe of the rare talent and art shown at Her Majesty's Theatre over on the other side of the Haymarket by Mr. Carl Rosa's new Carmen, Miss Lillian La Rue."

"That's rubbish!" fumed Henrietta. "No one will remember this La Rue woman in the years to come. But I think you ought to talk to reporters more—the critics, too. Ask them to dinner at your home and charm them in your own surroundings. They're just men, you know, and quite susceptible to beauty. Flattery goes a long way."

Lillie found great satisfaction in her increasing self-sufficiency and in a weekly income earned through her own hard work. It was good to be in a position where she could buy pretty clothes, and not have to hide from creditors. While she still had debts, the nightmare of financial ruin was behind her; she meant to ensure that it would never rise again. Jeanne Marie would have a careful upbringing, a good education, every benefit. It was exciting to be back in London, her past fame enhanced by her present celebrity as a professional actress, her beauty extolled as always, her wit, charm, and simplicity acclaimed. She was stared at, followed, and pointed out as never before. It was noted that Mr. Langtry was no longer about to squire her. Gilded youths, unattached males, aristocratic men-about-town like Lord Lonsdale or Sir George Chetwynd vied for her company, showered her with flowers and invitations, and haunted the stage door of the Haymarket.

But, like it or not, she was an actress and her spare time was limited. Her meals were regulated, she had to be at work while others played, and, to look and act her best, she had to rest regularly. No more dancing till dawn, then riding in the Park. Those who wished to come were welcome at the intimate five-o'clock suppers prepared at Ely Place by Dominique. After the performance she was tired and, while she did accept certain invitations, she could never stay at a party long. She gave interviews freely, found reporters interesting men quickly won over by her easy, friendly manner. She had to accept the fact that she couldn't please everybody, and she learned to ignore such gibes as: "The difference between Madame Modjeska and Lillie Langtry is that the first is a Pole and the other a stick."

She had always got on better with men than with her own sex. Never was this more evident than on the Haymarket stage. The actors accepted her at face value and found that she did her job adequately and was pleasant to work with. That was enough for them. However, the actresses were prone to be catty, jealous, and to find fault with a newcomer given star billing. They could be viciously patronizing, too. One rainy night when Lillie was giving a young woman of the company a ride home in her carriage, the talk revolved on the Louis XV period.

"Such a wicked, exciting age, Mrs. Langtry, when beautiful women swayed kings and empires trembled before them. I should think you would find it fascinating." A smirk crossed her face. "After all, you might be called the Madame Pompadour of this age."

"Oh, come," said Lillie gently, "aren't you a little severe?"

"I think you're in a better position to answer that."

For answer Lillie pulled the carriage string, and the coachman stopped his horse, in the middle of Westminster Bridge.

"Mrs. Ogden gets out here," his mistress called.

The actress stared at Lillie as the coachman struggled with the door in the wind and rain.

"Good night," Lillie said in a voice of iron amiability. "I look forward to discussing French history with you again, Mrs. Ogden."

Lillie greeted Mrs. Ogden warmly the next day, but that actress was distant—so different from Henrietta who was a doer and a fighter. Henrietta was full of plans for Lillie, and her latest had to do with an endorsement for Pears' Soap: the company was prepared to pay a big fee for a few words of praise from Lillie. The money was fine, but, Henrietta insisted, as in the case of Adelina Patti, the fact that her pictures would appear in advertisements in England, France, and America, was much more important. At first Lillie was not convinced. Society would think it undignified and inexcusable. But now she was Mrs. Langtry, the actress, and she needed capital. The publicity and constant reminder to the public were important, and what if it did set Society's pearly teeth on edge? Could *it* sell soap?

No fan clubs existed in the eighties, but there were plenty of stage-struck young men and women. They patterned themselves on Oscar Wilde—wearing long hair, vivid clothes, and affected drooping mannerisms—or they had the Langtry knot, toque, shoes, and gloves, or imitated the make-up and attitudes of other prominent stage figures. Lillie was attended by a number of these acolytes, such as Justin Huntly McCarthy. He asked nothing more than to help her in and out of her brougham, obsequious as a lackey.

All manner of people felt they had access to an actor's or actress's dressing room, no matter how shaky their friendship. Still, Lillie was hardly prepared the night the custodian knocked and announced, grinning and gesturing inanely, "Some queer old bloke is waiting to see you. Got 'is 'ands full o' books, 'e 'as. Says 'is name is Gladstone."

Lillie sat up. "You mean Prime Minister Gladstone?"

The man shrugged. " 'E don't look like no minister to me."

Gladstone entered, greeted her solemnly and put down the books he was carrying. White-haired, stern-visaged, he looked a fierce Old Testament patriarch until he smiled. At seventy-three he had already served ten years on and off as Prime Minister. Just why this great man should take the trouble to see her puzzled Lillie.

"You no longer suffer from dizzy spells, I take it?"

"Not since Lord Beaconfield's demise last year. He was a good man and a worthy opponent. God teaches us that even our so-called enemies are His children."

"Even my critics, too, I suppose," she said with a laugh. "But they have such immunity and I have no Parliament in which to answer them."

"You must never answer them, Mrs. Langtry. Never! In your professional career you will receive attacks, personal and critical, just and unjust. Bear them, never reply, and, above all, never rush into print to explain or defend yourself. It is truly 'nobler in the mind to suffer the slings and arrows of outrageous fortune.' And God will help you. I have the simple religious faith of a child. It sustains me." He handed her a book. "I want to leave with you the *Memoirs of Sister Julienne*. You must study her life in similar context." He picked up the other books. "Now I'd like to read you several passages from the immortal Shakespeare on the same subject—what I like to call fighting the good fight."

They were familiar passages, and they recalled the evening recitations with her father in St. Saviour's rectory. But as William Ewart Gladstone read them, his dry voice ringing with sincerity, Lillie pondered the astonishing fact that here was the busiest and most powerful political figure in England, perhaps in the world, in her dressing room. He was a godly man in the best sense—who else but a Gladstone would roam London's dark alleys giving prostitutes money and trying to reform them? She could feel his goodness in his peace of mind and utter lack of self-consciousness as he read to the notorious Jersey Lily. Why, he was just like Papa—only he had a world-wide reputation.

143

Knuckles rattled the door. "Ten minutes, Mrs. Langtry!"

"What does that mean?"

"Ten minutes until curtain time, Mr. Gladstone."

"Then I must go. Keep this book as long as you wish, and good luck in your acting. Just ignore criticism, as I told you, and you'll succeed." He collected his other books. "I hope you'll do Shakespeare soon."

"I hope so. It takes great ability to portray his roles, but Rosalind appeals to me."

"Just the part for you! Be sure to play her as a high-spirited girl of sensitive intelligence, not just a hoyden."

She took his arm as he moved awkwardly toward the door with his burden of books. Sweet old thing! Lillie kissed him impulsively on the cheek.

"Well!" he said, reddening but pleased. "Well! What would happen in Parliament if they knew the Jersey Lily had kissed me?"

"You'd be ruined?" she hazarded, laughing.

"I'd be given three cheers by all the members! Good night. I look forward to your Rosalind."

Several times that year she saw him, always the aged Voice of Experience advising Miss Innocence-on-the-Stage.

ten

CONTINUING at the Haymarket, Lillie alternated as Blanche Haye in *Ours* and Kate Hardcastle in *She Stoops to Conquer*. Henrietta insisted on sitting in the wings every night, taking notes and swamping Lillie with suggestions between entrances. Her dogged interest was annoying, but she meant well. She was aiming at the next phase in her protégée's career. The Haymarket engagement would be concluded by early spring. The rest of England clamored to see Mrs. Langtry, and theater managers of the leading provincial cities were eager to book her as a star attraction. The terms were high. The country was the place to learn more and to experiment, buttressed by the successful London début, and Henrietta was convinced her star was ready to go it alone.

The prospect distressed Lillie. The Bancrofts' management and reputation had done extraordinarily well for her. She had paid attention to nothing but acting. The tour would call for the additional worries of casting, producing, directing, and a hundred other details. Henrietta insisted that those responsibilities would be hers, but Lillie felt she was being pushed too far too fast. She held off a decision, although a confidently aggressive Henrietta went right on with the business arrangements. It was Edward Langtry who forced the issue.

His trip to New York had been a wild-goose chase, he declared. He had hoped to perform a valuable service which might lead to a position that would save them financially, but the Adelaide Neilson affair had proved to be a farce. George Lewis' senseless telegrams had kept him in America five months, although he had settled the Neilson business in five hours. Outraged, he accused Lillie of having been in collusion with her lawyer. Slovenly, unkempt, an alcoholic grossness to his features, he made an unprepossessing victim. Poor Edward, she thought. He called her a liar and a cheat, and she let him work off his anger without replying.

"Good-bye, Edward," she said finally. "I see no use in our meeting each other again. If you want to believe those things about me, you can. I bear you no ill will, and I'm sorry I made you such a bad wife."

"Hold on. I don't like to ask, but since you helped ruin me I must. You have plenty of money now, and I have next to nothing left of the fee given me for that miserable trip. And I've no place to go—Father's turned me out—and you know the Irish estates pay only a pittance." He strained to meet her pitiless glance. "You're established now, Lillie. You've got to help me until I can get on my feet."

"I'll gladly help you," she said dully. "I'll see that you get a regular allowance, but only on the condition that you leave me alone."

"Whatever you say," he replied hoarsely. "But I'll never give you a divorce. You'll be free of me only after I'm dead."

George Lewis agreed that she'd done the only possible thing. He drew up papers for an adequate monthly allowance, contingent on the arrangement that Edward Langtry would never molest his wife again. After that Lillie was willing to tour. She needed money now—all she could get—to support Edward as well as Jeanne Marie and herself. She was once and for all committed to the stage.

Henrietta had already planned and organized everything, demanding for the Jersey Lily sixty per cent of the receipts collected by provincial managers. Wisely, she had decided on plays which would not tax Lillie's budding talent but which would show her in the best dramatic light. She would repeat *Ours* and *She Stoops to Conquer,* then prepare *As You Like It* and Tom Taylor's *An Unequal Match* for the end of the tour.

The local critics turned handsprings for Mrs. Langtry. The houses were sold out weeks before she appeared, and at her re-

146

ception in Manchester, which Henrietta apprehensively regarded as the key city, she was cheered, mobbed, and followed on the streets. On the last night of her engagement the audience refused to let her leave the stage. She took curtain call after curtain call, bouquets and floral tributes pyramided near her. Her curtain speech was greeted with tumult. The theater manager and custodian had to barricade the stage door to keep it from being battered down, and they warned her not to go out till the police came.

"We want Mrs. Langtry! Hurrah for the Jersey Lily!"

Her carriage was waiting outside, but the coachman and horse were missing, their places taken by young men and boys fighting for the privilege of pulling her. Henrietta hung back, frightened, as Lillie was hoisted into the carriage. Tumbling over itself, fighting, trampling, yelling, the procession inched up hill, on the flat shuddered along grunting and straining, and then struggled to hold back the carriage on the down slope to her hotel.

Lillie was alarmed as the speed increased. The vehicle careened nearly out of control, and young men dropped off left and right just as if they'd been run over. Pedestrians went flying as one wheel mounted the curb. The carriage zigzagged across the street, bounced off the opposite curb, teetering on two wheels, righted itself, and shot past the hotel entrance as Lillie held her breath. The crowd cheered triumphantly, hauled the carriage around, and wouldn't let her go until she had made a speech. Then she blew kisses to all.

What a night! she thought, looking down from her hotel room window as she waited for Henrietta. Better than anything she had known in her reign as queen of beauty. If this could happen in Manchester, what greater conquests lay ahead? The night wind caressed her burning cheeks. Down below, the rioting youths slunk off slowly, screaming taunts at the police. The clear sky blazed with stars—how uncannily bright they were! She thought of something a fortune teller had told her 'way back at some forgotten fair in Jersey: "You will rule in three dominions; you will conquer by these possessions and live three lives." Superstitious nonsense, but— She had been queen of society; with the same incredible luck she might attain to queen of the stage. That left the third dominion a tantalizing mystery. What a divine night! Blurred singing reached her. She saw two young men clinging to a lamppost and drunkenly fending off the police. Lillie laughed aloud. They were wonderful and she loved them. And she loved the stage!

She had to break the Edinburgh engagement because of a hurried trip to London at the telegraphed command of the Prince of Wales, who had sent flowers and congratulatory notes for every provincial opening night. Lillie felt bound to obey his wishes, although the idea did not sit well with Henrietta. Sunday train travel was restricted in Scotland. The station master was flattered to be visited in person by Mrs. Langtry, but the railroad schedule was inflexible. There was only one way around it: Lillie calmly ordered a special train from Edinburgh to London at a cost of some one hundred pounds.

To her it was a simple business, but the procedure was so unheard-of that it was newspaper material in England and even in America, where the cost of the special was said to be $625. The New York *Mirror* went further, printing Joaquin Miller's now-famous spur-of-the-moment stanza under a cartoon showing an unmistakable Prince-Alberted figure, wearing a coronet-encircled high hat, and holding a lily with Mrs. Langtry's head coyly protruding from the petals.

Bertie was grateful that she made the trip, because an African king, splendid in tribal robes and with an Oxford accent, had arrived in London and expressed a wish to meet the beautiful Mrs. Langtry. Society had gazed on his black face with trepidation but had meekly taken its cue from the Prince of Wales, to whom a king was a king no matter what his color. So long as people behaved like gentlemen and proved diverting, Bertie welcomed them to his set. He had already shaken tradition by befriending wealthy Jews, self-made industrialists, and up-from-nowhere *nouveaux riches*.

"So you see, Lillie, I'm delighted you're here to do the honors. Kings and royalty are my profession, and Umanadi is worthy of ceremony."

148

It was odd to be back in Marlborough House. She had never been happier nor looked more beautiful. At dinner, she sat next to King Umanadi and did her best to amuse him. He was enraptured. When he belched at one point, after telling her that in his country a belch was a sign of deep appreciation for a fine meal, she too managed a ladylike belch. Umanadi came back with a dish-rattling eructation beyond anything she could possibly duplicate.

"Ah, madam," he said, lost in admiration, "if heaven had only made you black and fat, you would be irresistible."

Bertie assured her she had done much toward repairing the Empire's political fences on the Dark Continent.

Burbling with satisfaction, glowing with pride at Lillie's unbroken success in one provincial city after the other, Henrietta went on with her long-range plans by secretly cabling producer Henry E. Abbey in New York. He took the next boat, hurried out into the hinterlands to watch the Jersey Lily perform, then sat down to talk terms with Lillie's indefatigable business manager. The project was presented to Lillie more or less as a *fait accompli*, a typical strategic maneuver of Henrietta's. The idea of acting on the American stage had never occurred to Lillie, and the thought of leaving England was appalling to her.

Yet there was wisdom in Henrietta's impetuous methods. Lillie was already famous in America, she would be a big draw, and she would make far more money there in a much shorter time than she could at home. Oscar Wilde was getting big fees on his lecture tour under D'Oyly Carte's management. The idea of paying all her debts, including that sticky obligation to Sir Allen Young, was a great inducement; besides she would for a while be far removed from the vexing and potentially troublesome Edward.

Abbey was an amiable man, with black eyes, hair, and mustache, highly personable except for his flabbiness. He was eager to sign Lillie as his exclusive attraction. One of America's leading theatrical producers, he had sponsored Bernhardt's fabulous American tour the previous year. Henrietta was determined to procure the same terms as the Divine Sarah. She had clawed her way through many a theatrical battle, including one in which she had worsted William S. Gilbert before he teamed with Arthur Sullivan. Now she held out until Abbey agreed to sixty per cent plus expenses.

"I think we can do better," she told Lillie. "He's a *grand seigneur* in his dealings and no haggler."

"That's more than enough, Henrietta. I'm no Bernhardt."

"Certainly not! You're the Jersey Lily, and there's no one like you. Try for five per cent more. That's what they expect from a real star."

Lillie liked playing for high stakes. Not that she was greedy, but the challenge was there. Some day she'd have to make her own financial arrangements, and she wondered if she could learn to influence the producer. When the moment came she charmed Abbey easily; when she mentioned sixty-five per cent plus expenses, he capitulated without argument. He said he would send her the contract and would expect her to open in New York that fall.

Because Lillie was still a doubtful quantity professionally, or perhaps because Henrietta held salaries to a minimum basis pending the outcome of her American début, the Langtry company varied from merely adequate to second-rate. Henrietta had engaged her experienced sister, Kate Hodson, as the wheel horse, while the others in the cast were to present a competent background for the star who had to shine brightly at all times. They would not eclipse Lillie, who was still learning.

This cast now set about rehearsing three plays: *As You Like It, An Unequal Match,* and *The Honeymoon.* Henrietta leased the Imperial Theater (always doomed to be a white-elephant house) for a London tryout. The Pears' Soap advertisement ("I have much pleasure in stating that I have used your soap for some time and *prefer it to any other.* Lillie Langtry.") had been plastered in magazines and newspapers for some weeks and had set off much scathing comment. Lillie was paid one-hundred and thirty-two pounds for the endorsement, a sum she always remembered. It was exactly her weight at the time. Now the announcement of her forthcoming American tour revived all the old gossip—including the ice incident—and the London critics happily prepared to repudiate the high praise of their naïve provincial colleagues.

They lifted their noses at the circulation of "prurient rubbish concerning bald-headed men rushing to buy tickets to gloat over Mrs. Langtry's nether extremities" as Rosalind. One said she was graceful but posed too much and that her acting was tame and studied; "devoid of passion and deep feeling, wants heart and dwells in mediocrity forever." Another said she was clever, lovely, had a marvelously distinct delivery—then spoiled it by tacking on that she was "studied and artificial." A third was of the opinion that she lacked the "fire divine, the life, the passion, the heart which alone make the great artist." But several praised her beauty and thought she would become an above-average actress because she had perseverance and energy, had learned her lessons and—of all things!—had an admirable teacher in Henrietta Hodson.

Ellen Terry admired Lillie very much as a person; as to her acting naturally her feelings were mixed. In her autobiography, she quoted Henry Irving as saying that an actor should never criticize or pass comment on a fellow actor. But she did venture that "Just at this time, there was a great dearth on the stage of people with lovely diction. Lillie Langtry had it."

The Imperial engagement closed September 30, with Lillie scheduled to sail on October 14 and to open at Abbey's Park Theater in New York on October 30. The company was given a holiday, and Lillie saw to her own last-minute affairs, including a farewell dinner by Bertie. Henrietta, too, was busy, her spirits seeming to rise as their departure drew near. She sang to herself as she bustled about Pope's Villa putting linen away, packing china, and draping brown dust covers over the furniture. With an utter disregard for her husband, she cheerfully sacked the cook and most of the other servants, leaving the big house barely habitable.

As Dominique packed, misgivings filled Lillie. America was an unreal, uncivilized country, and the prospect of going there chilled her. Oscar had written that "For the American, Art has no marvel, Beauty no meaning, and the Past no message." It was the unknown that bothered Lillie. She remembered her days in London with Edward as a nonentity among a forbidding people. She was still far from widely traveled. England had seemed immense to her after tiny, isolated Jersey, her family and friends close at hand, and now the idea of having to prove herself all over again in a barbaric land depressed her.

The night of her departure swarms of friends saw her off at Euston Station. The railway carriage brimmed with flowers, and everyone but Lillie pitched into the special meal Henrietta had ordered from a caterer. Reporters took notes, jotted names of illustrious well-wishers, and wanted a statement from the Jersey Lily. Finally the whistle tooted. Kisses, hurried fare- wells, people crowding the windows to wave, and the midnight mail sped off into the darkness. One by one, members of the company fell asleep, and in her saloon-carriage Lillie stared numbly at the black window.

She hated leaving London, she hated what lay ahead—the strangeness, the raw, alien quality that was America—and it struck her as folly that she was risking her dramatic career on such a mad project. She had left everything and everybody she loved for a whim of Henrietta Labouchère's. And how pitiful her accomplishments! A wrecked marriage, a heartbroken hus- band, a notorious reputation, a darling child she hated to leave in the care of others, a lucky stage début, and now a shot into the unknown. She began to cry softly, glad no one was awake to see her misery, and she cried for a long time, thankful for the release as the tears dried on her burning face.

I must get used to depending on myself, she thought, pre- paring for a sleepless night. I'm just as alone in the daytime, but the composed, imperturbable Mrs. Langtry never breaks down, always remains cool, unemotional, and beautiful. Oh, yes, she told herself, I'm an actress, I am. She had just dropped off, it seemed, and then Dominique was shaking her. It was six o'clock in the morning, and they were in Liverpool.

The *Arizona,* pride of the Guion Line and known as a "Grey- hound of the Sea," looked much more like a lap dog in the damp grayness of the dockside. The long sea trip, Lillie's first, was exhilarating. When the weather grew foul, Henrietta collapsed in her cabin, but Lillie's spirits rose. She looked after Henrietta, dueled with the rats that infested the ship, sat at the Captain's table, and enjoyed the company of William Cutting, a young New Yorker.

Toward the end of the trip, the weather improved and passengers were ready to be entertained. Besides Lillie's company, there was another group of actors aboard headed by Charles Wyndham, who was taking his successful *Fourteen Hours* from London's Criterion to New York's Union Square Theater. As soon as she heard his actors were to give a benefit performance on shipboard, Henrietta roused herself and Lillie to give *A Fair Encounter,* the duologue that had brought Lillie to the stage for the first time, a long year ago at Twickenham.

In New York Henry E. Abbey knew that he had a big attraction, although he also knew that the Jersey Lily was still a gamble. A lot depended on publicity; even Jenny Lind might have been a flop if Barnum hadn't handled her. So Abbey played all the angles. While he stressed an admission of Lillie's that she had never set herself up as a great beauty or actress, his press agents ground out all the variations of the Langtry legend, including the ever-fascinating aura of scandal which clung to her. The self-righteous complained of the "erotic dodge" being used by publicity men circulating through clubs and drawing rooms that Mrs. Langtry, "who is an entirely honest woman," was no better than she should be. All this was sure to draw that section of the public not impressed by the arty approach, which on the other hand deplored that Mrs. Langtry was being sold as "an object lesson on the beautiful, as though she were a statue unearthed at Crete or Mitylene, transported from town to town for the instruction of the United States in the art of Phidias and Praxiteles." In any case, her acting was acknowledged secondary to her notoriety and the accenting of the poise of her head, the curve of her arm, and the fall of her ringlet.

As exponent of the aesthetic position, Oscar Wilde had given the press agents a boost by being Lillie's advance man ever since his arrival in New York on January 2 of that year, on the same *Arizona.* Newsmen had been prepared to do a fitting axe job on this grotesque, effeminate cultist, and Oscar had cheerfully anticipated them by downgrading, contradicting, startling, and shattering everything and everyone American. Accenting every fourth syllable, Oscar had replied to the inevitable "How do you like the United States?" with a hearty haw, haw, haw. He said he had found the ocean voyage intolerably dull, had continually hoped for something exciting to happen like the ship's bridge being swept away, but all he had seen was a lot of water and empty sky. He defined aestheticism as "the search for the secret of life," then warmed to questions about Lillie.

"I would rather have discovered Mrs. Langtry than to have discovered America. She will be a beauty at eighty-five. Yes, it was for such a lady that Troy was destroyed and well might it have been destroyed for such a woman."

At 4:30 A.M., October 23, 1882, word came that Lillie's ship was in the harbor. Henry E. Abbey and his party went aboard the reception boat *Laura M. Starin* to meet the *Arizona* at quarantine. With him were his partner, John Schoeffel, his business manager Marcus R. Mayer, Manager James Morrissey, frisky Mr. Howell of the Romany Rye Company, and about twenty-five other gentlemen "with footlights in their eyes," plus a squad of reporters. At five o'clock, just as the *Starin* was casting off, a cab pulled up by the quay, Oscar Wilde heaved out his bulk, and "the able representative of the sunflower" hurried aboard.

"Nothing on earth would have prevented me from welcoming the Jersey Lily to these shores," he announced. "She will brighten this gloom with a radiance that only the sun can match and warm the chillness of the coming dawn with the divine glow of her gorgeous presence."

The welcoming party had settled down to breakfast and had just begun the first course, oyster soup, as the *Arizona* loomed up in the fog. The band on the deck of the *Starin* burst into "God Save the King." Steerage passengers on the *Arizona* rushed to the rail in amazement, no doubt thinking this was the ordinary American reception to a shipload of immigrants.

Alerted by a message from the Captain, Henrietta woke Lillie and urged her to dress quickly for Abbey's welcome and an "interview" by the press. Lillie rose sleepily. Dominique fluttered over her, and Henrietta showered her with shrill advice which she ignored at such an impossible hour. It was dark and cold, her mind as congealed as her body, and she dreaded talking to inquisitive American reporters.

As Mrs. Langtry appeared on the motionless deck of the *Arizona* in the foggy darkness of that October morning and heard the band booming for her on the *Starin* alongside, she remembered another early morning when she had dressed hurriedly and rushed off to the harbor of St. Helier to board the *Red Gauntlet*. Her wedding day eight years ago! Edward flushed and happy, and she—how silly to remember it now.

Abbey stepped from a packed group of staring men, spoke to Henrietta briefly, then welcomed Lillie to New York. He asked her whether she preferred to go up the Bay on the steamer or on the reception boat. She chose to remain on the *Arizona* and, before the reporters could close in on her, Oscar catapulted forward, presented her with a bouquet, and kissed her hands.

"How good to see your beautiful face again in this land where I have starved for beauty!"

Now Lillie had to face "the party of American managers, actors, reporters, and the others who wanted to look at her and see what they thought." She did well because "in five minutes she convinced all she had earned the reputation she had made." She was simple as a farmer's daughter, graceful as a queen. "There was nothing theatrical about her, she shook hands with all, not as a petted actress or spoiled beauty but as a sensible, intelligent woman. Her navy-blue dress was a model of plainness and neatness, fitted her closely as rubber, and she wore no ornaments, not even a collar."

Because no loyal American would admit to an Englishwoman's being the fairest in the world, the reporters, the *Times* man included, were critical of her beauty. According to him, "One may see a hundred as pretty on Fifth Avenue at any time, but if they could carry themselves with the ease, grace, and self-possession of Mrs. Langtry, they are to be envied. She was asked all sorts of questions, sensible, idiotic, impertinent, irrelevant, and good-naturedly answered them all." Lillie's relationship with Bertie was the only thing none of them mentioned.

The interview at an end, the formalities of quarantine concluded, the officials left on the *Starin* with the reporters and the others eager to bring first-hand news of the Jersey Lily to a breathless New York. Lillie ate breakfast and went back on deck with Henrietta, Willie Cutting, and Oscar Wilde as the *Arizona* proceeded up the Bay.

"What a magnificent harbor!" Lillie exclaimed. "There's so much to see I could stay here all day."

"An accident of nature," said Oscar. "One harbor is much like another. The first I saw gave me a surfeit of harbors. Oh, Lil, some journal called the *World* has requested me to be guest-critic for your play. You don't know how much I look forward to extolling Helen again."

"See that you do then, Mr. Wilde," said Henrietta in her tart-sweet voice.

"I could write it now," he said, gazing at Lillie rapturously. "How could Lillie on stage enchant me any more than Lillie off? Perfection can only become pluperfection."

eleven

As Lillie came down the gangplank of the *Arizona* alone, another band broke out with "God Save the King" in stepped-up American tempo. A mighty shout came from the hundreds of people jamming the musty Guion Line pier. They pressed forward against the fence, reaching for her and yelling. Lillie smiled, waved, and Abbey led her to a landau. The crowd surged forward here, too, but the police kept them back until the horses started off at a trot. It was a jolting ride, since the streets were paved with cobblestones (Belgium blocks). She stared in fascination at this strange city, about which she had heard so much, as she and Henrietta rode with Abbey to the Albemarle Hotel on Madison Square.

"How do you like our fair city, Mrs. Langtry?" Abbey asked.

"You're as bad as the reporters asking how I liked America when I'd just arrived at six o'clock on a dark morning. I find the question surprisingly premature, but I think I like it. Only everyone's so busy and running about so, I don't think anyone'll have time to come to the Park Theater to see me act."

"They'll be there, I can promise you. They can hardly wait."

Big, commodious, boasting an elevator and all the modern luxuries of 1882, the Albemarle impressed Lillie. In London, hotels were commonplace and served transients without distinction. There important visitors stayed with titled friends in the metropolis or at country estates, and only the middle class had to content itself with ordinary appointments. Lillie was delighted to have Sarah Bernhardt's suite and to learn that nearly every bedroom at the Albemarle had its own bath.

"What a convenience," she marveled. "The Americans know how to live."

"Pure ostentation," said Henrietta, implacably British.

After unpacking and enjoying a good lunch, with the manager doing all he could for his famous guest, Lillie stood at the window looking out at New York. The sky was invitingly blue, the air refreshing, the sun so warm she wanted to go out. Abbey had sent his shay, a curious high-backed vehicle, so that she and Henrietta could take an afternoon drive. The coachman headed up Fifth Avenue toward Central Park, and to her surprise she was recognized immediately. Carriages turned to follow her, and she was hemmed in by a procession.

More reporters were waiting to interview her on her return to the Albemarle. They came in relays all day, repeating all the questions she had been asked on the ship, and she tried to accommodate them. They would have kept on after dark, but she had to dress for her dinner engagement with Willie Cutting.

Delmonico's was grander than any restaurant she had seen in London. Located at the corner of Fifth Avenue and 26th Street, it was one of *the* places in New York to see and be seen in. Willie had organized a party, including the wealthy businessman-sportsman Pierre Lorillard whom Lillie had known in London. People came from other tables to meet her, and she was showered with invitations she could not accept because she had promised Henrietta in England not to go anywhere without her. She refused them all by saying she had to work.

The food was delicious, the company brilliant. The women made her feel dowdy because when dining out, at least, their taste in dress was lighter than in England. Her first night in America seemed a great success, good omen for the tour.

Then came her first snub. Recognizing the handsome Mrs. Paran Stevens, whose daughter she had met, she went over to her table. Mrs. Stevens, a prominent society woman and first-nighter, looked up coolly as Lillie introduced herself and said she had known her daughter in London. Since Lillie was now no longer in society, but a professional actress, the blue-blooded

Mrs. Stevens said icily, "You are mistaken. I am quite sure my daughter doesn't know Mrs. Langtry." She turned back to her companion, ignoring Lillie, but not before the instant reply registered: "Perhaps, Mrs. Stevens. Your daughter knows so few people in London."

Lillie was composed as she resumed her seat. Actually, all she cared about at present was the stage. The other world would return to her later, and she'd have both for Jeanne Marie's sake as much as her own. The devil take Mrs. Paran Stevens!

Abbey's Park Theater, Broadway and 23rd Street, was not the first of that name, its predecessors having burned. It was a first-class house, and Lillie was pleased with it. As with all first rehearsals in a new location, the next morning was difficult and confused. Henrietta assembled the cast, searched for missing props, upset trunks looking for costumes, and drove relentlessly to put *An Unequal Match* into shape for opening night, Monday, October 30. While Lillie had her lines, movements, and business letter-perfect, the company behaved as if it had never heard of the play. Henrietta fumed. Lillie left early and, glad to be free, she decided to take a walk on her own.

New York was already coming down with a virulent case of Langtry fever. As in London her photographs were in the shop windows, here posters advertising her opening were plastered everywhere, and music publishers were turning out hundreds of copies of "The Langtry March," by Fred T. Baker, "The Jersey Lily Waltz," by H. Le York, and J. Albert Snow's "Langtry Waltzes." She was followed this afternoon, but she persisted to Lord and Taylor's big dry-goods store on the corner of Broadway and Grand Street, a sumptuous establishment described by the *Times* as "more like an Italian palace than a place for the sale of broadcloth."

The manager took charge immediately. He proudly showed her the huge chandelier over the staircase made by Tiffany at a cost of $500, but the crowds pushing around her made it impossible for her to get near the counters to make any purchases. Going back on the street, it was worse. She was pawed, accosted, and pursued. In desperation, she jumped into the first hansom cab, urging the driver to gallop away from the mob. His horse was quickly surrounded, and it seemed that everyone wanted to get into the cab with her.

In days to come it was even worse, for people sometimes became hysterical, and always demonstrations broke out when she appeared in public. Newspapers reported that the city had gone wild over Mrs. Langtry, and the stores sold out her pictures. Abbey's zealous press agents were partly responsible, but no more so than Lillie's own romantic appeal, her reputed fabulous beauty, and the fantastic stories about her. "Men and women fought for the privilege of following her through the streets to gaze at her face, and she revolutionized feminine costumes and coiffures." Hairdressers worked overtime duplicating her Langtry knot—a single, heavy plait halfway down the neck, balanced by bangs shortened and curled—and women sought to equal the utmost simplicity of her clothes which breathed the special chic "of the most smartly dressed woman of the age."

No sooner had she returned to the Albemarle from Lord and Taylor than the hotel manager scurried up. He begged her to do something about the pianos that were blocking the main staircase. Lillie was mystified until she came on four men arguing about two pianos that lay across the steps at a precipitous angle. One pair represented the Marker-Atloff Piano Company, the other the Fleming. They rushed her simultaneously, mouthing commercial claims, insisting that it was their particular instrument she required.

"But I have no need of any piano except at the theater, gentlemen."

"No!" shouted the man with the loudest voice. "We mean you to have one. Everything that Langtry touches is gold."

They began wrangling again, and hotel guests grouped around the combatants. To pacify them, Lillie agreed to have both pianos installed in her suite.

Reaching the haven of her drawing room, she came on Dominique screaming at a man who sat as if he belonged there. He presented her with a card introducing himself as the head salesman for two concoctions called Fillipin Fiz and Bongo Beer,

"America's finest carbonated drinks—delicious brews, sweet, mellow, and positively non-intoxicating." Pointing to four cases of his soft drinks piled in the corner, he offered her $500 for an endorsement on behalf of his company. He was so serious that Lillie wanted to laugh. She refused his offer, then helplessly agreed to "think it over" and in the meantime to accept the cases as a tribute.

"The Americans are mad!" said Dominique, slamming the door on him.

So they were. Cocky, alive, hustle-bustling, and terribly time- and money-conscious. Maddening, yet disarming, she thought, looking around at her rooms transformed since she had left that morning—awash with flowers, boxes of candy, assorted gifts, baskets of letters, the two pianos, and the cases of Fillipin Fiz and Bongo Beer. Smiling, she glanced at the throw-away which Abbey had shown her at the theater. Lily-shaped, with white flowers and green leaves on the cover, it opened to a picture of her against a giant lily with the message: "Mr. Abbey announces that seats for the first appearance of Mrs. Langtry, October 30, at the Park Theatre, will be disposed of at public auction to be held at the Turf Club Theatre, Madison Avenue and 26th Street (formerly Union Square) Tuesday evening, October 24, at 8:30."

Why, that was tonight!

She looked out at the lights twinkling luridly in Madison Square. Barbarians, Oscar called the Americans, ruffians apathetic to art and beauty with no past to speak of. Oh, yes? A horsecar rattled across the Square, the sidewalks resounded with busy footsteps, the frantic, murmuring clangor of New York wafted up to her, its exciting pulse beat a siren melody. Vibrant, twanging with vitality, aglow and aglitter. How could Oscar—how could anyone?—fail to respond to this New York, a metropolis next to which London seemed to have slept for centuries?

Billy Oliver, a Wall Street operator, handled the auction for first-night seats and disposed of tickets at inflated prices. Charles Wyndham, the fellow-passenger on the *Arizona,* set a record as high bidder with $320 for a first box, a generous gesture by a fellow countryman, since he could only remain for part of the first act before racing down to the Union Square Theater for his own performance. The first-nighters of the Union League Club, led by Herman Oelrichs, took eight orchestra seats at $17.50 each. The remainder went from $10 to $5 depending on location, and speculators were rumored to have pegged the house from $15 to $3.25.

These were unheard-of prices. Lillie remained consistently on the front pages and, with Abbey, came to believe that she might have been overpublicized. To hedge against this, she gave interviews stressing that she was not a great actress and denying that she was inspired by any overpowering passion for the stage. She said truthfully, "It was necessary for me to make money, and friends advised me that the stage was the easiest way." Some critics had anticipated this strategy; they said little was expected of her début and that a pupil of Henrietta Hodson's was sure to be conventionally correct.

James Gordon Bennett's New York *Herald* had become a mirror for Lillie's every activity. The paper had covered her London début on Bennett's orders. It had assumed a proprietary interest since her arrival and now had an "exclusive." A *Herald* reporter had been specially assigned to follow her throughout the day, recording every thought, every move.

The publicity build-up included a charity "coffee clatch" at Sherry's. Lillie was required to sell tickets for it accompanied by a voluble, enthusiastic reporter with the improbable name of Bury Irwin Dasent. A personable man, he was frank in his unqualified admiration of her as a woman. He also showed amazing editorial industry, taking her straight to the Stock Exchange to begin her in-person sales.

"Money means nothing to these big financiers and money changers," he told her. "I've got them primed, and it'll be a big story for the *Herald*. I can write the headline now: MRS. LANGTRY PANICS WALL STREET."

His imagination was prophetic. Their carriage was dogged by crowds as soon as they came into the financial district. People closed in as they inched along Wall Street and, as they

162

turned into Broad Street, diagonally across from the Stock Exchange, progress was made impossible. The coachman had his whip stolen. The crush nearly lifted the horse from his traces, and brokers, runners, clerks, messenger boys, and stenographers besieged Lillie with requests for autographs, a ribbon, glove, or memento. They pulled at her sleeve, yanked at her shoes, shook the carriage as the coachman cursed helplessly.

A shrill tweeting of police whistles set the crowd muttering as New York's Finest plunged to the rescue. Men fell back before the night sticks, jeering good-naturedly. Lillie entered the Stock Exchange with a blue-coated escort and mounted to the gallery. An official cupped his hands and, screeching like a hog-caller, announced Mrs. Langtry's presence in the big, high-ceilinged chamber. All eyes swung to the balcony. There were hoarse cheers and pandemonium as everyone broke for an advantageous position beneath her.

The stock market suspended operations while Lillie sold her tickets. She might have been offering some get-rich-quick shares, they went so well. She was stuffing bills into her purse and not bothering to make change, since she didn't understand American money. The crowd was still waiting outside, and Dasent asked the police to make way as they started back across the street.

Lillie asked, "Where are we going?"

"The Drexel Building. J. P. Morgan's office. He's God down here, and we're going to 'crash' his office."

Because the great financier did not like reporters, Dasent made Lillie introduce herself after they pushed open the ornate, frosted-glass door.

"Have you an appointment, madam?"

"Tell him it's Mrs. Langtry. I've come all the way from England to see him."

The attendant was gone about a minute, then motioned them inside. James Pierpont Morgan had evidently been slouched comfortably in shirt sleeves in a swivel chair before his massive, mahogany roll-top desk. He had hurriedly put on his jacket, and his suspenders were visible as he finished buttoning it. He was dressed in severe black wool with a stiff-bosomed white shirt, a wing collar, and something resembling an Ascot tie on which a diamond stickpin glittered. A bulky, portly man, his scruffy white hair was carefully brushed, his forceful features were flushed, and his big, bulbous nose was a red beacon over his short-clipped mustache.

"Mrs. Langtry," he said with a little bow, taking the cigar from his mouth.

"So nice of you to see me, Mr. Morgan, but then all you important American men are so charming."

With a girl-like verve that astonished Dasent, she chatted blithely about the coffee clatch, the tickets she was offering, British financiers, and her friends the Rothschilds. Morgan listened, not smiling, not frowning, his eyes on Lillie and unaware of the reporter. Like any connoisseur of beauty, he majestically took her measure. He asked the price of the tickets, was told there was no fixed price since it was for charity, grunted and reached into his pocket. The left, the right of his jacket, then his trousers. He hadn't a penny on him, this millionaire many times over. A silvery peal of laughter came from Lillie. Morgan gave a wisp of a smile. He called out to someone, money was promptly loaned him, and he handed her the bills without looking at them.

"I'm sure you will come to my coffee clatch," she said, thanking him.

"I'm not sure whether I will or I won't, Mrs. Langtry."

They shook hands then, Morgan's reticence and courtliness somehow speaking volumes. Lillie and Dasent went outside, past the secretary whose eyebrows were still level with his hairline.

"What a story! That's what I call really bearding the lion in his den. You were magnificent, Mrs. Langtry."

"Mr. Morgan is a delightful man," she said airily.

The excitement continued during the week. Rehearsals improved, and so did Henrietta's mood. Dasent scored a beat by mentioning the cordial telegram Lillie had received from the Prince of Wales. She continued her conquest of New York. David Belasco, an intense-looking youth with a great shock of

164

hair, invited her to the Hudson Square Theater to see the new double stage. He was stage manager, and he, the other actors and officials were waiting on stage when she arrived, "all in tuxedos with fast-beating hearts under white shirts."

The next afternoon she asked Belasco to tea as a return courtesy. Henrietta did not hide her annoyance. Lillie's costumes weren't back from the dressmakers, American stagehands were incompetent, Mr. Abbey was upset over the to-do of providing opening-night seats for provincial critics. Nothing was going right.

Dominique had just begun to serve tea, when Pierre Lorillard and Willie Cutting burst into the drawing room, both so agitated they waited for each other to speak first.

"I'm afraid the Park Theater is on fire," Lorillard blurted.

"What?"

"It's true, Lillie!" said Cutting. "We just came from there and thought you should hear it firsthand."

Lillie rushed to the windows, followed by the others. The darkness of late October had fallen, but the flames leaping from the roof of the Park Theater were lighting up Madison Square. She could see a mass of people gathered on Broadway, intent on the fire except when they turned their heads toward the Albemarle where they knew she was staying. The flames were blazing higher and higher, giving the Square an awful brilliance, but the sign she had gloried in—the sign proclaiming MRS. LANGTRY, fixed on iron standards above the roof— seemed safe enough from the angry, licking tongues of fire. Belasco saw her hands clench and tears in her eyes as the Park, in which she had hoped to triumph in a few days, burned to a shell.

"All our dreams gone forever," Henrietta moaned. "What are we going to do?"

"The sign's still there," said Belasco.

The sign was a symbol. If it toppled and went down, then she—no! *Nothing* would stop her, *nothing* could. She watched breathlessly as the flames leaped for the sign, her name lambent with fire.

"We're ruined," Henrietta wailed.

"Never! Whether it burns or not," said Lillie huskily, "I shall succeed."

The crackling of flames was audible across the Square. The crowd gave a collective "Ooh!" as a wall collapsed and crashed down in an extravaganza of sparks and hot ash. The Park Theatre was gone, her opening night there turned to a permanent closing, but it did not matter—look, a miracle!—*the sign still stood.*

"Well," she said loudly, above Henrietta's sobbing, "don't let's fuss. We'll try again some other way. You Americans don't give up easily, or you'd still be part of England. Neither do I. I'm sure Mr. Abbey will find some solution, and we'll go on as planned."

Lucky Langtry. It was not enough to have reams of news about her, a cable from the Prince of Wales, and that the first night seats sold for the highest prices since Jennie Lind's American debut, but now the Park Theatre has burned down to give her additional éclat. To crown all, Manager Wallack gallantly postpones his new piece, sends his company to the provinces, and places his handsome house at the disposal of the Jersey Lily. It might all be Langtry luck, but one of the Park employees died in the hospital of wounds attempting to escape the burning building, and the ruins are now being searched for the remains of the burned carpenter.

Lillie tossed the newspaper aside angrily, picked up another, and began to read.

There were fifteen people in the Park when it caught fire from a lace curtain at 4:30 P.M., Monday, shortly after Mrs. Langtry had left the theatre. Four hours later it would have been a tragedy. But as it is, Manager Abbey has lost a cheap and pretty theatre for which he paid $12,000 a year and had fitted up elegantly for about $30,000. Mrs. Langtry has lost nothing but a week's time and the spear she carries as Rosalind, and both manager and star stand to recoup from the tremendous advertisement of the conflagration. A benefit will be held for the families of the deceased and injured in a fortnight, Mrs. Langtry has volunteered her services, and—

166

She crumpled the newspaper into a ball, slashing at it with her fingernails as she would the face of a man who had attacked her. The week's postponement caused by the fire, the reorganization necessary to find another theater and arrange for new scenery, Henrietta's domineering ways, and being hounded by the press had stretched Lillie's nerves thin. She had had enough. Now to be subtly accused of arson—!

The other producers were all good friends of Abbey's. He was offered the Grand Opera House at Eighth Avenue and 23rd Street, but it was much too big. Abbey accepted Lester Wallack's offer of his theater at Broadway and 30th Street. Wallack had once wanted to sign Lillie, and now, ironically, she was to act in his theater after all.

The postponement would put her opening close to the New York gubernatorial election. Abbey gave his press agents their head to counteract it. Lillie still felt she had had too much publicity, but she was in no position to stop it. The other papers panned James Gordon Bennett and his *Herald* for its hour-by-hour coverage of her, condemned it as a cheap circulation stunt. They sneered at "a gilded youth who waited for hours outside the Albemarle to see Mrs. Langtry and was rewarded by opening the door of her carriage."

Besides the election, in which there was much interest because one of the candidates was the highly regarded Democratic Mayor of Buffalo, Grover Cleveland, Abbey was faced with another threat to his big attraction on that night of Monday, November 7, 1882. Adelina Patti, now thirty-nine, an international singer and New York favorite, was opening that night at the Academy of Music. A true prodigy, she had made her début in her teens and was such a lovely thing she had attracted the favors of New York's important men—among them Leonard Jerome, the father of Lady Randolph Churchill, who had scandalized the smart set by presenting her with a fine barouche and two handsome white horses to draw it.

Tommaso Salvini, the prominent Shakespearean actor, was another competing attraction that night. But Lillie was already a sell-out, and some swells were planning a theatrical double by taking in both Patti and the Jersey Lily. As to Lillie, the press agents had done well where age was concerned. A bare year on the stage and a sensation, she had just passed her twenty-ninth birthday—hardly a tender age for a star, since Lillian Russell was twenty-one. Because she looked to be in her early twenties, everyone assumed that she was.

It was New York's biggest theatrical opening. President Chester A. Arthur had been sent complimentary tickets, couldn't come, and permitted Chester A. Arthur, Junior, to represent him. In her dressing room, Willie Cutting kissed Lillie's left cheek for luck, Pierre Lorillard her right, while Oscar Wilde presented her with a single lily and boasted of his guest-critic assignment.

"If you say nasty things about me, Oscar, I'll never talk to you again."

"Perish the thought, Lil! But we mustn't let a hint of collusion stain my artistic integrity. Anyway, the *World*'s giving me *carte blanche*. I had to translate it for them. White card, you know. Haw, haw, haw!"

"I predict an ovation—an evening in the theater New York will never forget," said Abbey.

"It's after eight," said Henrietta pointedly. "It's almost time to go on."

Lillie smiled. "Well, I'm going on, but I don't know how I'll come off."

The men filed out, calling their good wishes, and Dominique took Lillie's first costume off the rack.

"I wish you'd tend more to business," Henrietta grumbled. "An actress never stops being an actress. This is the most important night in your life."

"Every night is the most important night in my life."

Both outside and inside Wallack's Theater, the atmosphere was charged with first-night excitement. Lights burned brightly under the marquee bearing Lillie's name. Photographs and huge reproductions of the Jersey Lily flanked the entrance, and the doors were choked with smart men and women in evening dress. Police made way for vehicles and kept the street clear, but no provision had been made for the overflow crowd surrounding the theater to stare at the arrivals. Drunks staggered about, sleazy speculators hawked real and counterfeit tickets at $35 each, an enterprising small boy offered "the only correct photograph of Mrs. Langtry" for five cents, and inside a uniformed attendant sold a better one for a quarter. Four immense bouquets, among which were propped tinted photographs of Lillie, stood in the lobby, to be deprecated later by a reporter who insisted that their "size betrayed the managerial hand . . . and deceived nobody."

In 1882 New York had morning, evening, weekly, and fortnightly newspapers and magazines by the dozens. Besides a phalanx of local critics, there were special correspondents from Boston, Chicago, Philadelphia, St. Louis, Cincinnati, and other major cities. They were a headache to Henry Abbey, who had been criticized for not allotting two press tickets to every publication, and he had taken the usual precaution of asking them all downstairs "to take something." Now they milled around the lobby, looking at everything and everyone with professional skepticism, and duly noting the arrival of well-known society people and celebrities such as young Chester Arthur, Mr. and Mrs. Cornelius Vanderbilt, Perry Belmont, George Gould, William Cutting, Gerald W. Cutting, Pierre Lorillard, and Abe Hummel, famed criminal lawyer and an inveterate first-nighter.

The house was packed. Programs rustled, the audience rippled with anticipation, friends chattered like squirrels as the house lights dimmed and the footlights came on. The string orchestra swung into "Old English." Many eyes were on Oscar Wilde sitting "conspicuously" (how else would he do anything?) in Henrietta's box. As for Henrietta, her thoughts were backstage with Lillie and she could hardly listen to the poet's patter as he cut a peculiar figure in his Little-Lord-Fauntleroy, knee-breeched lecture costume.

Waiting for her cue, Lillie was extraordinarily calm and resigned. It was a mercy not to have a carping Henrietta underfoot. She circulated among the cast, telling everyone this was just like any performance in England. It wasn't, however; they knew it and she knew it. A circus of publicity had led to this night, an incessant barrage of front-page comment that had left them all a little shell-shocked.

Frenzied applause greeted her appearance and followed afterward at the slightest pretext, quite belying one critic who insisted, "That foolish fribble Mr. Oscar Wilde sat with his back to the stage and tried at intervals to start the applause, but the audience did not respond."

To Lillie things seemed to go no better or worse than usual. It was well over a month since she had acted before an audience. Both it and the circumstances of her appearance were different from any she had faced before. She went through the familiar paces faultlessly—or so she thought—put off by the sporadic bursts of applause, doing her best to portray the silly character of Hester Grazebrook in the old-fashioned play Henrietta had chosen for her American appearance.

Henrietta bobbed up backstage between acts: more voice shadings, beware of looking at the audience, use bolder gestures. Lillie listened dully and nodded. Henrietta had heard only the most flattering comments. Abbey was pleased. Salvini was playing to an empty house, and late arrivals who had gone to see Patti first said she sang Lucia to a small audience in poor form, clearly put out by the Langtry fever.

"It hardly matters what the critics say," Henrietta went on. "The people love you. In any case, Mr. Abbey says the reviews will be lost in the election news because of this man Cleveland. Lillie, are you all right? You seem so listless."

"I'd like to forget the theater for a while—and have some fun."

Taking her first bow, her eyes went immediately to Oscar, leaning far out of Henrietta's box, his expression ecstatic, his big arms flapping like a symphonic conductor as he appeared to lead the applause. Ushers walked down front with armloads of bouquets, one of them so huge it had to be taken apart afterward to get it backstage. The audience clapped harder, quieting finally while Lillie made a demure speech of thanks, appreciation, and praise of America.

Then she called Abbey from the wings. She smiled shyly as

he extolled her and thanked Lester Wallack for the use of his beautiful theater. Whatever judgment would be passed on her, Lillie had excited more attention than any other dramatic star who had appeared in New York. She had filled Wallack's Theater with its greatest audience and brought in $6,800 at the box office—$1,000 more than Madame Bernhardt's record first night. More than that, she had created a favorable impression, been applauded to the echo. "Over a wagonload of flowers were showered on her, and she was called out twelve times."

"Superb!" said Oscar, his voice booming through her dressing room. "Absolutely superb. And I shall say so in my review which I shall write later—much, much later. We've planned a little party for you, Lil, and guess who's going to be there! Moreton Frewen, your old cavalier who's been living a primitive life in the West. He's married now, but he's bringing a man who's been dying to meet you."

Henrietta's lips were a thin line, and Lillie pretended not to notice.

"Oh, you're to come, too, Mrs. Labouchère. There'll be gaiety, champagne, and good English talk with old Frewen. Just the thing after this ordeal." Oscar detached a flower and presented it to Henrietta with a charming bow. "You'll like Freddie Gebhard, Lil. The press regards him as a playboy, an enchanting term. They say he has an income of $80,000 a year, which is equally enchanting, eh what? as Jimmy Whistler would say."

The first review Lillie read was that of William Winter, the dean of New York critics, who had been connected with the *Tribune* since 1865 and who pushed higher on his ivory tower each year. He gave his customary lecture on the drama, ranging all over his field, obscuring and reserving his opinions except to say that while the crudities of Mrs. Langtry's performance were obvious, "the freshness, charm, and promise of them equally so." The *Times* was guarded and not too complimentary. Neither, strangely enough, was James Gordon Bennett's *Herald,* nor his *Telegram;* and the *Post* dismissed her performance as the "work of a clever amateur subjected to a brief course of intelligent training."

171

The New York *Spirit of the Times,* a sporting sheet, noted that the clever Mrs. Labouchère had chosen the play because its main character was easy to act, an old-style piece with a slice of comedy followed by a slice of pathos, with Hester on stage only three-quarters of an hour. *Music and Drama* called attention to the number of bald-headed men, obviously prurient and lecherous, in the audience, then hit hard:

> She cannot rival Mary Anderson or Miss Adelaide Neilson. She can never be an actress. She lacks heart, passion, and inspiration. She is always the beautiful Mrs. Langtry, playing a parroted part to make money out of foolish Americans. She is an amateur, a novice who has tried to begin at the top of the ladder. Compared to Jumbo, the elephant, well—he is worth seeing.

Oscar's review for the *World* dragged in such artists as Whistler, Jean François Millet, Albert Moore, and Frederick Leighton, the Pre-Raphaelites, the Greeks, the Romans, and all art. It said much of Lillie's beauty, little about her acting. Those in the know took this as a purposeful evasion, showing how little they understood a man to whom appearance and externals were everything.

> It is only in the best Greek gems, on the silver coins of Syracuse, or among the marble fringes of the Parthenon frieze that one can find the ideal representation of the marvelous beauty of that face which laughed through the leaves last night as Hester Grazebrook.
>
> Pure Greek it is, with the low grave forehead, the exquisitely arched brow; the noble chiseling of the mouth, shaped as if it were the mouthpiece of an instrument of music, the supreme and splendid curve of the cheek, the augustly pillared throat which bears it all. . . .
>
> The character of Hester requires no small ability on the part of the actress who sustains it. . . .
>
> If I was to express the opinion, in which I think all who were present last night might well honestly agree with me, it is that Mrs. Langtry went through the phases with taste, feeling, and force. I do not see what higher commendation I can pay her.

172

Don't you, now? thought Lillie, skimming his extravagant lines. Dear, sweet Oscar, writing just as he talked. But what did it all come to? The few who praised her unanimously were countered by the many against her. Rare were the critics who fell in between. This William Winter, now. She hunted for his review and thoughtfully read it again. Henrietta—how shrill, tiresome, and demanding she was getting to be!—said critics didn't matter. Abbey said it was just what he had expected. There was a good advance sale, but he had the tour to think of, and he was worried. Of course, Mrs. Langtry was an interloper and still learning. All that tedious amateur-top-of-the-ladder business. What were Winter's words? "Freshness, charm, and promise . . ." Hmm. As with Clement Scott in London, here was a critic worth cultivating. Lillie had a plan.

It was not easy putting off the young Gebhard, but first things came first. Lillie slipped away from the Albemarle alone. She took a carriage to Delmonico's and earnestly requested an inconspicuous wall table. As agreed, Abbey came in later with William Winter, seeing her immediately but putting the critic so that his back was to Lillie. Toward the end of their meal, Abbey lighted a cigar, looked around the restaurant, and recognized her with a pleasant start.

"Why, there is Mrs. Langtry dining alone," he told Winter. "Would you like to meet her?"

Lillie took it from there. Winter, a preacher away from his dramatic pulpit, proved as impressionable as the man on the street. All attention, all charm, Lillie belittled herself, praised his discerning review, and congratulated him on the great work he was doing for the theater. He listened, as spellbound as an infatuated adolescent, his eyes never leaving her face so that he missed Abbey's wink. Everybody was looking at them, and Broadway's dean basked in Lillie's radiance. She had melted Winter's critical frost; he would never be able to see her as an actress without thinking of her as a warm and lovely woman.

"Acting is not a static art sufficient unto itself," he pontificated. "Talent is to be appreciated and admired, but better still it must communicate visual enjoyment and delight—and merely watching you is a guarantee of that."

"True, true," Abbey muttered through his cigar.

"Oh, Mr. Winter, how wise and clever you are!"

The critic's smile was fatuous and summary. "I only do my duty as I see it."

Abbey choked on something, gulped water, and apologized.

twelve

Lillie's *affaire* with Frederick Gebhard lasted close to eight years. She undoubtedly would have married him, had she been able to secure a divorce from Edward Langtry during that time. She loved him deeply, but even in mellow old age she was curiously contradictory about Freddie and their highly publicized romance. In a revealing 1913 interview during which she admitted what she had indignantly denied so many years—dropping the ice down Bertie's back—she said, "There was a lot of pother about Freddie Gebhard and me. I give you my word with my hand on my heart that we were just good friends—nothing more." Three years later, a youthful sixty-three, she told Somerset Maugham on shipboard of her world-shaking love for Freddie, and she confessed to Alfred Lunt, her young leading man on the last of her many "farewell appearance" vaudeville tours, that he had been "her great love."

In 1882 Freddie was twenty-two years old, seven years Lillie's junior. His social position in New York and Baltimore was unassailable. The son of dry-goods merchant Frederick Gebhard, who had left a $5,000,000 fortune, it was common knowledge that he had an income of $80,000 a year. Automatically in the upper brackets through his wealth and social connections, he was the counterpart of an English scion, enjoying his patrimony and leading a gentlemanly club and sporting life.

Freddie was shy, even retiring, "a tall, slim man who carried himself with a certain air of quiet distinction." He was over six feet tall and weighed close to 190 pounds, his black hair neatly parted in the middle, his eyes small and sullenly level, his nose good and snubby, his mustache thin and slight, his lips prominent and protruding. He ordered his clothes from London, and "the cut and texture were not in the mode; they were the mode." He took seriously his duties as a young gentleman of fashion and leisure. He was in the New York Social Register, he belonged to every important club in and near the city—the Metropolitan, Union, Coaching, Knickerbocker, Racquet, New York Yacht, Larchmont Yacht, Tuxedo, and the Westminster Kennel Club—and his interests revolved around pretty women, horse racing, gambling, yachting, and all the fun and games of the man-about-town.

Lillie was as grateful to Moreton Frewen for Freddie as she had been for his gift of Redskin. Expansively young and gay, Freddie was different from Edward, Bertie, and every other man she'd ever known. No matter that he was younger than she. He was her first friend in America, a balm to her ego after the critics' hatchets, a relief from Henrietta, her querulous duenna, exactly the source of the fun for which she longed. Freddie sent flowers every day, boxes of candy, baskets of fruits. He took her driving. They went to look at the mighty towers for Brooklyn Bridge, and they watched the skaters in Central Park. When she mentioned her skates that had been sold at the Norfolk Street auction, he immediately went out and bought her a handsome pair. They were stared at as they glided over the ice to music, as they sat together in Delmonico's, in their carriage, and as they walked along Fifth Avenue.

Henrietta had been shocked at Lillie's lack of jewels when she made her stage début. It was incomprehensible to her that the sensation of three London seasons possessed nothing more than several bracelets and a few insignificant rings and brooches. Her contempt had annoyed Lillie who had thought that jewels were lovely but superfluous for women naturally endowed—something Henrietta certainly wasn't with her bulldog features. Lillie thought differently now. Freddie watched her as she studied a matched diamond necklace and bracelet set in Tiffany's window at 15th Street, and it was delivered to her Albemarle suite the next morning along with a note and big bouquet. She protested—oh, not too strenuously, because he was such a dear—but Freddie insisted that he wanted her to have it.

Henrietta objected, just as she had to the flowers, candy, and the rest. She did not like Freddie. There was talk about their friendship, and she wanted Lillie to concentrate on the forthcoming production of *As You Like It*. Freddie worked on Henrietta, but she was impervious to his charm. Lillie was going out without her, keeping late hours, breaking all the rules just when she should be straining to confound the critics and redeem the bad reviews threatening her tour.

"I don't want to fuss, Henrietta. You can direct me on stage and do as you like there, but not off."

"You'll spoil everything I've tried to accomplish for you, if you don't listen to me. You ought to be grateful that I—"

"Henrietta!"

"As you please, then! But this afternoon before rehearsal you're coming to Napoleon Sarony's with me for another sitting. His photographs can do a lot for you. And I don't want Mr. Gebhard along!"

Lillie's Rosalind was not well received. The repercussions reached Bertie, who had been worrying about her. Edwin Booth, appearing in London then, had done badly both with his *Hamlet* and *Richelieu,* but the Prince and Princess of Wales were in the royal box for his *The Fool's Revenge.* Hustling to receive what he expected to be royal congratulations, the flustered American actor was speechless as Bertie said, "I am glad to see you, Mr. Booth. I sent for you because I wish to get your opinion about Mrs. Langtry's chances of success in America."

On mild days, Lillie went riding in Central Park with Freddie, strikingly smart in her riding habit, her lovely face flushed in the crisp late November air. They were besieged as they mounted at the stables, mobbed along the street, and followed by a persistent throng right to the bridle path. Reporters even tracked them down on horseback, and Freddie felt toward them as he felt toward the critics.

177

"If I weren't afraid of hitting all the front pages and hurting you, I'd attack them with my riding crop. I may do it, anyway!"

"Don't for both our sakes," said Lillie sweetly. "It's just what they want."

Hoofs pounded behind them. There were cries of "There they are! Hey, Freddie! Lillie! Wait!"

Lillie yanked at her horse's head, swung him sharply about, and galloped down a wooded trail. Freddie followed, Lillie reining in until he was abreast, and they cantered on together.

"Yoicks and away!" she said, laughing. "They're no horsemen." Sure they had eluded their pursuers, Lillie dismounted back of some trees deep in the park. Freddie hastened to assist her. She felt him tremble as their bodies touched.

"You don't like reporters, do you?" she teased. "I need them in my business."

"I'm just a target. They jump on everything I do because I'm rich and marked as a playboy. Even if I wanted to, they'd rather I didn't amount to anything."

"Do you want to?" she asked idly.

"Oh, I'm young and there's plenty of time. Would any of them work if they had my income? They're just jealous, but let's not talk about them. You're the loveliest, the most wonderful woman I've ever known in my life. I want you to know how much I—"

"Let me guess, Freddie." She patted her horse's muzzle as he tossed his head. "Besides, I'm a married woman."

"You think that's going to stop me?" He snorted. "By God, Lillie, I'm a man and I'm human. That's why I've got to—"

She put her fingers over his mouth, taking them away before he could kiss them.

"I've got to be with you, Lillie. If the critics are going to butcher you wherever you go, people crowding you, men flocking around—" He grimaced. "What's to stop me from touring with you? I could help."

"I know you could." She stroked his cheek; had he been a dog, he would have thumped his tail wildly. "But think of Henrietta."

"You think of her!"

His vehemence made her laugh. "Get on your horse, Freddie. He's pawing the ground."

"So am I, Lillie."

Hoofbeats came around the bend. "Hey! There they are!"

Lillie mounted swiftly and started off, Freddie behind on his horse, cursing and shaking his fists at the reporters.

The critics had scored, for America and for art, and they knew it. The Jersey Lily had been oversold. She was neither the great beauty nor actress publicity had claimed (her honest protests to the contrary being ignored). The critics felt justified in outdoing each other in vindictiveness. The few conspicuous exceptions, such as William Winter who praised her loveliness and charm while saying little about her art, were not enough to stop Henrietta from frantic worry, which she communicated to Henry Abbey.

Until Freddie had come into her circle, Lillie had always given in to Henrietta to whom she owed her professional career. Both were stubborn, independent-minded women, and Lillie had gladly acceded to her wishes in order to keep the peace. But no more. Mrs. Labby was querulous and domineering, intolerant, and intolerable as the indispensable woman in charge. Why, only this morning she had taken it upon herself to refuse the receipt of Freddie's usual basket of fresh fruit. Lillie had had to get it from the hotel manager later. She was in no mood to argue that afternoon as Henrietta held out a batch of press clippings having to do with Freddie and herself.

"I'm not going to discuss it, Henrietta."

"Well, I am! Mr. Gebhard is an unworthy young man of dubious morals and background. He's going to ruin you, particularly now that the critics have been so vicious. You could beat them by being the hard-working innocent, but not by associating with a notorious playboy."

"Oh, rot!"

"It is not rot! This man is dragging you, your acting, your whole future down in the dirt with him."

"Don't let's fuss about this. I'm going to take a bath."

179

"Not before you hear me out." Red-faced, her bulldog features set in implacable lines, Henrietta was not going to give an inch. "If you don't break up with this Freddie Gebhard, if you don't give him up for good right now—fruit, flowers, jewels, and all, mind you—I'm leaving you and you can go on tour alone! I wash my hands of you, do you hear!"

"I hear," said Lillie softly. "You're screaming."

"I have to when I talk to a willful, selfish young woman who owes everything she's accomplished to me!" She stopped for breath. "You are an indiscreet woman. It will be the ruin of you."

"And were you indiscreet when you lived with Labby before you were married?"

The insult, for so Henrietta conceived it, struck her like a great blast of air. She held on to the back of a chair. Air rasped in the back of her throat as she sucked it in to speak, but she couldn't make it. After flapping her mouth like a fish, she slammed out of the room.

Dominique came out of her bedroom. "The dragon she bite?"

"Yes, but she'll get over it."

Dominique laughed. "Oh, you think so, madame?" She helped Lillie undress. "Mr. Gebhard. He will be pleased."

If the company noted Henrietta's absence from her familiar box, it took no notice. Lillie seemed unaware of them that night. Her acting had a peculiar intensity which made demands on their own interpretations and improved them accordingly. The audience applauded her loudly. Freddie thought she had never been better, but he was put off by her silence as they drove to Delmonico's to join his friend, Jim Brady. Later on, she was feverishly gay, laughing at all that was said, keeping a circle of men around her like Circe. Freddie wisely kept away and, as she glanced at him with smiling gratitude now and then, he was glad he had successfully judged her mood and let her alone. For once she was in no hurry to return to the Albemarle. She sat back as Freddie instructed the coachman to drive around New York's dark streets. She let him hold her hand, but she was in a dream of her own.

180

Henrietta's announcement the next day hardly surprised Lillie. The reaction to it was something else again. It was a bombshell, linking Freddie and herself, publicly and inseparably in the most lurid light, and was published under the heading "The Langtry Scandal." Mrs. Labouchère "officially announced that she didn't approve of Mrs. Langtry's proceedings in this country, had no further connection with her or her engagements, and would go back to England after visiting friends in Washington." The "proceedings" which disturbed the good lady were not identified, but the press had long conditioned the public mind to them and reaped a circulation bonanza. The unprecedented situation resulted in the most unparalleled outbreak of club and newspaper gossip in years. Editors took time off Lillie's acting to print denunciations of her morals, play up Henrietta as the injured party, and blacken the character of Playboy Freddie.

Mrs. Labouchère was sanctimoniously described as "compelled to remonstrate and finding her remonstrances received with contumely, withdrew with dignity." She had to drop Lillie because as a duenna she "had no value unless she were obeyed, or seemed to be." Thus in the specious Victorian pattern, Henrietta was the good woman, Lillie "naughty," Freddie "unspeakable." What a story! what scandal! what copy! and this was only the beginning of a fabulous saga which would outlast the Victorian age.

Oscar Wilde was in the act, too. "I knew something was going to happen," he was quoted. "When I was talking to Mrs. Langtry recently, my intaglio ring cracked. That was a very bad sign. Then again she came to the theater the other evening looking very pale and uncomfortable. She had broken her looking glass, a distressing omen."

Life at the Albemarle was sticky that day, reporters clamoring at the door for a word with either of the two women involved. Henrietta wore an inviolable mantle, treated her protégée like a fallen angel, and insisted that she would never, never reconsider her decision. Lillie never expected her to. She tried to offer some sort of severance pay and passage to England. The offer was dismissed. Mrs. Labouchère had no need of money, certainly not Mrs. Langtry's. She was so aloof that Lillie had to laugh at her airs.

As for Freddie Gebhard—infatuated, genuinely in love, or both—his devotion to Lillie was unstinting. Thin-skinned and rankling at the newspaper vilifications, he worked himself up to a bubbly boil as he sought to retaliate in defense of Lillie. He was used to being pilloried, but no one was going to soil his Lillie and get away with it. Without consulting her, he wrote a letter to the New York *Sun*, a paper he felt was taking the lead in defaming her. His emotions running away with him, his grammar and spelling no match for his honorable intentions, luckless Freddie only provided further ammunition for his critics.

Garbling what he heard in part from Lillie, Dominique, chambermaids at the Albemarle, cast members, friends, and reporters, he attributed Mrs. Labouchère's premature departure all to the harmless presentation of "a basket of fruit." As for the so-called scandal, he stressed that "She [Lillie] could do no wrong, even if she wanted to, watched by Mrs. Labouchère, by a younger sister of that woman, by Miss Pattison, by the manager, and by the hotel servants." Implying that Lillie had been spied on and kept under guard, he hinted that the Labouchères were not married and Henrietta, thus, in no position to criticize.

This further snarled things. More reporters descended on the Albemarle for a riposte from "that woman," but Henrietta towered on her high horse and refused to talk. Not so another cast member, Emily Faithful. She wrote to the *Sun* in defense of her friend, Miss Pattison, denying she had ever spied on Lillie; saying she had lived in a different hotel and that her activities began and ended with her performances in the theater. This was published on December 9 with many more columns on the "Langtry Scandal." Abbey, caught in the middle, played the blusterer, vainly shrugging off the imbroglio as a tempest in a teapot. But he looked like a man who had aged overnight. His reputation was on the line, his funds were tied up in Lillie's tour, and he got nowhere as peacemaker with Henrietta.

She had always handled the business details arbitrarily and dictatorially. He had thought of his star as a temperamental, cosseted actress. He said he would be willing to cancel the contract if it weren't for the tour plans being arranged so far ahead, and then he was gratified at Lillie's reply.

"I fear neither the critics, the newspapers, nor the scandal they've foisted on me. I feel quite capable of managing my own affairs. You've taken a big gamble, Mr. Abbey. Neither of us wants to lose money, and I see no reason why we should."

"No need at all if you feel this way. I must say it pleases me, Mrs. Langtry. You might like to know that your receipts at Wallack's for your four weeks come to some $61,803.63, which is exceptionally good, considering—" he smiled broadly—"considering everything that has happened. As for the scandal, you know the press as well as I do. I have nothing against Mr. Gebhard whatever. It occurs to me that on the whole this may be helpful publicity."

"I've thought of that. Freddie wants to come to Boston and make the rest of the tour with me as a sort of—how shall I say it?—bodyguard."

"Hmm." Abbey smoothed his mustache. "You realize what you're letting yourself in for?"

"Most certainly, but all's fair in love and war. The press has made it the latter. I'm going to use every weapon I can to make this tour a success—not only for my sake, but because of the loss of your theater and to justify your confidence in me."

"You have done that already, but two problems remain. Mrs. Labouchère served her purpose as a chaperone, you know. Then there's the matter of transportation for, uh, Mr. Gebhard."

"I am doing something about both those things," she assured him.

"Good." The producer looked at her differently, not impervious to either her beauty or charm, but now as one shrewd businessman belatedly recognizes another. "You are a remarkable young woman, Mrs. Langtry."

"Not so remarkable. The laws of survival demand that I fight my own battles in my own way from now on. I am certain that I can."

183

Having Freddie along would titillate the public, and a chaperone was necessary to counteract loss of the puritan element at the box office. From time to time, Lillie had received several pleasant letters from Edward's sister, Agnes Langtry, who was now living in London. Thinking she would be flattered, Lillie immediately sent her a cable inviting her to come to America and make the tour at no expense.

The matter of transportation she left to Freddie, after explaining she wanted more comfortable accommodations for the long trip. He put the problem to his friend, James Buchanan Brady, who sold railroad supplies and had many influential friends in the business.

A stout, amusing man, Jim Brady doted on food, pretty women (especially Lillian Russell), and diamond jewelry. Eschewing alcoholic drinks, he accepted only root beer and orange juice at parties. He had gratefully accepted Lillie's gift cases of Bongo Beer and Fillipin Fiz, which he gulped down six bottles at a time. Jim could not resist giving Lillie as presents various diamond trinkets he "picked up" on business trips: a ring, a brooch, a bracelet. He asked nothing in return for his lavish generosity, something outside of Lillie's experience with men and diamonds. His motives puzzled her.

It was just like him to be sympathetic to Freddie's plea, to arrange instantly for a special train for the Langtry company, with a luxurious palace car for the exclusive use of the Jersey Lily, her maid, and Freddie.

Reporters covering the troupe's departure from New York noted with pleasure Freddie's scowling presence. The company raised its collective eyebrows, but said little. Henrietta's walkout had shaken it. Some had feared being stranded jobless in America, and they were impressed at the loyalty of Kate Hodson, who seemed delighted to be rid of her sister, just when the opposite might have been expected. Looking serenely at the New England countryside through the windows of her private car, "The City of Worcester," Lillie left behind a shocked, bewildered New York still eager for every bit of news about her.

Literary Boston assembled on December 9 for a banquet in

Lillie's honor given by the Papyrus Club, but the excitement over Henrietta had caught up with her, and she pleaded indisposition. It was a struggle to perform the next day. The second act intermission was stretched to half an hour, but Lillie made it and played to the end with spirit. The haughty critics damned her as a rank amateur and called her acting "shockingly shallow and insincere." All the same, long lines formed outside the Globe Theater. Every performance was sold out.

Lillie disarmed the public with her beauty, clothes, and composure. The scandal might have been glossed over except for the fact that her gruff, impeccable escort checked in at the same hotel. Boston papers reported this casually, while some in New York excitedly allowed readers to assume the pair might well be occupying the same rooms. Freddie attracted much attention at the Globe, his eyes never leaving the stage, and Lillie had most of her meals with him. She set herself a strict regimen. Appearances to the contrary, she made Freddie understand that their outwardly intimate relationship entailed no special privileges. This was a business trip. There was money to be made, and the responsibility was all hers.

In love and marked as her favorite, Freddie was content. He railed at slurs as any proper gentleman should. At the same time his male pride was soothed by the general belief that he was sharing the bed of the world-famous beauty, and he was relieved that no one was the wiser. If he was being used—and Lillie took no pains to deny what he may have known—Freddie didn't care. He felt privileged just to be near her; the future was paved with promise. It didn't matter that Lillie was driven about Boston by Sir W. Anstruther Thompson, the British consul. What mattered was not to overdo a good thing.

In Philadelphia next, Mrs. Langtry "was brought into the city privately to avoid the crowds which were waiting at the railroad station." She and Freddie put up at the Bellevue Hotel, which had kicked up a storm a year earlier by refusing admittance to Sarah Bernhardt, "an actress." But the couple were both of high society and hence qualified, scandal or no. Once again the critics disparaged her. But the rush to see her in action and Freddie in person continued unabated.

Christmas was gayer than she could have imagined. She had sent gifts to Jeanne Marie and her family. Agnes Langtry was on ship coming to join her, and, off Henrietta's leash, Lillie could enjoy herself as she pleased. Freddie found fun everywhere. His upper-bracket standing gave him license on both sides of the tracks, as it were. He was a convivial, discriminating companion. She did feel a twinge of homesickness mingled with maternal guilt, but there was a job to be done and she had to be ruthless with herself. Freddie was her mainstay. For all the vicious talk about him, he was innocent and lovable compared to the titled, playboy roués she'd known in England, including a kind, fat, balding king-to-be who had such a proprietary interest in Jeanne Marie.

It was inevitable that the scandal should reach Congress. On January 6, 1883, the Honorable Richelieu Robinson took the floor of the House of Representatives to denounce Mrs. Langtry and all things English.

> This is only one of the follies which indicate the poison, the pyaemia, the malaria that are dosing our American manhood to death. This worship of everything English is a new and dangerous disease. Our government was founded in opposition to everything English. Republicanism can be preserved only by preserving that healthy hatred of everything English, and all her ways. Not that we have any hatred of Englishmen. We owe them pity, not hatred. . . . Is it desirable that we should forget our American manhood in the worship of everything English whether in the way of a profligate lord or a more profligate representation of English nobility coming to demoralize our stage and corrupt our society?

Back in New York a harried Henry Abbey faced press inquisitors who demanded a comment on the Washington thunderbolt. He repeated what he had said about Mrs. Langtry's lack of pretension as either a great beauty or actress. What about Gebhard, though? Was he officially associated with the venture? Abbey flushed and wriggled in his chair.

"Mr. Gebhard can do as he wants. He has plenty of money, and he is free to go where he pleases. That is all I have to say on the subject, gentlemen!"

186

Agnes Langtry joined Lillie in Chicago, ignorant of the scandal or her intended role as chaperone. A timid, naïve woman, she was welcomed warmly. Freddie did all he could to be nice to her.

Chicago reporters treated Lillie roughly, the critics throwing their spears like headhunters. But still the public flocked to the Haverley Theater.

After a matinée, Freddie walked from the theater to the hotel with Agnes Langtry without being recognized, while Lillie and her road-tour manager, Frederick A. Schwab, were mobbed. "There go Langtry and Gebhard!" someone yelled, and the crowd ran after the carriage.

It was icy cold in Chicago, yet neither the weather nor the critics nor the press kept Lillie from enjoying herself. Oscar Wilde had said that the most beautifully decorated house in the entire West belonged to Mrs. Herbert Ayer. Lillie dined there and enjoyed her talented hostess, the former Harriet Hubbard. She went roller skating at the local rink, ice skating at Lincoln Park, and ignored the people trailing Freddie and herself. She had rooms 3, 5, and 7 at the Grand Pacific Hotel. Freddie's rooms were 133, 135, and 137, and they could never get together without stumbling on groups of reporters. And she had to keep reminding interviewers that she came from the Island of Jersey, not the State of New Jersey.

Business was fine, totaling $29,000 for the two weeks, but some trouble in Chicago made the last night of her engagement memorable.

The trouble began before the curtain as the audience took to guying George Bowron, the orchestra leader, for his baldness. It burst into full flower as Lillie appeared in the doublet and hose of Rosalind. No one in the cast was spared from loud, unfavorable comment, the stage was pelted with candy, and a large piece of taffy thumped against the bass drum. The actor who tried to sing a solo was howled at, Charles the wrestler was dubbed "Muldoon," and everyone in the house became a referee in the bout that followed. The cast, being upset, chopped up and cut its lines. Lillie was interrupted with constant squeals for "Freddie!" She ordered the curtain pulled down before the epilogue, and the audience mingled satisfied laughter with its own smug applause.

"Americans are very strange," said Agnes Langtry primly, as they sat in the private car en route to St. Louis. "I don't think I shall ever get used to them. What an audience that was!"

"Oh, there are good ones and bad ones. I'll admit that was an especially bad one, but they all paid for admission. An actor must get used to that sort of thing."

"I couldn't! I wouldn't want to."

Agnes sounded so much like Edward that she turned Lillie's stomach.

"It's an occupational hazard of people in the limelight, Agnes," she said calmly.

"I don't see how they can say such terrible things about you and Mr. Gebhard. They're indelicate and indecent."

Agnes looked to Freddie for assent. He growled something, his teeth clamping tightly on his cigar, his eyes twitching angrily. Agnes went on and on in her plaintive voice.

Lillie was relieved when she finally excused herself and went to bed. She turned to Freddie and laughed.

"Don't be so gloomy."

"My God, Lillie, how do you do it? How do you take such treatment, anyway?"

"Because I have to. As simple as that, Freddie."

"But that scum tonight!"

"They're nothing. Only a tiny segment of the big audience."

"The scandal, all the trouble you've had, starting with Henrietta. Every bit of it is my fault."

"We're not going to fuss about this. I want you with me."

"You're sure?"

She kissed him swiftly on the cheek and moved away.

"Very, very sure."

"Sometimes I don't know. But I love you, Lillie, you know that. And this is no *affaire* or anything. I want to marry you."

"Freddie." She was touched. "I'm flattered, although I couldn't marry you if I wanted to."

"I'll make you want to, if you let me," he said softly. "Did you hear me?"

188

"I did. You're very sweet, Freddie."

"I've got to be a lot more before I'll be happy. I want you to talk to Abe Hummel when we get back, Lillie. He'll get you a divorce, if anybody can. He can put innocent men in jail and free guilty men."

"Just the kind of lawyer I need. Oh, Freddie, let's not talk of marriage. I can't think of anything but this tour and my career. I'm going to make money, and I'm going to show those bigoted critics I can act. Everything else has to fit in piecemeal."

"Including me," he said bitterly.

"If I sound horrible, it's because I have to. I have to rely on myself now, Freddie, as director, star, manager, producer, and everything else. I need you to remind me I'm a woman."

"Then why not act like one once in a while? Everybody thinks we're lovers. Let's *be* lovers. God, you don't know how much I want—"

"Shh!" Lillie warned.

"Do you know where Dominique put those clothes she ironed?" Agnes inquired from the doorway to the sleeping compartments. "I can't find my nightgown." She smiled self-consciously at Freddie.

"I believe it's in the cupboard in your room."

"Thank you, Lillie. Good night. Good night, Mr. Gebhard."

"Good night, Miss Langtry."

They waited until she'd gone, then spoke together, and stopped.

"That's one answer to your questions, Freddie."

The private car twisted as the train rattled around a curve in the night, the engine whistling mournfully, the lights of an isolated farmhouse blinking like cat's eyes in the blackness. Freddie yawned.

"Nobody else could make me do things I don't want to do and like it."

"Don't I ever seem old to you?" she asked.

"Old? You're wonderful, that's all. Do you think you could give me one cool, piecemeal kiss before I go to bed all alone?"

Telegraphic accounts from St. Louis, appearing in the New York papers January 21, 1883, told of the blizzard which struck the town as being "only a sideshow alongside the Lily and Freddie combination." They added that the farce had almost become a tragedy—because of Colonel A. B. Cunningham, a hard-boiled newspaperman and one of the editors of the St. Louis *Globe-Democrat,* who had insisted on interviewing Mrs. Langtry in her rooms at the Southern Hotel. He had knocked at her suite, been refused admittance. Then he had rudely brushed past Dominique, Roberts, the second maid and dresser, and had come on the pair having breakfast together.

Freddie was dressed, but Lillie was in her dressing gown. Her long, gleaming chestnut hair unbound, she was fresh-faced, smiling, and adorable. To Cunningham, they looked like a couple deeply in love. He started to ask questions and stood his ground, although Freddie repeatedly and angrily ordered him to leave. Cunningham wanted answers to his pointed queries. Lillie would make no comment, and Freddie threatened to throw him out. The editor left, convinced that everything about the scandal was true. The *Globe-Democrat* printed his scathing findings in its afternoon edition: that Mrs. Langtry's success was solely due to her notoriety. Her relationship with Gebhard was exactly what it seemed; to protect the city's morals, the newspaper urged citizens to ban her performance.

Preparing for her opening at the Olympic Theater that night, Lillie had no time to read the papers. She knew that Freddie was upset about something in them. She asked him to ignore whatever it was and stop carrying on whenever he read derogatory remarks. Freddie said he couldn't help it. He wished her luck, then went down to the lobby of the Southern to buy some cigars.

The place was filled with hangers-on, club men, and admirers of the Jersey Lily, all talking about the inflammatory Cunningham piece. A stranger came forward, called Freddie by his first name, and slapped him on the back. Outraged, Freddie gave the fellow a shove that sent him staggering, and lighted a cigar. As the man moved away, there were murmurs of approval and then a pregnant silence that brought Freddie's head up. What he saw enraged him, and he acted instinctively. An account of what followed was best described by a tensely melodramatic eye-witness story printed in the New York *Sun*.

At half past 7 o'clock last evening Mr. Fred Gebhard, who has gained distinction through his acquaintance with Mrs. Langtry, was smoking an after dinner cigar in the rotunda of the Southern Hotel, when he espied Mr. A. B. Cunningham of the *Globe-Democrat*'s local force standing near the west end of the office counter. He stepped up to Mr. Cunningham and an excited scene ensued, which attracted the attention of nearly all of the large number of persons who thronged the rotunda. Changing a cane which he carried to his left hand, Mr. Gebhard shook his finger in Mr. Cunningham's face and called him an infamous liar. Mr. Cunningham also shifted his cane, and putting his hand in his trousers pocket, waved Mr. Gebhard off with his left saying: "I don't want anything to do with you, sir," at the same time stepping backward. "But I want to have something to do with you, sir. You are an infamous liar," said Mr. Gebhard, advancing again on Mr. Cunningham.

"Keep away from me. I don't want to have anything to do with you, sir," said Mr. Cunningham, continuing his retrograde movement eastward along the counter and waving the enemy off with his left hand while he still kept his right hand in his trousers pocket. In this manner they proceeded around the corner of the counter and down to its south end, the epithet being repeated several times by Mr. Gebhard, and Mr. Cunningham's conservative answer following each time. At one point Mr. Gebhard was led aside by a friend, who advised him to desist, as he had gone as far as he could in denouncing Mr. Cunningham publicly; but he was returning toward the latter, when a policeman, who had been summoned by the clerk (Mr. Willard) interposed, and by Mr. Willard's order Mr. Cunningham was led out of the hotel. As Mr. Cunningham is a very powerful and active man, and as Mr. Gebhard is a vigorous six-footer weighing nearly 200 pounds, the spectators, who had expected to see a gladiatorial exhibition, were disappointed by the interference.

. . . It is said tonight that Cunningham has challenged Gebhard to fight a duel.

Freddie had again created a news sensation from coast to

coast. Given such a drama, editors enlarged upon it freely. They claimed the two men had been locked in mortal combat in the lobby, that Mrs. Lantry had come on the scene to find Cunningham pulling a revolver from his trousers pocket; that she had thrust herself forward and begged for her lover's life. At any rate, Cunningham did send a note to Freddie, through his friend Tobias Mitchell, challenging him to a duel with pistols and giving the place and the time.

A wounded Confederate veteran and a crack shot, Cunningham's challenge gave Freddie pause. It irritated Lillie that he had again become embroiled. But he loved her, it had all been for her sake. They were sold out for the week at the Olympic, and his impetuosity, worthy of a true Lochinvar, was endearing. She didn't want him to fight a duel and possibly be killed over the mendacious scribblings of a newspaper man. As Freddie stalled, Cunningham placarded him as a coward, and the newspapers made the most of it pro and con. In New York, there were columns reflecting the opinions of members of the Union League, Union, Manhattan, New York, University, Knickerbocker, and Lotos Clubs on whether Freddie should recognize the code duello. Their feelings were mixed, with the majority feeling that Freddie did not need to fight: he was a gentleman and the reporter was not. While in St. Louis Freddie risked being called a coward, in New York, which mattered, he was regarded as a plucky young man who had avenged an insult.

Freddie was deluged with telegrams, even one from his brother offering to come out and act as his second, but he listened to the advice wired by his influential friend, Jim Brady. The latter promptly sent a few telegrams of his own to certain important people in St. Louis. Behind the scenes, pressure was brought to bear on Cunningham. So Freddie did not reply to the challenge, nor did Cunningham press it, subsiding with the statement, "I'll admit that if I had wanted to fight I had plenty of opportunity." Freddie said only, "I simply declined to pay any attention to the note from Cunningham. He lied about me, and I denounced him publicly."

The fine hand of Jim Brady was evident in Chief of Police Campbell's call at the Southern Hotel. He and Freddie had a a glass of wine together. Campbell invited him to visit police headquarters, and the whole matter simmered down, to the disappointment of St. Louis, the press, and the nation. Freddie held court at the Southern, and was entertained by the St. Louis Club. He denied he was parting company with Mrs. Langtry, but ever so casually volunteered that he was accompanying her only as far as Memphis, then planned to go to Denver, Cheyenne, and points West on his own.

While the critics cudgeled her as a poor actress who was not surpassingly beautiful and expressed sympathy for the "much abused public," the Olympic played to a neat $15,000 for the week. It was jammed for every performance, the space back of the last row packed five and six deep, and the Jersey Lily was never more celebrated. All in all, it was a good, explosive week, but there was safety in cooling off. Freddie was reluctantly leaving, and Lillie would miss him.

"You won't get into trouble alone, will you?" she asked him.

"I hope not, but it's going to be dull."

"I think we'll both find it a welcome change," she said, laughing. "Be good, Freddie. I want you back in one piece. No more duels."

thirteen

ALTHOUGH Lillie had luxury accommodations, train travel was exhausting. Springs and roadbed were hard, and the special rattled, pounded, and swayed. A strong woman with emotional and physical reserves, Lillie forgot discomfort in watching the fascinating countryside unrolling outside the window, the size and variety of America as to people and climate continually sparking her wonder.

Freddie turned up from time to time as she played New Orleans and other Southern cities. The ripe transcontinental scandal continued, and in Milwaukee she was forced to deny that he was becoming her manager. Sometimes he was reported to be with her when he was actually sitting in a box at Tony Pastor's in New York. In early February he was with her in Cincinnati, where there was an advance sale of $5,800 at Robinson's Theater.

Working her way back East, Lillie was delighted to find Oscar Wilde playing a lecture date in Buffalo when she was to appear there. He stayed at her hotel, along with Freddie. From the yellow press, one might have inferred they were carrying on a sordid *ménage à trois*. As always warmly and cheerfully amusing, Oscar excoriated American tastes, cast-iron stoves, wall-to-wall carpeting, and everything he had seen. Lillie visited Niagara Falls in company with him and a band of reporters. The English celebrities were watched for their reactions to this great American phenomenon, so Oscar showed that he was disappointed and unimpressed.

"It's simply a vast unnecessary amount of water going the

194

wrong way and falling over unnecessary rocks with a vulgarly loud and wet rushing sound. Nature at its unaesthetic and barbaric worst."

"At least you'll have to admit they're wonderful falls, Mr. Wilde?" said one offended newsman.

"My dear chap, the wonder would be if the water didn't fall. Every American bride is taken here, and the sight of this stupendous waterfall must be one of the earliest, if not the keenest, disappointments of American married life."

This heresy having satisfactorily startled his hearers, Oscar provided a caption as photographers aimed their cameras at Lillie: "Mrs. Langtry was photographed with Niagara Falls as an unpretentious background."

They took the traditional boat trip across the gorge dressed in oilskins, then visited the cavern under the falls through thunderous spray. Looking the roly-poly Ancient Mariner in protective boots and clothing, Oscar happily disparaged the spectacle, haw-hawing appreciatively at his own witticisms. If struck dead by a thunderbolt, with his dying breath Oscar would have criticized it as a cheap, unconvincing electrical display.

"The very best thing Americans have is money. And so much of it." He clutched his forehead. "What we geniuses must suffer for our art!"

Lillie's stop at Buffalo was also memorable for the anticipated blow-up with Agnes Langtry, the circumstances being much the same as they had been in Henrietta's case. For a long time afterward feline gossip had it that Agnes was so shocked at the relationship between Freddie Gebhard and her famous sister-in-law—now finally revealed in all its sordid horror—that she had fled over the border to Canada with Lillie keeping all her luggage out of spite. Fiction, of course! But Lillie's idea of bringing her to America had been uninspired. She had never been well acquainted with Agnes, anyway, and she should not have been surprised to find Agnes as spiritless and ill-prepared for life as Edward had been.

Perhaps some reporter had been pumping Agnes. At any rate, she took to snooping and making exigent demands à la Henrietta. She finally succeeded in surprising Freddie and Lillie in nightclothes, sharing a bottle of champagne. Thus establishing the ugly truth she had long suspected gratified Agnes. She tried Henrietta's either-or gambit and nearly cried as the two "sinners" laughed in her sanctimonious face. By the next morning she packed and went, and that was it.

Of course the episode embarrassed Lillie. She felt sorry for Agnes—the only attitude she found herself capable of adapting toward a Langtry—and, as in the case of her husband, she was irritated at the twinge of guilt deep inside her. The Langtrys were a pitiful clan.

Abbey suggested a supplementary season at the conclusion of his tour. Interest in the Jersey Lily was still high, the heated transcontinental romance had added to her glamour, and he was convinced she would do good business.

A new vehicle was in order, however, and Lillie set about presenting William Gilbert's *Pygmalion and Galatea.* Casting herself as a Greek statue come to life was a shrewd choice. Still, it was the first play she had put on without the influence of Henrietta, and it was something of a gamble. She opened at the Fifth Avenue Theater on April 21 with the usual critical reception.

Even an erstwhile friend, Helena Modjeska, managed to snipe away in her curtain speech after the last performance of her *Romeo and Juliet* at the Booth Theater. She praised Edwin Booth, expanded on the art of the theater and the seriousness back of good acting, and added that *some* stage figures ignored the fundamentals. "Don't study and work for fame," she concluded acidly. "Become notorious and make a fortune." She mentioned no names; she didn't have to.

Lillie paid return visits to Philadelphia, to Boston, and to other New England cities and was always the bane of critics and the delight of audiences. She settled at the Fifth Avenue for a long engagement, alternating her new play with *She Stoops to Conquer.* The public admired her beauty, was entranced by her lovely voice, and "those who heard her wistful, waning cry, 'Farewell, Pygmalion' in Gilbert's pathetic comedy never lost

196

the sound out of their ravished ears." For all this, Lillie was not altogether satisfied. As a businesswoman, she knew that commercial success was vital—more important than mere art if she meant to stay in active production—yet she wanted critical approval also.

She thought hard over the problem and discussed it with William Winter and Dion Boucicault, the Irish actor and playwright who had come to America in 1853 and prospered in his writing and producing of such plays as *Rip Van Winkle* and *The Sidewalks of New York*. He knew the theater and had originated the idea of the traveling company with one play and one star.

It was Boucicault who suggested that she study at the Conservatoire in Paris with Professor François Joseph Régnier, a renowned teacher of dramatics and the Stanislavski of his day. Besides softening the critics and erasing the amateur stamp, her pilgrimage to Paris would demonstrate her seriousness of purpose and desire to learn. Whether or not she really needed it, whether or not Régnier could help her, he argued, it would create a climate of forebearance and stimulate interest in the "new" Langtry.

"It's the *cachet* that counts, the Régnier *imprimatur*. And right now young stage aspirants find it indispensable to study under him, talk over an acting point, or at least have the great man advise them. But the thing is, Mrs. Langtry, he's a theatrical oracle, and you can't lose."

With Boucicault she was convinced that "from the actor's point of view, America was the promised land." There was freedom here, money, and an unlimited audience; not just in New York, but all through this tremendous country. After winning over the American critics, she would tackle the London ones. First, there was Freddie to consider—the poor dear really wanted to marry her—and perhaps if she became an American citizen she could free herself of Edward. Perhaps, perhaps . . .

After Henry Abbey graciously canceled her London contract for the fall, Lillie announced her plan to study with Régnier at the close of her New York engagement in June. She disbanded her company after the traditional party, during which she presented her manager, Fred Schwab, with a diamond-horseshoe stickpin, distributed gifts to her leading man and cast members, and heaped praise on Producer Abbey whom she greatly admired. The press gave her net receipts for the tour as some $102,000, and said she planned to "go the rounds of watering places, beginning at Coney Island, for rest and recreation," before going abroad.

After giving a tea for William Winter and other friendly critics, lengthy interviews for reporters and magazine writers, Lillie was free to enjoy herself and to give Freddie his head. He took her to Tony Pastor's, Delmonico's, the Fifth Avenue Hotel, and all the other smart places. They rode horseback in the park, and he took her to the tracks at Morris and Jerome Park, Sheepshead Bay, and Brighton Beach, always impressed with her knowledge of horses and her betting sense. Freddie had a small stable of his own and talked of expanding it and raising winners—the perfect gentleman's vocation—and Lillie encouraged him.

Freddie was set on going to Paris with her, and it was not easy for her to change his mind. He had been loyal and loving, in spite of having been subject to the most frightful gossip and the butt of ridicule. He deserved better. The tour had been business, as Régnier was going to be, but there was a time for every purpose—even to embrace, to love. She didn't love Freddie. She was fond of him, very fond, and she might have felt more deeply if she hadn't had to concentrate on making the tour successful. Freddie, in his ardent, bumbling, scandalously controversial way, had helped her accomplish this, and she was more than grateful. In fact, she hated to leave him behind, so when he suggested that they go off in the country alone for a little while, she agreed.

Giving herself to him she found so unexpectedly pleasant that she wondered how and why she could possibly have held out so long. It had amused her to live innocently while the press and public assumed otherwise, and she had admired his gentlemanly reserve. He had been pictured as a rake and yet, while touring together, they had attracted attention by their proper

198

behavior. All the time Freddie's arms had been there to tumble into, but he had left the choice to her. This was why she was compliant now.

She had never known such passionate kisses with Edward or Bertie, nor had any man ever really aroused her. Edward had been a limp, apologetic fumbler. Bertie had worked himself up like a steam engine. Freddie was ever-considerate—how big and handsome and young he was! Ah, but what a revelation it was. An expert at flirting, a professional at leading a man on, Lillie discovered now that she was actually an amateur at love.

Ignorant of technique as were most "decent" women, never awakened by her timorous, ineffectual husband, frightened of the Prince, her emotions had been hidden deep under protective layers of prejudice and false concepts. To be brought out of herself was a tumultuous experience. Here Freddie was master, she subject. While she luxuriated in the delicious sensation and longed for further delights, she feared her weakened senses and the male dominance that played with them. She had to depend only on herself; she could not afford the craving for this wonderful drug. She would have to fight it lest passion tie her fast to Freddie or any man. Let love make slaves of others, but not of Lillie Langtry. Not until her career as a real actress was set firmly could she abandon herself to this lotus land.

And yet what could compare with loving and being loved? She was a woman; she, too, was human.

When they returned to New York, all tension gone and intimately at ease, their appearance still snapped heads around wherever they went. Neither critics nor editors could forgive her for winning over the public and making piles of money after being branded untalented and immoral. Her name and Freddie's were linked in newsprint daily. The consensus was that Lillie's actions more than justified "all the scandals about her which drove first Mrs. Labouchère, then Miss Langtry from her company." How wise was Gladstone's advice! thought Lillie again. One ignored everything said, went on as before, and everything worked out for the best.

Boucicault arranged a big farewell supper for her. There

were gifts, speeches, demonstrations of affection, and she thought about Oscar as she listened. There was cash in America, yes, but kindness, too. These were all good friends who found her a lovely, estimable, charming woman no matter what was printed about her.

She sailed on July 28 "to see her husband and take lessons from Régnier" just as her fellow professionals were preparing for the new season on Broadway. A big party was given for her on the boat, and a sarcastic reporter wrote that a delegation from the Union Club kissed her hands to the end of the gangplank. Freddie was said to have tipped her servants, arranged flowers, and given instructions that her bedding be aired.

Lillie and Freddie stood apart while Willie Cutting, Pierre Lorillard, and the rest of the male contingent sipped champagne and watched Freddie enviously. Ah, to love—correction, to freely partake of the charms of—the loveliest woman in the world! Who could ask for anything more? That lucky Gebhard!

"It kills me letting you go like this, Lillie, after we just—"

"Hush, Freddie. That's one reason I'm going away."

"Talk to your London lawyer about the divorce, will you? And don't forget me for a second."

"How could I?" she said, her voice so thrillingly husky that Freddie quivered. "You're the best thing that happened to me in America."

Lillie was in London briefly. She conferred with George Lewis, saw her parents, then left for France by way of Jersey, "my quiet island." Jeanne Marie was a sweet toddler learning to talk, and was in excellent hands. Struggling with the guilty feeling she always had after touching home, Lillie went on to Paris. There she spoke the language like a Frenchwoman and loved the country, so it was natural she should be lionized. Admirers flocked to her, Sarah Bernhardt fêted her, she met members of the Comédie Française and the Théâtre Français—Coquelin, Jean Mounet-Sully, Frederick Febvre, and even the playwright Victorien Sardou. All of them admired Régnier, then seventy-six, a theatrical legend, a *cher maître* whose

200

wheezes were histrionic and whose benign glance was a form of dramatic benediction.

She was received at the Conservatoire with fanfare, Régnier kissing her hands and mumbling praise of her beauty with tears in his eyes. As she had guessed, there was little he could teach her. She walked, talked, and acted out scenes alone and with other actors. Only time, experience, and hard work would bring a change, and *le système Régnier* hardly amounted to more than a series of catchwords glued with cant. It had all the benevolent flatulence of a political speech by a party wheel horse, meant to be applauded and not listened to.

"You have a beautiful face, a lovely, expressive body, perfect carriage, graceful movements, charm, chic, the ability to wear clothes well, and a way of weaving enchantments like a goddess. For you there are no lessons, no mysteries. Simply use the sublime things *le bon dieu* has given you, and you will have the world at your feet."

Gone forever was the Emilie Charlotte Le Breton of the stiff, white skirts and homely woolens, the country girl Belasco recalled whom "butter would choke and milk intoxicate," the repressed rustic who "to her own bewilderment became the rage of society." With self-realization came the knowledge that, lacking the step-by-step childhood training of a Bernhardt, Terry, or Modjeska, she would never be a great actress. But she could be a competent one, her beauty and presence making up for whatever she lacked. While she always accentuated the positive in her make-up, she was entirely sincere in publicly envying the Divine Sarah's ability. "Bernhardt is not beautiful," said Lillie, "but she has all the world at her feet for the sake of her great art. I would give all my beauty to be just one part as great an actress as she."

Good clothes pointed up the Jersey Lily's beauty and were important to the personal production in which she appeared daily. The fittings were bearable now. Nothing could be slipshod—the color, the fit, the handwork, every piece had to be perfect. In those days no couturier could compare with the House of Worth at No. 7 Rue de la Paix, and Lillie patronized it exclusively, very often with some striking original designs of her own. Pins in their mouths, the dressmakers bustled about her, tucking this up, letting down a hem, lifting a bodice, and making alterations.

Jean Phillipe Worth, who with his father, Charles Frederick Worth (originally an Englishman born in Bourne, Lincolnshire), operated this popular monument to style, later recalled her affectionately in his book, *A Century of Fashion*. Typically French in rejecting the aesthetic view, he refuted her classical beauty, granting only that the line of her nose was Greek and that she was most fascinating.

With her eye for the novelty that would look best on her, Mrs. Langtry introduced the first jersey costume, "a blue pleated skirt united to a tight-fitting bodice with a red sash." She wore it to the races at Longchamps that summer, and the Jersey Lily in jersey created the sensation she had foreseen. Worth was swamped with orders, although he knew that "two-thirds of its success was due to her perfect body." But few women had the magnificent figure necessary for a close-fitting suit, and Worth mourned the tragic physical shortcomings it revealed during its reign.

"I'm going to America this fall," Lillie announced, "and I shall want a special wardrobe for each play. It will be a wonderful advertisement for the House of Worth. Your name will be in every program."

The Worths promised the beautiful, striking, unique.

"I do not mind the cost, but I am not your usual do-nothing, rich-lady customer. My wearing of your clothes will bring many inquiries and orders, marvelous publicity for the House of Worth. I ask you to bear this in mind when you send the bill."

Father and son looked at each other and shrugged. A seductive figure, a face to make the jaw drop, speaking French like a native—and yet a mind like a man, a businessman. *Incroyable!*

After two weeks in Paris Lillie decided that she must have gained the Régnier cachet. There was no use wasting time; Freddie was waiting, so were her audiences. She cabled to a producer, who had approached her earlier through Abbey, to make immediate arrangements for a long American tour. Back came an answer that he would put into effect the itinerary he had set up "just in case." Her first engagement would be in late October. Much too soon, she thought, hardly time to engage a company and rehearse. Awful to have to rush, and—Freddie!

The usual crowd of reporters covered her arrival in New York, a restless Freddie struggling to remain aloof until they had finished with their silly, probing questions. He was tremulously happy to see her. Lillie, too, was beside herself (could it really be love?) but decided for appearance's sake merely to clasp his hand. Freddie aimed for her lips, however, and she was conscious of actor Arthur Elwood giving a start on her left. She had a premonition of trouble to come and then dismissed the notion. She was his employer, and on-stage endearments would have to suffice the jealous idiot.

Her reunion with Freddie was joyous, so wonderful she could not understand how she could have left him behind. She spent her first night in New York at a hotel, then was offered a handsome apartment at 120 West 13th Street by Harriet Hubbard Ayer. Mrs. Ayer had left her husband Herbert in Chicago and had started a business in cosmetics. Leasing the apartment was contingent on Lillie's endorsing her Madame Récamier Preparations, adding her name to those of Patti, Bernhardt, Lillian Russell, and Mrs. Cora Brown Potter. She was delighted to do this for the convenience it afforded Freddie and herself.

The New York reviewers were still highly critical without the maliciousness of the earlier reports. William Winter was kind, as always, and Dion Boucicault was gratified at her reception. She was no fly-by-night now, but a serious actress, and he said that winning over the press was only a matter of time. The audiences were all with her, and the critics would have to come about.

Except for Arthur Elwood, her tour of the provincial cities would have been a pleasure. Her leading man hated America. He bridled at his notices, and he couldn't stomach "that bounder Gebhard." He blew his lines, forgot important bits of business, and threw Lillie off so much that she had to prompt him in whispers.

The first flare-up occurred in Boston. Lillie pleaded with him to stay with the company, calling on Jim Smyth-Pigott to help as peacemaker. Young and imperturbable, this Jim had a casual approach to life and the stage, and Lillie had grown fond of him. He would do anything required of him, including such an outrageous publicity stunt as dreamed up for Daniel Frohman's *The Highest Bidder* at the Lyceum in New York. Smyth-Pigott was taken out near the Atlantic Highlands by tug. Here he jumped overboard and swam toward an incoming liner. Crowds lined the rail as an officer threw him a lifeline, but the actor pushed it away saying, "I don't want this." "Then what do you want?" the officer shouted. "I want to know if you have seen *The Highest Bidder* at the Lyceum Theater in New York." Then Smyth-Pigott struck out gracefully for the distant tug. Frohman saw to it that the press front-paged the story.

Lillie did more than just play a town and run. She liked the open air and exercise and was happy to get off the train and stretch her legs. Besides, she was the best possible walking advertisement and could also check on the work of her advance man. William E. Sage of the Cleveland *Leader* years later recalled Freddie and Lillie striding down Euclid Avenue, a quiet young woman and a normal-looking young man with nothing scandalous about them—Freddie "a man of much physical attractiveness and possessed of most charming manners."

St. Louis newsmen, hoping for another episode as sensational as the one which had involved Colonel Cunningham, missed the scene Elwood had with Freddie. She led her leading man away to cool off, but his acting did not improve. His contract expired April 26 and, although it had an option of ten additional weeks if the tour should be successful (and it was), Lillie let him go in Chicago on that date.

It was no surprise to Lillie when she was served with a court summons. Freddie wanted her to engage an attorney, but she saw no need. The action came up in New York's Third District Civil Court. The place was crowded with spectators, "some to get a glimpse of the Jersey Lily, others to learn the validity of a verbal contract or agreement." Elwood insisted that in Boston and again in St. Louis he had been assured his contract would be extended.

On the stand Lillie coolly testified that she had discharged Elwood for incompetency since he stammered through sentences and marred her theatrical effects. She admitted their conversations, alleging that she had changed her mind about his option. Here Elwood's lawyer decided to hint at a liaison.

"Did you chaperone Mr. Elwood on the occasion of a certain St. Louis walk?"

"No, there was no chaperone," she answered sharply.

"Then he was the chaperone?"

"Put it anyway you like." The papers added that she blushed.

Passing her former leading man, Lillie "looked into his eyes and passed on without word of recognition." The jury was out about an hour, returning a judgment in her favor.

"You see, Freddie, I don't need a lawyer."

"Just wait. We'll need Abe Hummel sooner or later."

The tour resumed. Lillie sent a telegram from Denver to the *Spirit of the Times:* "Arrived safely thus far on my journey. Have seen buffaloes and prairie dogs." The American West delighted her, especially California, but she could not take time just now to see more of it. She had plans—one of which called for finding a first-class leading man and a superior company in England. By July 4 she was back in New York, and she and Freddie stole a week in the Catskills. Then they visited training farms in upstate New York to buy horses for his stables. The newspapers reported she was "sensibly spending her vacation in New York, lunching on the steamship *America,* and witnessing the races at Monmouth Park." She sat for Sarony again, and for Mora, another photographer, who conceived the idea of putting her in Japanese costume. Press agents had her meditating on a tour of the Far East.

Then came another lawsuit, this one brought by the management of Niblo's Garden Theater, which was represented by Abe Hummel. She had failed to appear at a matinée, and it had been necessary to return the money at the box office. Freddie warned her that she would have no chance against such an antagonist, but Lillie was not too worried. So long as juries were composed of men she was confident.

Because Lillie later became his esteemed client, Abe Hummel liked to tell the story of how he first met her "on the other side of litigation." Lillie pleaded that the condition of her health had prevented her acting on the day in question, and Hummel, a bear at cross-examination, set out to prove she had been perfectly well at the time. He quickly saw that the jury regarded her beatifically, that not one of them doubted her, and he *had* to trip her in a lie.

"Tell me truly," he demanded, "isn't it a fact you were out riding that day?"

"No."

"Do you mean to tell me you were sick?" he drove on.

"Oh, no." The slick, sinister-faced lawyer sat down in triumph. Lillie turned with a gracious smile and said gravely, "But, Mr. Hummel, you in America use 'sick' in a different manner than we do in England. In saying I was not sick I meant that I was not sick at my stomach. If you intended to ask if I had been ill, I wish to tell you that my health was so precarious that it would have been impossible for me to act."

Hypnotized, the jury gladly accepted her version. It was one of the few cases Abe Hummel ever lost in good grace. He congratulated Lillie and ingratiated himself with compliments (he was a first-nighter of repute). He begged the right to represent her hereafter so that she might be spared "iniquitous complaints, the chastisement of evil-doers, and the thousand and one claims on fame, fortune, and beauty incumbent on a celebrated person such as yourself."

"He's got a way with words, Freddie. I didn't say yes or no, but I'll gladly use him if more trouble comes along. But another thing—you've been talking to him, haven't you?" He mumbled something. "You asked him about divorcing Edward, isn't that right?" He nodded, the bashful boy with his hand caught in the cookie jar. "Why?"

"I'm an optimist. You said it was impossible, and I had to know. I want to marry you, Lillie. In fact, I've got to!"

"What if we can't ever get married?"

"Then it doesn't matter, if only we're together. I know I'm not as bad as the newspapers wish I were, but I'm not as good either. You must love me a little, Lillie, or else you wouldn't have me around like this."

She gave an infectious laugh. "I do love you, Freddie, and it surprises me. But how can you love a woman who can think only of the stage, her career and herself—who uses and abuses you and hasn't much time for love?"

He opened his arms, and she slid between them.

"So long as you make the time, why should I kick? We'll go a long way, you and I. If we can't have anything else, we'll have a happy scandal together. I'll never make the rules. You can do what you want, go where you want, but you'll never shut me out."

"Then you're coming to England?"

"Of course. Not on the same boat—it'll break the reporters' hearts—but soon enough. I want to be with you, see England, meet your family, everything."

"We'll have to be careful. I'm still Mrs. Edward Langtry."

"Damn him, anyway! Why does he want to hold you when you don't love him and don't want him? It's humiliating for both of you."

"Edward believes the marriage bond holds forever. It should, but not for him and me. There are other complications, as you know."

"Jeanne Marie, eh?"

"Yes," she said gently, telling herself she would have to learn to live with half truths. "If he knew about her, he'd never have consented to our separation, such as it is. He'd have so strong a claim he'd compel me to take him back. The publicity would be terrible."

"One thing I can understand. You could act and all, but if you were my wife, I'd never let you out of my sight."

"I don't want to be owned, Freddie. People have to respect each other's personalities." He started to protest, and she shushed him. "I trust you more than I've trusted any other man. That ought to mean something. You know things about me no

207

one else knows, things that could blacken and ruin me. I can't be more to you than I am."

He kissed her passionately, and Lillie did not hold back.

"The door's locked, the maids are off, and the rest of the afternoon is ours."

He kissed her open-mouthed, running a warm, tingling hand over one breast, then the other. "Let me love you, Lillie!"

"In broad daylight?"

"Makes it more sinful. The papers make us the glorious personification of vice, so let's sin a little. Besides, I like to look at that marvelous body." He kissed the pulse twitching in her throat. "You're the most beautiful thing in the whole world, and I'm the luckiest and happiest man to have you."

When she was in London, Freddie wrote that he would be delayed because his horses were running in the tracks around New York. He hoped to enter them at Saratoga in August, unless she wanted him to come over right away. This delay fitted in nicely with Lillie's plans, for George Lewis had told her it might not be wise for Freddie to visit London just now, not only because of Edward but mainly because of her own career. She reluctantly agreed, for she had a great reputation now, and it was important that she live up to it. She had the money to do so.

Lillie began by moving into a big, comfortable town house at 86 Eaton Square, S.W., furnishing it luxuriously, and acquiring a staff. Dominique was retired with honors. Beverly, her new butler, ran the place like a military post, fending off intruders for his famous mistress. It was wonderful to be self-sustaining and able to indulge in the beautiful clothes and expensive jewelry so necessary to a star. They were part of the show, something she felt she owed to her audiences. She did not want them to be disappointed in the Jersey Lily. Clothes were her department; so were her favorite pieces of jewelry. The baubles given her by Bertie and others had all gone when the Norfolk Street house was "sold up." Now she had Freddie's glittering gifts, plus assorted items donated by rajahs, foreign princes, dukes and nobles, and other wealthy admirers who felt it incumbent upon themselves to contribute some token to her beauty. It was hard to refuse these worshippers, who could expect nothing more than a dazzling smile in exchange, so she simply added their bracelets, rings, and brooches—many of them ostentatious —to her treasure.

In her search for a suitable leading man, Lillie got in touch with Charles T. Coghlan through Clement Scott, the writer and critic, to whom she had turned so often for advice that he liked to look on her—as she had foreseen—as a sort of protégée. Coghlan, then forty-three, approached every role like a scholar. His moody temperament made his performances uneven, and he was either outstanding, adequate, or downright bad. But he had a fine professional reputation and would bolster Lillie's productions without overshadowing her. At the time of Bernhardt's first appearance in England, acting was affected and grimly formalized. Sarah's divine fire, passionate manner, and headlong technique had started a revolution on the London stage. Excesses followed before actors simmered down and reverted to British restraint. Critics praised this particular native quality in Coghlan, who was considered "a brainy actor and the apostle of reserve force."

He and Lillie got along splendidly from the beginning. He was no Arthur Elwood. Coghlan had no romantic interest in her and was flattered by her dependence on his judgment. Whatever the flaws in his own acting, he could examine her work objectively. They toured the provinces with great success that fall, the pressure off Lillie now that she no longer felt the entire responsibility of the production resting on her own shoulders. Coghlan was a dependable co-star. The provincial critics, who had always praised her, noted a startling improvement in her acting. She was ready for London now. Freddie was champing to cross the Atlantic to be with her, but she told him to wait until she was established.

She rented the Prince of Wales Theater on Coventry Street, and opened with *The Lady of Lyons*, January 24, 1885. The critics beamed at her "ripened experience" and praised her Pauline as "broad, natural, and sympathetic." Much heartened, she waited for their reaction to her Séverine in *Princess George*, an adaption from a play by Alexandre Dumas the younger. But its reception was not too favorable, some critics annoyingly referring to her as still amateurish.

In Sheridan's artificial *The School for Scandal*, with Coghlan as Charles Surface and Beerbohm Tree as a hilarious Joseph, she was better than in the pretentious Dumas drama. The critics, for the first time, found her agreeable throughout, "an interesting and picturesque Lady Teazle." To be taken seriously at last was delightful.

And Sardou's *Peril* was a high point. Well received in the United States and a staple in her repertoire (in six years she was supposed to have realized $300,000 on this play alone), it was such a hit that she had to extend its run. She was "sincerely congratulated for the marked improvement over any former effort she has made in London." She had always liked this play, and it was no accident that it had been translated from the French and adapted by the critic Clement Scott. Ever shrewd in combining friendship with enlightened self-interest, Lillie wrote him, "The Prince of Wales was delighted and finds me immensely improved since the first night." She had also received a letter from Sardou about the magnificent reception of *Peril*, and so she astutely suggested to Scott, "Don't you think it's worth a paragraph?"

Scott obliged, only too glad to accommodate the lovely charmer who sought his influential advice. She had begun writing to "Dear Clement Scott." Now it was "My Dear Scottie," and she was sending "some of the whiskey you liked." He was invited backstage with: "Do come round—the door (promptside) into my dressing room is open. You can walk through without asking anyone—Lillie." Or she asked him to dinner at 86 Eaton Square, putting her invitation irresistibly in her wonderfully bold handwriting with its big, swooping, plunging letters: "Do dine with me at *8*. I shan't ask anyone else. I want you all to myself."

A London magazine, describing Mrs. Langtry's theatrical career, told how she had "set half of New York crazy and other principal cities had an attack of Langtry fever, while the charming actress scooped in the almighty dollar by the thousands. Mrs. Langtry was able to smile at her early criticism while she turned over the leaves of her bank book."

"I owe it all to Mr. Coghlan," she told Jimmy Whistler, glowing over her notices. "He's done so much for me."

"Rot! How could anyone *not* like everything you do anywhere any time? Drama critics know even less than art critics. They're all scum, do y' know? Have you seen our friend Oscar lately, most beautiful Lillie?"

"Not since his marriage."

"Constance Lloyd is a handsome woman. But Oscar married! I never thought he liked women except aesthetically. Contemplation and all that, y' know? Not that Oscar was ever a true artist. He's a fancy critic and lecturer who reflects the views of others tinctured with his own. He picks from our platters the plums for the puddings he peddles in the provinces."

"And how is your work, Jimmy?" she asked, changing the subject.

"Still incomparable, still genius, still unappreciated. Situation normal, eh what?" He gave a harsh cackle and adjusted his monocle. "But what about your portrait? When can we finish 'Arrangement in Yellow'? Soon, I hope. So you liked my country, eh? I wouldn't have expected it of you. Noisy people, aren't they?"

"Noisy and *nosy*."

fourteen

Now that Lillie was living in London she sent for Jeanne Marie. The little girl who called her *Tante* attracted very little notice. The dean had aged greatly, but he enjoyed his limited duties in Marylebone parish and never missed an opportunity to see his daughter perform. Lillie loved walking back from the theater, applause still ringing in her ears, Papa leaning on her arm and talking about the happy alliance of Church and Theater which the two of them represented.

Mrs. Le Breton looked the part of the perfect stage mother. Pretty, well dressed, and imperturbable as always, Mama inspired Lillie's devotion by never listening to gossip, never asking questions. Sometimes Lillie worried lest they run into Edward on the street, but from what she heard he spent most of his time in and around Southampton drinking, sailing, or reading as befitted a gentleman of leisure. Clearly, the Le Bretons felt he had wronged both Lillie and Jeanne Marie and was unworthy of them, so they never mentioned him.

Freddie, still building up his stables, had a number of good wins, but he was restless and panting to see Lillie. However, George Lewis still advised caution, and she dared not risk a visit from Freddie. She wrote to him often, assuring him of her faithful love, and warning him over and over not to believe what was written about her—a wise precaution, since she was shortly involved in another notorious affair.

An ugly situation had arisen between Lord Lonsdale and Sir George Chetwynd, both of whom knew the details of Lillie's friendship with Bertie. Besides, Sir George knew far too much about her husband, while Lady Lonsdale (later Lady de Grey) was one of Lillie's best friends. Lillie had to be nice to these noblemen and they knew it; they seemed to think they should decide on *how* nice. Lord Lonsdale amused the public with his rakehell activities, and his turf winnings had begun to outstrip his boudoir accomplishments.

The attentions of both Lord Lonsdale and Sir George became so objectionable that Lillie wished Freddie were there to disabuse them in the good old punch-in-the-nose American way. All she could do to protect herself was to play one off against the other, and this she managed by dropping a word to one, an insinuation to another. Things came to a head on July 23, 1885, in Rotten Row, during the fashionable twelve-to-two-o'clock period while the Smart Set paraded on foot, carriage, and horseback. Lillie had told each of the men that she would be riding in the park that day and would meet him near the Achilles statue where she had once held court.

Sir George, a member of the Hurlingham and Turf Clubs, and High Sheriff of the County of Warwick, was thirty-six and married to a daughter of the Marquess of Anglesey. Lord Lonsdale, twenty-eight, was married to Lady Grace Gordon, daughter of the Marquess of Huntley, and was every bit as good a horseman as his adversary. Each arrived early on a fine animal and became infuriated at the sight of the other waiting at the Achilles statue. Lillie was there on foot, heavily veiled and unrecognized, highly amused at the fire-breathing pair facing each other like jousting knights. After learning that Lonsdale was waiting for Lillie as he was, Sir George said something about a sly bitch. Lonsdale took offense, replied in kind. Sir George struck him with his riding crop and knocked his hat to the street. Then, according to a newspaper account:

> . . . in delivering the blow, Sir George cried, "Take that, you devil!" "What in——do you mean?" rejoined Lord Lonsdale, smarting under the blow. "Don't meddle with my Lily!" shouted his assailant as he again struck Lord Lonsdale with his whip full across the shoulders. Lord Lonsdale returned the blow with his whip. The horses of both combatants became frightened, began to plunge and kick in a lively manner, and the

riders were forced to dismount. Dropping their whips, they continued to fight with their fists. Sir George soon got his opponent's head "in chancery" and pummeled him repeatedly. Lord Lonsdale struggled to free himself and both men rolled in the dust. They regained their feet, blood flowing from noses and mouths, their clothing torn, and renewed the fight . . .

They were punching away to an audience of rearing horses and shocked Rotten Rowers—Lillie astonished yet gratified at what she had brought about—as Sir William Cummings and the Duke of Portland, assisted by mounted policemen, separated them. Each man was forced into a closed carriage and taken home. Legal proceedings were threatened, but the disgrace was enough to satisfy all society gossip. Friends managed to keep the affair out of court. Sir George was around town the next day, bearing only slight marks of the battle, but Lord Lonsdale stayed home at Carlton House Terrace nursing a mahogany-black eye.

Nothing on the stage could have equaled such a grudge fight in Rotten Row. It was the talk of London. People flocked to the Prince of Wales Theater, and it was observed that the Jersey Lily had never looked so serenely beautiful. Now that she was rid of Sir George and Lord Lonsdale, she cabled Freddie Gebhard to disregard the affair and come at once.

The season was coming to an end, and she made preparations for a provincial tour while she awaited Freddie's arrival. Gossip over the fracas in the Park died down, but repercussions continued, and she was startled to be served with a court summons "for refusing to pay household debts contracted while living with her husband." Since she had settled all her early debts George Lewis told her not to worry—she was famous, she had money, and this was a nuisance case. A number of dressmakers' bills were mentioned in the summons with the statement that Mr. Langtry claimed he was unable to pay them as his only source of income "is an annuity allowed him by his wife on condition that he does not molest her."

Now it occurred to Lillie that Sir George Chetwynd was back of the suit, trying to strike at her vindictively. Lewis managed a postponement from October 20 to November 3 because of her stage commitments, and she did not have to appear in Brompton County Court when the case came up. A news item stated that the "plaintiff showed that Mrs. Langtry had, previous to contracting the debts, a check from Captain Allen Young, the Arctic explorer, for a large sum; that when plaintiff called on her for the amount of her indebtedness the defendant told the plaintiff that she was unable just at present to pay the bill, but would endeavor to do so at a later date. Judgment was given for the plaintiff."

Mention of the check infuriated Lillie. She had repaid the loan, and mention of the matter now could only embarrass the so-called explorer—as well as Bertie. Sure now that Chetwynd had engineered this attempt at character assassination, she paid off gladly without contesting the judgment. It worried her that Freddie had not arrived, but she smiled over his letter of explanation. Oh, Freddie was jealous, all right! He didn't like being held off, then being ordered to come at once. He wanted to make her suffer. So be it, she thought, and wrote him that he should come at his convenience. As a result of her mildness, his letters became more ardent than before. She loved his childish misspellings—so many men had faults; so few were as lovable as Freddie's.

Lillie's tour drew capacity houses all through the provinces, and she was back in London in January for a rest before the start of the new season. She had just returned from a clothes-buying trip to Paris when Freddie arrived at Eaton Square at tea time. They had time for passionate embraces and the tense exchanges between thwarted lovers too long parted, before Mrs. Le Breton, trailing her sewing, was introduced to Mr. Gebhard, "an old and dear American friend now visiting London." Young, good-looking, of good family, and prepossessing as Edward Langtry never had been, he instantly won Mama's admiration. She knew nothing of the American scandal; only that the man was in love with her daughter. What man wasn't?

Because London hotels were so poor, Lillie said, she wanted to save Freddie from them and let him stay in her house. Mrs. Le Breton agreed to stay at Eaton Square as chaperone, and

Freddie liked her. He sat with her in the theater watching Lillie, unaware that he was being observed by a lovely American girl he had once courted, Mrs. John Leslie, formerly Léonie Jerome, who noted in her diary about Mrs. Langtry in *Princess George*: "such a fiasco, can't act and is badly made up, red hands. Freddie Gebhard with the mother. Looked ashamed of her, rather disgraceful." Again: "Saw Freddie Gebhard looking too foolish at the Opera with Mrs. Langtry. She had paint on her face. Such bad form."

It was the consensus of Léonie and her sisters that Freddie was making a fool of himself over Mrs. Langtry. It never occurred to them that their mother had bustled them out of the United States because of their father's like propensities. Leonard Jerome, diplomat, financier, part owner of the New York *Times,* horseman and yachtsman, had made something of a fool of himself over many a beautiful woman (Jenny Lind, Adelina Patti, Minnie Hauk, the siren-like Fanny Ronalds, and others).

These girls rode high in society and were supremely conscious of form, particularly Jennie, Lady Randolph Churchill, whose husband was still on the Prince of Wales's blacklist. Jennie knew the gossip, and decided that Freddie Gebhard was no gentleman.

Happy together, Lillie and Freddie couldn't have cared less. He was an eager American tourist interested in seeing all the right places, pleased to spend heavily on clothes in Savile Row, and proud to be seen with Lillie. His presence held off her puzzled admirers ("Dash it all, who is this plagued American monopolizing our Lillie?"). He met her at the theater every night after being with her most of the day. They liked being alone. He was a house guest, Mrs. Le Breton was an ideal chaperone, and the niceties were outwardly observed. Who heard the footsteps down the hall, the doors closing softly early in the morning, the faint cries of pleasure?

Freddie was easily persuaded to tour the Continent with Lillie. In Austria, she sent word of her arrival to Crown Prince Rudolph, who rushed down from his shooting box at Mayerling. Wearing a gay, feathered hat and Tyrolean shorts, he was tanned and heavier than she remembered, a beard giving a touch of manliness to his pinched, feminine face. Just the same, he struck her as still pathetically unsure of himself.

"At last you've come to Vienna, madame," he said in warm French. "How many years has it been—seven, eight?—and I've never forgotten you. So lovely, so charming."

He liked Freddie immediately. They were given the royal treatment and fêted at parties where Viennese orchestras played and special artists entertained at the command of the Crown Prince. No longer the brusquely rude, impulsive young man of London, he was pleased Lillie had kept her promise to visit him. The suppers he gave for them in a private villa on the grounds of the Café Sacher in the Prater were hilariously gay. Lillie noticed, however, that Rudi had to force himself into the mood. While everyone else sang, he remained silent, staring fixedly at a pretty, dark-haired woman across the room.

"Isn't she lovely?" he said to Lillie. "Over there. The Baroness Maria Vetsera."

The young woman flushed under their gaze, turning to her escort in transparent animation. Lillie wanted to ask about her, but Rudi was lost in thought, his mouth set and ugly.

The next day he insisted on taking her through his palace, although it had been closed for the summer. He pointed at paintings and tapestries with his cane. He showed her the sumptuous rooms with their glorious furniture under dust covers. The mantel gewgaws, little clocks, and relics in glass cases seemed to belong more in a museum than in a palace. Lillie remarked on this, and Rudi scowled.

"You don't like them, madame?"

"They belong to a hideous inartistic period," she said casually.

He stroked his beard. Then suddenly he raised his cane and shattered one glass dome after another, each article crashing noisily to the floor. They were alone in the empty palace, the furniture wrapped like so many ghosts; and his red-faced fury and avenging cane, the tinkling of glass, and the needless destruction of every knickknack frightened her. It was as if she were witnessing a series of small, wanton murders. Rudi seemed more than ever a strange, volatile young man.

"Sounds like a queer bird to me," Freddie commented when she told him.

"I don't know. He did it to please me, and if you'd known him years ago—well, he's gentler, more human and attractive than he used to be. But sad where he was gay, gloomy instead of impetuous." She looked at him. "People change, don't they?"

"I won't, Lillie," he assured her. "Not about you."

Lillie returned to New York in September, 1886, with Coghlan and her company. On the ship she was surrounded by reporters who were obviously disappointed not to see Freddie, but he had returned long before. Lillie's manner charmed them as usual as she answered their questions frankly. She recognized Bury Irwin Dasent, who had accompanied her to the Stock Exchange and J. P. Morgan's office on her first American tour. Dasent was eager to do some new feature articles about her and, knowing they would be favorable, she agreed.

She dined with Freddie at Delmonico's that night, and all her old American friends seemed to be there to greet her. After England and the Continent, it was refreshing to be welcomed with such informal warmth by society figures, financiers, actors, gamblers, and just about everyone who had the money to get into New York's smartest restaurant.

As they drove back to the hotel in a hansom, Freddie told her excitedly, "I was going to write you all about it, but I know how you love surprises. You've got a house, Lillie, one of the best."

"How wonderful!" She kissed his cheek. "I'm sick of hotels and when I like a place, as I do New York, I can't wait to have a house there. I love you, Freddie!" Then she was reminded of the expenses of the tour, costumes, scenery, transportation, Coghlan's salary, the cast's. "Did it cost much?"

"Enough," he said airily. "But you don't have to worry. It's a gift, darling, from me to you." She protested, but he cut her off. "I want to do things for you and, by God, you've got to let me! I may not be a crown prince or a duke, but this is one way

218

I can show how much I love you. Besides, we're practically husband and wife now—we're going to be if Abe Hummel can work it. Now, what do you say?"

"All right," she said quietly, squeezing his arm.

"And that includes alterations, redecoration, furniture, fixtures, *everything* you want. I want it to be the very best. With your eye and good taste you can make it a show place."

"It's your house, too, Freddie. But may I see it now? *Please.*"

"At two o'clock in the morning?"

"We'll find out if it's haunted. Please, Freddie, show me my house by moonlight."

Lillie's house was actually two houses, Numbers 361 and 362 West 23rd Street near Ninth Avenue in the Chelsea district, close to the site of the present London Terrace apartments. Built in 1829, when 23rd Street had been called "Millionaire's Row," they were presented to Clement Clarke Moore, author of the ageless " 'Twas the night before Christmas." Moore leased them to Edward Fox, who combined them into one big house and later sold it to David Beach Grant, who in turn sold it to Freddie Gebhard.

Red-brick, turreted, three-story, Lillie's spacious New York residence had a plain but aristocratic appearance, a French-type mansard roof, large windows, and fancy iron grille work. With a fifty-foot frontage and a ten-foot setback from the building line, there was room for landscaping. Lillie put in a small lawn, shrubbery, plants, a gold-flowering laburnum tree and a big ailanthus tree (both of which were still in front of the gloomy, boarded-up house as late as 1929, the year of her death). An intricate wrought-iron entryway led to a double white front door. A portico protected visitors arriving in carriages, after they pulled into the crescent-shaped driveway whose entrance was flanked by handsome brick pillars on which were mounted pagoda-like lamps.

As the house became a landmark, hundreds of people and hangers-on gathering every day to see Lillie leave or arrive— or perhaps Freddie or, oh joy! *both*—she ordered an iron picket fence erected along the street connecting the gateposts. Because she had failed to secure a permit from the city, this iron fence became a coast-to-coast *cause célèbre* and resulted in endless litigation. The newspapers devoted so many columns to it that it became a stock joke. ("It'll keep everybody out except Freddie.")

Given a free hand, Lillie took Freddie at his word. He was mad about her, anxious that she have "a setting quite worthy of her beauty and charm," and insistent that he pay for everything. Since this was going to be her home for some time to come—in fact, she and Freddie might live there permanently if things worked out—it had to be exactly as she wanted it, inside and out. She arranged to knock out interior walls, enlarge rooms, and install large marble bathtubs, marble fireplaces, and carved mantels. The quality merchants were pleased to serve the Jersey Lily. She chose only their best furniture, rugs, draperies, and paintings.

Of course the job of decorating the house was a plum. Lillie consulted with the candidates and chose James T. Mitchell, a young English architect and contractor. A good man eager to make a name for himself, he clashed frequently with his client, who was under the Wilde-Whistler influence. He complained of the difficulties of "trying to translate the passing whims of the beauty into wood and brick." Years later he told a feature writer for the New York *Sun*:

> The interior was to be finished entirely in highly polished walnut, and it all had to be imported from a certain English forest. We were kept on our sharps for a year in getting the wood just the right grain, and then the interior graining and polishing was a tremendous job. This was a big commission for me. I worked on it day and night and when we finished that beautiful walnut job, I was the proudest man in New York.
>
> But my troubles were only beginning. Mrs. Langtry looked over the work, but she seemed hardly to notice it. "The very latest thing in interior decoration." she said, "is hard, finished white enamel. I want this all covered with white enamel. You will have to send to England for the right kind. I am sure you won't be able to get it here."

I tried to beg off, but she was accustomed to just waving her hand to get things done. I could have got it here, but it had to come from England.

It almost broke my heart when my men set to work covering the walnut with this hard, white finish. I don't know where she got the idea, but at that time women were copying her hats and gowns and imitating her speech, and before long all the moguls in New York were smearing their houses with enamel.

Freddie had suggested black walnut because it was the prevailing motif in the homes of the American wealthy. For Lillie its effect was cold and gloomy, particularly on dark days, while the white enamel gave the rooms light, warmth, and a freshness that set off her draperies and furnishings. Because the polishing and graining of the walnut paneling had taken hundreds of man-hours, Mitchell's frustration was understandable.

Lillie occupied the house on and off for only three years, then only occasionally after that, but she always said these were the happiest hours of her life. Certainly they were the most carefree.

She loved her comfortable, restful New York home in this lovely, unspoiled residential area. The house, set well back on the north side, made a refreshing picture with its green lawn, shrubs and flowers, and framing shade trees. Substantial rather than pretentious, it was given a severely austere aspect by the high iron fence in front, which truly made her New York headquarters "an inviolable retreat." Those who hung about hoping to see her arrive or leave in her carriage in the daytime were disappointed by the quiet of the place. The curtains were always drawn as though it were unoccupied. Reporters found it "more difficult to get into that house than to go through the eye of a needle," but the House-of-Usher appearance was deceptive.

During the daytime Lillie was either resting, going over a new part, or attending to her duties as manageress. Things changed at night, however. After the theater she and Freddie frequently entertained. Carriage after carriage drew up under the portico, and the windows were brightly lighted until the early morning hours. The gay parties were in keeping with the sumptuously furnished house and the talk of the neighborhood long after Lillie had abandoned it. Gossip had it that Freddie spent "$200,000 on liquor *alone*" during those hectic years.

How pleasant it was now to leaf through the favorable reviews, sniff the fragrant verbal bouquets tossed at her. The New York *Star* capsuled her as "Venus costumed by Worth." *The Spirit of the Times,* in a complete change of heart, stated that she had "won the dramatic diadem fairly and wears it worthily."

"And listen to this, Freddie!" Lillie said excitedly. " 'The ladies forgot their admiration of Mrs. Langtry's Directoire costumes in the admiration of her acting, and gentlemen applauded her art as well as her beauty. Her performance from beginning to end was a triumph. For almost the first time, Mrs. Langtry's good looks and fine dresses seem to be accessories to her dramatic ability.' " Lillie's eyes shone with pleasure. "I can't believe they're writing about me!"

"I knew they'd come around," he said. "When you put your mind to it, no one can resist you—and I ought to know."

A magazine writer, describing a mass interview at the 23rd Street house where he was admitted by a flunky (Beverly in a tailcoat), spoke of the portieres of yellow silk, the tapestries on the walls, the carpets of thickest velvet, and "in all directions quaint little tables loaded with bric-à-brac."

Lillie froufroued into the room wearing a tight-clinging gown trimmed with fur.

"I am dying of thirst," she confessed, "and after my journey I must have champagne. Don't think this awful of me, but I am truly fatigued, and if you are charitable and want to put me at my ease, you will join me."

It took no urging. Tactful, lovely to look at, she made no enemies with such an approach. The reporters sat about sipping champagne in midafternoon and succumbing to her charm. Some realized she was a clever woman, others felt "she calculates the effect of everything she does, but in an artistically imperceptible manner," but nothing could dilute their admiration. And some, like Bury Irwin Dasent, fell in love with her.

Of course the scandal was not forgotten (and could hardly be with Freddie still around), nor was her *affaire* with the Prince of Wales. To the prurient-minded, it followed that she was a low, common woman. Most galling was her radiant beauty and clear complexion. A candle burned at both ends should look like—a candle burned at both ends: shriveled, gutted, raddled. Orgies, late hours, endless parties and debaucheries, hard drinking—and still Lillie was lovely and youthful. It was a phenomenon that would annoy the righteous increasingly as Lillie grew older and continued to look younger. Lost on them were the lengths she went to in order to take care of herself, to sleep long hours, to watch her diet, to keep her lithe, well-muscled body in trim.

She had mentioned the importance of exercise to reporters questioning her on the secret of her beauty, but the subject was overlooked or ridiculed, as in *Punch* for January 5, 1887:

> "Mrs. Langtry's horror is adiposity, which she combats with dumbbells." So says the evening paper. Had the information been given with regard to any other woman, it would have been said—"She's afraid of getting fat and has taken to dumbbells." But fancy a fat lily. An adipose one is bad enough in all conscience. And a lily working dumbbells! How Oscar must shudder.

The dumbbells were fiction, as were many stories of Lillie's drinking and sinning. She did both in moderation and was usually in bed before midnight during her engagements. She was blessed with a strong body and blooming health and had the good sense to protect both. She was a great walker, enjoyed brisk outings wherever she was, always dragging a devoted, puffing Freddie along. An account of her athletic activities was set down in a letter to the New York *Sun* after her death:

> During the metropolitan racing season Mrs. Langtry lived at Manhattan Beach, at the time the most famous seaside resort in the United States. Rain or shine, hot or cool, every morning shortly after daybreak, she came jogging over the long wooden bridge that spanned Sheepshead Bay, which separated Manhattan Beach from the mainland, clad in heavy woolens, swathed in a sweater, muffler and heavy woolen hose with

clumsy-looking pedestrian shoes. She never once slowed her gait and continued straight on to the Sheepshead Bay racetrack. The mile-and-one-eighth track circled without let-up, she then jogged back to Manhattan Beach. In all this she was accompanied by Freddie Gebhard, though he never seemed to get the same enjoyment from the slog that Lily did.

It is true that Lillie never strolled but always stepped right out, even along Fifth Avenue but, for Freddie, this jogging, while dazed with sleep in the obscene brightness of daybreak, was murder.

"My God," he complained, puffing at her heels, "you're worse than a jockey exercising his horse. Only in this case you're the horse."

"You don't have to come, Freddie. I told you."

"I'm not letting you out of my sight, ever."

"Anyway, it's good for you. Breathe deeply and get the poison out of your system. Loosen up your muscles, make your body limber."

"I'm the spectator type, Lillie. I don't like to sweat."

"It's good to sweat. Listen to the birds, look at the dew glistening on the grass. What a magical time it is, and no one around but ourselves! Don't you love it?"

"No!" How could she keep dogtrotting so effortlessly, arms and legs pumping, head outthrust and high, sniffing the air like a pointer? And she looked so damn lovely in that clumsy runner's get-up that it hurt. What a woman!

Sweat trickled down his red face.

"Every dog has his day, and so apparently have women like Mrs. Langtry." This was said of Lillie in the early days of the Gebhard scandal and the first money-making tour. She had come back bigger and better than ever each time, undeterred by snubs, vicious slanders, the nastiest criticism. The efforts to crush her by pointing a hypocritical finger and crying shame had come to seem pathetic.

It was said then, and later, that she had no respectable women in her circle. Lillie could hardly be blamed for her lack of feminine friends. She got on better with men because so

224

Emilie Charlotte Le Breton at fourteen.

Lillie at the time of her marriage to Edward Langtry.

Edward Langtry

"The Jersey Lily," by
George Frederick Watts.

Lillie Langtry during her
first London season.

Mrs. Langtry as Rosalind in *As You Like It*. (*Museum of the City of New York*)

Mrs. Langtry in *As in a Looking-glass*.

Frederick Gebhard. (*Museum of the City of New York*)

Hugo de Bathe

"Abington" Baird, by Joshua Deighton.

Lady Lillie de Bathe in 1900. (*Museum of the City of New York*)

Mrs. Langtry wearing some
of her fabulous jewels.

Lillie Langtry (*left*) and
her daughter Jeanne.

Lillie Langtry's house at 361 West 23rd Street, New York City. (*Museum of the City of New York*)

The White Lady. (*Museum of the City of New York*)

"Regal Lodge," Lillie's racing box at Kentsford, near Newmarket, England. (*Museum of the City of New York*)

Lillie Langtry's London drawing room. (*Museum of the City of New York*)

Mrs. Langtry on her last American tour, 1917.

Lillie Langtry in her garden in Monaco.

The last photograph of Mrs. Langtry (*left*), with her companion, Mathilde Peat, 1928.

few passed judgment on her. Women, on the other hand, were often mean, or subservient and unable to express themselves—horribly jealous, too, like Christine Nilsson, the great Swedish operatic soprano who first toured the United States in 1870 and sang at the opening of the Metropolitan Opera House in 1883. When it was suggested that they meet, Lillie was agreeable. She played the piano well, had always appreciated fine singing, and looked forward to being introduced to the soprano. But the singer broke that engagement, as well as all succeeding ones, with the flimsiest of excuses.

Lillie had neither patience with nor sympathy for women with neurotic artistic temperaments. She understood far better the solid, earthy people like Lillian Russell, whose zest made up for any lack of refinement. She was aware of being baited for an artistic feud when some reporters suggested that she meet the great Lillian Russell, conceived by some as America's answer to the Jersey Lily. Lillie yawned at the notion and avoided a direct answer. The same reporters, sure of feud material, approached Miss Russell with their gambit. She too shrugged, saying she'd think about it.

But later Lillian Russell wrote a note to Lillie proposing a quiet poker game "with two interesting mutual friends." Eight years Lillie's junior, Lillian had been born in Clinton, Iowa, as Helen Louise (Nellie) Leonard. In her way, she had achieved as tumultuous a success as Lillie's. Each woman had heard much about the other, especially from James Buchanan Brady and Freddie.

Lillie accepted the invitation to include Freddie, although he looked a little worried, since he knew that Lillian Russell liked games for high stakes. He took care to review poker play for Lillie before they left. Jim Brady flung wide the door of his friend's hotel room and gallantly introduced the women with an anxious glance at Freddie. The meeting went very well. Lillian praised Lillie's work, and Lillie hers. Then they had a snack of cold chicken, ham, and champagne—Brady substituting four bottles of root beer for himself—and settled down at the card table.

Reporters hurried to the hotel, their feud pieces already

225

written in their minds, but "When the argument committee looked in, they saw the two girls feverishly raking in chips and smiling warily at each other." No face-scratching, no hairpulling, no screaming—no story.

"Jim's almost as generous with his cards as he is with his diamonds, wouldn't you say, Miss Russell?"

"I would say neither he nor Freddie can play good poker, Mrs. Langtry. You and I have to work hard for our money, so we know how to take care of it. You either have it or you bluff it, but in any case bet sky high. It takes nerve to call."

"Just the way we do it in the theater," Lillie agreed.

"Looks to me like the girls got us right where they want us, hey, Freddie?" said Brady, looking at their chips.

"You can say that again." Freddie threw down his cards. "And I don't mean just at poker."

Brady's laugh boomed in the room. To Lillian Russell, the pink on Mrs. Langtry's cheek was almost a blush. Strange that this Englishwoman should look even younger than she; stranger still that while she had Jim, who at thirty-seven would be just right for Langtry, Lillie should have Gebhard, who was practically a youngster for all his cigar-smoking and big talk. And yet, with all his brains, Jim looked up to Freddie just because the kid talked smooth, dressed sharp, and belonged to the right clubs.

"You know the newspaper boys thought we'd be at each other like a couple of cats. I hate to disappoint them, but we'd have to like each other. I don't think anything nastier's been written about two women than about us two."

"Yes," said Lillie. "We're sisters under the sin."

Again Jim's laugh echoed in the room.

Lillie closed her New York season March 16, 1887, with *Lady Clancarty,* in which William Winter called her acting of the name part "superb." She prepared for a tour which would take her to California and back, averaging nearly 70,000 miles. She longed for a specially designed private car to make the trip more comfortable, something luxurious as well as expressive of her own personality. In discussing her ideas with friends she met the colorfully slippery Colonel William D'Alton Mann.

A legitimate Civil War Union colonel, a newspaperman with a skin-peeling style and a penchant for blackmail, he was also the inventor of the Mann railway carriage, a Pullman-rivaling sleeping car which he had patented in 1872. Colonel Mann hadn't done too well with his invention, but he talked Lillie into letting him design a special car for her. Freddie immediately volunteered to pay for it. He wanted his Lillie to have the best on the road as well as at home, but the expense was far more than he had imagined, for Colonel Mann outdid himself. He produced something that, even to Lillie, was on the gaudy side, lacking only purple sails to make it look like Cleopatra's barge.

She christened it the *Lalee,* East Indian for "flirt," and this dreamboat of a private railway car enhanced the Langtry legend as no other means of transportation could have done. Its circus quality struck the eye, its knockout garishness appealed to her theater sense (wasn't it the only one of its kind?), and its luxury rivaled J. P. Morgan's yacht, the *Corsair.* Seventy-five feet long, it was painted in Lillie's favorite bright Jersey blue with bas-relief wreaths of gold lilies twined on both sides around the name *Lalee.* The roof was sparkling white, and under it was worked a decorative brass frieze of stylized lilies. At either end there were massive platforms of teak imported from India.

Her bedroom in the car was upholstered in green silk brocade, and everything in it—ceiling, walls, dressing table—was curiously padded and bustled to resist shock in case of collision. The bathroom fittings were gleaming silver. The two sitting rooms had rose-colored silk curtains, trimmed with bunched Brussels lace, and they opened into a large saloon or drawing room in cream and green brocade imported from Lyons, France. This was filled with comfortable chairs, bookcases, tables, and a piano in one corner. Beyond were two guest rooms, a maid's room with sewing machine, Beverly's pantry, a kitchen, and compartments for the rest of the staff.

Beneath the car were huge ice chests "big enough to house a

whole stag," Colonel Mann explained proudly. He had also partitioned the frame with thirteen floors and eleven ceilings for extra safety. These were excellent "crash" precautions but made the *Lalee* so heavy it had to be rerouted around a number of shaky bridges along the way. Not even Queen Victoria had ever traveled in such high style, and Lillie grew fond of her home away from home. She asked Coghlan to take one of the guest rooms, but, mindful of Freddie's jealousy and newspaper gossip, he expressed his preference for regular accommodations, although he gladly joined her at meals.

She rarely stayed at hotels now, although the railroad yards were inclined to be noisy. She loved to watch the ever-changing "savage" American countryside—so different from England's parklike confines—through the *Lalee's* broad windows. The car brought her into contact with many odd characters intent on seeing the great actress at every whistle stop.

Freddie was in the San Francisco station when she descended from the *Lalee,* after the very remunerative tour. The provincial critics had all echoed the New York bravos: "the glamour of London drawing rooms was over her still."

In accordance with Abe Hummel's advice, Freddie had leased a house for her on 21st Street, just off Valencia Street. Now Lillie prepared to declare herself a resident and citizen of California with General W. H. L. Barnes, prominent San Francisco attorney and politician, representing her. Hummel was trying to speed up divorce proceedings, through George Lewis, by offering Edward Langtry a large sum of money not to contest the suit. Edward maddeningly refused to be bought off, and it seemed that a divorce on statutory grounds of desertion would not be legal in England. Whether she pleaded non-support or desertion, Edward could argue that she had left him. Then there was the problem of the child, which had to be handled with extreme delicacy. Perhaps her chances might be better if she bought property in California and became a bona fide American citizen. Freddie was all for that, but Lillie was reluctant because she thought of herself as an Englishwoman.

Like many Westerners General Barnes was genial and expansive. He knew of an ideal ranch property, a beautiful place,

228

just the spot for Mrs. Langtry and Mr. Gebhard to raise horses. As for the divorce, it was a question of time; sooner or later her husband would tire of contesting the suit. Meanwhile she would be an American citizen with a splendid investment in the booming West. The ranch idea was appealing. Though it would be expensive, Freddie was eager to pay his share and Lillie was making money "hand over fist," as the press put it. She looked forward to having a stable and encouraged Freddie in the joint venture. It was what he needed so as not to feel overshadowed by her stage career.

The ranch would also provide them with a retreat from prying eyes, a place where they could live as man and wife without subterfuge. Thus during the frantic two weeks Lillie performed in San Francisco during July, 1887, she bought the property with Freddie, sight unseen. She spent hours picking out furniture and decorations to make over her Western ranch home to the Jersey Lily's taste, and applied for her American citizenship.

General Barnes, in order to avoid publicity for his famous client, prevailed on the officials to bring the court books to her home on Valencia Street. But his efforts at secrecy boomeranged. The newspapers reported that, regarding Mrs. Langtry, Justice Field in the Circuit Court had crustily declared, "the method adopted in her naturalization was irregular and invalid"; "the right of citizenship was one of the most important which the people of this country possessed and it must not be jeopardized or cheapened by opening the doors to fraud," as carting off the court records seemed to entail.

Lillie felt she was being unfairly penalized, but when she went to court Justice Field was mollified and signed the document.

"I don't feel any different," she told Freddie ruefully.

"You don't have to, so long as this helps get your divorce. I don't care what country you're citizen of or where you live."

"You'd live in England with me?" she asked, testing him.

"I'd go wherever you go, so long as I could get back to New York now and then."

"That's just the way I feel about London!"

"We'll raise horses here and race them back East," he said enthusiastically. "We can even ship the best to England. By God, it'll be the most famous breeding farm in the world. The home of champions!"

Lillie smiled. Of course it was too good to be true—like all extravagant dreams and schemes—but Freddie believed it. And never had he looked so boyish and lovable.

fifteen

BEVERLY, the perfect butler, was sent ahead with the furniture and baggage to civilize the wilderness for his mistress. In black frock coat, wing collar, and high hat, he set out as casually as if sauntering into Rotten Row. Lillie dismissed her company, then followed with Freddie and a party of friends. She felt like an explorer pushing off into the unknown.

They left at sunrise on the *Lalee,* hitched to a special train, stopping at the edge of what Lillie thought was "a stupendous lake, with ferry boats crossing and recrossing in every direction." Actually, it was an arm of San Francisco Bay, across which Napa Valley trains were ferried. The *Lalee* was brought over in the usual manner and tied up to another engine. The *Lalee* reached the end of the line at a little whistle stop called St. Helena, all of whose inhabitants had turned out to whoop greetings at the Jersey Lily in her fabulous Cleopatra's barge.

Lillie was pleased to see Beverly, immaculate as always, waiting beside two ancient stage coaches he had apparently commandeered, ready to creak the party over the last difficult twenty miles to the ranch. The traditional Wild West vehicles were rickety, the road steep, rough, and winding, and the leather thongs that passed for springs absorbed few of the bumps. Teeth rattling, they clung tightly and fearfully as the coaches jolted along narrow cowpaths, lunged up corkscrew turns, shuddered around switchbacks, and skidded on mountain-goat trails bare inches from ravines. Some gasped and shut their eyes. Only Beverly remained impassive, arms crossed and expressionless, bobbing next to the driver on the lead coach.

231

Never had Lillie seen such savagely remote and inaccessible country! The press would never bother them here, nor any other intruder; it might as well be the end of the world. Surely, their purchase had been idiotic!

When they gained a pass, a saddle in the towering mountain chain, the huge plateau spread below them was impressively beautiful. The high, dry summer air had a sparkling tang, trees and vegetation a blinding greenness, and nature had never before been so magically lovely. Freddie took her hand and they looked at each other without speaking. This view was big, fresh, limitless, breath-taking. Like the Alps, yet unlike them. Untouched.

"By God!" Freddie shaded his eyes. "By God, this is paradise!"

Comprising about twelve square miles, the Guenoc Stock Ranch was located in Coyote Valley, in the southeastern part of Lake County near the Napa County line. It was about eight miles from the nearest post office in Middleton. Lillie's tract had once been three farms, 4,200 acres for which she had paid $81,000. Freddie had paid $44,000 for the 3,200 acres adjoining. The house on his property was about 100 yards from the larger ranch house on "Langtry Farms," and they shared an extensive lake closed in by mountains at one end, perfect for swimming and watering stock—of course they were going to have a lot of cattle.

Lillie's house was square and serviceable, high-framed and built of hand-hewn beams that gave it a pioneer look. She saw no gardens of any kind, only corrals along which about thirty cowboys were lounging. As the stage coaches pulled up, some were sprawling, some rolling cigarettes, some laughing, all staring hard.

Beverly turned apologetically to Lillie. "They're all in your employ, madam. A motley crew, I believe the term is, but hardly the ruffians they pretend to be." He helped Lillie down. "Dinner will be ready in due time, but you must make allowances for the service. Domestics are unavailable in this territory, so I have obtained Indian squaws from the reservation."

232

He gave a deprecating little bow. "There is a language difficulty, and they do not bathe. I am afraid madam will find them rather pungent indoors."

Under Beverly's sergeant-major supervision, a relay of stone-faced Indian women in pigtails, buckskins, and moccasins served the party a simple banquet of broiled trout, roast beef, quail, potatoes, and green beans—all products of the ranch—washed down with the champagne Freddie had nursed over the mountain pass.

So began an ideal existence for Lillie—informal, carefree, and unobserved by anyone except close friends. She explored every inch of her property on a cow pony, envisioning great avenues of eucalyptus, formal gardens with a swan pool, perhaps a hedge maze, the house modernized and enlarged on artistic lines. She "discovered" a sulphur spring. Remembering the benefits of Saratoga Springs water, she and Freddie decided to bottle their own and sell it for "medicinal purposes." Then they "discovered" what a cowboy claimed was a quicksilver mine. This too seemed worthy of development. There were apple, peach, and pear orchards, but especially the extensive vineyards delighted her, and she became intrigued at the possibility of producing Langtry wine. Telegrams were dispatched and, in time, an expert hustled over from Bordeaux to "cope with it," as she put it.

Most important was the hiring of a manager for the joint ranch. Finally they chose one Charles W. ("Doc") Aby, a good friend of Mr. Buck, editor of the New York *Spirit of the Times* (another dragon Lillie had tamed). Aby had been stud groom for Lucky Baldwin, a notorious gambler and horse plunger who had entertained Lillie and Freddie at his California ranch. Aby was one of the most voluble men Lillie had ever met. He fell in immediately with all of her ideas and guaranteed to Freddie that his ranch would indeed be the home of champions.

He talked Lillie into buying Friar Tuck, a fine English stallion by Hermit, plus some expensive brood mares. He brought in a crew of laborers from San Francisco to build a mile-long race track on Freddie's place. Besides raising good blood stock, he planned to put in 700 acres of wheat, barley, and oats, and run about 300 head of good graded cattle.

Aby made it sound like a gigantically successful operation. Lillie had the skepticism of the professional, but she was too happy to care. The first weeks were an idyll; then it turned into a grand house party when friends streamed in as they might have done at a resort hotel. Alterations were going on in the house, new barns were going up, construction and projects were everywhere in progress. Cowboys and guests rode, fished, hunted, and whooped it up at will. The only hazards were occasional rattlesnakes, someone with too much champagne falling off the front porch and breaking a leg, or a drunken cowboy pinking a friend with his six-shooter.

Beverly was now a hotel manager and leaned heavily on the French chef, Mézirand, especially when an elaborate Dutch oven was built to provide Mrs. Langtry with bread light in texture instead of the prevalent sour dough. Mézirand later complained about the difficulties of catering to Mrs. Langtry's tastes. (In addition to the regular meals over which Freddie presided, Lillie liked after-midnight suppers of cold cuts and champagne.) And he added with Gallic bluntness, "Mr. Gebhard is a mere figurehead. We look at him as the great bouncer, and he will probably remain until he gets the grand bounce himself."

In that golden time the ranch was paradise, any idea was feasible, and damn the expense. They were prodigal children in a prodigal land. They were in love, nothing was impossible, and dreams came true. But idylls end and snakes sneak into Eden. Lillie was an international figure, a famous actress in mid-career. The bags of mail forwarded to the ranch—crank letters, proposals, requests for money, gushing letters announcing the christenings of Lillie Langtry Joneses, Smiths, and Browns, as well as business and legal communications—all reminded her of that fact.

She looked at Freddie, scowling over his cigar as he read the racing results in old New York newspapers. He looked tanned and fit, but he couldn't forget Fifth Avenue, his clubs, the

234

bright lights. He was a party man and the West—big, empty, and beautiful—was probably dull to him. Now he sighed, glanced at Lillie, and smiled. How lovely she was with her shirt opened at the throat, her eyes a deep blue-gray, her lips half-opened. Soft and alluring, and her tight trousers fitting so seductively. And how that woman could ride!

"Any more from Judge Roy Bean?" he asked, indicating her letters.

"Yes," she said excitedly, "and the best yet. He's changed the name of Vinegaroon to Langtry! The greatest honor I've ever had." She laughed delightedly. "I gather it isn't much of a place, but it will be now that the Southern Pacific goes through. He wants me to visit Langtry the next tour I make."

"We'll have to do that just to see the old fraud."

"The old dear, you mean. You know, I wrote offering to present the town with a handsome drinking fountain, and this is his answer. Listen! 'If there's one thing the folks don't drink out here in Langtry, it's water. If you could make that there fountain spout whiskey, then we'd sure snap it up quick.' Don't you love that, Freddie?"

Judge Roy Bean, the Law west of the Pecos, barkeep on the side, subscribed to a New York theatrical weekly and tacked every picture of Lillie he could find on the walls of his saloon-courtroom. Every article about her went into his scrapbooks. He became an authority on the Jersey Lily, and even took to trimming his grizzly beard like the Prince of Wales's. Judge Bean made a special trip to Chicago during Lillie's first tour and returned home with a prized picture of her as Kate Hardcastle. Once a cow thief appearing before him claimed to have seen Lillie on stage and was promised a pardon if he told all about the lovely lady.

Langtry, Texas. What a conceit! And yet how heartwarming to be immortalized, to imagine her town on maps in the years to come, prospering, turning into a big city . . .

"Lillie," Freddie was saying. "Aren't you getting restless?"

"Maybe a little, darling. I've been thinking of rehearsals and the new season. Coghlan says—"

"I know. We've been here about six weeks now, but we could

235

still make the big races at Saratoga. I'd like to see my horse Eole run in the late classic. My trainer thinks he has a good chance. What do you say?"

Aby told them not to worry, and Henri Descelles, the vineyardist, kissed his fingers and assured Lillie she would soon be tasting her own *vin extraordinaire*. Then came the jolting ride back to St. Helena, sanctuary in the *Lalee*, and the long trip across the continent loaded with souvenirs, fruit from Langtry Farms, and a 400-pound buck in the ice chest.

Back in New York, it was hard to believe they had ever been at the ranch. Beverly looked no different, and operated just as efficiently at 23rd Street as he had done in the wilds. More interviews, then Saratoga, the races in the broiling late-August sun, gambling at Dick Canfield's Casino, side trips to buy mares for Aby, and then rehearsals.

Sarah Bernhardt was in town accompanied by her son, Maurice, who acted as her interpreter and cleared everything for her in his capacity as secretary-manager and back-rubber. She was pleased by Lillie's success, and she fascinated dinner guests in the 23rd Street house. Few grasped her rapid French, but her magnetism was a universal language. Freddie was tickled when she caressed his cheek and called him *"beau garçon."* Lillie often breakfasted with mother and son in their Hoffman House suite, gabbing about Paris, New York, the stage, and *la boxe*. The handsome Maurice, who had seen Charlie Mitchell, the English heavyweight champion, fight John L. Sullivan, the world champion, to a draw at Baron Rothschild's Chantilly estate that year, was wild about the sport.

Sarah ridiculed boxing with all her laughable intensity, then at the urging of her son she challenged Lillie to a bout. Maurice produced some gloves, tied them on the actresses' hands, and squared them off. Sarah went at it with her usual dramatic gusto, forcing Lillie to flailing, while Referee Maurice dodged about, grinning and shouting *"Bon! Bon!"* as they swatted and lunged clumsily.

"But yes," Sarah decided breathlessly, *"la boxe* is a great art."

236

In spite of Sarah's exaggerated eccentricities, the baroque whims press agents dreamed up to publicize her, and her satin-lined coffin, which Lillie had seen in her cluttered trophy room in her Boulevard Pereire home, she was the gayest and most mischievous of companions. They sat for Sarony together, although Lillie was irked with the photographer for making her "simply look pretty when she was beautiful." The bearded Bohemian had his troubles posing them. Singly or together, Sarah unintentionally spoiled shot after shot, breaking them up with jokes and funny remarks in French, most of them at Sarony's expense.

"Ah, these Americans," she told Lillie. "They are vulgar and we are supposed to laugh; we are witty and—*pouf!*—they explode." And she pointed derisively as Sarony inserted another plate and cursed to himself. "They are serious at the silly and silly at the serious."

Bills for expenses at Langtry Farms kept coming, plus legal fees for General Barnes. She discussed these matters with her lawyer—bald, gargoyle-faced Abe Hummel of the incredible firm of Howe and Hummel. She kept hearing how these attorneys freed murderers and robbers, made judges apologize to pimps, whores, and madams, besides operating a profitable blackmail business in breach-of-promise cases. She did not doubt these scabrous stories. But Abe was always charming, thoughtful, and helpful to her. He continued hopeful about her divorce and thought the ranch a poor investment.

"Better let me take care of your money, Mrs. Langtry. Invest it in mortgages on Manhattan Island, and I'll guarantee that some day you'll be a multimillionaire. Real estate's moving uptown, and every tenement, warehouse, and brownstone will ultimately be worth a fortune. But good luck tonight! I'll be there. You know, I never miss an opening."

As in a Looking Glass was one of Lillie's greatest successes and her first portrayal of a sophisticated bad woman. Although it was said she played the cruel, despicable Lena Despard "to prove her art is not limited to comedy and to satisfy the public greed for novelty," she exulted in the change from former sweet, willowy, ingenue parts. It was a switch, too, for Maurice Barrymore, already known as a matinée idol, to play the wicked Jack Fortinbras. He was married to the actress Georgiana Drew, and was an attractive man. A *most* attractive man.

Barrymore and Robert Hilliard, another member of the cast, were a high-spirited pair. They carried on a joking rivalry, happily igniting Freddie's jealousy by caressing Lillie more ardently than was called for. He said nothing until the night he came upon them in her dressing room, which he regarded as forbidden territory to all males but himself. Barrymore and Hilliard egged him on to fight. Freddie would have agreed if Lillie hadn't interfered. He couldn't afford to stay angry with her, and she knew exactly how to handle him. The story leaked out after a reporter pumped Lillie's dresser. Then it appeared that Maurice Barrymore and Robert Hilliard were both madly in love with her, the former going so far as to kiss her shoes before every performance. Freddie was pictured as gunning for both of them, Lillie waiting serenely for bodies to fall.

It was gilt-edged rot, of course, with the papers running columns of denials, denunciations, and variations, until the triangle was turned into a catchy music hall song with the chorus, "He kissed the popular actress's shoes, but it wouldn't agree with me." Given such a great box-office boost, the run of the play was extended. It was amazing, Lillie reflected, how Freddie's impetuous blunders turned to gold.

By February she was off again in the *Lalee,* and the provincial theatergoers poured in to see her. She had reached such an eminence and become such an attraction that it hardly mattered what the critics said about her. People *had* to see Mrs. Langtry who personified beauty, glamour, and the stage. Freddie joined her now and then, but spent most of his time in New York, living in the 23rd Street house and tending to his own nebulous affairs.

Everything went smoothly except at a one-night stand in Oswego, New York, when the theater caught fire. The house was jammed, but the audience kept its head. Everyone filed out into the snow and bitter cold to watch the house burn to the ground in twenty minutes.

Frightening enough, but nothing like the fire in Bridgeport,

238

Connecticut, where she was playing *Pygmalion and Galatea*. The green baize curtain, concealing the pedestal on which she stood as the living statue, suddenly blazed up. It seemed the stage was on fire. The audience screamed and started to bolt in panic. Lillie continued in her part in a loud voice. Miraculously, the audience was reassured, and the fire was extinguished without damage. Afterward, P. T. Barnum, who was in a box, congratulated her on her coolness.

During the tour a newspaper trumpeted that from an investment of Mrs. Langtry's in Carson City, Nevada, (a speculation Hummel had arranged) workmen boring for water on her property had struck a vein of silver assaying at $510 a ton. Called typical "Langtry luck," it was assumed she could now "build her 23rd Street fence with silver brick posts."

She was reported ill with neuralgia in Chicago on February 25, 1888, and was forced to miss several performances. The neuralgia business was not true. She had just received a telegram notifying her of Dean Le Breton's death, and she was deeply grieved. She had loved her father, happy memories of him flooded back, making what she was doing seem terribly unimportant. She regretted not being able to drop everything and go to England, but going would serve no purpose. Besides, Mama was as capable in distress as at other times. One thing she did know: she would see to it that her mother and Jeanne Marie came to America to live with her.

In Texas, Langtry luck was again evident as their train broke down. It was a crisis because they had to be in Fort Worth within an hour or cancel the engagement. The entire house was sold out at top prices, and Lillie had learned that failing to keep commitments often influenced timid theater managers on the itinerary. Stranded miles from any settlement in a countryside flat and arid in the baking sun, the company fretted as Lillie sat reading in the *Lalee*. If there was nothing to be done, then there was nothing to be done, and "Don't let's fuss, *please*." But the instant she heard a train tooting in the distance she was out on the track.

It was a special chartered by Colonel Tom Ochiltree, a prominent Texas politician, newspaperman, and public speaker, taking out a hunting party. Here was a made-to-order situation, with Lillie the Lady in Distress and the colonel as White Knight. Within minutes she was sipping bourbon with Colonel Ochiltree in his private car, the company and baggage aboard his train and heading for Fort Worth.

"It is not so much her beauty that appeals to me," he later told James Smyth-Pigott, her fellow actor, at the Carleton Club in London. "It is the splendid dignity and frankness of her carriage and her superb brain. She knows more than all of us put together."

Regretting she hadn't the time to visit Roy Bean, she went on to Los Angeles for a week at the Grand Opera House. The critics welcomed Lillie as "one of us" and heaped praise on her. They expected her to rest at her ranch. "There under the blue skies and golden sunshine of this Italy of America," one newspaper editorialized, "Mrs. Langtry will find recreation after her long season of work and travel and will reign, like a queen, over the hundreds of men and women employed on her princely estate, all of whom vow allegiance to the most beautiful and popular of California's adopted daughters."

She played another week in San Francisco, ending her season there. Much as she wanted to, she had to forego visiting Langtry Farms. Mrs. Le Breton and Jeanne Marie were on their way to New York, and Lillie was determined to greet them at the pier. The decision was hard on Freddie, who had joined her and was eager to stay at the ranch, but he readily agreed—one of the things she liked best about him. Voluble as ever, Aby came on with news of the ranch, seeking money for improvements, more barns and breeding stock. He brought fish and game as gifts, and several bottles of excellent wine from the vineyardist with her picture on the label. Descelles was optimistic, but a new California bonding law prevented the sale of Langtry wine.

Lillie was back in New York June 16, 1888, "bringing ample supplies of venison, killed by her own fair hands for friends" and was "now nestling in her charming metropolitan cottage with its historic fence." She was supposedly to remain only long enough to meet her mother and daughter (and her brother

Clement, who was going to Langtry Farms to see to her interests there) and let Freddie enter Eole in a few races before returning to Langtry Farms. Rumors of her secret marriage persisted, and she was forced to make repeated denials.

It was satisfying to live as a family. There was plenty of room in the big house for Mrs. Le Breton, Jeanne Marie, and her French governess. Mama accepted New York as equably as she had accepted London after her long sojourn in Jersey. Everything Lillie did was right; she knew little of her daughter's theatrical career, looking on it "from afar as a glittering pastime of her wonderful progeny." A pretty, dainty, little woman, at seventy she was plump, pink, and white as a baby. She held her husband in reverence, praising him in "a quiet, proud, wifely way . . . as my dear husband William Le Breton, the dean, as if everything identifying the man was in the title."

She wore simple, expensive clothes and always ate her meals in state wearing her best dress and family jewels. If no one were present except Lillie and a woman friend, "both of them in tea gowns or deshabille, Mrs. Le Breton put them to shame, with her lovely silver hair elaborately dressed, gloves on her plump hands, and at least a fan or bouquet." Without any thought of herself, petted and adored and given every luxury by Lillie, she had a commendable innocence and lack of curiosity concerning her daughter's affairs.

Lillie entertained only intimate friends now, people like Jim Brady, Porter Asche, or Mrs. Baron Frederick Blanc, as the newspaper referred to her. Occasional parties disturbed no one in the rest of the house. Freddie was always discreet, and his impeccable clothes and good-natured charm pleased Mrs. Le Breton. He played with seven-year-old Jeanne Marie, helped her learn English, fitted in smoothly as a member of the family. Mama found this praiseworthy, and she gushed to Lillie about it: this was exactly what the little girl, lacking a real father, needed.

To escape New York's deadly heat and be close to a track where Freddie's horses were running, they went to Long

Branch, New Jersey, then a popular ocean resort, Presidents Grant and Garfield both having owned summer homes there. They arrived July 4, spent a week at the West End Hotel, and then confounded puritan minds and revived marriage talk by renting the big house of George Washington Brown, a former mayor. "Gebhard's trunks went in then with the same load as Lily's," an observant reporter noted, "his horse and carriages into the barn, and he is a completely homelike dweller. So are Mrs. Langtry's mother and two nieces [Jeanne Marie and her governess], confirming the wedlock theory in assemblage of Mrs. Langtry's relatives under the same roof as Gebhard. A positive announcement of a marriage in September was made by ex-Judge Bedford and two other members of the Union Club, but Mrs. Langtry said this was a lie."

Still the headlines kept asking IS MRS. LANGTRY MARRIED? And it seemed she had to be to condone so casual and cozy a living arrangement. The gossip was that she and Freddie had been married, following a quiet divorce on the Coast in June, that this was their honeymoon. A close watch was maintained on the handsome, spacious, wooden house "surrounded by wooded grounds an eighth of a mile from the shore." The secluded couple were not there often. They went driving on pleasant afternoons, usually in an open victoria seated side by side, "a sightly pair for Gebhard is a handsome fellow and the Lily's beauty is heightened by becoming summer toilets." They drove to the races at Monmouth Park three days a week, dropped in at the West End Hotel morning concerts, and stopped by there for the evening dances. Freddie sometimes waltzed with lady friends, but Lillie never danced. They were always mobbed by staring people, and she was described as "invariably ladylike."

One hot moonlit night they walked along the sandy beach of Pleasure Bay and took a swim in the raw. Frolicking happily, Freddie was the first to see neighborhood Peeping Toms stealing up on them. He called to Lillie. They bolted out of the water, and she had only time to slip a petticoat over her dripping body as they fled down the beach with their clothes in their arms. They were never positively identified, but for a long time afterward a certain newspaper liked to refer to her as "the heroine of the memorable nightgown imbroglio at Pleasure Bay."

Porter Asche, who was once married to Aimée Crocker of San Francisco, was often with them in Long Branch. His feelings toward Lillie were obvious, although, because of his friendship with Freddie, he kept them to himself until he could get her alone. Lillie made sure this rarely happened. The two men regarded themselves as rival sportsmen and made much of their stables. Freddie's horse Rosarium was a consistent winner that year, as was Porter's Geraldine. They quarreled hotly about their horses' respective superiority, and it was Lillie who suggested a match race at Monmouth Park. It was arranged, with their friends betting heavily. Lillie had to back Rosarium, but she hedged by secretly placing a larger amount on Geraldine. The result was just as she expected—Geraldine outran Rosarium with ease. Freddie was bitterly disappointed that his good Eastern pony fell far behind the great sprinter from the Pacific. She never told Freddie about her second bet, nor about Porter's impassioned proposal.

Freddie reveled in parties—talked, planned, and was obsessed with them. The New York *Evening Star* for July 21, 1888, reported that Lillie had visited Hollywood, John Hooey's Long Branch retreat, on Thursday night for the first time and that she and Freddie were guests of honor at a dinner given by Colonel Michael O'Brien, the agent of the Southern Express Company. The private dining room was changed into a bower of roses for the event, and

> Mrs. Langtry was accompanied by Mrs. Le Breton and two other ladies. The gentlemen in the party besides the host were Freddie Gebhard, T. Henry French, Fred Gould, and Edwin Thorne. There was fine music, Mrs. Langtry delivered a dramatic recitation, and Mr. Gebhard likewise. It was the first time Mr. Gebhard had given evidence of ability in dramatic delivery.

Freddie's offering was a surprise he had prepared for Lillie, and he did well—indeed she thought he might be a good actor

243

if he worked hard. He was as pleased at her approval as a second-grade boy given a gold star in reading.

James Buchanan Brady, who arrived late, said "Whyncha tell me you were gonna perform, huh, Freddie?" his swollen bowling pin of a body shaking with laughter. "You got yourself another leading man there, Lillie. He'll rock Broadway back on its heels."

"This is positively my last appearance," said Freddie.

"You were delightful," said Mrs. Le Breton. "My dear husband, the dean, would have loved it."

Then Brady took Lillie aside. "I got a little trinket for you."

"Another?" she said, incredulously.

"I pick 'em up all the time in my travels, and I know you appreciate diamonds like I do." He held out some handsome diamond earrings. "And I ain't wearing these things on my own ears yet!"

He guffawed. Lillie studied his ballooning porcine face. Jim was so homely, but so amusing—a shrewd, generous, loyal, and lonely man who gave diamonds to women he admired and expected nothing in return but a picture for his gallery of beauties. Strange he should do so well at business—he was an unbeatable salesman for a railroad-supply company—and be so attracted to Freddie, the nonchalant man-about-town. Not so strange, perhaps, since socially Freddie was all the things Jim wasn't.

On the way to Saratoga in August, they entertained a large party at a box in Tony Pastor's. The variety performers Rice and Barton in singing a tropical song came to a risqué verse about Lillie and Freddie, hesitated, and broke down as the audience smirked at the couple in their box. Freddie glared until Lillie whispered to him.

Abe Hummel called on them at 23rd Street to admit there was nothing new on the divorce. Edward would not be bought off and had successfully fought off every effort to bring suit. Abe also assured them on the blackmail attempt of Colonel William D'Alton Mann, who liked to make the rich share the wealth by exposing the lurid incidents in their past. His biographies were masterful jobs, colorfully written, bound in Florentine leather and stamped in gold. The price always seemed absurdly high for a book until the colonel brought out the juicy pages he had so kindly omitted. He had made as much as $90,000 on his biographies, and now he had written what he learned about Lillie while discussing plans for the *Lalee*. He felt it was worth $200,000.

Abe Hummel was the perfect lawyer to squelch Colonel Mann. He knew something about everybody, and what he had on the colonel was worth an equal $200,000—perhaps more. Faced with a stalemate, Mann reluctantly agreed to destroy his biography, but he had a long memory. Undoubtedly he would get back at Lillie in time.

Freddie took her in his arms to soothe her and led her to an upstairs bedroom.

"You really think this solves everything, don't you?" she said, prepared to give in, as she always had to, in the thing he did best.

"It always has, Lillie. It always has."

Clement Le Breton wrote that he was enjoying himself at Langtry Farms. The hunting was marvelous, and he had many trophies. He was proudest of a huge grizzly bear which he was having stuffed and mounted. Clement was now as proud of his sister as he had been in the old tomboy days. As a lawyer he understood her difficulties with Edward, and he liked Freddie, although he didn't like the idea of her becoming or marrying an American. Now he asked when she was coming back to California.

Now that Mama and Jeanne were acclimatized to America and prepared to stay in New York, after their summer in Long Branch, Lillie wanted to go out to the ranch. Freddie was planning to ship his best horses out there, and Aby had joined them at Saratoga to buy some new ones. Everything was decided—they would follow Aby and the horses in the *Lalee*. Then came the shattering news of an accident: Aby's train jumped the rails at Shohola Glen, Pennsylvania, plunged down an embankment, crushing some of the cars and burning others. From the first telegraphed reports, it seemed a ghastly tragedy, and Lillie and Freddie hurried to the scene.

No one was killed, but many passengers were seriously injured. Doc Aby had been pinned down by one of his precious horses and had cradled the head of the dying animal. He was hurt and had lost blood. Arriving in the atmosphere of doom, Lillie tore her petticoat to bind his bleeding head. Describing her attentions afterward, Aby said she was the only angel he had ever known on earth—so she must have seemed as a lovely, cool-headed nurse.

Freddie was dazed over their losses. Her mare, Pauline, worth $1,500, which she had ridden in Central Park only a week ago, was dead. He had lost ten good horses, including his fine champion Eole, all of them winners at Long Branch, Monmouth Park, and Saratoga. Their total value was estimated at $300,000. Aby had lost an animal of his own, and it looked as if a few others were so badly injured they'd have to be shot.

"It's a mess," Freddie said, and never had he been so subdued or serious. "My horses are just about cleaned out, and they weren't insured. Why in hell did this have to happen to us? We were just getting started out there, and now I'm through."

Playboys weren't made to wrestle with disaster, but it wasn't in Lillie's nature to lie there tasting dirt after she'd been knocked down. Of course, Freddie's loss was far greater, but they had been looking forward to a time alone and to building up the ranch—and they'd do it yet! Their imminent departure was in all the newspapers—even in a sheet as small as the *Calistogan,* a weekly in Calistoga, California, a little town at the head of Napa Valley and nine miles from St. Helena. Its headlines proclaimed "The Lily and Fred are traveling to California in their special car."

"We're not beaten yet, Freddie, believe me! We'll buy more horses, and we'll keep at it. We'll succeed together. I feel awful about the horses, but I'm glad no one was killed. And we'll find another champion as good as Eole!"

246

He clutched her in desperation. She felt like a mother as she caressed him, a sensation she did not particularly like.

"There's nobody like you, Lillie."

"Thanks. You can have my autograph."

"Don't make fun of me," he pleaded.

"Freddie! I only want to have fun with you."

The blow was too much for Freddie. He hadn't the stomach to go out to the ranch after that accident. The trip was canceled, and Lillie began to plan her fall season. She was tired of handling all the business and financial details of production and, hearing of a suitable manager, telegraphed to Frank Carlos Griffith who was running a summer attraction in Camden, New Jersey. Lillie interviewed him at her home. Young Griffith, excited at his rise in fortune in being summoned by such a great star, "found her a beautiful, gracious woman who put me at once at ease." She hired him at the then comfortable salary of $60 a week. A month later, in late September, Lillie again took to the road with her company for the much-in-demand *As in a Looking Glass*.

Freddie stayed in New York, living with Mrs. Le Breton and Jeanne Marie, supposedly rebuilding his stables. Occasionally he surprised Lillie in faraway cities. She'd return to her hotel suite, or the *Lalee* when the railroad yards weren't too far from the theater, and find him waiting for her, a satisfied smile on his face. Doc Aby had recovered and was keeping them posted about the ranch. The place was still being run like a hotel. Freddie's friends were free to visit any time, and their antics were written up in newspapers in scandalous detail.

This tour was as successful as the others, Griffith being especially helpful. All the time Lillie looked ahead apprehensively to the opening of *Macbeth* on Broadway after Christmas. She was said to have invented a new style of costume, "robes of coarse stuff covered with splendid jewels as was the custom of the time." The play was to be mounted in a sumptuous manner hitherto unknown in New York, the scenery and props budgeted at an unprecedented $8,000.

"How do you think it looks?" Lillie asked Griffith at dress

rehearsal. The manager was optimistic, and she put a hand on his shoulder. "From now on your salary will be $100 a week," she said, moving off to her dressing room and leaving Griffith staring, since he hadn't asked for a raise.

Because of Coghlan's Shakespearean experience and the fact that he'd played Shylock to Ellen Terry's Portia in London, he took care of the staging and was listed as director in the program, Lillie as manageress. There was a special note saying that the scenery, costumes, and properties were the exclusive property of Mrs. Langtry. General admission to the Fifth Avenue Theater was 50¢; orchestra, $1.50; first balcony (first two rows), $1.50; first balcony, $1; second balcony (four front rows), 50¢; second balcony, 25¢, and boxes $12 and $15.

The play opened on January 21, and the loyal *Spirit of the Times* threw its riding crops in the air and acclaimed Lillie's Lady Macbeth the sensation of the week *and* the season. She was "admirable and rose to greatness; grand and exquisite." She got away from the established Siddonian traditions in the sleep-walking scene by trying to arouse pity for the poor, weak, dying Lady Macbeth, rather than in thrilling the audience. Dion Boucicault, who had seen all the great Lady Macbeths, threw up his hands and cried, "She is astounding."

All in all, the role was a vindication for Lillie. The critics might quarrel with her about nuances and that rot, but she had played Lady Macbeth and carried off the part triumphantly. What more could her detractors ask of an "amateur?" No, for this she hadn't relied on her beauty, ability to wear clothes, or her charming drawing-room manner. She was prouder of her acting than she had ever been before.

"Did you like it, Mama?" she asked Mrs. Le Breton.

"You were fine, but I don't like gloomy, unhealthy plays. Give me gay plays about happy people. There's enough sadness in the world without going back to murders of hundreds of years ago."

248

sixteen

Mrs. Langtry in *Macbeth* was such a novelty that she attracted the intellectual playgoers who had sniffed at her as a popular actress. Lillie enjoyed her *succés d'estime,* although she noted a slackening at the box office. The general public preferred her in glamourous, exciting roles, rather than in the old classic chestnuts expected of Ellen Terry, Helena Modjeska, and the other dramatic "institutions" of the day. *She* was the Jersey Lily. They could accept her Rosalind with its girl-boy twist, but, please, no more heavy, tragic roles for the scintillating, scandalous beauty!

Lillie took note of the tremendous gap separating the critics and the public. It was hard to please herself and be a good businesswoman at the same time. Ah, well! She toured the eastern cities in the spring of 1889, but her thoughts were on England, where there was a great demand for her. She hadn't been back in three years; she was homesick. She had had enough of her adopted country for a while. Freddie would just have to bear with her. He wasn't pleased, but she was going anyway. He'd come around, as always, and tag along. Everything would be so much easier if she were Mrs. Gebhard. Hummel had pulled wires and trumped up schemes, but the law was arbitrary. What could be done when Edward filed a convincing defense against her every time she brought suit?

Hummel urged her to be patient, but she had already waited close to nine years. Surely Edward must be getting some warped satisfaction from his stubbornness, while poor Freddie suffered because he would never believe her completely his until they were married. Always scandal, an illicit relationship, the whole divorce question tangled in the existence of Jeanne Marie. How good it was to work and not have the time to brood about things! thought Lillie. How much better it would be for Freddie if he could do the same!

This time her tour was interrupted by a siege of colds and grippe which caused a postponement at the Walnut Theater, Philadelphia, and she returned to New York for another engagement still feeling seedy. All the same, she was determined to go to England and surprised Griffith by asking him to stay on as her business manager.

"Book me sixteen weeks in the provinces, and London after that," she ordered.

As an American he was not familiar with the English theater, but he agreed to make arrangements by cable.

Lillie opened in *Esther Sandraz* in Chicago on June 14, a new play by Sidney Grundy, an English attorney. It was an immediate hit and potentially as durable a vehicle as *Looking Glass,* which it resembled. Grundy, in a congratulatory cable, reminded Lillie that she had refused the play four years earlier.

Esther Sandraz, the title character, was another good-bad woman in the daring tradition expected of Lillie, a type she was to portray in many variations over the years. It was overripe melodrama, but the audience loved it. They cheered her Esther more than her Lady Macbeth. Just as there was a law for the rich and one for the poor, so, Lillie thought, there were plays for critics atwitter for culture and other plays for an unsophisticated public thirsting for pure entertainment with a mild erotic kick. She couldn't please everyone, but it was good to have the paying majority in her favor.

"Do you *have* to go back to England?" Freddie grumbled.

"I need a change, darling."

"Who doesn't?" he said irritably. "Honest to God, it's hard living the way we do—on the front pages."

"You'll come on the next boat, won't you?"

"Sure. Why not? I've got nothing else to do."

"You could act, Freddie. I'd help you. It's not good spending all your time on fun and games. I've seen what it does to young

Englishmen. Or if acting doesn't appeal to you, I'm sure Jim Brady could find you something."

"You want me to work—is that it?"

"A steady diet of parties is bound to be tedious. I don't want to reform you, but everybody does something."

"Only because they have to, and I don't! Do gentlemen work in England? Does the Prince go to the office every day?" he sneered. "By God, Lillie, are you getting tired of me?"

"No, but what can we do? Live together like other people, keep house, raise children, go about as mister and missus? We can't. I'm no home girl, and you're no man about the house. We both have things to do. I have the stage, which I love, and you have—"

"You!" he exploded. "That's all I have. You!"

"Then keep me, Freddie. If you want me, keep me yours."

Freddie was so upset at the prospect of her leaving that she let him persuade her to rent the Oliver Doud Byron cottage in Long Branch. Things weren't easy between them now. He made love in desperation, hoping she would call off her trip, and they had bitter arguments. Lillie, who had always been so healthy, became ill with a nasal and bronchial condition close to pneumonia.

THE FAIR LILY IS VERY ILL, read the headlines, HER LUNGS SAID TO BE AFFECTED—A WRECK OF HER FORMER SELF. Doctors were quoted as saying her stage career might possibly be nearing a close. In any case, the Lily had wilted. On July 10 the Boston *Herald*, speaking as the mouthpiece of the strait-laced, happily announced:

> Those who saw her when she first came to this country hardly know her as the same woman now. She looked a blooming English Hebe then, her eyes still bright with youth, her complexion willowy and superb. She looks old now, her eyes are dull, the crows have come to stay, her face is colorless, and her complexion is like that of all actresses after years of excitement and late nights and stage paint, and her figure is portly and unharmonious.

The editorial *coup de grâce* expressed the righteous triumph of those who wanted to see her sins catch up with her.

251

The truth was that Lillie's mind, always clear and quick of decision, was benumbed as she was caught in a crossfire of treatments at the hands of incompetent doctors and Mrs. Le Breton, a great one for old-fashioned home remedies. The temperature was in the high eighties outside the Long Branch cottage, but Mama insisted on shutting all the windows, piling on the blankets, and making Lillie's room a Turkish bath. Lillie lay red-faced and sweating, tossing feverishly, too weak to resist.

"Freddie," she begged, "if you love me, do something. Get me a good doctor, somebody who knows something."

Jim Brady suggested a Dr. Curtis of Staten Island, who had cured his belly trouble "good." That doctor entered the bedroom and shuddered at the terrible heat. He looked into her eyes, palpated her, and ordered every window in the house flung wide open. Mrs. Le Breton was horrified.

"The newspapers have you all but buried, Mrs. Langtry, and no wonder. A simple summer cold's been turned into a crisis. I prescribe an immediate walk on the beach. Breathe deep of that sea air and eat all you want."

Lillie's strength quickly revived, her mind functioned with its old lightning efficiency. Freddie almost regretted having called Dr. Curtis when she cabled Griffith her approval of the tour itinerary which had been gathering dust. She confirmed her steamship reservations and superintended her maids in packing thirty trunks.

Accompanied by Mrs. Le Breton, Jeanne Marie, and a retinue of servants, Lillie sailed for England on the Cunard Line's *Servia*. On that July 13 the *Spirit of the Times* observed for posterity that her fame "was assured beyond all critics by her wonderful performance of Lady Macbeth." Reporters seeing her off remarked that her beauty was intact, her charm persuasive, and that of the two staterooms reserved for her use one was completely filled with gifts of fruits and flowers. Lillie assured them she would be back in a year. She spotted Bury Irwin Dasent.

"I'm not afraid to ask," he said with a smile. "Where's Freddie?"

"Just shy. He'll be along on the next boat."

"What would you say if *I* took this boat?" he said in a low voice.

"Ah, Bury," she chided, touching his cheek as the *Servia* blew a preliminary warning blast. "You poor, dear romantic! Don't you know when the play is over?"

Freddie did not take the next boat, nor the next, nor the next. He did not write, nor did Lillie as she impatiently awaited his arrival before her provincial tour. She conferred with Griffith and Coghlan. She went to Jersey for a holiday, rented a house outside St. Helier, saw mother and daughter settled, and returned to London. Sir George Lewis (he was now baronet) thought it wise to keep Jeanne Marie away from England for a time.

All her friends flocked around, and it was pleasant to be welcomed back so effusively. One would have thought she had returned from the dead. There was no use describing the beauties of America, its vastness and variety, the excitement of New York, Chicago, and San Francisco, because it would have been lost on them. She now preferred the leisurely British pace to the frenzied American tempo.

One of her early callers was Oscar Wilde, apparently bursting with news which he tried to conceal as he fished in his gaudy clothes for a cigarette case. Lillie indicated that she wanted to smoke, and his eyebrows rose comically.

"I smoke on stage—I might as well off. I like the taste of cigarettes."

"Amazing, aren't they?" he said, puffing happily. "But it's my corrupting influence. They'll say of me what that woman said of Byron: 'mad, bad, and dangerous to know.'" He giggled. "What a perfect epitaph!"

"How is Constance?"

"I'm the ideal husband, never under foot. In married life three is company and two is none. Didn't I tell you that the one charm of marriage is that it makes a life of deception absolutely necessary for both parties? And you know how I love deception."

253

"But aren't you in love?"

"Naturally. With you as always. One should always be in love. That is the reason one should never marry."

"That's real Wilde. Only I'm sure you've used it before."

"It's time-tested." He fumbled inside his bright jacket, withdrew a rolled-up manuscript, and gave it to her importantly. "There is a play I've written for you."

"And what part do I play?" she said, teasingly.

"It's called *Lady Windermere's Fan* and you play a woman with a grown-up illegitimate daughter."

"Now really, Oscar, do I look old enough to have a grown-up daughter of any description?" said Lillie, unconscious of irony. "Don't open the manuscript and don't read it to me. Put it away for twenty years."

"But, Lil," he said, with a theatrical groan, "I wrote it just for you. I've already spoken to George Alexander about it, and he's interested."

She knew Wilde as a poet. She had many times listened to his idle, amusing chatter, often seen him concocting trifles and intoxicating himself with his own words. But never had she conceived of him as a playwright. An older woman with an illegitimate daughter riddling the opposition with epigrams—no! It was impossibly grotesque.

"Just read it," he pleaded, looking hurt. "Tell me if you like it."

"My dear Oscar, I'm no critic, but I'm sure it must be good."

"Certainly it's good! Full of poetry and paradox dancing together. It's for you, and it'll make money—just as much as those flatulent travesties of Sidney Grundy's." He picked up the manuscript. "Listen to this scene."

But Lillie wouldn't let him read any of it, and he left brusquely, refusing her offer of tea. Perhaps she hadn't been tactful, but it seemed unlikely that his aesthetic talent was capable of turning out a commercially successful play of her stripe. And that role!

She shuddered, smoked another cigarette, and rang for tea. Drinking it alone, she thought of Freddie. She missed him, his presence, his charm, his cheerful indulgence of her whims and—why hide the fact?—his accomplished love-making. How important love was in one's life! She felt only half alive without Freddie, yet she had never been able to make him feel how important acting was to her.

Freddie still did not write, and the business of "the next boat" began to seem like a very bad joke. Lillie still looked at the "arrivals" in the newspapers every day and expected him to show up at any moment. He didn't, but she kept hoping, surprising herself and her admirers with her fidelity. It was a battle of willful spirits. Without a doubt Freddie loved her; she loved him more than she had ever loved any other man. If she should send a cable begging him to come to her, she knew he would. But she didn't want to beg. Freddie might as well understand, even if it meant—but she wouldn't think about that. Freddie would come because he wasn't constituted to hold out on principle. He would be along on the next boat, or the next.

She had played Rosalind in London almost eight years before, and the reviews had been merciless. This time it could be no ordinary production.

The day *As You Like It* was to open at the St. James, Lillie awoke with a high fever and a racking cough, but she was determined to go on in spite of the doctor's advice. She ate little that afternoon, waiting for her brother Clement to drive her to the theater. He had returned to his London law practice, and his presence saved a lot of talk. He came in at five, and his anxiety at her looks annoyed her. Her eyes burned, her throat pained, her joints ached, but she had to have her way.

"I'm perfectly all right, Clem. I'm going on!"

"What? It's measles, old girl. Plain measles, so it's all off."

Whether it was the turmoil of production that had exhausted her or worry over Freddie, Lillie was susceptible to complications and came down with a serious case of influenza. Four doctors attended her, stroking their beards and shaking their heads. England was shaken. The press ran daily front-page bulletins on her condition. Queen Victoria's health couldn't have excited any more interest. Out of danger at last, she was weak and depressed. She chafed at the long recuperation which

255

required her to stay in bed. It was pleasant to look at all the flowers and remembrances, the letters, cards, and get-well messages from kings, princes, and dukes. But they were meaningless until she finally heard from Freddie.

His cable was penitent. He had been wrong, unhappy, begged her forgiveness, and—Lillie had to smile—he was taking the next boat. The New York reporters noted Freddie's close-mouthed departure and improvised to the effect that "at her cabled request, Fred Gebhard sailed last week on the *Majestic* to escort her to this country. She will rest at her 23rd Street villa, then go to the California ranch for the summer."

She had missed Freddie's comforting love. She longed for his protective solidity and now looked eagerly forward to his arrival, although she had second thoughts. She loved Freddie. She'd certainly marry him if she ever got a divorce, and yet just how necessary was he? The gap in her life had not proved the yawning abyss she had envisioned. She had managed quite nicely without him and, whether or not he came—granted a certain amount of hurt—she could go right on doing so. All of this brought up the disturbing thought that if she didn't need Freddie, then she didn't need any man *permanently.* Men got in the way like Edward, like Bertie, like Freddie, like . . . Oh, dear, why did it have to take so long to cross the Atlantic!

An equerry brought a message on crested paper bearing a symbol with three feathers and under them the motto *"Ich dien."* The impending visit was a royal command to which Lillie could reply only in the affirmative. She gave Beverly strict orders that afternoon.

The butler was flabbergasted an hour later when Freddie Gebhard, just off the boat and in London, showed his grinning face. He brushed by as if he owned the place. Beverly protested, but Freddie only clapped him familiarly on the back and tossed his hat on the hall table.

"Great to see you after all this time, Bev. Just great! I was really worried about Mrs. Langtry, and I'm happy she's all right now. I can't wait to see her. Where is she?"

Beverly drew back stiffly. "Mrs. Langtry is occupied, Mr. Gebhard. She cannot see anyone this afternoon."

"Well, you can jolly well un-occupy her, as you British say." Freddie laughed. "Just tell her Freddie's here. That'll do it quick."

"Mr. Gebhard!" The butler's jowls quivered. "You cannot see her. If you want to leave a message, I shall make certain she gets it."

"Say, what is this?" Freddie looked suspicious. "That fancy carriage outside. Who's up there with her? Who is the bird?"

Beverly shuddered at this unseemly reference to his future sovereign. "I can't say, sir. I have my orders."

"What!"

Voices came faintly from upstairs, Lillie's lilting tones and a guttural male rumbling. Beverly put a warning finger to his lips, then pointed pleadingly to the door. Now Freddie heard the voices, cocked an ear, recognized Lillie's, and grinned happily.

"Hey, Lillie!" he shouted. "It's me. Freddie! Come on down."

Although the owners of the voices were not yet visible on the stairs, they halted their descent. A shocked silence flowed toward Freddie like an icy wind. He looked irritated and bewildered. Beverly threw out his hands and looked as if he were going to cry.

"Lillie?" Freddie called again, his voice lower and tentative.

There was no answer. The lilting voice hurriedly resumed, the guttural voice filling in appropriately. Then two figures came in view, their eyes on each other as they talked on, like actors oblivious to some unprecedented stage catastrophe, a ghastly incident that might panic the audience if they took cognizance of it. Now they were at the foot of the stairs and still talking easily, as Beverly came out of his horrified trance at an imperious gesture from Lillie.

"At least I'm glad you're well again and looking so lovely. The Princess and I shall certainly be there on opening night."

"Thank you, Your Highness."

Beverly tendered a handsome black overcoat, black silk top

257

hat, and walking stick, assisting the Prince deferentially, clucking and bowing in his attentive zeal. Like Lillie, he ignored the American intruder. The portly man, with the aristocratic nose, the thinning hair parted in the middle, the beard and mustache streaked with gray, kissed Lillie's hand. He smiled at the bobbing Beverly holding the door, and looked through Freddie glacially as he made his exit.

A cathedral hush followed. Beverly fled, crumpled as if by a bullet and preferring to die off stage. Lillie glared, and Freddie cleared his throat. It was like thunder.

"This is a fine welcome!"

"How could you?" she spat at him. "You've disgraced me! Breaking in, deliberately making a scene before the Prince of Wales! You fool!"

"Now wait," he said, recoiling at her white-hot anger. "I'm sorry, Lillie. I didn't know who—"

"You did it to embarrass me. Get out!"

"I'm sorry," he said abjectly.

If Freddie had grabbed her hard, shaken her, bruised her lips with a kiss expressing his love and pent-up longing, he might have moved her. He might have blunted her fury with his passion, helped her trample on her dignity, taken her to bed laughing. But this contemptible apologizing . . .

"Get out!" she repeated.

"Not unless you come with me. I came over three thousand miles to take you back."

"Back to what?" she said with a withering laugh.

"You're an American now. It's your country, and you belong to me."

"I'm Lillie Langtry. I don't belong to anyone."

"Save your speeches," he said, stung. "You're not in the theater."

"And you're not my leading man. You never were."

"Who is?" he sneered. "That fat old joker? Where would he get with a woman if he wasn't going to be king of this stinking country some day?"

"That's a terrible insult! It's the greatest country in the world."

258

"Oh, it is, huh? Tell that to the reporters the next time you come over to dig for the gold you can't get here."

"Oh, get out, Freddie. Get out!"

"I suppose you were having tea up there with the Prince. Locking the doors and putting Beverly on guard. Fine thing! He had it once for free, so he can get it now whenever he wants. A command performance. Sure, I'm a fool. You act high and mighty with me, but when he whistles you lie down and roll over. This is 1890, Lillie. Kings don't mean a damn thing any more."

She slapped him and he laughed. "Thanks."

"You're disgusting!"

"But it hurts, doesn't it?" he gloated. "Gets under that thick skin of yours." He looked at her and for a time neither spoke. "I am sorry, Lillie, but you can't blame me for being jealous. You don't know what love does to a man."

"Don't I?" she said dully.

"This isn't the stage. This is something real that's happening to us. It's been wonderful, and you know it. Let's not kill it."

Something Oscar had said occurred to her, something about loving acting because it was so much more real than life. She laughed inside, a painful, tearing laugh as she looked at Freddie.

"Lillie!" he said, supplicating.

"No."

She went upstairs slowly and calmly, not looking back and unmindful of the hurrying footsteps, then the front door slamming. She had half hoped Freddie would follow her, then she might . . . Unable to resist, she peeped out the octagonal window facing the street. The momentum of "the grand bounce" had apparently carried him out to the middle of the street. He had regained the sidewalk and was looking about uncertainly. He quivered with anger, his black eyebrows contracted over his blazing eyes, his mouth moving. From her perch, Lillie watched under tight control as Freddie kicked at a lamppost. He walked off, head bowed and shoulders slumped. She followed him until he was out of sight, her eyes prickling, as she told herself over and over, "I will not cry, I will not cry."

259

"We're both fools," she said, not knowing she'd spoken aloud.

For some reason she thought of their first meeting in New York, the fun they'd had, the scandalous comedy of her first tour, with Freddie following from city to city. Unbidden, a speech of Rosalind's from the second scene of Act Five came to her: "No sooner looked, but they loved; no sooner loved, but they sighed; no sooner sighed, but they asked one another the reason; no sooner knew the reason, but they sought the remedy."

Everyone commented on the seriousness with which Lillie approached the postponed opening of *As You Like It* at the St. James. Never had she demonstrated such perseverance and concentration in seeing that everything in her performance and the production was exactly right. And her labors were evident in the reviews she received for the first night before "a large and fashionable audience" that included "the Prince and Princess of Wales and their daughters, with the Duke of Fife and many well-known figures in Society."

"The skill and fascination of her Rosalind" were noted, as well as the presence of Mrs. Henry Labouchère in the center of the stalls, "the clever lady who first instructed Mrs. Langtry in the histrionic art." The improvement in her acting was called remarkable; in the forest scene, wearing doublet and hose, she was "bewitching." She was credited with having learned much since last seen in London, and "constant study and practice in America and the provinces have imparted to her style power and ease to a remarkable degree. Mrs. Langtry is the crown of the feast; and more than one male auditor seemed to wish she would carry out her agreeable threat in the admirable spoken dialogue."

Lillie had been deliciously appealing in speaking the lines: "If I were a woman, I would kiss as many of you as had beards that pleased me, complexions that liked me, and breaths that I defied not; and, I am sure, as many as have good beards, or good faces, or sweet breaths, will, for my kind offer, when I make curtsey, bid me farewell." Enraptured males took her promise to heart, one of them bringing down the house with his hearty cry of "Hear, hear!"

Ah, but that first night was a night—enough to drive the gnawing memory of Freddie away for a few hours—what with endless curtain calls, a curtain speech, accolades, bowers of flowers, a summons to the royal box, and even an obeisance from Henrietta, stouter and grayer.

"Lillie," Henrietta said ecstatically. "You were sublime."

"I owe it all to you, Henrietta. You started me on the way."

"But it was always in you, and now you're a real professional. By the way, whatever happened to that troublesome Gebhard person?"

"Who?" said Lillie, going on to shake the next hand.

With her professional life again happily launched, Lillie set about filling the breach in her private life by accepting most of the invitations rained on her. She attended important seasonal functions, appeared at Marlborough House, and was escorted by a multitude of men, all of whom she treated with maddeningly casual familiarity. After Freddie, most of them seemed foppish nonentities with superficial charm, galling conceit, and effeminate mannerisms. But they were diverting. A beautiful woman could not go it alone. She preferred these spineless clotheshorses to the confident idiots who took her notorious reputation literally, never doubting their ability to woo her into bed as a sort of sport.

Freddie was pushed out of mind until it was time to turn out the light and lie in bed waiting for sleep, defenseless against memories, against the voices that came out of the darkness to haunt her. (Oh, why had he listened to her? Why hadn't he come back?) It was always Freddie talking. "I'm a man; I'm human." Was she?

She had written the ending, and she was going along with it. No changes, no rewriting, no epilogues. She cabled to Abe Hummel to have her furniture, horses, and carriages shipped to England. She bought a handsome house at 21 Pont Street, one of London's smartest and most exclusive residential districts. This was home now—permanently. Beverly was no longer in her employ—the scene with Freddie and Bertie having upset him so much that he turned in his frock coat—and it had been difficult to replace him. His first successor was incompetent, the next kept breaking into the liquor closet and serving her guests drunkenly. That one was succeeded by her young French chef, Louis Barrerya, who liked to call himself *"votre petit cuisinier"* and was an imperturbably resourceful majordomo.

It was Louis who outwitted the Marquis de Vrémont, her most fanatic admirer, who hounded her after the theater and wanted no other man to share her company. To make sure of her he hired an apartment across the way, where he sat at the window with a revolver and threatened to shoot any male who entered the door of Number 21. With a hotheaded man like the Marquis, one had to take his murderous vigil seriously. Louis devised a side entrance out of his view by placing a plank from a window railing to the ground so that male visitors could be ushered directly into the dining room, safely out of revolver range. Louis had a Gallic appreciation of the situation.

"This way, monsieur," he directed. "We are under siege from the front."

To be one of those who had "walked the plank" for Lillie was a badge of honor. She thought of prosecuting the Marquis, but there was something pathetic about him. With Louis she admired the spirit of the man, yet he was a nuisance. She was finally able to persuade him that any prospects of love between them were doomed because of her unrelenting husband. Then he was all for turning the gun on himself. She let Louis talk him out of that—with the assistance of several bottles of good cognac.

Other admirers were as persistent, but gayer and more imaginative. Lord Dudley was always trying to spirit her off to the country. One night after the performance, he waited for her disguised as the driver of a hansom. He drove at a furious clip through the West End, rather than toward her home as directed. She thought her cabman out of his mind until she recognized Lord Dudley, very much pleased with himself. Lillie pretended to be frightened and finally persuaded him to pull up at No. 1 Belgrave Square, where Reuben Sassoon lived, and there she dashed inside. Informed of the trick, Sassoon came out and berated the cabbie, who had to expose himself as Dudley. Then they all went inside. Sassoon cooked bacon and eggs, and they talked half the night away.

Lord Dudley, Claude Lowther, and Robert Peel loved practical jokes quite as much as Bertie and the others in the Marlborough Set. Claude talked her into whiling away a dull, rainy afternoon by passing herself off as a flower girl on the Strand, while he trailed her as a match boy. They went to Clarkson's, where they were given old clothes and made up for their parts. Lillie began to like the idea of acting a real-life role. She sold a few bunches of violets, then had trouble with a man who tried to pick her up for the same price. She saw Claude arguing with a policeman, and then the man turned her in for accosting him. The incident became embarrassing, with the policeman refusing to believe she was Mrs. Langtry. Claude had to take them all to his barber, Gilbert of Truefitt's on Bond Street, for proper identification.

Lowther was indefatigable. Lillie gave a dinner, after which the guests were playing for small stakes at a roulette table in the drawing room. She loved gambling, and spinning the wheel with a titled croupier crying *"Faites vos jeux"* was a novelty in London. No one heard the doorbell.

"The police!" Louis shouted. "The police, madame."

Everyone froze. Sir George Arthur swept the money off the green baize cloth and disappeared behind the curtains. The women rushed for chairs, trying to look unconcerned, and two men hid under the table. It was left to Lillie to explain matters to the two fierce-looking policemen, whose gruff voices sounded familiar. There was feeble laughter as Claude Lowther and Robert Peel removed their beards.

"Did we fool you?" said Peel joyously.

"Oh, no." Lillie sighed. "It happens every night."

The St. James repertoire drew good houses. Bertie came frequently, so did Princess Alexandra and Prince George (later George V), although he did not have his father's enthusiasm for the theater. Their arrival was the cause of feverish preparations and much scurrying about by the management. Each time the official word came to Griffith two or three days in advance. It was his duty to meet the Prince and his party the instant they arrived and to conduct them to the royal box. Here they were seated while the audience stared; special programs, printed on satin, were distributed to them, and the ladies were given bouquets.

Bertie always paid more than the scheduled rate. His appearance was the best kind of advertisement for the theater, and every effort was made to cater to him. Behind the two royal boxes, a private lounge was available. Here, he and the other gentlemen in the party could smoke and talk, and Griffith kept it stocked "with the very best Scotch whiskey—only Scotch—and the finest cigars."

During one intermission, the Prince went backstage to show the light of his royal countenance to Lillie and other members of the cast, who were grouped on stage in the order of their importance like a battalion under inspection. Bertie was popular with the actors, and even Griffith found him a "most affable charming man." Tonight the Prince congratulated Lillie and the others, and then he singled out "Daddy" Averill, who was a friend of long standing. Lillie enjoyed this ritual—a sort of godlike, paternal blessing, unlike anything in America. (Had the President ever come backstage in Washington?)

More often than not during the long evening, the Prince and his party had a snack in the lounge. A sumptuous cold supper was served on royal china by a battery of footmen and flunkies, the whole operation under such conditions being a triumph in culinary logistics. Cold chicken, pheasant, roast beef, cakes, and other delicacies with wine and champagne to wash them down. Bertie saw to it that a few carefully chilled bottles were sent down to refresh the Jersey Lily. This gave rise to stories concerning her heavy drinking. They were nonsense, but as late as 1934 Griffith still felt he had to deny them in an interview. He insisted he had never seen anything but the greatest dignity and good taste in the conduct of either the Prince or Lillie. He had heard the rumors about her dissipations but never once had seen her even slightly under the influence of liquor. In fact, she had disliked seeing anyone drunk and once or twice had fired someone from her company for that reason.

Tragedy and grand spectacle drew Lillie to Shakespeare's *Antony and Cleopatra*. In one sense it was a good choice. At thirty-seven plus, she did not look her age; her spirit was youthful, her beauty never more evident. Any number of men were agreed that age could not "wither nor custom stale her infinite variety." The St. James was too small for the spectacular production she planned, so she rented the great, barnlike Princes Theater on Oxford Street. An episodic, disjointed play at best, Lillie hoped to redeem its defects with elaborate costumes, striking effects, and authentically gorgeous scenery.

The cost of milk-white horses, Roman chariots, purple galleys, and massive architectural pieces was far more than Lillie had anticipated. Just before the opening she found herself some 300 pounds short of funds. Because the carpenters and costumers demanded their money, there was no time to cable her New York bank for funds. Griffith warned that the production would have to be called off unless the bills were paid immediately.

Weary from rehearsing, Lillie couldn't think of a soul who would lend her the money with no strings attached. She knew plenty of wealthy men who would be only too happy to put her under obligation, but she didn't want to waste time and words. Then she remembered the bountiful Rothschilds and hustled from Princes Theater to the bankers' headquarters in New Court. The few times she had visited Alfred Rothschild in his office he had never been too busy to see her. A bachelor, soft-voiced, gentle, and eager to please women, it seemed to Lillie he spent all of his working day signing checks. The pile grew, secretaries shuttled in with more, and he went right on chatting as he endlessly scratched his name. She imagined him leaving for home twitchy-handed, his fingers involuntarily scratching his name on air. Now she was convinced that one more little check would be only a matter of automatic reflex.

An important meeting was taking place, however; the Rothschilds couldn't possibly be disturbed. Lillie's insistence that it was a life-and-death matter only sent the clerks into a dither.

She was finally allowed to write a note, and in her sprawling, distinctive hand described the "crisis." The clerks timorously waited until lunch to deliver the message. Alfred read it aloud to his confrères, and her use of the word "crisis" was like comic relief. Baring Brothers had taken a heavy loss on a rash investment, every big bank in London was somehow involved in the transaction, millions of pounds were at stake, and that was why the Rothschilds were in solemn conference. Lillie's request was ludicrous in contrast. A puzzled clerk was instructed to give her the money in cash with the compliments of the Rothschilds.

Saved by the financiers, *Antony and Cleopatra* opened on schedule to mixed notices. A bewitching flirt and man-eater, Cleopatra has only a few brief love scenes in the play, spends most of her time arguing with Antony. Her mercurial personality was so different from Lillie's that she found it hard to portray. Cleopatra was no Rosalind; hectic scene followed hectic scene with a shifting of scenes between Rome, Alexandria, Messina, Syria, and Athens—enough to bewilder the audience. Coghlan was an acceptable if subdued Antony. The spectacle and costumes were effective enough, but the piece was troublesome both to stage and to enact. All in all, Lillie was most satisfied with her death scene. Herbert Beerbohm Tree, scrambling over after the last act of his play at the Haymarket, applauded her portrayal of the dying queen. She trusted his judgment.

There was an aptness in Lillie's playing the part, and Max Beerbohm, critic and satirist, knew what he was talking about when he later referred to her as *"cette Cléopatre de son siècle."* She had just broken with her Mark Antony, and Caesar had recently been in the audience and congratulated her. Yet London flocked to see her Cleopatra mostly for the sumptuous production. Lillie was gratified: she had accepted the challenge of another complicated Shakespearean role, in which few actresses had truly triumphed, and she had brought it off.

One night the past repeated itself: The theater custodian knocked at her door and said there was an old man who wanted to see her.

"Claims his name is Gladstone, but he can't be. He ain't in

evening clothes, and he don't look distinguished. Not like no prime minister."

It was Gladstone. White-haired, his face lined, his nose forbiddingly truculent, he came in just as if he'd seen Lillie the day before, took some reference works from under his arm, and pointed at a passage.

"Take Scene Five, Act One, where you say 'My salad days, when I was green in judgment:—cold in blood, to say as I said then!' and so forth. This is not a reflective, contemplative commentary, Mrs. Langtry. No, no. Cleopatra is a scheming minx. The words reek of bitterness and scorn at herself."

"I'm sure you're right, Mr. Gladstone. You know, it seems so fitting to have you visit my dressing room tonight. Do you think I've improved since the old days at the Haymarket? Some critics don't think so."

"Of course you have, but retrogression appeals to pessimists. Some people think I was inept when I was first prime minister and that I grew progressively worse. But the public knows best, or they'd have voted us both out of office the first time, eh?"

The play had been so expensive to mount that, to meet operating costs, the big theater had to be filled to capacity at every performance. Griffith was worried. He came to her dressing room looking embarrassed and holding some photographs so that she couldn't see them.

"I feel I had to speak to you about this, Mrs. Langtry. It's a shocking thing." He gave up the photographs reluctantly. They showed her as Cleopatra—nude from the waist up.

"Hmm," she said, glancing at her manager's flushed face. "Do you think these do me justice, Mr. Griffith?"

"They're obviously faked," he said, looking off. "Your face has been set on another woman's neck and shoulders. It's a scandal. Indecent! You should prosecute these people."

"Disregard it, Mr. Griffith."

"But it's an outrage. And there are a lot of rumors about you in circulation. I think you would be wise to deny them."

"Ignore them too. Mr. Gladstone—he was here the other night—once told me never to rush into print with denials. It's the best advice I ever had."

"As you wish. But these photographs!" He crumpled them. "I've bought every one I could find and destroyed it."

"That's very kind and admirable of you, Mr. Griffith, but you shouldn't have gone to such trouble. Any *perceptive* person would know at once they are faked. So do, please, charge it up to expenses."

All the Rothschilds were good-natured, and Lillie was grateful for their assistance. Alfred was probably the most popular —a small man, delicate and soft-voiced, a bachelor who lived at Seamore Place in a house filled with priceless *objets d'art*. He liked to entertain at small dinner parties consisting of three men and one woman. The lone woman was always made much of. Alfred invariably took her aside and with great secrecy presented her with some small knicknack. Lillie had compared notes with his other feminine guests, and when it came her turn she decided to tease him.

After dinner he whispered his stock question, "What shall I give you, beautiful lady?" Without hesitating Lillie picked up an enameled Louis Seize snuffbox studded with diamonds and worth hundreds of pounds, the prize of his collection. "Oh, this will do," she said calmly.

Alfred blanched. He had a bad heart, and for an instant she feared she had brought on an attack. He got his breath finally, promised Lillie something much prettier, and out came one of the familiar little tokens.

"I still prefer the other," she said, looking at the inexpensive gift box. "This one has no stones."

"But what would a woman do with a snuffbox?"

"It's just the thing for hairpins and such."

Alfred frowned. "And you'll be heartbroken if you don't get it?"

"You asked me to choose, you know."

"B-b-but—are you serious?" he said plaintively.

Lillie laughed and he caught on.

"I do believe you're pulling my leg. I'm going to propose putting you on our board. We could use you. There's no humor in finance."

seventeen

In April, 1891, Lillie fell seriously ill with pleurisy. She was rumored on the point of death. Once again medical bulletins on her condition were featured daily, and newspapers on both sides of the Atlantic prepared her obituaries.

Whether she was sick or dying, Lillie's admirers had to see her. Louis turned away one determined male after another from her Pont Street threshold—all but Luke White, who was more headstrong and infatuated than the rest. Luke was in charge of the St. James's Palace Guard. It was a chancy business, but his friends kept loyally mum as he sneaked off in civilian clothes. Nothing was going to keep him from his beloved, and he talked himself past the butler to reach her bedside.

His charming small talk and flattery perked her up. She felt better after his call, then worried at hearing how narrowly he had escaped royal censure. No sooner had he left his post than Queen Victoria had decided to visit London. Luckily another officer in the same regiment, to save Luke's skin, jumped into uniform and hurried to St. James's Palace minutes before the Queen arrived and barely managed to turn out the Guard.

"I would have been cashiered," Luke proudly told Lillie afterward, "but I had to see you—and it was worth it!"

Men were such lovable fools. As she convalesced, she found no interest in the hundreds of letters, postcards, telegrams, and cables that were delivered to Pont Street. Then she came on a long, pleading letter from Freddie. Spent and lonely, she read it over and over. Freddie, Freddie. She would go to him gladly now, but first she had to get her divorce. Nothing had developed through either Abe Hummel or Sir George Lewis so the only thing left was for her to go to Edward herself. She could make other men do practically anything she wished. Why not her husband?

Lewis innocently supplied her with the address to which he mailed Edward's monthly checks. She wore her plainest dress and a heavy veil, doing everything she could not to look like the Jersey Lily. Once off the train, she posed as Edward's sister and asked directions to his cottage. He lived alone and was apparently out. The door wasn't locked, but Lillie couldn't bear to go in and wait. She was leaving as she heard footsteps and ducked out of sight into the shrubbery. She saw only his back. His hair gray, his neck thick, his body gone to fat. He wheezed as he walked.

He stopped at the steps, swaying a little. She could smell the whiskey on him, the fumes like poison among the sweet-scented green leaves. Now he turned. Lillie stifled a cry. His face was bloated, his skin an unhealthy yellow, his dead eyes sunken and lined, his body humped in dejection. Off guard, he was naked to the world. In the sag of his shoulders, the petulant droop of his bedraggled mustache, the hair growing over his collar, she saw he had stopped caring for anything. His clothes were soiled and rumpled, his boots cracked and caked with mud. A thoroughly defeated man. He might have let go completely, if breathing hadn't been a natural process.

He sighed and pulled at his nose, now grown gross and bulbous. Fumbling at the knob, he forgot to step up and stumbled inside the cottage. He mumbled incoherently. There were the indistinct sounds of books and objects tumbling to the floor, then the clink of a bottle against a glass.

Lillie turned blindly away, hurrying through the woods to the road, unaware of briars tearing at her dress or branches slapping her face. It was worse than the shallowest revelation scene in any contrived melodrama in which she had ever played. Her eyes were blurred with tears; self-contempt overcame her. Ask this wreck for freedom? This hulk that was her husband?

Oh, my God, she thought, have I done this to him? Have I *really?*

Although she was late and had forgotten about it, the reporter was still waiting for his interview in Pont Street. Lillie went in, composed and radiant, saying she would oblige as promised if he would be brief. The procedure was cut and dried, stilted question leading to stilted answer, except that she let drop a bitter remark that was long afterward associated with her. It was hard to say exactly to whom she referred, but the statement was quite foreign to the Jersey Lily's personality. Dominique had said it long ago, and now Lillie brought it out without thinking.

"What do you think of men, Mrs. Langtry?"

"Men are slaves. The most foolish thing a woman can do is to permit herself to care even a little bit for one of them."

"Just what do you mean, Mrs. Langtry?"

Lillie smiled and got up. The interview was over.

She met him at the track. She was placing a sizable bet with a bookmaker and he overheard her. He told her she was betting on the wrong horse, making a serious mistake. And what was the right horse? His, or course! Thank you, but she always picked her own winners. Not this time, Mrs. Langtry. If she bet on his, she'd win for sure. And, if she lost, he'd pay her triple the bet out of his own pocket—he showed her the money to prove he was able to do so. Lillie hesitated too long. He took her money, placed the bet with the bookmaker for her, then joined her at the rail without being invited. He didn't say a word during the race, nor did he display the faintest emotion as his entry won easily: not even an "I told you so."

And now here they were dining together for the third night in a row. Impossible to ignore, this forceful man with his hair cut short and, unlike her admirers or other men of the period, with neither mustache, nor beard, nor side whiskers. He was smiling amiably, eyeing her with possessive fondness. Slight and wiry, a hard drinker and given to other vices according to reports (all bad), but nonetheless in the top physical condition

271

necessary for his reputation as England's finest gentleman jockey. Brown-haired, boyish-faced, the skin stretched tight over his bones emphasizing his hardness and the steeliness of his flinty gray eyes. His warm smile did not soften the tough, durable quality he exuded, that maleness which both attracted and repelled Lillie. Truthfully, she had never known anyone like him. He frightened her. She didn't mind, though—not too much.

He called to the waiter who bowed low and hurried away. Bottles of champagne were grouped around their table, sentinels turned to frosted silver in the ice buckets. The best champagne, the fresh bottle would make it an even half dozen, and none was three-quarters empty. Strange, strange man.

"There's still plenty left. Why order more?"

"Because I like to. The best is at the top anyway, so I only take a glassful from each bottle."

"Doesn't money mean a thing to you?"

He laughed. "Not a damn thing." He reached for her hand, but she pulled it away. "You go around with the wrong people, Lillie. You think too much."

"I go around with the best people! At least, I always have until—"

"—you met me, eh? You never got over being a society beauty, did you?"

"And you never got over *not* being a gentleman!" she flashed back.

"Ah, but I am. If a man worth some five million pounds ain't a gentleman in the eyes of what you call society, then I don't know what the hell he is."

"Your millions don't mean anything to me!"

"Oh, don't they, though? And you're not impressed, either? What a damn liar you are, but I love you just the same."

"Don't speak to me of love!"

"Did any of your gentleman friends ever hit you, Lillie? Or was it always tenderness?" He squeezed the fleshy part of her arm. "You're not fragile, you know. You're solid, all-woman, and used to getting what you want. It's time you got what you deserved."

272

"And what might that be?" she said haughtily.

"Me, of course." He smiled and looked the charming boy.

"You'd hit me?" And he would. Oh, *he* would.

"If necessary—just like a horse. The master must master."

"No one masters me."

He snorted. "Just what kind of men have you known?"

Lillie tried to say good-by to him at her door, but he pushed inside with her. Then she threatened to call Louis and have him thrown out.

"Can he box?" said her escort. "I'm pretty good at it."

He followed her upstairs, ever more outrageous, and yet she felt sure she could control him. After a little while, she ordered him out. He was immovable. He put his arms around her from behind, his palms closing over her breasts. Lillie broke away, raised her hand to slap him, but he cut under her arm and caught her along the face. She had never been struck by anyone in her life since her youthful battles with her brothers. She whimpered with hurt and covered her face. He let her stand thus for a minute, then took her solicitously in his arms and let her sob against him.

It seemed she couldn't stop crying until he crushed his mouth to her tear-streaked lips. A kiss like a hammer blow that made her cling to keep from falling, her pulses quickening, her breath sucking deep in her throat. She stood weak and helpless. He undressed her quickly with all the ease of a man long practiced in the art.

"You've got the longest hair," he marveled, unbinding it. He lifted it in two great wings and swung it over her shoulders so that it crossed over her chin and breasts to her navel, a luxuriant, honey-colored mass. "Beautiful, beautiful. What a woman you are!"

"And you're a rotter," she said feebly.

"An unmitigated one and a proper cad to boot."

"I'm not at all sure I like you, Squire."

"Don't try so hard. I'm an acquired taste."

"How old are you?"

"What do you care? Thirty in September."

"Infant!" she sneered. "I'm nearly thirty-eight."

"What the hell are numbers? It's what people are that counts. Come here!"

"No."

"I can outtalk you, outrun you, and outfight you, Lillie. You don't have a chance."

I don't, she thought fearfully. How did this ever happen?

"I'm not sharing you," he went on, pressing his hot, demanding body implacably against hers. "Do you understand?" he said fiercely. "Anything different and that slap'll seem just like a kiss."

Lillie tried to reply, but taking her answer for granted he gave her no opportunity.

George Alexander Baird, Laird of Auchmedden and Stichill, preferred to be known as Squire Abington. A true British eccentric, he was born in the wrong century and conducted himself like a figure in a Restoration comedy. He was fop, rakehell, devil-may-care cynic, tosspot, morally lax woman-chaser. Descended from one of Scotland's oldest families, he was devoted to horses, women, racing, boxing, games, and gambling, not necessarily in that order. He was the last and, in his astounding way, the most memorable of the Bairds.

Born in Bany's British Hotel, Edinburgh, September 30, 1861, he was nine years old when his father died, leaving him everything. Spoiled by his mother, doing as he pleased, he was so willful and uncontrollable he gave fits to the trustees managing his father's estate. He hung around the stables. He followed the grooms about and steeped himself in horseflesh. Much against his intentions, he was persuaded to enter Eton. Young George hated conformity, so he committed heresy by leaving school to visit his mother in London. He amazed the authorities by refusing to accept the usual flogging as punishment. He threatened to hit back—and was expelled.

Somehow he was admitted to Magdalene College, Cambridge, but six terms there made no dent in George. He distinguished himself only by running the 100-yard dash in ten and a half seconds, participating in such sports as cock-fighting and dog-fighting, gambling and chasing women, and as a gentleman jockey or amateur rider. He entered the Lincoln races as "Mr. Abington," prudently adopting the name of a Lanarkshire village to fool the gimlet-eyed trustees.

He left Cambridge without a degree and went to live at still another Baird estate, Whittington Hall, Lickfield. Here he perfected his riding and built up his racing stables. He bet on himself as a jockey, his champion gamecocks, and his Donald, reputedly the best fighting dog in England. He came into his millions in 1886, with an income of close to 250,000 pounds yearly from coal mines in Scotland.

Baird rode as hard as he did everything else, and he was warned off the course for two years at Wolverhampton for foul riding. In another race he was disqualified for trying to shove Lord Harrington through the rails. His apology—"Beg pardon, my lord; thought you were a bloody farmer!"—was the Squire at his best. Harrington's reply is not recorded.

To keep fit and make his ideal riding weight of 136 pounds, the Squire adopted a strict training regimen that was agony for a Regency-type sporting gallant who wanted to be a champion by day and a hell-raiser by night. Preparing for a big race in 1890, he dined on three ounces of sweetbreads and took a dose of a special medicine prepared for him by a Marchmount Street "turf" druggist. The reducing mixture was turned out by the vat for the Squire. Enough was stored at his many residences "to supply a county hospital."

During the racing season, not a day passed that the London newspapers didn't mark up a major win for Mr. Abington. He had a fine string of over 150 horses at Moulton Paddocks, Newmarket, the best quarters of their kind in all England. Even those who despised him rated the Squire as the best-informed horseman in Europe.

Anyone throwing around as much money as the slim, boyish-looking Squire was a perfect mark for turf sharpers, tinhorns, and deadbeats. His innate Scotch caution protected him to a point, but not where boxers were concerned. He loved the sport, admired the pugilists, and considered himself one. Baird was agile enough, but too small and slight to be effective. Still, he liked barroom brawls and had "an engaging habit of throw-

275

ing brandy and soda over total strangers in West End bars." Time after time it cost him 20, 30, or as much as 50 pounds to have the police and court charges dropped.

He dreamed of an Englishman dethroning the American, John L. Sullivan, as world heavyweight champion, but the effort seemed as beyond British brawn in the nineteenth century as it has been since. The Squire hadn't much luck with his stable of fighters, but Charlie Mitchell, a wily, 160-pound middleweight who had come close to beating the much-heavier Boston Strong Boy in one of their fights, was by far the best prospect.

Baird was fascinated with his pugilist characters. They, their friends, and their hangers-on formed his entourage in London, living and brawling comfortably at his West End home, which was a sort of boxers' country club. The Squire liked to boast that their upkeep cost 1,500 pounds a week. Besides these minor expenses, consorting with his sluggers involved him with the law almost as often as his love affairs did.

Rough, tough, brazen, and dashing, he had great success with women and treated them brutally. He preferred actresses like Agnes Hewitt, Bessie Bellwood, and Gladys Leslie, who once had him arrested for knocking her down. Then there was the lovely ballerina, Dolly Tester, with whom the Squire eloped. (A costly business, since he had to settle 15,000 pounds on her husband, the Marquess of Aylesbury, but he said it was worth every penny.) He always made up for his beatings with generous gifts of jewels or cash. Only the insatiably greedy tried for more.

The Squire was the most flamboyant of a group of restless young hotheads of varying backgrounds, some from the old aristocracy, some from the new, some from the trade (ugh!) who suddenly emerged at that period as heirs to great fortunes. Drunk with their millions, they seemed determined to squander all they could and tie a can to the world's tail.

Society with a capital "S" frowned on Baird and his affairs, equine, feminine, and fistic. But he was a popular figure in England. Bold, handsome, romantic, and victorious, a commoner with ten times a duke's wealth, he was one of the people.

Outside his boxing coterie, his friends were divided in their

276

affection. His trainers, jockeys, and hostlers were enthusiastic save one who said, "If he had a redeeming feature, he had it overlain at birth, for he was a dyed-in-the-wool swine." Perhaps an extreme view and a truer one might be the posthumous comment:

> "Poor old Squire; he was not a bad sort in the main." He paused, and then added, thoughtfully, cautiously: "But the main was such a long way underground that dashed few turncocks would trouble to look for it."

But it *was* there—and probably accounted for his hypnotic influence over the Jersey Lily. As she came to be seen more and more with him, their names intimately linked in notorious dalliance, the blackened pot of gossip boiled over. First Gebhard, then Baird! With pleasure Society ruled her out. She had put herself beyond the pale. The *haut monde* could never condone such an association. And the men who worshiped and pursued her were dismayed, humiliated that this bounder had succeeded where they had failed. Her greatest sin was that the Squire was no gentleman.

To many the attraction of the "impossible Abington Baird" remained "one of the mysteries of Lillie's career." W. H. Leverton, who managed and was associated with the Haymaket Theater for fifty years, thought it lamentable and inexplicable.

> The keynote of her character was her worship of beauty, of the refined and pleasant things of life. She was essentially fastidious; her surroundings, her *décor,* were chosen with studied and exquisite taste.

And here she was allied to this moneyed monster who was every ugly, appalling thing she was not. How could she stand this Yahoo—a woman of fine breeding, keen mind, and brilliant wit? This lovely idol who was intelligent, well read, who never used profanity, hated the risqué, "detested gossip; . . . never indulged in it, and was impatient of it in others." It simply did not add up.

While his coarseness appalled her, the Squire had a bedrock masculinity, a shock appeal that overwhelmed Lillie. Spitting on propriety, abhorring the amenities, lacking every refinement of culture, he was conspicuous for boldness, assertiveness, and the direct, frontal approach to every problem. Neither spineless, nor a pussyfooter, he cut straight at life, living hard, loving hard, playing hard—and always to win. The only man she had ever known who could not be molded, led, toyed with. Not that she would ever dream of marrying him! But Edward was a jellyfish in comparison, Bertie a voluptuary grandpapa, and Freddie—darling Freddie! Ah, why hadn't he a pinch of the Squire's slashing vigor and decision? Hateful and disgusting as he could be, Mr. Abington was electrifying. He breathed fire, made her tingle. He would never have let her get away as Freddie had done. Never an explanation nor an apology, but action all the way for a winner.

Having always loved horses and races, Lillie learned much from the Squire. She went to the track with him, watched him place his bets, and spent hours watching him work at his sprawling Newmarket stables. But she could never be idle long. She had arranged for a provincial tour that fall, much of it in Scotland. The Squire was delighted because he had large estates in Ayrshire, Aberdeenshire, Derrickshire, and Roxburghshire. It was time he had a look, got in some hunting and race riding.

"Of course, it's dull as hell after London," he told her, "but if you like beautiful country, I know Scotland to the bone. I own most of it."

The Squire was a great contract man. He doted on written agreements. He wanted to finance part of her tour and insisted that his lawyers draw up a statement depositing 2,000 pounds to her account. Lillie presented her recent London repertoire, the Dundee *Journal* calling her tour a triumph. Taking over for Coghlan, Frank Worthy was highly capable, and she was given ovations in town after town. The impossible Abington must have been good for her, because critics thought she was as radiant and compelling as ever.

With a baby waist and sleeves, low bodice shimmering with embroidery, shawl of apple green carelessly over her lovely shoulders, poke bonnet fastened to her perfect arm with a wide,

278

pink ribbon, white and red roses in her belt, Mrs. Langtry is the embodiment of spring.

The Squire did not attend every performance as Freddie had done, thus saving her embarrassment. The theater rather bored him. ("I can't stand sitting there," he told her, "watching the adventures of damn strangers when I have better ones myself.") He was more jealous than Freddie but refused to worry about it: he would use her for a punching bag if she looked at another man. Lillie trembled and believed him.

Most of the time they were able to stay at one or another of the Squire's estates, each a small palace in a gem-like setting of green fields, woods, and hills. Superintendents, caretakers, head gardeners, grooms, and housekeepers rushed up to give an accounting of their stewardship. He cut them off brusquely. When he wasn't shooting, he was riding hard at the race meetings he set up wherever Lillie had an engagement. A string of horses followed them by rail, and the Squire exhausted one mount after another. He projected himself into the race like a missile, crashing to an explosive finish. It seemed to Lillie he was intent on killing himself and the horse, never slacking the pace or the whip no matter what the condition of the course. The opposition had to speed up, give way, or be ridden down and over by the Squire.

"You're so hard on the poor beasts," Lillie complained.

"No more than on myself. The horse is just a means to get to the finish line first. If he can't do it, I don't want him. He might as well drop dead. I've had gamecocks and fighting dogs, and I know what I'm talking about. They're the sweat and blood of sports; we're the brains. Never get sentimental about animals, Lillie."

They were riding up a lovely, spottily wooded valley cut by a winding brook, called Six Mile Bottom. It was an area in which he had hunted a great deal. They raised a lot of birds with their horses, and he regretted not having brought a shotgun.

"But it's so cruel. I can't kill animals and call it sport."

"Hell, all life is cruel—and it's better than killing men."
He squinted ahead. "What's that smoke?"

They went through a patch of woods, crossed a clearing, and came on a tiny settlement where an ancient thatched-roof house was blazing. The flames had a good start—too much for the shriveled old woman hopping frantically about, dragging out her possessions. Sweat and tears poured down her dirty ravaged face. It seemed the height of futility to bother snatching her rickety wooden chairs, battered tables, filthy bedclothes, and other seedy horrors from the flames. She grunted and moaned, struggling to salvage her ridiculous things. A pathetic scene. It annoyed Lillie to see the Squire howling with laughter.

"Better if it all burned. Stinking rubbish."

"Not for her, the poor old thing. Oh, Squire, do something!"

"All right." He swung around in the saddle and whistled to those of his coterie who had been following them. "Jimmy! Get a move on there. Help the old girl."

A squat frozen-faced young man with cauliflower ears, Jimmy lurched from his horse. He shoved the octogenarian aside, pulled and hauled, darted in and out until the cottage was empty and the roof nearly fell on his head. As he finished, the local firemen charged in with their hand pumper. It was too late for them to do anything.

The captain courteously tried to interrogate Jimmy and suddenly landed on his back, his brass helmet bouncing on the scorched grass.

Jimmy walked over, grinning and rubbing his knuckles. "The old girl didn't thank me, and then I *had* to whang him in the beezer."

The promise of a good fight amused the Squire. The captain's nose was bleeding, but his three-man brigade wanted none of it. Baird, who hadn't stopped laughing, nearly fell off his horse. It was just a show to him, thought Lillie sickeningly. An impromptu, open-air performance with clowns and slapstick. She hated him enough then to hit him with her riding crop.

"Well, that's that?" he was saying, jerking at his horse's reins. "Wait a minute!" he called to his followers. "Any of you got any money on you?" Most of them had. "Poor old bitch. Better set her with a pony, Fred! You, too, Jimmy, George."

Then he motioned to Lillie, drove his spurs deep, and galloped off, still laughing. Looking back, she could see the old woman still wailing over her personal junk pile, fifty pounds in bank notes sticking out fanwise from her fist: no more than a ten-thousandth of a drop in the Squire's golden bucket.

Coming back from his stables, Lillie spoke wistfully about wanting to have her own horses and racing them under her own colors. She told him of her efforts with Freddie, about their horses on the California ranch. She had thought that a big investment, and Abe Hummel was still forwarding bills from Doc Aby, but Lillie didn't think she'd ever have a winner there.

"Probably not," the Squire said. "They all sound like roarers to me. How'd you like it if I started you with a horse? A good one?"

"I'd love it, Squire! Which one?"

That night as they dined in a restaurant he made up his mind. A distinguished-looking man came over to their table, nodded to her, and then began to bargain over a horse called Milford.

"I'll give you eight thousand pounds, Mr. Baird, and that's more than he's worth."

The Squire grimaced his no and added, "I like a good horse myself, sir." The man went off, mumbling. "I'm going to give you Milford, Lillie. He's the son of Saraband and should be a winner. He'll stay at Moulton Paddocks. Morton can train him."

The gift of the two-year-old chestnut colt pleased Lillie. The fact that he'd turned down a big offer didn't impress her, however, for the Squire was made of money.

Returning from her tour, Lillie rested while looking for a new play. She had still not come up with anything worthy of production during the winter of 1892, for the Squire monopolized her. He could be a lamb, as he was with Mrs. Le Breton when he visited Pont Street; he could be brutal in his cups, although he made it up to her in diamonds; he could be incredible. One evening they attended a party at Sir George Chetwynd's home, 9 York Terrace, Regents Park. The bitterness of the Lonsdale fisticuffs had been more or less forgotten. Sir George was still captivated by Lillie, and the Squire was the impetuous sort who interested him.

It was hard to say just how it happened. They were at the table when Baird admired Sir George's home, its size, location, everything. He offered to buy it then and there. Lillie knew he had been drinking heavily, and Chetwynd laughed off the offer.

"I'll make it ten thousand pounds even," said the Squire.

"Nonsense!"

"All right, fifteen thousand pounds."

"Go to the devil!"

"Twenty-five thousand pounds."

Chetwynd gulped. The Squire held up his glass for a footman to refill it. Lillie said nothing, and the others at the table watched in awe. She wouldn't dare caution or interfere. The Squire meant what he said. He had the chips; drunk or not, he was enjoying himself. Again Chetwynd turned him down, but weakly. The Squire raised the ante, grinning as the baronet wiped the sweat from his forehead.

"Done." He had to say it.

"All right, we'll draw up an agreement immediately." He called to a footman and asked for pen and paper.

"I say, Baird, can't we wait? Lawyers and all that, you know."

"No—right here tonight. We'll sign, and I'll give you my check and take possession tonight. You're to leave everything as is. Don't move, take, or touch a thing. Just leave, and I'll be the new lord and master here."

"B-b-but—I say!—you can't!—really!"

"You said done, didn't you?" The Squire had a snarl in his voice. "And you want the money?" Chetwynd babbled something. "Then I'll trust you to keep up your end like the noble gentleman you're supposed to be."

Sir George flushed, looked around the table. The knowing smiles forced him to subside uncomfortably. Baird drained his glass and demanded more.

282

"How do you like my new house, Lillie?" he asked. "I always wanted to live in Regent's Park."

It was a very late party. The Squire grew surly and vicious. Lillie thought it wise to sneak away before he noticed. Sir George was perhaps the last to leave, clutching his check, but he was a stunned, bewildered man. He was allowed to take an overcoat, hat, and walking stick, nothing else.

Then the Squire was assisted upstairs by his valet, William Monk, who had come in from the carriage outside at Lillie's suggestion. He awoke late the next day in terrible shape. Blinking sore, inflamed eyes, he made out Monk watching him.

"Where am I?" he growled, shading his eyes.

"At home, Squire, in your own house."

"What the hell do you mean? This ain't my bed!"

Monk explained, then offered to bring his master—*what?* Coffee be damned! The Squire demanded whiskey. He was an original hair-of-the-dog man.

Lillie continued to see Baird often. He expected her to be on call, although he saw fit to absent himself frequently, hang around his West End pals, and get drunk at Romano's. His boxers always carried him home after he passed out, going on to become involved in more London brawls. He was absurdly jealous, forbidding Lillie to go out with anyone but himself, and her visitors made him violently angry. She was virtually under house arrest, always prepared to be his on his own gross, arbitrary terms. It was galling. She was at loose ends anyway from not working, hating to be taken for granted by the brutal Squire.

He had no business thinking he owned her and being so sure of himself. Like most men he was mostly talk. At bottom, she was no longer afraid of him. One morning, after she learned from Monk that his master had gone to Scotland for a few days, she decided to break free. On Regent Street, she ran into Robert Peel, later baronet, who was delighted to see her. He was bound for Paris that very day. Wouldn't it be a lark if she joined him?

"Paris!" he bubbled. "I love the city, simply adore it. I say, why don't you just pop over with me? We'll 'do' it together, what?"

"I don't know," she said pretending doubt. "But I could use some new Worth gowns."

Called "that prince of muttonheads" by the American newspapers, Bobby Peel in his silly way was a fourth-rate, road-company Mr. Abington. He had recently come into a great inheritance, also derived from coal mines, and had a cozy income of 100,000 pounds a year. There was a slight difficulty though; he had fantastic tastes and a desire to impress women that cost him 300,000 pounds a year. And now that the Jersey Lily was his at last he was going to buy Paris for her.

He banked her hotel suite with flowers, gave her gaudy jewelry. Gift after gift came by special messenger. He reserved entire night clubs, commanded special performances by singers and dancers, insisted on paying for her dresses at Worth's, and left a paper chase of ten-thousand-franc notes from Montmartre to the Tuileries. A thoroughly fatuous performance, but amusing as farce comedy. Bobby was sweet. He tried hard, and he was a change of pace. A few kisses and the implied promise of more sufficed him. Lillie had no trouble keeping him in hand.

But the game was afoot; coming events cast great shadows. The Squire would certainly follow, assume what he would assume, and take the proper steps.

Lillie expected him with a curious, anticipatory distaste. She was concerned about Bobby, but his brow was unclouded though he must have known the risks. They were having tea in her suite after a long day of shopping and fittings. There was a flurry of excited French in the hall, then a gruff English voice—an unmistakable voice. The teapot was steady in Lillie's hand as she poured, but Bobby Peel shot up as if he'd been bayoneted through the seat of his chair.

"My God, that's Baird, isn't it?"

"One lump or two, Bobby?"

"He'll kill me!"

If it had been locked, the door would have been battered open. As it was, it banged wide with such force the hinges

284

screamed. The Squire was flushed with rage and drink, aflame in his most dangerous mood. Lillie chose to disregard it.

"Come in," she said blithely. "How nice to see you in Paris, Squire. Do you know Mr. Peel?"

"I don't want to know the bastard!"

Bobby paled. He melted in his chair.

"Sit down and have some tea with us. It's so refreshing after a long trip."

"I'll refresh both of you!" the Squire snapped, snorting and pawing the carpet like an aroused stallion. Bobby darted for the door. "No, you don't!" The Squire intercepted him with the flat of his hand against Bobby's face. He shoved hard. Peel toppled backward over a fold in the rug, and the Squire began kicking him. He continued, Peel giving a grunting bleat each time and struggling to get up. Lillie tried to pull him off Bobby and was pushed roughly aside. Then the Squire dragged Bobby to the door, propped him up, and booted his terrified victim into the hall. "That takes care of one of you!" He slammed the door shut, bolted it, started after Lillie. "Come here, you!"

She backed away, the same sort of classic retreat she'd done hundreds of times on stage, except that this was painfully real and she was almost too frightened to move. She talked quickly, she tried frantically to disarm him with words. The Squire gave no sign of hearing. He was too intent on playing spider to her fly.

Drunk with anger, maddened by jealousy, he knocked her down with a blow to the left eye. Lillie staggered up and went down again with a smash to her right eye. Methodically, he cut open both cheeks with his knuckles, split her lips, and paralyzed her vocal cords with a punch to the throat. To complete his mastery, he ripped off her newest one hundred pound Worth gown, tore off her underthings, and pounced on her. Then, like a juvenile vandal maliciously eager to wreak the utmost destruction, he made a shambles of her suite. He turned over the bed, upset tables and chairs, scattered her possessions, ruined everything. Vaguely aware of his sound and fury, for perhaps the first and last time in her life Lillie fainted.

A knocking at the door brought her back to consciousness.

She couldn't speak. She was half blind from congealed blood, her face felt torn to pieces, her body used, bruised, and vilified. Some of her hair had been torn out by the roots. Her back was raw from fingernail scratches, tooth marks throbbed on her breasts and shoulders, and the reek of male musk was nauseating.

More knocking. The chambermaid, towels draped over her arm, came in and screamed. Her screams brought more maids, the hotel manager, followed by several doctors. Lillie was covered with blankets, the air blue with excited French as people stumbled over the débris in the room. Before she was removed to a private hospital, some shocked policemen appeared at her excruciatingly scrawled request. She scribbled a demand for the arrest of George Alexander Baird on charges of brutal assault, the manager adding hysterically that he would sue the *salaud* for damages to his property. The *gendarmes* took it all down, and shrugged. They asked where they might find this unspeakable creature.

"In any bar," she wrote. "Anywhere boxers or women congregate."

By the time Lillie awakened in the hospital the next day, bandaged like a mummy, so stiff and sore that she couldn't move, the story had spread from Paris to the London and New York newspapers. The distortions were wondrous. The beautiful Jersey Lillie was scarred and disfigured for life. She would never act again, perhaps never see or walk, and the fiendish, unrepentant Mr. Abington was all but committed to Devil's Island.

Actually, the Squire was in jail recuperating from a colossal hangover after a mélée with four policemen in a brothel. Lillie was resting as comfortably as possible for a lovely woman with two purple-black eyes, contusions on the face, a swollen nose, mashed lips, a croaking voice, an aching body—and the hideous thought that she might be pregnant.

She was under a sedative with three doctors conferring over her when a sorry, penitent Squire was led into her room under police guard and manacled. He was filthy, bedraggled, all the fight out of him. The police asked her to make formal application for the arrest of this Baird, this *canaille*. Lillie whispered that she wanted to speak to him alone. The doctors protested, the police expostulated with much head-shaking and shoulder-heaving. But, being French, they understood, and she had her way.

Lillie waited, fighting the sedative, and the Squire did an impossible, astonishing thing. He looked at her dazed—the ghastly eyes, the bandages, the wreck of a beautiful woman—as if for the first time realizing the bestiality of his attack. Then he burst out sobbing. Tears streaming from his bloodshot eyes, he ran toward her, clanked his handcuffed arms on the bed, weeping and accusing himself incoherently.

Her lips cracked as she smiled. She tried to laugh at what couldn't possibly be happening, and fell asleep.

It was two weeks before she was able to leave the hospital, heavily veiled and on her solicitously humble assailant's arm. According to the effusive hotel manager, everything was for the best. Her suite had been refurbished and redecorated by Monsieur Baird, he had also contributed generously to help the hotel forget the, shall we say, unfortunate incident. To avoid publicity the move was under cover of night. All tenderness and apologies, the Squire was a remarkably changed man.

"When I saw what I'd done to your beautiful face," he said in a shaky voice, "I could have killed myself. I swear I'll never hit you again."

"You'll go to prison if you do, Squire."

"Then don't make me jealous. For both our sakes, stay mine."

In ten days Lillie was ready to show her face outside the hotel. The Squire stayed close, finding time to attend the races at Longchamps and Auteuil, ride against amateur riders, buy some good mares for his stables, and mix with the Parisian boxing fraternity. When it came time to go home, they went to Cherbourg for the channel steamer. At the waterfront, the first thing to catch Lillie's eye was a huge white yacht riding at anchor in the sparkling blue waters of the harbor.

"Oh, isn't she lovely!" she exclaimed.

287

"Well, she's yours, and we're going back on her." Lillie was speechless. "I heard she was for sale, so I sent a telegram to the owner. She belonged to Francis Edward Baring, Lord Ashburton. You know those damn aristocrats—always out of pocket. He paid forty thousand pounds for her new. I got her for twenty thousand."

"She's so big. Why, you could go anywhere in her."

"Around the world and back! You wouldn't expect me to give you a small yacht, would you?"

They were brought out in a launch, and Lillie was piped aboard and welcomed like an admiral. The captain saluted, the crew—so many of them!—stood straight at attention for her inspection. Immaculate white uniforms, shining brass, gleaming decks. She was a floating palace.

"Captain Jones, this is Mrs. Langtry, the owner and your employer. Show her around this tub, and then spin us across the Channel."

"Very good, sir."

After handing her such a huge gift so casually, it was just like the Squire, with his indifference to yachting and all traditions, to use crude landsman's terms.

Lillie loved the yacht immediately, although she was big and showy for her taste. She would have preferred a racing sloop like—she thought of Edward's lovely yachts, the memorable *Red Gauntlet,* the *Gertrude,* the slim *Ildegonda.* Why, out on these very waters in Le Havre they had won the International Yacht Race in a gale—when was it?—eighteen years ago. With a pang, she concentrated on what Captain Jones was saying.

". . . and she's graceful as she is seaworthy, madam. Three years old, three-masted and schooner-rigged, as you can see, but what people call a steam yacht. She's two-hundred-and-twenty feet long with a twenty-seven-foot beam, and a burden of seven-hundred-fifty tons. Burns twelve tons of coal a day at sea under average conditions, lighted by modern electricity, and carries a crew of thirty-one men under my command."

"Is she the finest yacht in the world, Jones?" asked the Squire.

"Without a doubt, sir."

"Damn good thing. I don't want any second-bests for Mrs.

288

Langtry. Any whiskey on her?" Captain Jones hastily gave an order to a crewman, and Baird took Lillie's arm. "Funny, I still don't know the boat's name."

"She looks to me like a great white lady."

"Sure, the *White Lady!* Jones, order some new bronze name plates when we get in and get the painters busy."

Below in the handsome salon, the Squire paced up and down, scowling and gulping Scotch from a crystal tumbler. He was serious, an unusual mood for him. He helped himself to more whiskey, took a folded piece of paper from his wallet, and handed it to Lillie. A check for 50,000 pounds.

"Squire, what in the world! A magnificent yacht and this fortune."

"It's little enough for what I did to you."

"Suppose I refuse to accept it?" He looked so grim that she laughed. "Will I be knocked down and have my eyes blackened all over again?"

Now he pleaded with her.

"Very well," she said gaily, "then I won't. But money means so little to you. It's almost as if you were trying to bribe me."

"What the hell, Lillie! How else can I prove how much I love you?"

"There are subtler ways, deeper and more expressive."

"You know I'm not the subtle kind," he complained. "I don't trust emotions. Did you ever feel the same about something Wednesday as you did Tuesday? Not that I'll ever feel differently about *you*," he amended quickly, "but money's real, and so are yachts. They won't let you down."

"You can lose money," she reminded him, "and boats sink. Do you think love is real?"

"Ours is."

He sprang to embrace her, but Lillie shrank back as if she expected him to hit her.

"Stop being silly!" he said petulantly. "You know what else I'm going to do? I'm changing my will so you'll be one of the principal beneficiaries."

"There's no need for that, Squire."

"Damn it, I say there is! You're going to be taken care of, and

289

we're going to be married. The perfect combination. You want to act and be independent; I've got my own eggs to hatch. We'll never get in each other's way."

He meant it, and she was touched, even if the idea repelled her. She couldn't marry a man like Abington Baird.

"I'm not free. I can't marry anybody."

"I'll see Langtry when we get back. *I'll* make him listen to reason. He will at what I offer him, and if he won't—" He clenched his fist. "I'll pound sense into him. One punch should do him."

"Promise you won't touch him! Have a little decency for my sake, *please.*"

"Decency! You ought to hate that sniveling, weak-willed son of a bitch for messing up your life. If he had any guts, he'd blow his brains out and do the whole world a favor."

"You're cruel."

"A man's got to be to get what he wants!" He took her hand and trotted her up on deck, stopping along the bow rail out of sight of the crew. "Look there," he said, pointing at the black, oily swells streaming past. "If you said the word, I'd jump in. You don't believe me?" He put his leg over the rail, hoisted himself up, and straddled it.

"Squire!" Lillie clawed at him.

The yacht was rolling, and he balanced himself as easily as on horseback.

"Are you going to marry me?"

"What's the use of talking about it when I can't?"

"Answer me!" he shouted, leaning over the water.

Lillie gasped. The engines of the great *White Lady* throbbed under her feet, the 50,000-pound check crinkled in one trembling hand.

"Yes," she said with her most alluring smile. The Squire slid down off the rail and strutted toward her. "Of course."

eighteen

THE arrival of the *White Lady* generated much excitement in England. Pictures of the yacht were featured in newspapers and magazines, long stories stressed her luxury and, because of the sensational Paris fracas, she was sarcastically referred to as *The Black Eye*. While Lillie's detractors hoped that her beauty might have been impaired—something they felt her disgraceful association with the Squire more than justified—she returned to the stage lovelier and more radiantly youthful than ever. The London season was particularly brilliant that May of 1892, the theater boasting some scintillating attractions.

Henry Irving and Ellen Terry were at the Lyceum, alternating productions of *Henry VII, Hamlet,* and *Othello.* Oscar Wilde's *Lady Windermere's Fan* with Marion Terry was still a surprising hit at the St. James, and Lillie was at the Criterion in the provocatively named *The Fringe of Society* playing—what else?—a sophisticated good-bad woman.

The theater was sold out for every performance. The play was a shaky, showy vehicle propelled to success by Lillie's beauty and wardrobe. Much was made of the "simplicity of her frocks, youthful little gray skirt with a white lace blouse, apparently patterned by gray satin ribbons striped slantingly under the arms to fasten with choux rosettes behind." Her lovely hair was "brightened by a hat covered entirely with scarlet poppies and velvet bow of the same vivid glowing red, only relieved by a carelessly tied sheaf of young green barley." And she wore "another frock of creamy fawn shade with twin brooches of immense turquoises set with diamonds as spots of color at her throat and breast." With this went several "new black lace hats which remain level with her hair, but come out in the prettiest, picturesque poke in front.

The Squire had told her Milford was fast, and he promptly won several trial races. Lillie had given her horse little thought in the rush of mounting her new play. Now he had been entered in a big race for two-year-olds at Kempton Park. The officials had asked her to register her colors, and she mentioned it to Baird.

"So you got your notice from Weatherby's, eh? Well, I had Milford transferred to you last week. Any colors will do so long as they're original. Give me the form, and I'll fill it in."

Lillie smoothed the fawn-colored dress she was wearing, then her eyes went to the brooches the Squire had given her.

"Fawn and turquoise," she said deliberately. "How's that?"

"What the hell's fawn?"

"The same color as my dress. Light, yellowish brown."

"All right, fawn and turquoise." He wrote it down. "I'll make that turquoise with fawn hoops, turquoise cap."

"Hoops?"

"The circles on the sleeves of the jockey's blouse," he said impatiently. "Do you want to run under your own name?"

"Oh dear, I hadn't thought about that. The papers will puff it, and actors will be asking me for racing tips. No, but what would be a good *nom de course?* The Jersey Lily would never do, and they'd know—"

"Try Mr. Jersey."

"Perfect!"

He put it down. "You won't fool them long, Lillie, but what the hell do you care? You're going to have a lot of winners before you're through. Now, about your leading man," he said nastily, changing the subject. "I've been hearing some funny things."

"Charles Wyndham and I are old professional friends. Did you know he paid over sixty pounds for a seat at my New York début? He's a sweet old thing."

"See that you remain professional friends—*distant* professional friends. For your own good and mine, too."

Women race-horse owners had always been a rarity in England. The turf was regarded as a masculine enterprise, the only woman owner of any consequence at the time being "Mr. Manton," the Duchess of Bedford. The Criterion buzzed the night of June 4, 1892. Milford had won that afternoon at Kempton Park! The fact that Mr. Jersey was the Jersey Lily was known all over London. So was the Duchess of Bedford's pre-race remark, loudly expressed from her box: "I hope Milford drops dead."

"Sour old bitch," the Squire dismissed her. "Hasn't had a good win in years, and you're just beginning. You can't beat Morton as a trainer."

Where horses were concerned the Squire could be trusted, and Milford cooperated. He was a leading two-year-old. He won the Coventry Stakes at Ascot, the July Stakes at Newmarket, and his winnings approached 10,000 pounds. She was unable to see Milford run, because of the play, and contented herself by betting on him. The Squire took care of all details. Racing seemed easy, and Lillie was ecstatic at owning a winner. Nothing could be more gratifying.

After closing her season in August, she pried Baird away from his horses and boxers, and they went cruising in the *White Lady,* formerly Lord Ashburton's *Lady Mabel.* The yacht had been completely refitted according to Lillie's ideas, the alterations coming to some 20,000 pounds which the Squire paid. She was the biggest yacht at Cowes. Bigger than Bertie's or Queen Victoria's royal yachts, bigger even than J. P. Morgan's *Corsair.* Lillie found secret pleasure in outdoing them. The papers wrote that she was going round the world in her and would later steam to the United States for her next tour.

In the fall, Lillie looked for another theater. To be herself, to preserve her individuality in the face of the Squire's tyrannical possessiveness, she had to continue acting. She liked the Haymarket, where she had begun with the Bancrofts, but the management asked a big rental. Lillie postponed a decision until Baird insisted on paying all her expenses to five hundred pounds a week. She opened with *The Queen of Manoa* by Haddon Chambers and Outram Tristram, a poor play but the best available in a dreary field.

Baird did not have Freddie's lovable charm, yet she continued to admire his strength and impetuosity as much as she deplored his vulgarity and endless round of pleasure. Nor was he the man she would have wanted to marry—if she had been free—except that the subject did not seem to bear analysis. Edward's attitude in blocking the divorce was inexcusable, but she was grateful for the marital brake which kept her from becoming Mrs. Baird. How could one live on a seesaw with a man who could change from being warm, generous, and adorable to vicious, brutal, and hateful all in the same hour? To herself, Lillie refused to admit she loved him. Still, if life could be outrageous, people as well, why couldn't love?

Boxing had little interest for her. Society liked it as a novelty, especially because it was outlawed. Lillie had even been to a big party where the evening's entertainment was a fight between two well-known pugilists in the grand ballroom of a duke's castle. The titled guests had watched in dress clothes and, of course, several ladies had fainted at first blood. Thrilling. Too all-but. Lillie couldn't share the Squire's excitement on September 7, 1892, over the news that James John Corbett had knocked out John Lawrence Sullivan in twenty-one rounds at New Orleans. "Gentleman Jim" was thus the new heavyweight champion of the world and the first under the Marquess of Queensbury rules. The Squire disputed this claim: Charlie Mitchell was the true world's champion. Sullivan had avoided a third, rubber bout, but this was Mitchell's big chance.

"Gentleman Jim's a boxer, not a bull like Sullivan. He's made to order for Charlie! We'll go over to America and officially bring back the title where it belongs."

"When will you go?"

"Not till next year now. Charlie's in jail, you know."

The Squire had a spectacularly iron constitution and could discipline himself when he wanted to. But he wanted to less and less often. That fall he was puffy-faced and thick around

294

the middle. Lillie knew better than to point this out. She could never have successfully maintained her own looks or stage career if she had lived as Baird did. He set his own pace in everything and was particularly fond of introducing novelties to his pugilist pals.

It was a miserably raw and rainy Sunday afternoon in December, when Faithful Wright went to the Haymarket to pick up some dresses from her mistress's dressing room. She was full of talk on her return. She had seen Mr. Baird and his friends in the lobby of the theater. There was a lot of loud talk, screaming, and barking.

Barking? Trust *him* to do all he could to affront the traditions of the old Haymarket! Lillie dressed hurriedly and took a hansom to the theater. She could hear the commotion from the street—undoubtedly the barking of dogs, plus a terrified screeching she could not identify—and she hastened into the lobby past the big posters bearing her name and photograph. She saw a number of men with flushed faces screaming encouragement like race-track spectators. She couldn't fathom what was going on. The noise, odor, and confusion sickened her.

"Hello, Lillie," said the Squire, suddenly appearing at her side holding a sheaf of bills. "Come down to see the fun?"

"Just *what* are you doing in my theater?" she demanded coldly.

"I thought we'd liven up the drafty old barn with a little sport." He drew her toward the circle of screaming men, from the center of which arose shrill barks and anguished squeals. "Don't think you've ever seen anything like it."

"I don't want to," she said resisting. "What is it?"

"A rat pit."

She abhorred the cock- and dog-fighting he indulged in, but this—this—and in the mighty old Haymarket.

"Have a look," he urged her, laughing at her horrified expression. "Watch the little beggars fight for their lives."

Lillie started to say something but fled. The Squire burst out laughing and turned back to the pit, where two terriers were having a roaring go at killing the thirty-two rats put in there according to the rules. The dog killing the most in the shortest time was declared winner. But if as many as four of the rats either dog had shaken dead or senseless was somehow able to crawl out of the ring, he was disqualified. At the end of that particular go, before fresh rats and dogs were put into the pit, all rats still alive and in place were bludgeoned to death by the officials. Teeth snapped, skulls crunched, blood spattered as the terriers shook their prey, and over all squeaking, snarling, and barking. The Squire smiled as he contentedly placed his bets.

Lillie visited Jersey periodically. The Squire allowed this because he was not fond of children, and it was a small island. If she went on to Paris alone or tried to deceive him in any other way, he would hear immediately. She must remember what had happened last time.

Mama was her darling, immaculate self, loving, forgetful, and serene. Jeanne Marie was something else altogether: a gentle, well-bred girl of eleven, good manners and lessons stamped on her by governesses and tutors, totally different from the scrappy tomboy Lillie had been at her age. And she was beginning to ask embarrassing questions which never occurred to Mrs. Le Breton.

Why do I have to call you "ma tante" when people are around? Why do you say "my poor little niece" about me? Why can't I see my father if he's alive? Why doesn't he live with you? Why can't I live with you in London? Will I ever see you on the stage? Can I be an actress? Who is Squire Abington?

Who *is* Squire Abington? Why, that nice man who runs a rat pit, blackens my eyes, drinks heavily, has a stable of boxers and horses, showers me with money and jewels—and owns me. How could one satisfy a troubled, intense little girl living her childhood in secret, motherless exile? Lillie loved Jeanne Marie deeply. The maternal failures brought on by circumstances—most of them more or less of her own making—pained her. She was conscious of her responsibilities and wanted to do her honest best for the child, so far as she could. Her sudden, unannounced arrivals were happy interruptions in Jeanne Marie's placid, isolated existence.

296

Because she was growing up, Jeanne was a different person every time Lillie saw her. Adapting themselves to each other, assuming a mother-daughter relationship was not easy, but they managed—Jeanne because she admired her beautiful and mysterious mother, Lillie because she worked as hard in the role as she did in perfecting a new stage part. They came to feel very close, walking the beach hand in hand, Lillie talking convincingly in her melodious voice and Jeanne all eyes and anxious to please. Each time it took several days to accomplish this transformation, and Lillie was fairly pleased with herself. How easy it was to lose oneself in Jersey! People minded their own business, no reporters snooped about. One lived as one pleased, not to please others. It occurred to her that she could retire here if she wished and be a real mother to Jeanne. It would be good for both of them, and yet . . . Always "and yet."

George Alexander Baird was the last person one would choose to be the father of a sensitive, imaginative eleven-year-old girl. But how on earth could Lillie rid herself of the persuasive madman? She owed so much to him. Not that she wasn't wealthy in her own right, but it took a great deal of money to conduct an up-and-down business like the theater, dress and live like a first-magnitude star, and bring up a daughter like an aristocrat. Jeanne was going to have the finest education possible. In time she would come to London for the season, be presented at court —Bertie would have to see to that—and make a fine marriage to a rich nobleman of impeccable background.

And now here was the fantastic figure of the Squire become a fixture in Lillie's life. How ironic that the Jersey Lily, known to be so self-reliant and independent, was actually a prisoner in legal bonds to her long-estranged husband and to the Squire in possessive compulsion that passed for love. Neither jailer would ever let her go "until death do us part." She had rationalized that to leave Jersey it was necessary to marry Edward, to maintain her pre-eminence as a professional beauty it was necessary to give herself to Bertie. Now she was convinced that for the "love" she needed and insurance for her daughter and career it was necessary to surrender to the Squire. If she believed any of it, she was even weaker than Edward who had never been stronger than in his present sterile, self-defeating steadfastness.

"It's all settled," the Squire told her, shortly after Christmas. "Charlie Mitchell gets out of jail this week, and then we'll leave for America to beat Corbett. Why don't you come with me? You're going to tour there in the fall, anyway."

Lillie's mind moved with lightning precision. "I can't. My contract with the Haymarket runs through the winter—then there's the company."

"To hell with all that. I'll buy off the contract and take care of the salaries."

"It's nice of you, Squire, but the theater doesn't work that way. I just can't close up shop." He was angry, and she smoothed her hair, thinking hard. "But I could join you." Seeing this sat well with him, she pressed her advantage. "You'll be much better off looking after Charlie Mitchell and preparing for the fight without me. It's just like rehearsing a play without distractions."

"We can go on to your ranch after the fight, then."

The thought of the Squire possibly bumping into Freddie Gebhard at Langtry Farms intrigued her. What would these two say to each other? She had no intention of accommodating the Squire, but to keep the peace . . .

"All right. It's a lovely place, and your advice would help on the horses. Doc Aby is wasting my money."

"We'll set him right," he said cheerfully, now that things had gone his way. "And I'm going to see Lumley about changing my will. A codicil. Those family solicitors are a damn nuisance, but he did see your man Lewis. There seems to be no way of taking care of your husband. I wish you were Mrs. Baird, Lillie. I'd leave you all the money."

"I don't care about the money."

"Oh, come off it, sweetheart! But anyway, I'll fix it so you'll be taken care of if anything goes wrong."

"What could go wrong, Squire?"

"You never know. America's still a wild country." He laughed and pulled her close. Lillie was wearing a peignoir,

298

but she might as well have been naked. "God, how I love you! Gorgeous mane, perfect muzzle, fine chest, good hip, sound haunch, nice withers, wonderful legs. First prize, the blue ribbon on every point."

"I won't neigh my thanks."

"It's the highest compliment—horse- and woman-flesh. What is lovelier? Which reminds me. You're going to have a Derby-winner this year."

"You really think Milford has a chance?"

"Not Milford—Meddler. He won the Middle Park Plate his last time out, and he's going to run under your colors in the Derby. I'll make the arrangements when I come back, but I'll have Lumley draw up an agreement before I leave."

The Squire was terribly rushed before he left. Lillie was excused from seeing him off at Liverpool because she had to appear at the Haymarket. They spent the last night together. She thought he seemed far from his ebullient self. He hardly touched his champagne at dinner, and he was disturbed.

"Damn that Walter Lumley. He made out a codicil to my original will but talked me out of having you as a legatee. You see, my mother's still living and so is my grandmother, and—well, I couldn't do anything different. You tell lawyers what to do and then they don't do it. But as soon as I get back, I'm going to get around Lumley by transferring to your account what I would have left you. He'll call you about Meddler."

"I told you it doesn't matter."

"It does to me. You mean more than my family, and yet they have the right, Lumley says. What do I care about my first cousins?"

In bed, the Squire never stopped talking, saying how much he loved and wanted to marry her. It was an uncomfortable time for Lillie, but her nerves did not fail her. The occasion was such a sentimental one she almost convinced herself that she loved Mr. Abington. As he kissed her good-by, she handed him a little package containing a handsome stickpin in the shape of an owl's head in onyx and diamonds.

"It's because you're so wise, can see in the dark, and play with rats."

He caressed it lovingly as he put it into his necktie. "If the ship sinks, it'll be the first thing I save." The Squire looked at her wistfully. "I want to marry you. Marriage is about the only thing I haven't tried."

"Some men aren't cut out for marriage," she said gently.

"It's a natural state, isn't it? And how could I miss with you?"

Baird sailed for America on the *Majestic* Tuesday, February 8, 1893, with Charlie Mitchell, Jem Hall, and an entourage that included his secretary Joseph Bailey, valet William Monk, the trainer Billy Woods, the bookmaker George McDonald, and assorted secondary boxers. His departure was the occasion for frenzied farewell scenes on the pier and in various staterooms. All the Squire's West End set was in attendance. The big White Star Line steamship was crowded with carnival performers, hooting, shouting, and drinking champagne from the bottle. A band played, songs that made women passengers blush were bellowed, and drunken fighters squared off for hilarious rounds all over the ship. One fell off the stern into the Mersey and had to be fished out. The Squire gleefully played his favorite part as master of the revels, now and then thoughtfully fingering his new stickpin.

Perhaps Baird thought of Americans as hayseeds or he was merely confident of his own sharp strategy. As it was, he outsmarted himself. After Mitchell's challenge to Corbett was accepted, the Squire agreed to bet on the side as much money as all the sports in the United States could raise. At the contract signing in Gilsey House, New York City, Richard Canfield handed over fifty thousand-dollar bills representing the betting money riding on Corbett. The Squire stalled. Al Smith, one of the fight promoters, told him flatly to put up or shut up. The Squire had only $10,000 to show. His bluff had been called, and now the fight arrangements were snarled in misunderstanding.

As negotiations resumed, Mitchell urged Baird to match Jem Hall against Bob Fitzsimmons, a fellow countryman who had fought successfully in Australia and New Zealand before coming to the United States in 1890. Baird liked the idea. It would whet the public appetite for the big brawl between

Mitchell and the champion and be remunerative as well. New York frowned on boxing, however, and the Squire put out feelers. The best offer came from New Orleans which put up a record $27,000 for the fight.

A more cosmopolitan and less censorious city than New York, New Orleans appreciated pugilism as a fine art. The Squire and his contenders were guests at many banquets before the Hall-Fitzsimmons fight on Wednesday, March 8. A partisan crowd of 12,000 people gathered in a big, drafty hall to watch. The Squire bet a wad on Jem. He sat at the ringside wearing evening clothes in the atmosphere of sweat, blood, cigar smoke, and harsh screaming that he loved. From the start, Hall showed little against the aggressive Fitzsimmons, who was to take the title from Corbett at Carson City, Nevada, in 1897. Fitzsimmons took a lead in the first round, knocking him down. The Squire was alarmed.

He stripped to his silk undershirt and insisted on acting as his man's second. He ministered to Hall between rounds, shouting advice to no effect. Fitzsimmons connected solidly in the fourth. The crowd roared as Hall went down—and out. Mitchell jumped into the ring to nurse his friend.

It was some time before Hall recovered.

"What round was it, Charlie, when I got knocked out?" he asked.

Mitchell told him.

It was an ignominious loss. The Squire paid up. Chilled and soaked with sweat from his exertions, he went right out and celebrated in the same clothes, exactly as if Jem Hall had won. He hadn't ridden since November, he was fleshy and soft, but he thought nothing of it when he began to cough the next day. That night early he took to his bed in the St. Charles Hotel, racked with fever and trying to kill it with whiskey. Friday he was worse but sure he would shake this illness as he had shaken all the others. He refused to call a doctor. By Monday he was delirious, so sick that his worried valet and secretary called in a Dr. Fitch, who at once diagnosed pneumonia.

Dr. Fitch said later that "his constitution was too weak from dissipation to rally from the increasing severity of the attack." It is significant that the Squire lingered six more days, fighting a last-ditch battle and refusing to believe he would die. Toward the end, he kept asking, "Is she here? Is she here yet?" This made no sense to the doctor, and no one bothered to explain.

He died on Saturday, March 18. The boxers grouped in the hall outside his room sobbed at the news. Iron men like Squire Abington weren't supposed to die, and he was dead at thirty-two. Perhaps the wonder was that he had lived so long.

The body was sent to New York on one train, the superstitious Bailey and Monk following from New Orleans in another. On March 29 the *Majestic* brought the Squire, embalmed and fittingly dressed in evening clothes, back to Liverpool which he had left among scenes of great hilarity only seven short weeks before. And on April 1 the last curtain was drawn on the short, happy life of George Alexander Baird, who had been born in a hotel room and had died in one. He was buried next to his father in Stichill churchyard near Kelso, Scotland.

Lillie was not so much bereft as shocked. The Squire had entered her life like a thunderclap and was gone just as suddenly. No doubt he had loved her in his way. Now that he was dead she could safely admit that, because she had tolerated his domination as she had no other man's, she must have loved him a little, too. Yet marriage had always been out of the question, and relief was part of her mixed feelings. She never had any intention of going to Scotland for the funeral, nor did she show any signs of grief. Yet Lillie was only too aware of the gap he'd left. Never had anyone been so violently alive as the Squire; one would have expected him to die violently, not of a natural cause.

"Such a nice young man," said Mrs. Le Breton. "So vital. Really a shame."

The servants saw and understood a great deal, Lillie decided, when Louis, her chef-turned-butler, expressed his sorrow. Honest Frenchman that he was, Louis added, *"Il était fou, mais je l'aimais malgré moi. Cependant, Madame a de la chance."* They were exactly her own feelings: She was lucky. Still, she had come to depend on Baird in so many ways. Now she was dissatisfied and at a loss. She was off the stage and had no desire to act or do much of anything. She had come to a new phase of her life unprepared. It was imperative that she re-orient herself without the comfortable if forbidding bulk of the Squire to bolster her.

Financially, his death made a big difference. Owning a big yacht and running a racing stable were expensive luxuries over and above the demands of the theater. She had used Milford's winnings to buy more horses and now, since the Squire's magnificent stables at Moulton Paddocks would be broken up and sold, she had to find quarters for her own animals. So she bought a house called Regal Lodge in the village of Kentford as a "racing-box" and turned her horses over to Sam Pickering, a well-known trainer. The yacht, which she now thought of as *The White Elephant,* was put up for rent, but she still had to pay the salaries of Captain Jones and his crew on a stand-by basis.

Long the despair of the trustees of his father's will, the Squire had been the bane of his solicitors. His business dealings had been careless, complex, and complicated. He had left his personal affairs in a mess. When the will was finally probated it was learned that as he had told Lillie, his fortune was left first in trust to his mother, then to the children of his first cousins. The gross value of his personal estate was given as 846,051 pounds, 12 shillings, and 11 pence. The amount was considerably under what had been estimated, leading friends to observe that in his wasteful, fun-loving fashion the Squire had gone through close to 2,000,000 pounds.

Lillie had been requested to visit his lawyers. Walter Lumley, the principal executor of his estate, was as difficult as the Squire had described him. Neither beauty nor sentiment moved him, and her session with him was marked with unpleasantness, in spite of Sir George Lewis' protective presence. To make sure Baird was right about the codicil, Lillie asked if she had been remembered. The lawyer informed her coldly that only the family was mentioned in the will. She nodded.

Lumley amended his statement: no *strangers* were mentioned in the will.

The Squire's death had voided the agreement over Meddler as her Derby winner, and Lumley added that there was a serious question about the ownership of Milford. The newspapers reported that the executors were planning legal proceedings against her, claiming that the horse belonged to the estate since no deed of gift was found. But Lewis saw to it that she kept Milford.

There was additional argument about the 50,000-pound check Baird had given her, since he was legally bound not to distribute such largesse without approval of his solicitors. The inference was that he had been blackmailed. As late as December 16, 1893, newspapers both in England and America were telling how the notorious Mrs. Langtry had settled out of court a suit "involving the late 'Squire' Abington's estate." The story was that he had regretted his generosity and employed a friend, at 20,000 pounds, to get Lillie to surrender the check. On delivery of it, he paid 5,000 pounds, and the suit now brought against the estate was for the remaining 15,000 pounds.

Lillie knew this was all fiction, for the canceled check was among Baird's papers.

She tried to bid on Meddler at the sale of Baird's horses and was prevented by Lumley's representatives. He was sold to W. H. Forbes of Boston, then to William Whitney, and died the property of Clarence H. Mackay in France, although Lillie several times dickered for him.

Furious at being blocked from buying Meddler, Lillie did obtain Lady Roseberry at the sale of the Squire's stables. A good horse, nothing to compare with Meddler, but she found some satisfaction in the way Lumley botched an opportunity to make money for the estate. By St. Gatien out of Busybody, Meddler had won the rich Chesterfield Stakes the previous year over the best two-year-olds in England. He had been an 1893 Derby favorite. The Squire had predicted he would win, and the bookmakers had believed him. A lot of money was put on him in advance, but Lumley was anxious to keep the horse from Lillie. Meddler failed to start because Sir George Lewis was demanding a settlement to drop his client's claim, and Lumley vacillated. As a result, Meddler's backers lost thousands of pounds when he was scratched, or so the reports had it.

With the Squire out of her life and Lewis' word that there was now little to fear from Edward, Lillie brought Mrs. Le Breton, Jeanne Marie, her governess and tutors to live in Pont Street. She also kept the house in Jersey, using that and Regal Lodge for vacations and change of *milieu*.

Lillie had had no manager since Griffith had gone back to America during her last illness. Her personal and business records were in a muddle; she needed a combined business manager and personal representative. The man she chose was the amiably resourceful Edward Michael. Just returned from the United States and determined never again to truckle "or hitch his wagon to any woman star," the breed of which he'd had a bellyful, he kept the appointment at Pont Street only to say No in person.

Mrs. Langtry appeared almost immediately, and the hard-headed Michael was undone. He later said she never made an entrance: there was no opening or shutting of doors, no noise, commotion, posing, or "effect." The Jersey Lily was just suddenly there, "a vision of beauty and grace." Dresses then had long trains, always awkward to handle, but Lillie's way with hers was "a rare exhibition of grace." And ". . . once on the scene and the train 'set,' she never touched it again; it seemed a part of her, and was maneuvered as though it were a rudder obeying its helm."

"And so you are to look after my business?" said the lovely vision, smiling bewitchingly and putting out her hand. "I am sure we shall get on well together. And now we have to talk about money—most unpleasant, is it not? But we will soon get it over. What are your views?"

Michael could only give them. They proved identical to hers, and they turned to business. Accustomed to flighty actors and actresses, he was "amazed at her grasp of affairs, her amazing insight, and her masculine power of instant decision." He signed on in spite of himself, "another scalp added to her girdle, and from that moment commenced a long period of willing and delightful slavery."

He prepared to leave, a little dazed. Lillie saw him looking at a watercolor on the wall of her drawing room. "Oh, that is my yacht, the *White Lady*. Isn't she a beauty? I wonder if you would mind taking charge of her. I understand you know about ships and things."

Michael knew nothing about ships but found himself mumbling in the affirmative. He chartered the yacht to a man who planned to turn her into a floating hotel, taking paying guests to see a naval review off Cowes. The man made a deposit, but couldn't fulfill the terms of the contract. There was "the most beautiful and luxurious vessel afloat," lavishly provisioned with hams, tongues, chickens, delicacies in aspic, and hotel fare, idle and tied up in Cowes. Beside himself, Michael telegraphed the bad news to Lillie. Back came a brief wire from Regal Lodge: IF YOU CAN MANAGE IT, PLEASE COME DOWN.

He came on her among the strawberry beds, her lips red from the fruit, lovely and unconcerned.

"Do eat some of them, Mr. Michael," she said in charming command. "They are just ripe, and the only way to eat strawberries is from the vine."

"But what about the boat?"

"Such a bore. How silly people are, to organize things they can't carry out."

"I know, but she's got steam up and she's groaning with food down at Cowes. Why don't you go out on her, Mrs. Langtry?"

"Oh, goodness, no! I hate naval reviews—all that pompous clanking and bustle. Besides, have you any idea how difficult it is to get a yachting party together? There's nothing in the world harder than to find just the right people—people who will mix comfortably. It's so much easier for a man to do these sudden things, anyway." She smiled brightly. "You go down, see the review, and eat some of those horrid provisions. I want you to, Mr. Michael."

The manager made good use of the yacht, then at her suggestion dispatched the *White Lady* to America in July. She was big, ostentatiously luxurious, and would surely be an irresistible attraction. Leaving Cowes in July, she reached New York in fifteen days averaging eleven knots an hour. She went on to Newport where she was leased to the millionaire Ogden Goelet for something like $2,000 a month with the option of purchase. And that was the last Lillie had to do with the Squire's impulsive gift for a time, although the *White Lady* continued to be associated with her as the press ran periodic stories about the Jersey Lily's projected voyages to every place except the North Pole.

Following the Squire's death, Lillie remained off the stage nearly a year, enjoying her leisure, establishing her stables at Regal Lodge, spending time with her daughter, and mending social fences. To the intense relief of her male friends, who had agonized over her affiliation with the unspeakable Baird, she began to be seen at dinners, parties, and receptions in London. She had no particular favorites. There was the usual struggle among her escorts to be top man, but as she had found them pale after knowing Freddie, so she thought them insipid milksops on the heels of the dynamic Squire. Still, their flattery and dancing attendance was soothing in comparison to the vulgarly passionate tumult that had surrounded her lately. She was content to shine again among old friends, holding well back this side of flirtation without discouraging any masculine hopes—a technique Lillie excelled in.

Her new admirers included a number of diplomatic attachés such as Portugal's Marquis Luis de Soveral, Austria's Prince Paul Esterhazy, and Germany's Baron von Dunkelmann. They were socially prominent, in solid with Alfred Rothschild's set, as well as with the Prince of Wales's Marlborough clique, and carried impeccable titles. Since the élite had ostracized her during the Baird phase, Lillie did not underestimate the prestige value of Bertie's friendship. Though she was cold-blooded in devoting herself to those men who rated highly with the Prince, she found some consolation in their charm and fastidiousness. They moved in the best company and they were influential— especially Luis de Soveral. This diplomat had sharp, sinister, dark features similar to Abe Hummel's, except for his Kaiserish mustache and swarthy jowls which gave him the nickname of the "Blue Monkey."

While men had always accepted her and taken a charitable view of her lapses, women were the true social arbiters. With them Lillie had long been *persona non grata,* and that July she faced many rebuffs at the Goodwood races. Walking among the dining tables set out under the trees at the Duke of Richmond's estate, where she had so often queened it in the past, she was quickly aware of the malicious undercurrent. There was nothing subtle about it. She was being read out of Society with the cut direct. Lillie stopped to talk to old friends and acquaintances at the tables, but Lady This or Duchess That deliberately looked away without deigning to reply. Callous, calculated to hurt, to put the notorious Lillie in her iniquitous place, to sink her socially once and for all without a trace. Not just the hostesses who had fallen over themselves to have her as their most honored guest in the professional beauty days, but women like Mrs. Sassoon whom she had respected.

Only an experienced actress of equable temperament, nerveless in crisis and expert in dissembling her feelings, could have taken such treatment. Snubbed repeatedly as she progressed, Lillie continued amiable. Her manner was charming, she was beautiful and enchantingly dressed, her voice melodious as she passed from one icy, speechless table to the next, presumably unconscious of the ugly whispers behind her. In the dappled summer sunshine playing through the leaves overhead, her endowments put all those feline watchers to shame. Scorned, dishonored, snubbed—and uncaring.

Oh, damn the Langtry! Who was that rushing toward her so eagerly? The Prince.

"How good to see you again, Mrs. Langtry!"

"Thank you, Your Highness." She curtsied gracefully, cats' eyes on her from every table, claws itching under long gloves. "You're looking very well."

"Goodwood always does that to me. Are any of your horses racing?"

"Not this year. Have you some entries?"

"As usual. You must join Princess Alexandra and me in our

box later." He said it loudly, bless him. "Are you sitting with anyone now?"

No, she told him carelessly, as if it were of no concern. "Then you *must* sit with me. I am at Mrs. Sassoon's table."

He took her arm, started back, then saw a lady he wished to speak to. With Lillie accompanying him, he stopped at table after table along the gauntlet she had just run. The change in the recent statues was so extreme Lillie could have shouted with laughter. They were *so* warmly pleasant, *so* friendly now. How lovely she looked, such a pretty dress, how wonderful to see her at Goodwood, how exquisite . . . Purr, purr, purr. Then she was seated next to Bertie with Mrs. Sassoon breaking her back to make amends, traducing herself with conviviality to impress the Prince. The Jersey Lily was back on the royal dais, and the others were all looking up to her. No matter what her feelings in her triumphal redemption, not a trace of smugness was evident in her lovely, untroubled face. Bertie was their leader and future king. Whatever he said or did was automatically right.

It was funny and it was sad. The relationship between her and Bertie had changed, as it had to, thought Lillie, but the foundation was solid. They were bound in tangible memories. Their friendship transcended the past and the present for reasons that were beyond these stupidly vicious aristocrats. Bertie would never disown her.

"By the way," he said in a low voice. "How old is she now?"

"She? Oh, all of twelve."

"That much. It doesn't seem possible."

He looked at her and sighed. He was fifty-three now, looked and felt it, despairing that he would ever be king as Victoria continued to reign endlessly. His mother's presence still struck a chill on him, she made him feel like a guilty small boy. But Lillie now so grandly beautiful at, it must be, forty. Incredible! All the figure and allure of young beauty—and much more.

"Nice to see all your old friends at Goodwood again, eh, Lillie?"

"Friends?" she said softly.

Bertie chuckled.

nineteen

Back in social favor through Bertie and his ardent diplomatic friends, Lillie returned to the stage in *The Social Butterfly*, a fuzzy, lightweight play by Robert Buchanan, a prickly poet with chips on both shoulders.

Sitting in at rehearsals for the first time, Edward Michael took note of her decisiveness and her "Don't let us fuss, *please*" at interruptions, and he came to recognize it as a danger signal. She hated hairsplitting and nitpicking, her manager learned.

> She never hurried, never flustered, never made unnecessary talk, but with great dignity and decision would on quick consideration pronounce judgment. Quite rightly . . . [she] exacted obedience and loyalty from those who served her. Once she had decided to trust, her trust was unbounded, and she never again considered the recipient of her trust but as one capable and to be relied on.

> For deceit there was neither palliation nor excuse; to betray her trust was inexcusable.

> She would be hurt, for she had far more heart than she was given credit for, but she could not and would not endure stupidity or incompetency, and any lack of straightforwardness was with her unforgivable.[1]

Michael was an observant man and found Lillie an absorbing study. He gave her the highest marks in every feminine charm: wiles, fascination, and moods. He credited her with "the iron will, immense courage, and a gift of instant decision which the

---

[1] *Tramps of a Scamp*, Edward Michael. London: Werner Lavrie, Ltd.

captain of a 50,000-ton liner in a critical situation might envy."

To his surprise, since she was a busy woman, Lillie was remarkably well-read. He found no topic which she could not discuss with specialists. She had "a big, broad mind which could not tolerate anything commonplace or futile," and, in business, she was "that rare phenomenon, a woman with a man's brain." She also impressed him as "one of the acknowledged wits of the world" with an unlimited sense of humor "rare in her sex."

Michael knew stage people and their way of acting off stage, and he had the skepticism of his profession. He had been reluctant to work for Lillie, but she had disarmed him from the start—and she continued to disarm him. To compound the mystery of her attraction to Abington Baird, her manager noted that "the coarse and sordid were entirely foreign to her nature and never tolerated in her presence." And the unhappy wretches whose comic reputation depended on coarse, dirty jokes were immediately exposed to Lillie's unequaled gift for expressing disgust or quiet contempt. "She could crush, destroy, and pulverize in record time, and in the smoothest, blandest manner."

Lillie could be thoughtful, as Michael had many opportunities to see. She was so appreciative of little services that people leaped to assist her. She had only to say, "Oh, thank you so much. How kind of you!" in her sweet voice, bestow her dazzling smile on her servitor, and he was her slave. Or she might press a sovereign into a dazed stagehand's fingers. "Now you will buy something for your pretty baby, won't you?" she'd murmur, and another had joined the legion who would "do anything for Mrs. Langtry." And it was never the money that clinched their lifelong devotion.

A sense of humor was particularly useful regarding a play as weak as *The Social Butterfly*. It opened at the Comedy Theater, Panton Street, on March 19, 1894. Lillie was praised for her clothes, beauty, and acting; the play was thumbed-down. As for Robert Buchanan, the aggressive playwright, it was recorded that "with his customary want of tact, he did all he could to spoil Mrs. Langtry's opening by a violent speech before the curtain accusing the London critics of trying to crush him." But it would take an outstanding author to compete against the Jersey Lily's loveliness *and* the House of Worth.

She was overpowering in a soft white woolen gown with a very wide, pale tartan ribbon and with a Zouave jacket; dazzling in a garden dress "of white muslin, the bodice trimmed with lace, a loose back in brocade with silver threads embroidered in a floral design and lined with yellow silk." To complete this eye-filling fashion show were two ball dresses, "one of pink and silver ornamented with long sprays of pink roses and green leaves; the other of ivory satin with huge butterfly bows of cream-tinted lace, caught here and there on the bodice with diamond clasps." With them Lillie shimmered in her splendid tiara and necklace of diamonds.

"It doesn't matter what you play in," said Oscar Wilde after the opening, at a supper at the popular Café Monico in Piccadilly Circus. "You're so beautiful people don't bother listening to what you're saying. They didn't listen to poor Buchanan either!"

Fame had changed Oscar. He was trailed by a task-force of sponging young sycophants who oiled him with flattery, repeated his witticisms, and behaved odiously. A biographer wrote later that as he became prosperous, he became preposterous—a description Oscar himself might have written. His conceit approached megalomania, and any criticism infuriated him. Always a big man, he had turned to swollen fat, his forehead was veined, his features flushed, his look apoplectic. In spite of it all, there were welcome flashes of the old Oscar who had never lost his love of life and sense of fun.

He and Lillie were still good friends. *Lady Windermere's Fan,* which he had allegedly written for her, had established him on the stage, and last year he'd had another success with *A Woman of No Importance.* Strange she was forced to appear in a piece like this empty showcase of Buchanan's, when Oscar was so much more talented. Perhaps she was truly foolish, yet she was glad Oscar had managed without her—and this quite apart from the ugly rumors circulating about him—things much uglier than had ever been said about the Squire.

"And why should they listen to Buchanan?" she said strongly. "It's up to the public. It always is."

"Ah, the amorphous *peuple ému*." He gave a mock bow. "I'm working on a new play, Lil. *An Ideal Husband*. What do you think of that as a definition of your Edward?" he said gently.

"Or Constance's Oscar?"

"*Touché*." He grimaced. "Beauty is enough for some women. Why do you have to be intelligent, too? But I've been a good husband. I've given Constance a home and children. She could have more, I suppose. As a wife, she's fecund to none."

There was laughter nearby, then succeeding waves down the table as his remark was savored and passed along. Fecund to none, fecund to none. Dear Oscar.

Abe Hummel had forwarded all the necessary information. Arrangements were completed for her forthcoming tour of the United States under the management of E. B. Norman. Lillie checked the playing dates and itinerary and went over the plans carefully with her staff. For Edward Michael she had "a Napoleonic genius for detail." In preparing a theatrical campaign or reviewing business affairs nothing escaped her all-seeing eye. He was in the habit of handing her the cashbook for inspection every Monday. He had never seen the equal of her gift for mental arithmetic. She knew her present credit balance down to the last twenty or thirty pounds, just as by the same magic calculation she could "estimate the worth of the house within a few pounds on the rise of the curtain."

Lillie did not like repetition. Once a decision was made, a question answered, it was over and done with. The oaf who revived the discussion or wanted some matter clarified was impaled with, "But we have settled that already, have we not? Let us not fuss, please."

Public relations were part of Michael's job. Gauging the attitude of the flamboyant American press was a complicated business. It had run both hot and cold toward Lillie, and her influence was tremendous. Not a day went by, even when she was in England, that there weren't columns about her in the American newspapers, and while she was in the Land of the

Free both male and female reporters were assigned to cover her every movement. They were not above extracting fanciful "exclusives" from waiters, chambermaids, carriage drivers, and others who chanced to attend her, however casually.

"Detachment is of great importance in these things," Lillie told her manager, "and, after all, I am an American. But we must sniff the wind carefully, Mr. Michael."

She left Liverpool with forty trunks of Worth dresses and twelve members of her company, including the dependable James Smyth-Pigott, on the American liner *Paris*. Jeanne Marie accompanied her.

In New York at the Holland House, reporters crowded into the flower-filled suite which Hummel had reserved for Mrs. Langtry. She spoke cordially to every man she remembered, telling them that she regretted her four-year's absence from the United States and wished she had never gone. She added much more truthfully, "New York is home to me, and I am interested in all its changes and improvements. My greatest surprise was to find 23rd Street considered downtown now."

The minute she mentioned the address she knew the reporters wanted to question her about her house there and Freddie, but she never gave them the chance. Hummel had told her the house was still for rent, but no tenant had turned up, and it was run down both inside and out. The house was still associated with Freddie and herself—and would be until it crumbled to dust—but she had no intention of going near the place.

"And what about Freddie?" she dropped casually, as she and Hummel discussed her long-aborted divorce suit.

"You must have heard he got married, Mrs. Langtry. She's a well-known Baltimore beauty—Louise Hollingsworth Morris. Good family and all that, but on the giddy side. It was a big, elaborate wedding. Friends of the two families came from all over the world to be there."

Lillie crushed the pang of remorse that started in her so unexpectedly. "I'm delighted to hear it. I hope he's happy."

She left Hummel's office with its autographed pictures of well-known actors and actresses and passed through the drab reception room filled with criminal-faced, seedy individuals who looked like the dregs of humanity. Howe & Hummel had an amazing clientele! Their reputation was invidiously heroic, and she was always relieved to quit their 89 Centre Street headquarters. As far as lawyers went, no two men could be such opposites as the shrewd, ugly Hummel and her English barrister, the courtly, aristocratic Sir George Lewis. Yet they both got results for her.

She spent less than a week in New York, seeing friends and showing Jeanne Marie points of interest, before boarding the familiar *Lalee*. Under the supervisory management of Joseph Reynolds her itinerary included sixteen weeks on the road, followed by four in New York City. The *Lalee* brought back disturbing memories. How gay, happy, and uncaring she and Freddie had been! She should never have let him go. If he'd had a quarter of the Squire's nerve—but perhaps it was for the best. The only thing was that she didn't quite believe it. She felt old and tired—until she looked in the mirror or saw younger women marveling at her youthful beauty or was asked by women reporters how she kept young.

Her tour began in Scranton with her old standby, *Peril*. Next Boston flocked to see her at the Park Theater in *Esther Sandraz*. Never before had she met with such enthusiasm.

In Chicago, a *Tribune* reporter, after interviewing her at the Auditorium Hotel, wrote of the spell in the room as his first glimpse of the Jersey Lily showed her to be the same radiantly beautiful woman, standing under the full light of the gas and slightly bending over a table.

The reporter was struck by the "very pretty manner Mrs. Langtry has of referring the question to her listener, which is flattering to him, and saves her tone from sounding didactic." She spoke of her London town house and writing table of which Oscar Wilde had said, "It is too pretty to be used for anything but writing poetry and love songs."

Lillie said there were few matinées in England, and the two a week in America plus performances every night she found tiring. She spoke of her "pretty house in New York" as if she still lived in it.

"But, after all, I prefer a nomadic existence. I am happier traveling. I am fond of a caravan life—the continual change pleases me. Is it a bad trait of character to love a change? Since I have to do it, I am fortunate in liking it, am I not? Do you know, there is something very pleasant about coming to a strange hotel, finding a different arrangement of furniture, the fireplace in a different place, a different kind of bed, a different kind of mirror there in the corner, where I cannot see to do my hair—everything unfamiliar."

"Mrs. Langtry," the reporter concluded, "is charming and witty. Her subtle attractiveness is not to be expressed in words. Her voice is as pure as crystal, and it is a voice the vibrations of which are as sweet as celestial music."

Town after town turned out in force for her. She was compared to Bernhardt, her acting called surpassing for "its dignity, its force, its passion, its delicacy, and its verisimilitude;" her art praised for its cleverness, intelligence, and the sophisticated manner in which she caught "the shrill intensity of the city."

In those days prominent touring stars overlooked few settlements, no matter how small, that could possibly offer a full house. Many a hamlet, whistle stop, or crossroads town had an opera house or civic auditorium of some sort, although some were ramshackle affairs. Looking back long afterward, Lillie was sure she was more familiar with their country than most Americans were; she could hardly put her finger on any town important enough to be on the map that she hadn't played in at least once.

"Well," she said, as they left Toledo, "next week New York."

"Will it be different there?" said Michael, smiling. "Even Queen Victoria herself doesn't get such red-carpet treatment."

"They order this matter better in America. You should have accompanied me in the old days, Mr. Michael. There were great civic receptions for me, an entire town was at the station, and Wild West mayors descended on me with jeweled stars as big as cheese plates and wearing outlandish, occult regalia. And some of the gifts I received you'd never imagine. Which reminds me—would you mind going to Salt Lake City?"

316

It was over a thousand miles distant, but the manager could only say yes. She told him of her talk with Hummel and her property there: on her 1883 tour some prominent citizens of Salt Lake City had given her deeds to land now "town lots" and presumably valuable. Michael made the jaunt with precise instructions to investigate and sell to the best advantage, if advisable. He joined her in New York holding a tax-free check for $40,000. Lillie looked at it and smiled.

"Thank you so much! And didn't you find that Utah city interesting? But I'm in heaven at my reception here, Mr. Michael. Let me read you just one sentence of William Winter's review in the *Tribune*: 'Mrs. Langtry conquered again, with the spell of her radiant beauty and the commanding grace and magnetism of her stately presence. There was not a trace of the amateur.' " She laughed. "Isn't that lovely—except that it makes me sound like a castle? I'm having the gentleman to tea this afternoon, and you must have a cup with us."

Being back in New York delighted Lillie. The city had vitality, a frantic pulse beat, a bursting at the seams. It had changed dramatically in her absence: uptown was downtown, stores, restaurants, theaters, and hotels had changed locations, and one had to learn where everything was all over again. It was the day of Charles Dana Gibson's Gibson Girl, America's lovely, outdoorsy, athletic ideal. The cycling craze of the nineties was in full swing. Everyone was on wheels, tooling along Riverside Drive, through Central Park, and the smart places to eat included Dorlando's, Churchill's, Rector's, Shanley's, Reisenweber's on Columbus Circle, and Bustanoby's.

Even Jim Brady, now known as "Diamond Jim," heaved his bulk on a cycle and took to the road of a leisurely afternoon. He came to pay his respects to Lillie with the usual jeweled trinket he had picked up on his railroad travels. His grizzled, porcine face beamed as she attached the diamond clip to her bodice. He was still the jolly Santa Claus. Tales of his gargantuan appetite were in circulation. When he laughed his huge frame shook, making his diamond cuff links, stickpin, watch chain, and the rings on his thick fingers shoot out dazzling light

317

rays. He talked gaily of Lillian Russell's brilliant successes, and he spoke guardedly of Freddie.

"You broke the poor fellow's heart, Lillie, but that's the way it goes. I dunno about this wife of his. Freddie's got talent, always did except he don't know how to use it. I got him working for me now—when he does work."

Lillie watched Brady consume enormous quantities of food, sluicing it all down with gallons of orange juice. After the theater, when others were drinking champagne, Jim was just as lively on bottle after bottle of root beer and sarsaparilla.

She had other escorts, the flashiest a slick, black-haired lady-killing Cuban called Antonio Terry. Tony had a fortune approximating the Squire's and an equal disregard for money. He had been having a headline love affair with young Sibyl Sanderson, the new operatic sensation who had rocketed to fame much as Lillie had done. It was said that Tony turned to Lillie to induce Sibyl to marry him, but Tony couldn't keep away from pretty women, anyway. He was a big spender and lavish with gifts. He squired many, including Lillian Russell, but he favored Lillie. He was persistent, and before long their names were constantly linked. Aggressive and explosively Latin, Tony had to have his way. He was hard to resist. Sibyl grew so alarmed at the reports that she hurried back from a Chicago tour to corral her fickle fiancé.

The final insult to the singer was the way Tony's wife named Mrs. Langtry as correspondent, rather than Sibyl, in her divorce suit. Lillie ignored the action, as she had ignored the newspaper insinuations. Tony was attractive and amusing, but hardly *that* amusing. Her experience with the Squire had made her determined never again to lose her head over any man. For sanity and peace of mind, she had to keep control. Never mind the press. She knew nothing of boxing terms, but she rolled with the punches.

Lillie had made herself so flexible and resilient that she hardly felt a tremor when a certain message was handed to her in her dressing room. Life seemed to be a round of running into people one had known earlier in different circumstances. With most, she had observed, everything had changed—mood, relationship, feeling, and sometimes even the memories were abhorrent. She asked her dresser, Faithful Wright, to show the caller in.

Then she resumed the brushing of her long, golden-brown hair. Neither nostalgic nor sentimental, she liked to think of herself as practical and realistic, a woman who could assign closed chapters to the file-and-forget corner of her mind. But she was human enough to stick at what-might-have-been. As the knock came on the door, a frown crossed her features and she took a deep breath.

"Hello, Lillie." Her back was to him and both looked at their reflections in her dressing table mirror. "Jim told me how beautiful you looked—so here I am."

"How well you look, Freddie!"

"I'm fatter. You must see that."

"You carry it nicely and dress as handsomely as ever. But a newly married man visiting my dressing room! I hope the newspapers don't get hold of it."

"When did you ever care what the newspapers said? Any way, Louise knows I'm here. In fact, she asked me to come back-stage."

Lillie smiled wryly and turned to face him. "Dared you, I suppose."

"I think you'd like Louise." She looked at him as he struggled to sustain the conversation. "Tell me, uh, about this Baird. Is it true he blacked your eyes and beat you up?"

"What do you think?"

"Maybe I should have done that. Things might have been different. But how was I supposed to know the Prince meant so much to you—an old man like that?" His mouth pulled down at the corners at the recollection. "God, did I get drunk that night!"

"It's a normal reaction." He flushed, and she waved away any intention to hurt. "I was upset too, Freddie."

"I saw the *Lalee* coming up from Baltimore the other day," he said, twisting his hat in his hands. "The memories it brought back! We had some wonderful times, Lillie. Maybe they were too good to last."

"Maybe."

"Anyway, I'll never forget you. How could I?" He crossed to her and held out his hand. Lillie took it and they stood there, looking into each other's eyes. Then he inclined toward her and hesitated. "May I?"

"Of course."

His lips grazed hers briefly. He might have been a new leading man impersonally rehearsing a love scene.

"Good-by, Lillie."

"Good-by."

Lillie was in a fog as she finished dressing for the first act.

"The overture is on," Edward Michael announced as he always did.

Usually Lillie acknowledged the warning. Now she sat calmly, staring at her empty hands. Michael turned to Faithful Wright, troubled by her worried gesture.

"Would you like another overture?" he asked.

Bernhardt liked to make the audience wait, curtain time depending on her mood. Michael had worked for other stars who "deliberately cultivated this idiotic fussing and futility," but Mrs. Langtry was never temperamental. What could have happened?

"Certainly not, Michael," she said with composure. "I know the clock, and I'm ready. Roll out the red carpet."

Michael smiled in relief. The red carpet was a Langtry trademark, dating back from the early days when she'd noticed how soiled her lovely gowns became trailing the grimy passage from her dressing room to the stage. Lillie always carried a piece of red carpeting in her baggage. Her last command before going on was to have it rolled out.

Faithful straightened her hem as she stood in the wings. Freddie had never mentioned the ranch or the 23rd Street house, Lillie thought, watching the stage manager for her cue. We ought to straighten it all out, but better let it lie. Good-by is good-by . . .

Then the curtain went up. Lillie walked on stage, a dazzling vision in white, a radiant smile on her lovely face. The audience broke into wild applause.

Lillie didn't have to be encouraged to stay on into the 1895 Broadway season. She needed a new play and accepted one offered by Clyde Fitch, a popular young playwright whose first big success, *Beau Brummel,* had been written for Richard Mansfield. He came to her with *Gossip,* which he and Leo Dietrichstein had based on an idea from a French play. She liked her part, a lovable Mrs. Fix-it and guardian angel to the entire cast. It seemed a good idea to appear in an American play by an American author. She went further and hired Effie Shannon, a rising young American actress, for the important role of Mrs. Stanford.

The curtain rose on *Gossip* on March 11 at Palmer's Theater in New York. Whether it was because of the fuss over her brief *affaire* with Terry or the almost unanimous critical approval she had received thus far, the reviews of this play were indicative of a change in climate toward the Jersey Lily. With the exception of the bemused Winter, she was scolded for her sumptuous dresses and dazzling jewelry. Comedy, said one critic, was not Lillie's strong point. He told how, at her entrance fairly blazing with diamonds, the sight of her tiara sent a murmur of admiration through the house, thus irretrievably ruining a strong scene. It was his opinion that hereafter she "must turn on her diamonds earlier in the play if she desires to produce any effect." Another critic stated flatly that it was a good play gone wrong and that Mrs. Langtry's tiara created a sensation in a New York audience not equaled in some time. "Every woman gave an involuntary 'Oh' of astonishment at the sight, and Edward Evangeline Christopher Rice fell out of his chair as the glitter of diamonds struck his eyes."

Reviews acted on Lillie like a barometer. These seemed terribly unfair after the early enthusiasm. New York critics were such petty, picky creatures! They didn't understand the hazards involved in mounting a new play. Even Fitch himself had been nervous on opening night. Though he had great faith in his writing he agreed with Lillie that she should wear a simple headdress in the big scene, providing the first two acts scored.

"But I will have the tiara on hand in case of emergency," she had promised.

"I don't think you'll need it," he said confidently.

But after the second act, which had limped to a curtain, he had hustled back to Lillie's dressing room.

"For heaven's sake, wear your tiara!" he had pleaded.

She had done so, her dazzling accessory giving a flimsy play a lift. It was not her fault that she had thereby undermined a strong scene.

In any case the public loved *Gossip*. People jammed the theater, if only to see the tiara. And Lillie could smile when it was rumored that in her forthcoming road tour she would be billed either as "Mrs. Langtry supported by an efficient 18-carat company of rubies, diamonds, and occasional sapphires," or "Mrs. Langtry's diamond fence, supported by Mrs. Langtry."

"Plain nastiness!" said Effie Shannon. "It's a pleasure appearing with you, Mrs. Langtry. The theater is more than just acting. It's romance and escape and beauty. Where else could the public see such lovely clothes and sparkling jewels? Those critics don't know what they're talking about!"

"So long as they're not running the box office, it doesn't matter," said Edward Michael practically. "And right now it's a very busy place."

Those who insisted on disparaging the Jersey Lily contended that diamonds were all she lived for, that she was never happier than when coercing her gentleman friends—if they rated such a description—from Bertie, Freddie, Baird, and down through Tony Terry—to give her jewels. It is true that Lillie understood the glamour and publicity value of jewels, but she did not flaunt them in greedy ostentation. She was, as Michael knew, a worshiper of beauty, with flawless taste and artistic instinct, typically feminine in her enjoyment of "pretty things." Jewelry was only part of her natural and ordinary equipment. "In their degree," her manager believed, "her shoes were equally important." He was quite sure that "she thought far more of, say, a rare piece of Louis XV furniture than any mere jewelry."

Besides boxes of ugly ornate pieces, all of them unsolicited gifts from admirers—many of them unknown to her—Lillie had a remarkable collection of diamond, ruby, and sapphire tiaras, bracelets, brooches, rings, pins, clasps, pendants, and clips. As keeper of the big tin box in which they were kept, Michael was intimately acquainted with them. (Griffith had been, too, and much worried over the responsibility, shunting them from bank vault to bank vault.) The black box, fireproof and portable, was two and a half feet long and two feet wide. Its contents were worth close to $200,000. The prize pieces were the huge *Gossip* tiara, practically a crown of large diamonds and pearls, a *rivière* of immense diamonds and sapphires in a Tiffany setting, a *parure* of big diamonds and emeralds which had belonged to the Empress Eugénie, and a brooch in which was set the largest ruby in the world. None of the jewels were insured.

Michael hated being entrusted with these valuables which the public regarded as part of the "show." On one Sunday morning at a railway junction, Lillie casually tossed the tin box at him from a carriage window and nearly caught him "in a vulnerable part." Then in her soft, appealing voice, she asked, "Do you mind taking charge of these things for me until the bank opens tomorrow morning?" Michael was always relieved when he could put them in the security of a hotel safe. On tour he traveled "with the wretched iron box" sticking into his ribs by night and nestling next to him on the long all-day trips, delighted on arrival when detectives met the train and escorted him and "these things" to the nearest safe.

"Perhaps you ought to have an armed guard," he suggested to Lillie. "That black box ages me every time I carry it."

"Then you must age beautifully, Mr. Michael. You appear in such blooming health."

Critical sneers to the contrary, *Gossip* was so popular in New York and on a subsequent New England tour that Lillie was tempted to stay on. But she had commitments in England and returned there in the fall. Knowing that the London critics were cognizant of the New York reviews, she decided on a tour of the provinces before opening in London, and it was a wise move, for *Gossip* did fine business. She let London wait. She wanted to rest and devote time to her horses, at any cost.

On the last week of the provincial tour, she summoned

Michael to her Birmingham hotel room at an early hour. She was perfectly groomed, immaculate and shining, and he regretted that he hadn't yet shaved.

"I'm so glad to see you. Oh, *do* please go into the passage, and ring bells and swear and do all the horrible things you men do when you want anything. I'm going racing, I can't get my breakfast, and I shall miss my train."

Michael raised the necessary hell to get room service. In a few minutes four waiters were running in and out with trays. Lillie glanced at the clock.

"I'm afraid I have missed it, Mr. Michael. I wish you'd arrange a special for me right away."

"Isn't that a rather expensive way of going racing?"

"Oh, no, I think I know what I'm doing. At least, I hope so. And, yes, I have another little request. I was going to ask you if you could go to America on Saturday."

"But the tour finishes on that day, Mrs. Langtry. I'll have a number of business matters to wind up. Would a later boat do?"

"Of course, but go as early as you can. So that is all right?"

Lillie finished her breakfast leisurely, as if the subject were settled. Her manager had to remind her that he didn't know the purpose of his trip to America.

"Of course, how absurd of me! Well, you know we have an American tour booked for autumn, and I don't want to do it." She smiled. "I think I have a racing coup for the end of the season, and I want to be here. So I want you to go to New York and compromise with them about it. Little Hummel will help you. Just let me know the amount required to settle, and I will cable it at once through the Knickerbocker Trust." She waited as he jotted down a few notes. "And don't forget my special."

That evening Edward Michael stood on the steps of the theater in Birmingham, watch in hand, looking anxiously up and down the street. Not a sign of Mrs. Langtry! The audience was streaming inside, curtain time dangerously near. Panicky, he fumed and fretted. Then he saw Lillie strolling toward the theater, nodding and smiling as men took off their hats.

324

"I-I-I've been terribly worried, Mrs. Langtry," he said breathlessly. "I was afraid I'd have to dismiss the audience."

"Oh, no. Of course I knew exactly what time I had to be back here." She favored him with an unruffled smile. "And even if you *had* to close the theater, the loss would have been mine, wouldn't it? So why were you so worried, Mr. Michael?"

She was so pitilessly logical that he could think of nothing to say.

"And you needn't worry about the expense of my special. I'm sure the fourteen hundred pounds I won will cover it—and leave a little over."

It was six weeks before Michael saw her again to report on how easily he and Hummel had settled the cancellation of her American tour. Lillie had been vacationing on the Continent and had returned to 21 Pont Street in September—to sustain a great shock. But not a twinge of anxiety was evident as she made "one of her fairy entrances from nowhere" and greeted him, composed, dressed strikingly, and lovely as always.

"How are you, Mr. Michael? I do hope you had a pleasant trip. I hope you won't mind a hurried lunch, because I have to catch a train. Sorry to be late, but I have had an accident."

"Accident? You don't appear to have been hurt, thank goodness."

Smiling easily, Lillie rang for the butler. "Nothing like that. I'm all right, but I have just come from Scotland Yard. I've lost all my jewels. This is absolutely all I have left in the shape of jewelry—" She fondled the pearl necklace around her neck— "plus a few personal things I always have with me."

"You mean the black tin box was stolen?"

"Yes, with the use of a forged order. A very neat job. There isn't a clue, and Scotland Yard is no help whatever. What I need is Sherlock Holmes." She rang for the next course. "I do so hate to hurry you, but I have to catch a train to Manchester where two of my horses are running tomorrow."

"You're going racing after *this?*" he said, aghast.

"Oh, you're as bad as Sir George Lewis this morning. His face was a study when I told him. He seemed to think the theft should be treated like a family bereavement. And I couldn't convince him that the loss made it all the more important for me to back my two potential winners. He thinks it most indelicate for me to be seen in public."

On the train her friends showed neither sympathy nor surprise when she told them the news as she might have discussed the weather. Not until the train pulled into Crewe Junction, where newsboys were shouting "Great Robbery of Mrs. Langtry's Jewels! Read all about it!" did they really believe her and express their sympathy.

"How can you be so calm about it?" they protested. "We thought you were trying to be funny."

Perhaps it was funny that the great vault of the Sloane Street branch of the Union Bank should be less safe than Edward Michael's lap or the strongbox of some drab Ohio hotel. The bank was only a short distance from her Pont Street house. On performance evenings or whenever she was going out, it was her habit to send her butler over in the afternoon with a signed order for temporary possession of the tin box. Lillie then would pick out the items she wanted and return the rest to safekeeping.

The day she learned of the theft she planned to attend the opera and followed the usual procedure. The butler returned, white-faced and jittery, to stammer that the jewels had been delivered to her on August 18.

"How can that be?" said Lillie in amazement. "I was on the Continent then!"

"Well, madam, that is what they say. And a bank representative came back with me to confirm the matter."

She hurried downstairs to face a thin, red-haired clerk with ashen features, who sagged with fright at her appearance.

"You have my order?"

He handed her the slip. The instant she saw it, she knew the signature had been forged from the facsimile used in the Pears' soap advertisements.

"This is forgery pure and simple," she snapped. "Do you remember what this imposter looked like?"

"Uh, well, uh, it's almost a month ago, Mrs. Langtry. But

326

he was fat and had a red face. A sporting gentleman, I'd call him."

"What stupidity!"

"But," he quavered, "I showed the order to Mr.—"

"Why in the name of heaven should you turn over my jewel box to someone like that when you have identification of my butler? It's a piece of reprehensible, criminal carelessness on someone's part. I won't stand for it!"

The robbery, so cleverly executed and undiscovered for so long, was front-page copy. Some American papers hinted that it was a typical Langtry publicity stunt. The police did what they could. Scotland Yard placed a notice in her name in the London newspapers, itemizing the jewels and offering a reward of 500 pounds for information leading to the arrest of the thieves or recovery of her property. No leads were forthcoming. Incensed at the bank's slipshod methods, Lillie asked her attorney to sue the Union Bank for 40,000 pounds for negligence.

It seemed incredible that the thief or thieves could dispose of such large stones without leaving a trace. Scotland Yard was of the opinion that the jewels would be broken down and disposed of separately, a process that would take time. They were doubtful of recovering any of the haul.

Then the case took a cloak-and-dagger turn. Lillie received a letter signed with initials claiming to be from a London attorney. He assured her she would get no satisfaction from the police—as she herself had come to believe—and he stated that her jewels were now in a safe deposit vault in the city. On payment of 5,000 pounds to his client, no questions asked, they would be returned to her. Lillie rushed to Scotland Yard and was told that if she should get her jewels back in this way, she herself would be subject to arrest "for compounding a felony."

The Union Bank also sniffed at the idea. Lillie thought it over and then proposed negotiations through the Public Notices or Agony Columns of a newspaper. After waiting impatiently for a reply, she received a message that the jewels had been shipped to Dieppe in France and must be ransomed there. By a combination of threats and charming appeals she obtained a 5,000-pound advance from the Union Bank. Two trusted friends, Lord Shrewsbury and James Smyth-Pigott, set out hopefully to redeem the jewels, but they had no luck.

"The whole thing was a hoax," they told her. "We did meet this so-called solicitor, a seedy fellow. He tried to lure us into the country with his talk of fifteen detectives trailing us on the boat. We held back because he showed us no proof that he had the jewels, and we thought he might knock us over the head and demand ransom money from you."

Lillie was leaving for Paris on a regular wardrobe-replenishing trip, when she received another letter—this time postmarked Dieppe—from a paroled convict who had "news." Lillie agreed to meet him. He came to her suite at the Ritz —a mild, meek man with nothing of the thug about him. He seemed genuinely concerned with her bad luck, but it immediately struck Lillie that he knew nothing about the missing jewels. However, he did know a great deal about criminals and criminal life in London. She felt he was lonely and merely wanted to talk.

There the robbery rested, except for a dozen theories which continued to crop up for years: it was an inside job, an outside job, a former butler did it, a spurned admirer did it, some crooks followed her to the United States and pinched the stuff—anything. The Union Bank took her negligence suit in bad part. Lillie couldn't understand their stuffy attitude. After all, her house was only two doors away, all the blinds had been down at the time, and it had been in all the papers that she was visiting Baden-Baden. Not only that: although the forged order had been written on her own personal Pont Street paper (pilfered by someone somehow), the name of the month had been spelled "Augst" with no second "u," a thing she never did. Nor had she any knowledge of any G. Watts whose signature had been affixed to the receipt for the jewels. The bank should never have honored such a signature, especially since the clerks were familiar with her butler's.

The morning of the hearing Lillie sat surrounded by lawyers. Sir George Lewis was late, and the bank's representatives were pressing hard for a settlement. Her counsel were Sir Robert Reid (later Lord Loreburn) and Herbert Henry Asquith (later

Prime Minister). Through Sir Edward Carson the bank offered a compromise of 10,000 pounds for the 40,000 she was asking. Reid induced her to accept it. Ten minutes later Lewis hurried in, and Lillie told him her reluctant decision. "Not enough," he said excitedly. "I can get twenty-five thousand pounds at least!" He ran off to find Reid, but the agreement had already been signed.

Lillie regretted settling for less. She hadn't realized that it was a good test case in regard to a bank's responsibilities and that the bank had been anxious to keep it out of court. In any case, the Union Bank stiffly demanded that she remove her account. This petty action annoyed her. She complained to Michael when he told her about completing a transfer to Drummond's Bank.

"I can't imagine why someone hasn't written a caustic play about bankers. But then what could possibly be dramatic about banking?"

"You don't know George Drummond. He was delighted to get your account and thought you 'a splendid customer.' So I sent him four complimentary seats to *Gossip,* and he came in person to give me a check for them. I refused, saying he was your guest, but he wouldn't hear of it. Impossible, he told me. You were a customer of Drummond's, and they made money on your account, so he *had* to pay for the seats. Mrs. Langtry," he concluded strongly, "in all my years in the theater such a thing has never happened before."

"It's the millennium," she agreed. "I hope they were good seats."

twenty

Before hitting the profitable provinces again, Lillie played Mrs. Barry in *Gossip* at London's West End and Comedy Theaters well into the spring of 1896. Once again the critics pooh-poohed the play, this time as "a poor sample of the American machine-made drama." It was a dressy vehicle for the display of her costumes and tiara—a newer and smaller one to be sure, but critically objectionable. The play had been showily mounted by Comyns Carr. The public was enthusiastic, feminine theater parties attending on the strength of Lillie's fabulous clothes. London's most fashionable dressmakers and milliners were so anxious to keep up to date that they sent representatives every night, sketchbooks in hand.

Her misfortune had done nothing to impair her sense of humor. She often joked about the jewel robbery.

Even the great teasers didn't like to be teased, Lillie discovered. At the time *The Importance of Being Earnest* was about to open at the St. James, George Alexander swore everyone to keep mum about the plot because Oscar Wilde wanted it kept secret. Lillie thought Oscar rather irritating when she tried to worm the details out of him at tea. So she told him airily that it didn't matter whether he told her or not.

"Arthur Bourchier lunched here yesterday and told me all about it."

Bourchier had a leading part, so Oscar, who was so arrogantly pompous these days, moaned. "Who else was here, Lil?"

"Only George Smalley," she said casually. "You know, the critic."

Oscar hurried away, and two hours afterward Bourchier burst in "almost crying with annoyance." "What's all this?" he demanded.

"Only my joke. I'll write to Alexander to explain."

She wrote an apologetic letter, and Alexander replied icily that he "did not understand jokes in business."

Beerbohm Tree heard the story that same night at the Garrick and laughed. "I'm sure the Lily did that," he said.

The tour got off nicely. Michael was always surprised because, without reminders, without prompting, Lillie turned up at the right theater in the right town at the right time. She was well received and no hitches developed until the week they played Manchester. There the director of the limited liability company owning the theater died, and the manager bustled up to Michael with a solemn request.

"We are burying the dear old guv'nor on Saturday, and we all think that as a proper mark of respect the theater should be closed for the day. Have you any objections?"

It was a ridiculous suggestion. Knowing Lillie and her practical, French-*concierge* mind, Michael referred the man to her with amused anticipation. The scrubby theater manager shuffled up to Lillie and repeated his request.

Her bright attention changed to ready sympathy. "Oh, most certainly. I quite understand, and I *thoroughly* agree. What a very proper feeling, and how nice of you to think of it! Of course it is the right thing to do under the tragic circumstances."

"Why-why, thank you, Mrs. Langtry. We-we appreciate—"

"By the by, Mr. Michael," she cut him off, "wouldn't you say if we took an average of our last six Saturday matinées and evening performances, that would be a fair way of arriving at the compensation the management must pay us for closing? Don't you think so?"

The manager began to expostulate, then slunk off. Lillie smiled.

"What an absurd creature! Does he really think that because a man I have never seen dies I am to cancel reservations and sacrifice hundreds of pounds to please the feelings of some officials in a limited liability company? Some people are really too silly for words, aren't they?"

After a week in Ireland, the company moved on to Kingstown for the night boat to Holyhead. Ellen Terry and Henry Irving were also on tour, returning on the same boat, and Lillie had a pleasant time talking theater and reminiscing before embarking. A supper party in her big cabin broke up early because the Irish Sea was kicking up. The stubby boat took the waves badly. Nearly everyone spent a miserable night, except Lillie who was unaffected.

They were a sad-looking crew as the boat tied up at the Holyhead pier in the raw grayness of early morning. Lillie came out of her cabin jauntily, smartly-dressed, hair immaculate under her perfectly adjusted hat, not a thing out of place. To Michael she might have been coming down the steps of her Pont Street house as she called out cheery good mornings, serenely pulling on her long white gloves. Ellen Terry stumbled along the deck, "a crumpled bundle of rags, disheveled, unwashed, with a dazed 'I wish I was dead' expression." Reacting to this priceless chance, Lillie sprang forward with a cry of sympathy.

"Oh, my poor dear! My dear Nell! Isn't this truly awful for us? What we poor women have to suffer! And don't we look *terrible?* But never mind; come down to breakfast in my cabin and you'll feel much better."

"Nothing to eat," Ellen Terry gasped. "Nothing!" She gulped at the thought of food. "Only fresh air." Tired and sick, she took in Lillie's bloom and perfection. "I think I better lie down," she murmured feebly, and fled below.

Lillie smiled at Michael as she realized he had overheard.

" 'This was the most unkindest cut of all,' " he quoted, chiding her.

"As you like it." She shrugged. "Or should I say much ado about nothing?"

Lillie had expressly taken Regal Lodge and moved her horses to nearby Kentford because Sam Pickering's stable was there and he had been recommended as a sound trainer. His record had been a fair one. Lillie had a moderate succession of wins,

332

none of them major. With Lady Roseberry she won the Lanark Cup, the Jockey Club Cup at Newmarket, and ran second in her favorite race, the Cesarewitch. After doing very well, Milford did not hold his early form, but she had Nobleman and several "platers" to keep up her record. She had "a satisfactory season, and realized more and more the fascination of the national sport of England."

Running a successful racing stable demanded good trainers, shrewd judgment of horseflesh, the ability to make ruthless decisions, the subordinating of everything else to win, and plenty of money. Lillie had learned much from the Squire and just as much by observation. Mr. Jersey would have to do better before she was satisfied. Just as she had been determined to succeed as an actress in spite of obstacles, she brought all her energy and resource to the fortunes of "the turquoise and fawn hoops and turquoise cap." Her first serious step was to change trainers.

One morning Sam Pickering was handed a note in Lillie's writing. "Please deliver my horses to the trainer Mr. William Robinson," it said. Having had no prior warning of her dissatisfaction with him, Pickering was shaken. Her friends asked why she had summarily sacked poor Pickering when she appeared to like him so much.

"I did and I do," she said warmly. "I've always liked him a lot. Nothing could exceed his attention and consideration whenever I went to the stables. Naturally, I think highly of Mr. Pickering!"

"But then I can't understand why you've taken your horses away from him."

"Oh, *that*. You see, he never won with them."

Few things gave her so much pleasure as racing, and she felt that making a success of her stables would be one of the greatest satisfactions of her life. Love of the sport impelled her, not the forgotten prophecy of the Jersey fortune teller, although it could be said that she had been queen of beauty, queen of the stage, and now aspired to be queen of the turf. She liked horses—the look of them, the smell of them, their polished flanks, their muscles moving rhythmically; the thrills, the excitement, the color, and the rough maleness of the trainers, jockeys, bookies, and touts.

This year (1896) had been good for Bertie's stables. He'd never before had so fine a horse as Persimmon, who won the St. Leger and the Jockey Club Stakes as well as the Derby. It had been a popular win. The crowd had bellowed itself hoarse for "Good old Teddy." He beamed with pleasure as he led his horse into the winner's enclosure, waving his silk hat and acknowledging the cheers. He was the people's prince, a middle-class idol, a real sport. He could do as he pleased and not be censured for his common-man's red-blooded vices. Let him smoke cigars, hop around the Continent, play with pretty women, drink and play cards with his racy set. Fundamentally, "Tumtum" was one of them. And the "upper ten thousand," who grimaced at his friendship with Jews, self-made men, and non-aristocrats had to bear with him.

Lillie hoped with Robinson that 1897 would be her own year on the track. Everything depended on her big Australian horse Merman, which she had been talked into buying though long-distance purchases were risky and the trip invariably hard on the horse. She had previously imported Maluma, a famous mare, only to have her overcome by the Red Sea heat en route and arrive sick and broken. It seemed foolish to bring a horse up from New South Wales after her experience with Maluma, but William A. Allison of the International Horse Agency pressed her to buy the stout chestnut colt by Grand Flaneur out of Seaweed. She was worried about the Red Sea—it was so hot there that Pat Sheedy, the international gambler, had told her he had sunstroke passing through at midnight—so Lillie ordered her 1,600-pound purchase to be shipped via the cooler route around the Cape of Good Hope. He arrived sound, and her example was followed by other owners. (The same year she imported Chesney. His ship, the *Thermopylae,* was wrecked off Robin Island near Capetown. Chesney proved his mettle by swimming eight and a half miles to shore, landing at Three Anchor Bay, and providing a feature story for Mr. Jersey.)

Robinson thought highly of Merman. After entering him in several proving races, he suggested that Lillie hire Tod Sloan, the great American jockey, to ride the chestnut in the big ones. She had put the theater aside for a while and was devoting herself to her horses and gardens.

Then came an unexpected development: she had been granted an uncontested divorce in California! The news reached her in a cable from the tireless Abe Hummel, who proudly flashed her return cable the next day: AWFULLY PLEASED. YOU ARE A CHAMPION! LANGTRY.

Well, she *was* pleased. It was hard to believe that she was finally free after so long—rid of poor Edward. She couldn't quite understand why he had not contested the suit after successfully blocking it for fifteen years. Maybe he didn't care any more or had been too drunk to file objection. At any rate, his reason wasn't important. Of course the press got hold of the story and trumpeted all the stale, old scandal with it.

Acting on Lillie's behalf, Henry C. McPike, a San Francisco lawyer, had appeared before Judge R. W. Crump in the courtroom at Lakeport, county seat of Lake County, May 13, 1897, with depositions alleging that Edward Langtry had deserted her and that she was entitled to a divorce. Lillie's sworn statements, taken in England and in America, attested that she was an American citizen, a *bona fide* resident of Lake County, where she had a large ranch bought with the proceeds of her dramatic career, and that "Mr. Langtry has never advanced a dollar to mend a fence or shoe a colt." She testified that her husband had deserted her years ago. From that time to the present date he had not furnished support for either herself or her child, and had declared he would not return to her.

In her statement, Lillie had sworn that she first went on the stage to support herself. She had always treated Mr. Langtry with affection and had never given him cause to disregard his duty toward her as a husband. She asked for the custody of her daughter. Other depositions affirming her charge of desertion and her residence in California were signed by Sir George Lewis, James W. Smyth-Pigott, Captain A. W. Williams, her mother Emilie Davis Le Breton, and her brother Clement Le Breton.

The courtroom was all but empty when Judge Crump leafed

through the papers. It appeared that Mr. Langtry had been served a summons and had failed to answer. Because he had not filed a defense in the time allowed by the California court, a default was entered against the foreign defendant and a divorce granted the plaintiff. A cut-and-dried routine case on the surface, but previous failures had made Hummel trick up his client's deposition and bring Jeanne Marie into the case. The press made ugly capital of this.

Edward Langtry was interviewed in England and didn't sound like a man who had been supported by his wife for fifteen years. Poisoned by the bitter grudge he had held so long and by the liquor with which he'd nursed it, he came out swinging. He refused to recognize the California divorce.

"You may say that I treat the decree with the same contempt as I did the citation, which I threw in the fire in the presence of the man who served me."

He felt Lillie's charge of desertion was particularly absurd, since he had remained at home while Mrs. Langtry had been all over the world with all sorts of fellows. He had successfully combated her charges of desertion and nonsupport in previous divorce attempts, and now he threatened to sue Lillie for bigamy if she married in his lifetime.

"My wife cannot remarry in England without committing bigamy," he was quoted. "I have been kind and fair to her always. She is my wife. They may treat me cruelly; they may lie about me, but she shall never untie the knot her father tied at the altar."

Brave words, futile and pathetic. However unrealistic and out of touch with life Edward Langtry had been, Lillie now stood out as a cruel, stony-hearted woman who had made a fool of her husband and dishonored his name. People talked. Friends gossiped. Reporters knocked at her door for a rebuttal. All the while Lillie clung to Gladstone's advice and busied herself at Regal Lodge. Mrs. Le Breton was too old and forgetful to be bothered by any of this. She had long since relegated Edward Langtry to obscurity. But Lillie fretted lest the scandalous outcry reach Jeanne Marie's tender ears.

336

Jeanne idolized her mother, appeared to believe what she had been told about her father, and asked few questions. Her education and bringing up had been under the loving supervision of Mrs. Le Breton whom Lillie liked to call "Sweet Duchess." Grandmother and granddaughter might be in Jersey, Pont Street, or Regal Lodge, Kentford—but always in strictest privacy, a remote, cloistered existence in which Lillie's social, dramatic, and personal affairs hardly set up a whisper. Jeanne was always surrounded by tutors, governesses, music teachers, and voice coaches, studying hard with "a college staff of her own," while Sweet Duchess officiated, cared for by her own servants as "one of the most beautiful old ladies in England."

Sometimes this system resulted in mutual over-protection, as on the occasion of one of Lillie's projected trips to Paris. The night before, the best Dieppe boat had rammed another ship in the Channel and sunk with heavy loss of life. The "Pont Street palace" retinue, Jeanne included, had been warned not to mention the tragedy to madame, lest she worry about her own crossing. The omnibus rumbled off with her ten trunks; the staff hung about, making diversionary conversation. Lillie climbed into her brougham and kissed her fingers in farewell to her trembling daughter.

No sooner had she disembarked at Dieppe than newsboys swarmed about hawking extras about the earlier tragedy. Lillie turned to a companion with one of her matchless smiles. "Well, now that the trip is done, I admit I knew there was a terrific disaster on one of those abominable little boats night before last. I didn't let any papers get into the house or have it mentioned by the servants! I knew Jeanne was safe, because she never reads anything later than Josephus."

Although the divorce came as a surprise, Lillie had known Abe Hummel was still trying. There had been prior notice in the American newspapers, but it was a stale story—as stale as the Langtry-Gebhard marriage announcements had once become. When the divorce went through, it was news—and there was hotter material to come.

337

On June 15, 1897, Edward Langtry put his former wife in the ugliest possible light in an interview published as a Hearst press exclusive and purporting to give his side of the case.

"However seemingly cruel it may be," he was quoted, "I affirm that I never heard that my wife gave birth to a child of which I am reputed to be the father, until I received the divorce citation which was served on me here five months ago. That should dispose of the question of desertion."

In the best yellow-journal style (all the more ironically poignant because for Edward it was the truth), he went on to say that the divorce had broken his heart. He told how he had made a $50,000 marriage settlement on his wife and had gone into the social swim only to please her. According to him the real estrangement took place in 1881, after he went to the United States to look after property belonging to the deceased actress, Adelaide Neilson. He had gone at the instigation of Sir George Lewis, his wife's attorney, who claimed it would be a good thing financially. Then he had been kept there five months by a succession of devious telegrams, after he had settled the business in hand in five minutes. His suspicions aroused, he had returned to England and seen Mrs. Langtry once in her Ely Place apartment. She had declined to live with him; they had never seen each other since.

Continuing in the same damning, titillating vein, the story had him denouncing Lillie's American divorce as invalid and explaining that he was planning a countersuit in which a certain exalted royal personage would be named as one of the correspondents. Then, tearing the veil aside, the newspaper said the royal personage was none other than the Prince of Wales.

"I don't see why you need submit to this libel, slander, and calumny, Mrs. Langtry," said her lawyer. "With all due respect to the poor fellow, your husband's been a commendably steady and reliable drinker for some time now."

"What about it, Sir George?"

"The truth should be known. This is the retaliation of a sick man who has long been a pensioner on the bounty of his wife. A dissipated man who's done nothing for a living and demanded your support. As a lawyer, I should like to pass on the information quietly to the press. A reminder. I see no need for this painful business to blacken your reputation as a person and an actress."

"No," said Lillie. "Say nothing in my behalf. I've never cared what other people thought, anyway, but my daughter means a great deal to me. Is there any way in which Edward could—?"

"None at all, Mrs. Langtry. You have nothing to worry about. She is yours legally. You've cared for her, clothed, fed her. She is all yours."

"Not quite all," she murmured.

McPike, who had handled the divorce at Lakeport, continued to speak loudly for his client. Mrs. Langtry was returning to Langtry Farms. She would spend four months attending to restocking the ranch and going extensively into breeding high-class cattle and the best strains of horse. Carrick, a racing stallion, had been shipped from England, had already reached New York, and would proceed to California after a brief rest. McPike expected Mrs. Langtry to arrive July 1. She would supervise refencing, putting up a number of new buildings, developing the sulphur springs, and other improvements.

Arthur G. Preston McNalty had succeeded Doc Aby in 1894 but hadn't done much better than his wasteful predecessor. In 1895 attachments of $7,000 had been placed on the property, and this accounted for the sale of all the stock. Langtry Farms had failed as both a breeding and a racing establishment, but there was great interest in the return of the Jersey Lily, which may have been a pipe dream of McPike's or else part of Hummel's strategy.

Lillie's thoughts often turned to her beautiful valley, but just now she did not plan to leave England. She had homes in Jersey, London, Kentford, California, and New York. Freddie had put the 23rd Street house in her name, but Hummel had had trouble renting it and she refused to pay for maintenance. It would have been wise to sell Langtry Farms, if it had not been such a landmark in memory. And she might go back some day.

There remained that colossal gift of the Squire's, which had returned a satisfying rental from Ogden Goelet for a few years. It had been fun owning the *White Lady*. She'd cruised the Mediterranean, visited Jersey, entertained the Island's governor aboard, made the royal yacht look like a tug as she steamed into Cowes harbor. But so expensive!

"What are we going to do about the *White Lady*?" she asked Edward Michael that summer, going over the cashbook with him.

"Well, if you want to get rid of her, I'd suggest consulting the yacht brokers who rented her."

"No. I know them. They'll fiddle along interminably while she eats us out of house and home. The only way is to put her up for auction and advertise well. Take that up with them, won't you?"

Michael made enquiries. The brokers wanted no part of an auction. No yacht had ever been put up for sale in this novel, modern way.

"They were horrified," he told her. "It just isn't done."

"Silly, old-fashioned muddlers! Instruct them to auction the boat and submit the form of their advertisement to me. If they're afraid of trying new methods, they can put the responsibility on me."

The big-yacht market was restricted, and the *White Lady* was already outmoded in engineering and design. The furnishings were removed and sold separately. The boat went for 280,000 pounds, which was better than the brokers had hoped for. It was all profit to Lillie, since the yacht had cost her nothing.

She used it to buy more horses and a stud farm at Gazely. Society still looked askance at Mr. Jersey. Women didn't belong on the turf. Like Lord Lonsdale she was accused of trying to overcome a bad reputation by pursuing the sport of kings. Who guessed that she had loved horses all her life, as a girl had bought a mare in secret with her brother Reggie, helped train the animal, and then watched Flirt win at the annual July race meeting on Jersey's Gorey Common?

Merman ran at Nottingham and lost. Then he was entered in the Lewes Handicap. She was watching him exercise in the paddock before the race when Lord William Beresford joined her.

"Fine-looking beast, Mrs. Langtry," he said, studying Merman, "but if I were you I'd have his shoes removed. Australian horses usually run barefoot in their own country."

She trusted Bill Beresford, although his advice seemed drastic, and sent for the track blacksmith. Merman's shoes were knocked off as bookmakers and onlookers stared. Lillie went back to her box, as if nothing were out of the ordinary. He won easily. She was greatly pleased and agreed with her trainers that his next outing should be the important Cesarewitch at Newmarket in October.

Mr. Jersey now had a string of thirty-five horses and supervised them carefully. She was out by the stables every morning before breakfast, visiting each stall, looking in at the mares and their foals, ready with a lump of sugar for her favorites. She would go walking briskly, much as she had done around the Sheepshead Bay track with Freddie, then would return famished to Regal Lodge. She would not tolerate cruelty to her horses. Her trainers and grooms and gardeners did *exactly* what she ordered.

Brayhead won the Liverpool Cup, and she suggested testing Merman against him. They raced a mile together just after sunrise. Through binoculars, Lillie watched the Australian horse win in a canter. He looked a real good thing. She was excited at her chance to win a big handicap and decided to back him heavily.

Then, on October 6, 1897, with the race burning in her mind, Edward Langtry literally tumbled onto the front pages again. He had been found wandering in a demented condition on the railroad line near Chester. His talk was rambling, his manner restless. He seemed to have lost his mind.

It was sickening to read about it. Edward had been traveling from Cork to London, stumbled off the train at the Crewe railroad junction, staggered along the track. Twice he was found in a dangerous position on the rails, dazed and disfigured. Warned away, he had wandered all Sunday night and been discovered in the Crewe cab yard Monday morning, delirious and with only a few copper coins on his person. All that was known was that he had fallen down a companionway ladder while

341

crossing the Irish Channel and been badly injured. The afternoon he was picked up, "the unfortunate man was taken before a magistrate and committed to an asylum for the insane, pending an inquiry into his mental and physical condition."

Here was another natural for purple prose journalism. The ruined, dishonored husband, spurned by his wife and left broken-hearted with nothing to live for. Disgrace, degradation, and now—the horror of it!—MADNESS. It was all there, black on white. Lillie had to take it, but her plans did not change a whit.

A week later, her head high, she did not shrink from public view as Merman started in the Cesarewitch, England's most important long-distance handicap. It was her forty-fourth birthday.

The favorite was St. Cloud, owned by James R. Keene, a New York stock speculator. Merman was quoted at a scornful eight to one. This was the big race. She had faith in her horse and in her jockey Tod Sloan with his new "American seat." She had to win. There were whispers as she went to place her bets. People ogled her, pointed and peered. They had newspapers under their arms, and Lillie knew what they were talking about. This notorious woman unconcernedly placing her bets, while one hundred and fifty miles away her wretched, wronged husband lay dying in a madhouse.

If there was one thing she had learned from the Squire, it was to plunge bravely and bet high. She put a bundle on Merman. She was completing the transaction with the grinning bookmaker as she noticed his big stickpin—an owl's head in onyx and diamonds. Unmistakably the one she had given Abington.

"Pretty thing, ain't it?" said the book, noticing her glance.

"Where—how did you get it?"

"Well, you know, it's a long story, but it belonged to Squire Abington. He gave it to Jim Carney, the fighter." He fingered the pin lovingly. "It was Jim's birthday or the anniversary of his confirmation, something like that. Anyway, I got it from Jim a couple of years ago when he was short a fiver for a sure thing." The fat little man chuckled.

"I see." She wasn't going to hold out now. "Make my bet ten thousand more."

The bookmaker blinked. "Sure you want to do that, Mrs. Langtry? You could ruin us if you won, but with St. Cloud and The Rush you haven't a chance."

"Just take my bet, will you?"

Outwardly calm, Lillie seethed with inner excitement as she watched the race. It was close all the way. Merman was neck and neck with The Rush at the judges' box, St. Cloud far back. Lillie knew she was second again and wanted to cry. She couldn't look—then the race was over. She heard someone shout "Merman by a neck" and, looking up, saw Number Seven, hers, hoisted up on the board. Shaken and thrilled but cool and smiling faintly, she let herself be escorted to the paddock by the old Duke of Cambridge as Tod Sloan was weighed and the panting Merman checked over.

She didn't know how she'd got there, but she did recall being overwhelmed with congratulations from friends, pseudo-friends, and suddenly admiring strangers. Was there ever such a feeling as leading in one's own winner! She remembered a horseshoe of flowers being draped over Merman's neck, pressing her cheek happily against his wet muzzle, smelling the good, clean-sweaty smell of the chestnut, and the Prince of Wales grasping her arm.

"Good for you, Lillie! I'm very pleased."

"I couldn't have had a better birthday present! I've never been so excited in my life!"

Bertie had had a good win earlier (Lillie having bet on his horse as well), and he was gutturally ecstatic. The track was bathed in October sunshine, the sky a bright blue. The crowds were cheering, stable boys running after her, and her bookmaker was gasping with a punched-in-the-stomach expression. (She had won over 39,000 pounds.) Trainer Fred Webb, Robinson's assistant, had his hand shaken by Bertie; a beaming Allison who had made her buy Merman said, "I told you so"; and then she was being brought inside the sacrosanct Jockey Club enclosure.

"I thought they *never* allowed women in here."

343

"They'll jolly well have to this great day. You're *Mr.* Jersey and my guest."

Fashionably dressed males grouped about Bertie and Lillie. The Prince called for champagne. He was in his best rollicking Teddy mood.

"A toast to Mrs. Langtry," he proclaimed. "All hail Mr. Jersey!"

To have breached the walls of the exclusive Jockey Club was an achievement. The members had to bow to Bertie this time, but later once again closed ranks around their masculine standard. Hereafter hard-to-get entrance cards plus an entry fee were necessary. Ladies were ruled out, but too late. The Prince had decided. Lillie was in—permanently.

"I heard about the poor devil," he said, before she entered her brougham. "A pity, Lillie. They're being terribly hard on you."

"I ought to be used to it."

"One never gets used to vicious lies. Remember, you can always count on me."

There was a party at Regal Lodge that night. Lillie blew out candles on a birthday cake that showed Merman edging out The Rush in decorative icing. The evening was festive, but the drama being played to a final curtain at the County Asylum at Upton, near Chester, was on everyone's mind. Two days later, on October 15, Edward Langtry died there at the age of fifty. In his obituaries, the newspapers painted a stark picture of a crazed man dying in agony as his wife "lived it up" at a birthday party celebrating her racing victory. In one, the statement he'd given the Hearst papers was taken out of context and made into a sob-story deathbed statement: "However cruel it may seem, I declare as I am about to die that I never heard that my wife had given birth to a child, of which I was the disputed father."

Then the supreme ironic parallel when it was reported that the pretentious wreath Lillie sent to the funeral was a cluster of turquoise and fawn blossoms, the colors of her jockeys! This brought further outcry at her shocking humor, the august London *Times* even seeing fit to comment editorially on the bad taste of the macabre tribute. Lillie said nothing except to

344

friends. It seemed silly to refute the lies the press so happily concocted to picture her as a bad woman. Actually Mr. Michael had selected a proper funeral wreath for Edward.

The public preferred the distortions—as grotesque as the plots of some of Lillie's plays. Stirred up by Edward Michael, Sir George Lewis decided to make a counteracting statement without consulting Lillie. Buried in the back pages, it stated that since their separation Mrs. Langtry had paid her husband an adequate allowance through her lawyer. Also that as soon as Mrs. Langtry had heard of the condition of Mr. Langtry's health, she had forwarded to the Chester asylum authorities enough money to assure him every medical care. Sir George pointed out that the allowance had been paid entirely irrespective of Mr. Langtry's properties in Ireland, that the coroner's jury had ruled accidental death (brain concussion), and that he had been placed in the asylum simply for diagnosis of what was wrong with him, *not* because of his state of mind.

Logical as a lawyer's brief, it made little impression and did nothing to efface another lurid chapter in the Langtry story.

twenty-one

THE day he visited Regal Lodge the Prince looked over Lillie's stables as if inspecting a color guard. She had made careful preparations. Everything was spotless; walls, ceilings, floors shone; the horses glistened. Each stable boy stood at attention in a clean, snow-white jacket next to the stall in his charge, looking straight ahead even if spoken to. Bertie grunted his approval, discussed his own stable problems, and then went inside where Scotch whiskey was waiting.

"So you think I ought to get married, Bertie."

"It's not good for a woman to be alone. Marriage has all sorts of advantages."

"I've always thought of marriage as one of the few things one can't help being impulsive about. And I've felt no urge to jump."

"Well, look at your stage career. You only pick those plays that have a good part for you, those that will be successful."

"Even then I can be terribly wrong," she said dryly.

Bertie was guest of honor at a small dinner party that followed. Jeanne came down, and Lillie was pleased at the impression she made. They had practiced her curtsey together, and Jeanne did it beautifully. She was pretty, well-spoken, shyly charming, always composed. Bertie couldn't keep his eyes off her.

"A lovely girl. You must be very proud of her."

"Oh, I am." She looked directly at him. "Only it won't be easy for Jeanne—having an actress for a mother, all the gossip —you know the sort of thing."

346

"She has the looks and the bearing. All she needs is the *entrée* which good backing can provide." He nipped off the end of his cigar. "When the time comes, I'll see that she has it."

Lillie sighed. "I want her to have the best of everything."

"Don't worry, my dear. We'll see that she does."

Since the divorce the newspapers never stopped predicting Lillie's imminent marriage. Speculation was so wild that after her victory with Merman it was announced that a money-making trip to America was now unnecessary. She would retire from the stage with her "50,000-pound winnings" and, following a period of mourning, marry Prince Esterhazy. Descended from an ancient, royal Hungarian family, Prince Paul Esterhazy de Galantha was sixty years old, twice widowed, and had long been attached to the Austrian Embassy in London. His duties involved buying horses for his government and prize stallions for the Austrian State Stud. He was well known as sportsman, gallant, and ladies' man. In the famous Sir Charles Mordaunt divorce suit in 1870—in which Bertie had been named co-respondent—Prince Paul had distinguished himself by declaring that where a lady was concerned he would "perjure himself like a gentleman." He had scraggly mutton-chop whiskers, and a broken nose from a steeplechase fall made his features uglier. For his age he was slim and straight. He rode beautifully and looked quite splendid in any of his two dozen Austrian uniforms with gold epaulettes, medals, and decorations.

Prince Paul squired Lillie about as often as she let him. He proposed a number of times, and she did give the matter serious thought. To be a princess in the cat-and-dog social world would be invaluable. It would banish all memories of past indiscretions. It would help Jeanne to move in the upper strata when it came time for her to marry. Then, too—the idea tickled Lillie—if she remained on the stage (and she would), she'd be the only actress ever legitimately billed as princess.

But Prince Paul was a pompous old fop incapable of arousing the slightest feeling in her. Lillie couldn't conceive marrying a foolish old man who was always discontented or disgruntled about something, forever taking umbrage at some imagined slight. It did no good standing on one's dignity when

347

it was as ridiculously insecure as this imperial horse buyer's. Take away the title, the uniform, and what did you have? Scarcely more than Baron von Dunkelmann, the German diplomat who gargled adoring gutturals at her, then belched happily as he swilled down a whole ham with gallons of beer.

Now, the Marquis de Soveral was a smooth one and knew his importance. A good friend of Princess Alexandra, confidant and adviser to Bertie, very witty, very shrewd. Sir Frederick Ponsonby, Bertie's secretary, wrote, "He was universally popular in England, where he made love to all the most beautiful women and the nicest men were his friends." One story had Bertie asking him if he'd seen *The Importance of Being Earnest.* Soveral came back with, "No, Sir. But I have seen the importance of being Ernest Cassel." (Cassel was a rags-to-riches financier who became one of Bertie's best friends, handled his investments, and was made baronet.)

The Blue Monkey, as the Marquis was called, danced and talked magnificently, his gay charm catnipped women, and he eventually leapfrogged to the premiership of Portugal. He was a great flatterer. When he took Lillie to an exhibition bullfight in Paris, he saw to it that they lunched with the two best matadors, who afterward showed off their prowess. Each took turns bowing to Lillie in the Portuguese Embassy box and shouting *"Madame, je vous offre le taureau,"* at which Soveral instructed her to bow acknowledgment.

"It is a great honor usually reserved for royalty," he said, teeth agleam. "But then, dear Lillie, that is what you are."

She could not see herself marrying any of them, or even sweet Jimmy Smyth-Pigott, one of her own kind and the best and most understanding of friends. She had noticed he was fond of her and she'd asked him how he liked the theater. Jimmy, who'd been tracing mysteries in the carpet with his cane, said, "Oh, it's all right, but it breaks into a chap's evenings so." He was a strange one.

Perhaps her divorce had come too late, thought Lillie. Maybe it was just as well and she had been spared from making another error. It was so hard to tell about men, what went on

348

beyond the amiable façade, the surface charm, the beards, mustaches, medals, and uniforms. As the Jersey Lily her beauty and reputation were enough to intimidate an ordinary good man, she supposed. None of her suitors were of her own age. They were either old men like Prince Paul Esterhazy, Prince Louis of Battenberg, and the others—or those suspiciously younger than herself like Hugo de Bathe, who was twenty-five.

Hugo she had met at the Duke of Richmond's estate in Goodwood. She had been walking with Bertie when a tall, thin young man came toward them. A handsome fellow with an elegantly swooping black mustache, who carried himself well and had a studious, fastidious manner that Lillie thought appealing. He bowed, and she noticed how beautifully his clothes fitted. Very much like Freddie.

"Young de Bathe," Bertie muttered.

"Who?"

"Hugo, the eldest son of Sir Henry Percival de Bathe, the retired general and Crimean hero. He said he wanted to meet you."

Lillie shrugged.

"Come along. Time you met some young fellows instead of old roosters like Esterhazy."

Hugo was pleasant and easygoing. Very charming, very amusing. His attentiveness was flattering, but he was just another man. Much, much too young in spite of his compliments and dogged insistence that she was the most beautiful and youthful-looking woman there.

Lillie examined herself carefully in the mirror that night. She had only to look at Jeanne to know how kind nature had been to her. She took good care of herself. Plenty of sleep, sufficient exercise, a sunny outlook, sound nerves, and excellent health and digestion did the rest. Lillie had always set little store by her esteemed beauty. Lack of pose and pretence about it had helped her stay lovely. And hadn't Oscar said she'd be beautiful at eighty-five?

Poor Oscar! He'd been doing so well. It was like him to brandish the dagger that had been used to cut him down. And even while *The Importance of Being Earnest* was still playing in London, with the author's name shamefully expunged from the program, he had been sent to jail.

She'd seen him once before he'd gone off to exile in France, a broken, embittered man. Society could forgive all sins but his. And was his failing really a sin or a sickness? His long hair was streaked with gray, smiling was an effort. He shrank before her.

"Aren't you afraid to come to see me?" he said, with a flash of his old gaiety. "People will avoid you if you're seen here."

"Nothing could be said about me that hasn't been said before," she said truthfully. "We're friends, Oscar. We always will be."

"Then you're one of the few. What's this?" He took the envelope she gave him. "Thank you, Lil. I won't pretend I don't need money."

They'd met later in Paris. She was coming out of Worth's and thought there was something familiar about this disreputably crumpled man lurching up the street. He tried to avoid her, then gratefully accepted her invitation to lunch. He was bright and witty during the meal, much like his old self until others looked at him.

"You're a wonderful woman, Lil, the true Venus Victrix of our age. You haven't said a righteous word. I saw Jimmy Whistler on the street the other day, and he almost tripped over his cane to get away. And Sarah Bernhardt's failed me by not going through with *Salome* just when I need money so badly. But you—you—would you be surprised if I wept?"

"I can remember when you wept because I hurt your feelings. Frank Miles had to lead you from the theater."

"Ah, yes, poor Frank." He fumbled for a cigarette, which he took out of a worn, scarred case. "I remember your first night in New York, the dinner with Moreton Frewen, Niagara Falls, all of it." His hand trembled as he lifted his glass. "I threw it all away, but I knew it would happen. I knew it." He stared at nothing for an instant. "You won't forget me, will you, Lil?" She told him never. "To think I was once in love with you. I would have married you like that! Thank God, I didn't appeal to you, but then I couldn't appeal to any woman long. Is that so very strange?"

"Nothing is strange, Oscar."

"The newspapers had their fun, didn't they? A jolly pillory but, as I always said, journalism justifies its own existence by the great Darwinian principle of the survival of the vulgarest." He stumbled against the table as he stood up. "Good-by, Lil, and thanks. I want to go first." He kissed her hand and slunk out.

Lillie sent him more money. She always refused to listen to anything against him. She felt much like Charles Frohman when he gave Seymour Harris two hundred pounds to pass on to Oscar: "Give him this if you can find him, and say it is on account of his next play. Of course, I know he'll never send anything, but—well, he was a great man and I expect he's in a pretty bad way—and that's all there is to it."

How quick people were to condemn! thought Lillie, brushing her hair before the mirror in her regular nightly ritual. Especially what they didn't understand. She had only been out with Hugo a few times and already there was talk—robbing the cradle and all that. What if she married him? A faint smile twitched her lips. What a fine frenzy *that* would arouse. She would be the triply notorious Mrs. Langtry.

Hugo's schooling had been at Radley, and he was a former lieutenant in the Third Battalion of the Gloucester Regiment. He had all the small, unimportant social graces which have a way of seeming important. A party type a little like Freddie, suave, charming to women, neat and nattily dressed, a bright and amusing lightweight good at games and at tossing chitchat like darts. Lillie saw him on and off, but her name continued to be linked to Prince Esterhazy's. Their engagement had been announced in one newspaper, and the flustered horse buyer had been forced to deny it officially in the press.

Lillie was enjoying herself socially, and her stables were prospering. Merman had won at Ascot while she was visiting in Jersey. She had been fishing for mackerel out in St. Aubin's

351

Bay and had forgotten all about the race till the old fisherman rowed her back to the dock in St. Helier. She found the town highly excited. Her fawn-and-turquoise colors were flying everywhere, even on the whips of cabbies, and the editor of the local paper rushed down to the boat with the good news. As usual she had placed a good bet on Merman. She promptly sent Michael a check for the cashbook.

She loved Jersey more than ever. She'd bought a new cottage from a fisherman and had it done over to her taste. It had a long, low parlor with flowered chintz hangings, a dining room big enough for serving three, two attic bedrooms and a toy kitchen. Outside, a steep white-washed roof, green trellised walls "which roses and pink geraniums literally smother." A great palm over the cottage and the sea washing the wall of the garden. Hugo thought it a lovely, romantic spot.

In September, 1898, she attended "Great Week," at Trouville, France, entering some of her horses in the races there. She was entertained by the Barons Arthur and Edmond Rothschild on their yachts, and who should be a guest but her old admirer, King Leopold of Belgium! White-bearded now, wearing a gay little hat and the baggiest of trousers, he cut a silly figure, but age had not withered his glands. He fluttered about Lillie, trying just as hard to land the prize he'd missed twenty years before.

Trouville was amusing, but her "retirement" was palling on her. Never before had she been so long absent from the stage. The stables were running themselves, Jeanne was just beginning to go out socially, Hugo—known to his intimates as Shuggy—was pressing her. She was restless. She disliked being idle. The spectacle of King Leopold, still typecast as a royal lecher, seemed to spur her into visiting Sidney Grundy who had written a play for her.

Grundy's *Esther Sandraz* had been one of her big hits. As he read *The Degenerates* aloud, she knew immediately this was just the thing. Her role was a fat one. The play was in the nature of a modern exposé, controversial, shocking perhaps, certainly bound to kick up a fuss. She told Grundy she wanted

352

to do it and called Edward Michael. It was arranged the play would open at the Haymarket in August.

First, however, Lillie planned a holiday. She went to Cowes, then back to Jersey where she was joined by Mrs. Le Breton, Jeanne—and Hugo. As rehearsals began, only two people outside of her family knew the secret. One was Bertie, who thoroughly approved, and the other was the put-upon Grundy, who gave the show away.

"Please go over that part again, Mrs. de Bathe," he said, nose in script. "Oh, excuse me!"

The cast stared, a woman giggled. Lillie smiled at Hugo, who looked sheepish.

Not that there hadn't been hints. Shuggy had been at rehearsals afternoon and evening, full of attentions, and had been allowed privileges denied the actors. Lillie had let him break her no-smoking rule, even ordering a stagehand to give him a light.

Now Lillie said it was time everyone knew. Hugo came on stage to take her arm, and she sent out for tea and cakes for the company.

Significantly, it was Lillie who faced the interviewers with Hugo Gerald de Bathe somewhere conveniently out of sight. For once she was on the defensive and to soften criticism of the May-December age difference did a little judicious lying that was unlike her.

"Yes, it is quite true. I am married to Mr. de Bathe. The wedding occurred very quietly at my old church, St. Saviour's on the Island of Jersey, where my dear father officiated so long. It was pretty much of a runaway match, as we kept it to ourselves, knowing it would leak out gradually. I see the papers put me down as forty-seven years old. Well, a few years either way does not matter. But I am only thirty-nine, for the old clerk at St. Saviour's took my age from the church register of births.

"I know nothing of Hugo's estates. Indeed, I have not been there yet. The newspapers, as a rule, do not spare me, and have often criticized me when I did not deserve it. I hope the newspapers will speak nicely of our wedding, now that the news has leaked out.

"The Prince of Wales was, as he always is, thoughtful. He remembered us kindly by congratulations. But I am sorry his name was mentioned, for what he did was done privately and out of pure friendship.

"Mr. Frohman is arranging with me for an American tour. I long to go, for I love the people of America. Of course, my husband will accompany me."

The papers quickly pointed out that if Lillie had been born in 1860 as she claimed, she would have been fourteen at the time of her marriage to Edward Langtry in 1874. The fact was that she was forty-six (her birth certificate proves she was born October 13, 1853) and Hugo twenty-seven. On their marriage certificate, however, their respective ages were entered simply "full age." Under rank, trade, or profession, Hugo was listed as "gentleman," an avocation to which he devoted his entire life with varying success. His condition was listed as "bachelor"; Lillie's as "widow of Edward Langtry, Esq.," which was an admission that her long-sought divorce was legally invalid in England.

It had been a spur-of-the-moment affair, with Shuggy pushing it and Lillie perhaps thinking oh-what-the-hell. She had chosen her old parish church from sentimentality and deference to her mother. She had happy memories of St. Saviour's. Besides, it was pretty and secluded and—how Hugo laughed! —"I always get married there!" The day was a happy one. As they raised a glass to each other that 27th of July word came of Merman's victory at Goodwood (with a big bet of Lillie's riding on him).

"That wonderful horse! Oh, Shuggy, from now on I'm calling this Merman Cottage."

"I'm delighted to begin married life with a victory," he said charmingly, smoothing his mustache.

It was Hugo's only victory and, as was always the case, it had nothing to do with him. But there were sighs and laughter that night in Merman Cottage "by the side of the turquoise sea which laps the golden sand."

354

Commenting on "a famous actress who, after a tragic domestic life, had married a fool," Oscar Wilde is supposed to have said, "She thought that because he was stupid, he would be kindly, when, of course, kindliness requires imagination and intellect." He might have been speaking of the Jersey Lily. While her marriage to Hugo de Bathe is as difficult to explain as her attachments to Freddie Gebhard and Abington Baird, she married him with her eyes open. She knew herself; she knew Hugo; she knew what would be said about them. And she probably didn't give a damn.

Living by oneself was a lonely business. Sweet Duchess was failing, Jeanne would marry, and what then? There were no strong men around—none strong enough to contain the Jersey Lily, anyway—and Hugo was the best available in the dubious circumstances. Deep down he had a little-lost-boy personality that needed mothering and appreciation as a dingy boot needs polish. He had severe good looks, a lovely mustache, a bubbling nature, and some day he would have a title—if things *ever* worked out as he meant them to. He spoke frankly—how he'd hoped to make a career of the army, then banking—and he asked Lillie to make an actor of him. He was worse than Lord Rosslyn on the stage, self-conscious and unable to apply himself. Outside of dramatizing himself, he had no dramatic feeling.

Whatever men thought of him, if they spared the time, women had always liked him for his humor, his dancing, and his manners. Hugo was smooth. He had pleased many women at first meeting and had been mildly astonished that Lillie hadn't found him irresistible. Shuggy couldn't know that his experience with women, his conquests, were as nothing compared to hers. It may be this indifference that intrigued him enough to propose. Quite a thing to be squiring the Jersey Lily, a miracle that she should marry him. And he was magnanimous about her age.

"Age differences are meaningless, Lillie. If our positions were reversed, nobody would think anything of it. And whose business is it but ours, in the first place?"

"Let's make it our business then. There may come a time

355

when it won't be easy for us. When it comes, I promise you I won't be hateful and possessive, Shuggy."

"But I want you to be possessive."

Being married again was pleasant and new. She felt very different living with a man, legally and officially, after nineteen years or more, since the last years with Edward hardly counted. Hugo was properly ardent although—she'd never tell him—hardly in a class with Freddie, the Squire, or—what did it matter? It didn't mean so much now. Hugo was sensitive, and she saw to it that his manly self-esteem did not suffer. As the older wife, she had her end to hold up, too. She wouldn't be faulted there, not as long as Shuggy's mustache swooped. The newspapers spoke of his inheritance and estates to come. Lillie didn't need money, but Shuggy wanted the record straight.

"Father hasn't a bean, you know, and all those estates are so much paper. It's a good thing my sisters married well. They're the ones with money. I'm afraid the old boy doesn't like me, Lillie, cutting me off the way he did. He'd take the title, too, if he could. That's about the only tangible thing I can offer you. You'll be Lady de Bathe, but what's that next to Lillie Langtry?"

Shuggy was all right. She didn't mind his living on her money. Did she love him? Why pinpoint love and the ideal married state at this stage? This was fine. Things were the same as before, and she was going on as always—with a husband. As for what others thought, let them think. Those who hated her would never change. Bertie had introduced Hugo to her; he approved. He had sent congratulations and a bracelet as one of the first-to-know. But he controlled society publicly, not privately.

The "old boy" was put out. General Sir Henry Percival de Bathe was the fourth baronet of the line created in 1801. He could trace his notable family back in English history to 1172, and did. He was reported enraged by his eldest son's marriage. The newspaper stories had him hurling all of Hugo's possessions out of the window of the ancestral home. Then he changed his will and snarled, "I wish I could die now so the will could go into effect at once."

356

The British raised-eyebrows and clearing-of-throats attitude was mildness itself compared to the virulence of the American press. Shuggy was characterized as "an empty-headed young noodle" and "typical English saphead." Lillie would have to wait years for her title; she should have married Prince Esterhazy, who had died most conveniently the year before. Most stinging of all were the comments of Colonel William D'Alton Mann—the blackmailing biographer who had designed the *Lalee*. He had bought *Town Topics* in 1891 and regularly enjoyed peeling society's skin with his outrageous reporting. He hated Lillie now and, speaking of dirty laundry, did he have a scoop on the Jersey Lily!

It seemed that Hugo's mother had never been received in English society. Why? She'd borne the old general four illegitimate children. Sir Henry had been the greatest dandy in London in pre-Crimean days. His description of skinning sheep in the trenches of Sebastopol had been a stock drawing-room story forty years ago. A hero. He'd married his mistress in 1871; Hugo was the first lawful issue, and his three pretty daughters, Lady Crossley, Mrs. Henry Lawson, and Mrs. Harry McCalmont, had married the millions ascribed to poor old Papa.

Lillie's marriage was in the American newspapers from coast to coast, most of them carrying pithy editorials on the subject. One prominent New York paper printed a trenchant one headed, "Listen to the Tale of Lily's Great Luck." Calling attention to Lillie's endless good fortune, it reflected:

> In young wifehood she was the courted of princes of the blood and her daughter, from the effects of association, perhaps, has many facial resemblances to the Guelph family. As the Lily grew wiser and stronger on her stem, she conferred her favors with a commercial perspicacity remarkable in a woman. She has estates in America and estates in England. Young millionaires die and leave her beside certain tumultuous recollections a large fortune. Even in her middle age, and possibly when she has passed the meridian, her rabbit's foot still retains its full efficacy.

The editorial called Hugo a millionaire and added that in

addition to her dower of lands and spectacular past, Lillie had brought her husband "the best wishes and congratulations of the Prince of Wales. Her daughter, too, who was at the wedding as a guest, says she is glad to have her mother settle down." Noting her father had been a dean and that she had been brought up in religious surroundings, he concluded with the bromide, "The nearer the church, the further from God."

Perhaps the soundest observation came from Broadway, recalling the famous Anna Held milk bath of 1896. It granted that Lillie had a new name, but would continue to be known as Mrs. Langtry "for de Bathe is virtually copyrighted in this country by Anna Held and her lacteal lavatory."

In her family, an even temperament and willingness to please helped Jeanne now in the awkward relationship with her new stepfather, who was young enough to be her brother—or husband. She didn't know whether to call him Mr. de Bathe, Father, Hugo, or Shuggy. He tried to ease things by treating her like a little girl, instead of a pretty young woman of eighteen. Mrs. Le Breton's memory was failing, but Lillie's instinctive tact kept the augmented household functioning as smoothly as ever.

The marriage and the spicy rumors concerning *The Degenerates* brought out a record crowd for the London opening on August 31, 1899. So great was the interest that a sell-out was assured for the entire Haymarket run, in spite of what the reviews might say. Hugo sat in a box with the Duke of Saxe-Coburg and Gotha and Prince Louis of Battenberg. Bertie sent a telegram from Marienbad: MY BEST WISHES FOR A BRILLIANT SUCCESS. BOOKED FOR A FORTNIGHT FROM TODAY. ALBERT EDWARD. This was the royal fillip the public loved. It amused Lillie to reflect that, even if the play were the worst kind of flop, she'd have to keep it running just so that the Prince could see it.

Lillie's acting was praised reservedly, the subject matter of the play deplored as well as the actress' lending her name and talents to such a shabby presentation. Still, it had the look of one of her greatest successes. The reviews, especially those that condemned the play most strongly, were of the sensational type that would make people fight to see it. Gossip said it was auto-biographical. It showed the "degenerate" aristocratic society of today's London, with Lillie playing a demi-mondaine forced to readjust her life morally because of the unexpected arrival of her virginal daughter who had been hidden away somewhere. To clinch things further, the set was supposed to be an exact replica of the sitting room of Lillie's sumptuous new house and the furniture her own, to add authenticity.

To deny the charges was useless; besides, they only made *The Degenerates* racier fare. In the *Daily Telegraph* Clement Scott, who considered himself her mentor, called the play a potboiler, its sentiments sickening, its lines cheap and disgusting. He suffered when Lillie as Lady Trevelyan said: "I was born a woman. I couldn't help it. Somebody blundered, and I have to suffer for it." He called this the statement of a vulgar, *déclassée* woman who insulted her sex with every word she uttered. All the talk of horses and gambling, the risqué remarks indulged in by the titled characters offended him nearly as much as their last-word slang.

The success of *The Degenerates* delighted Lillie. It was modern. It had a stirring shock quality that was critic-proof, and it would be durable. So far as Hugo went, things were working out beautifully. He seemed happy, and Jeanne was going through the preliminaries attendant on her first London season. As for herself, Lillie was convinced that the marriage had been fortunate. She had the looks, the drive, the vitality of a much younger woman. Slander aside, she had reckoned the consequences and looked into the future. Being Mrs. de Bathe made life easier for her daughter, effectively slammed the door on gossip's dirty face, and strengthened her position socially and on the stage. She could handle Shuggy. He was happy squiring her around and being the husband of a great star. He could go anywhere buttressed by Bertie's approval, enjoying himself as a gentleman. Tasting fame and fortune vicariously was highly agreeable to his gregarious nature.

The year before Lillie had moved to Number Two Cadogan Place, not far from her old Pont Street house. Supposedly once Charles Dickens' home, it was in one of London's best sections, a big, handsome structure. She had filled it with racing trophies, fine collections of silver and old china, and rare period furniture. Hunting trophies shot by her brother Clement in California adorned the walls of the study. The prize was Rameses, a great grizzly bear of the Rockies that had weighed one thousand pounds. Now he stood erect, some seven feet high, in the wide entrance hall, scaring people with his lifelike appearance. Lillie loved being photographed clutching one of his huge paws. Rameses was a monumental good-luck charm. He went with her on all her trips to America in a special trunk, startling reporters and keeping her in the news.

Lillie's boudoir had several walls lined with a continuous wardrobe for her hundreds of dresses. The walls of her bathroom were of turquoise and blue mosaic with starlike glints of gold, and her bath was marble. Off the dining room, there was a kind of formal throne room with a minstrel gallery where a small orchestra played for dinners. Naturally, there was a telephone, which Lillie often used, plus a device peculiar to her interest in the track—a tape to give Mr. Jersey the results of the various race meetings on which she had placed bets.

Novelties fascinated her. Along with her telephone, electric lights, and racing ticker, Lillie had several automobiles. She was still one hundred per cent horsewoman, but it was imperative that the Jersey Lily remain *au courant*. She had ridden in Bertie's autocar, which had carriage lamps and looked just like a carriage with its elevated chauffeur's seat. Later she learned to drive from Fournier, the famous French chauffeur. Shuggy was so taken with the new invention that she bought him one for his own use. He loved driving her about, sharing the hazards of motoring through the countryside. With other smart owners they attended various "motor meetings" at which he was the center of attention, with Lillie on the plush seat next to him.

The family motto of the old, tradition-encrusted de Bathe lineage was "Trifles deter me not." This was hardly applicable to Hugo who dealt with trifles all his life, most of the time winningly, though constantly deterred by them. He had always been ineffectual, but living with Lillie made him realize how much. It was not that she treated him condescendingly or humored him; he was a husband who could not impress his wife, overawe her, or come close to sweeping her off her poised, firmly planted, shapely feet. Anything he could do she could do better —an ignominious position at best. Shuggy chafed for some dragon to kill, some cause in which he could prove himself.

In October, 1899, the political situation deteriorated in South Africa. War broke out between England and the truculent Boers, and Hugo found his *métier*. Britain united over the issue. The country echoed and re-echoed with slogans, sabers rattled, the jingoists inflated themselves like barrage balloons on military propaganda and Kiplingesque poetry. There was nothing for it but for every young man to fight for the Queen. This was Hugo's opportunity, replete with melodrama like the buckling on of ancient armor. To fight, to kill—something his world-famous wife *couldn't* do. The papers later had it that his announcement threw Lillie into hysterics, that she appealed to the Prince to make Shuggy renege, and that he nobly refused with something of Sidney Carton's, "It is a far, far better thing I do than I have ever done . . ." In fairness to him, it probably was.

"It's wonderful of you, darling, but, really, you needn't, you know. You're no longer in the army, and I'd hoped so much you'd come to America with me. You'd love it over there."

"I know my duty, Lillie. I've got to go, and I know I'll get my commission back. They can use my experience in Africa. I want to make those rotters pay for what they've done."

Hugo's course resulted in a reconciliation between old General de Bathe and his son and daughter-in-law. Sir Henry's home, Wood End, was close to Goodwood. He met them at the door, eagle-eyed and ramrod straight at seventy-seven. His son's enlistment thrilled him. The old soldier belatedly congratulated the couple on their marriage and buried the axe with a great family celebration. It was an emotional time, as false in some ways as some of the trumped-up scenes Lillie had played in, but Shuggy was now Galahad off to the wars. The feverish excitement set off by the bad news from Africa had communicated itself to everyone.

In Paris Lillie was rushed, getting new clothes for the Amer-

361

ican tour. It was the last time she and Hugo would be together. The fittings were endless, but Worth was a perfectionist who wouldn't be hurried. One afternoon she received a message from President Félix Faure asking her to recite "The Absent-Minded Beggar" at a widows' and orphans' benefit. She couldn't refuse, but she had nothing to wear and called up Worth. He spluttered until he heard the magic words "the President of France." Then he told her to run over. He put his entire force to work on one of the second-act gowns. That night, fresh from Worth's, she said her piece, passed the hat to the audience, and raised 2,500 pounds beating her tambourine and chanting "Pay, pay, pay."

Hugo as departing hero was tight-lipped and stolid. Evidently traveling on shattered aplomb, he was observed by a New York *World* reporter on the same Africa-bound ship. He spoke proudly of his conquests over women and boastfully of his record, except for the Langtry part. He said he was twenty-eight, but looked thirty-five to the tart *World* correspondent to whom he described his marriage to Mrs. Langtry as a "youthful prank." Hugo confessed he rather enjoyed being known as the husband of Lillie Langtry, but he preferred to talk of the great things he expected to do fighting the Boers. In spite of his slight military experience, he took it for granted the Natal Volunteers would award a commission to the husband of the Jersey Lily. To ready himself for battle he engaged in daily signal and flag drills on the *Mexican,* running around the decks and climbing the rigging.

His gymnastics startled the passengers, one of whom asked why, with so many trained soldiers ready to fight the Boers, he should want to go. Giving the game away, Shuggy answered with great vehemence, "To show my wife I am a man!" The *World* reporter added that the inquiring passenger smiled and said, "I hope you'll succeed."

As Hugo swung industriously from the rigging, developing his muscles, Lillie assembled her staff and discussed the strategy of the forthcoming American campaign with that Napoleonic genius for detail which always amazed manager Michael. Taking the train at Euston Station for Liverpool, Lillie told reporters, "My heart is on the way to South Africa." It's quite possible that she meant it.

Nearby, Jeanne stood watching her mother wistfully. She would be in good hands, although some people wondered how Lillie could possibly leave her daughter with her old rival, Mrs. William Cornwallis-West. In truth, the two lovely women had always been friends with a warm common bond in the glamourous past. Besides, Mary Cornwallis-West's youngest daughter, Constance Edwina, was of the same age as Jeanne and the influence a good one. Mary knew the right people. Her eldest daughter, Mary Theresa Olivia, had made a brilliant marriage in 1891 and was now Her Serene Highness, Princess of Pless.

Jeanne was too old for tutors. Mrs. Le Breton was now an invalid in Jersey, and Mary had promised to ease Jeanne into society. She had spent several months that summer at Ruthin Castle in Lymington going to balls and enjoying herself with other young people. Now she would have a trusted chaperone while Lillie was away. Mrs. Cornwallis-West was one of the few women whose ideas on society and young men coincided with Lillie's own. She and Mary knew all there was to know about each other and had always kept the knowledge to themselves. And, knowing that Bertie would be king in time, Mary had nothing to lose by being kind to her old rival.

Despite the awe in which many Americans held English royalty, there was considerable pro-Boer feeling in the self-contented isolation of a country in which the distant war seemed unreal. Besides, the Boers were underdogs, always traditionally favored by Americans, and latent anti-British sentiment had been aroused by the humiliating military reverses of the Empire in Africa. Lillie took care to remind the reporters of her American citizenship at an interview in the Hotel Manhattan.

"I'm so glad to get back," she told them.

Trunks and boxes marked Lillie de Bathe littered the room, roses were scattered in random profusion, the Jersey Lily dazzling in an ermine-trimmed robe as she chatted in her "languorous hothouse voice."

363

"I don't mind the chaos. Isn't it deliciously upset? But do come in."

A few reporters had trouble spelling her new name. "Teddy" Michael wanted it right. "All the noble family of de Bathe has left is the final 'e,'" he was quoted. "It would never do to leave it out." No one thought to ask him his opinion of Hugo.

Compared to the rest of America, New York was liberal and sophisticated, with a secret pride in being known as a sinful city. News of the shocking and sensational aspects of *The Degenerates* had preceded Lillie. For January 15, 1900, the Garden Theater was sold out to an overflow audience judged as great and brilliant as her first back in 1882. Welcoming her back after a five-year absence, "Every seat in the house was occupied from the orchestra rail to the back benches of the gallery, and the standing room sale stopped long before the curtain. In the balcony, as well as in the parquet, the showing of toilets and the fashionable audience was stamped with society's *cachet*."

Sin-city or no, moral uplift was in the air. New York had been ripe with civic and political corruption, and a house-cleaning everywhere was in order. Newspapers reflected this pure attitude while reporting every scandal with salacious solicitude.

Anna Held's bath was still a scandal. Lillian Russell was a good source of scandal with her marital sweepstakes. And hadn't the lovely English actress, Olga Nethersole, been banned by the district attorney for kissing too "hot" in *Sapho*? Well, now! And here was that notorious woman, the Prince's favorite, Freddie Gebhard's playmate, and the currently infamous bride of a man young enough to be her son, flaunting herself in a degenerate play about degenerate people! Infamous! Hurrah for the healthy American Gibson Girl!

Kind words for Lillie were few, but the box office jingled gaily. She ignored the criticism and went ahead with her plans for the benefit *chantant* at Sherry's, which she had announced before leaving England. She couldn't go to Africa, but she could raise money. Lillie was determined to make the affair a success, but she was counting on society's help to put it over. She knew the Four Hundred were chary of association with actresses and

364

yet was surprised when her own charm did not win them. It seemed they were not prepared to lift a finger without the sanction of Mrs. William B. Astor, their acknowledged leader.

No woman had ever daunted the Jersey Lily—not even Queen Victoria—and Lillie expected no trouble from Caroline Schermerhorn Astor. But she underestimated the power of the queen of society who had long ruled from her command post in her luxurious mansion at Fifth Avenue and 34th Street. Here Mrs. Astor received guests before her full-length portrait, guided the fortunes of destiny's darlings, and supposedly set the magic number at four hundred because that was the capacity of her magnificent ballroom. Her parties in her new château at Fifth Avenue and 65th Street were fabulous. One *had* to attend to be anybody.

Mrs. Astor, however, would have nothing to do with Mrs. Langtry—a serious matter because without her name at the head of the list of patronesses, no one would sign on and the affair at Sherry's would collapse. It was a contest of wills. Lillie appeared to be defeated before she began. The upper echelon was delighted. Served that woman right! Lillie tried every way she knew. Mrs. Astor wouldn't answer her letters, her calls, or see her. The haughty butler told Lillie that his mistress did not see actresses *ever*. She took the insult casually enough and planned her strategy.

Society was closely knit in Manhattan. Shoddy and porous as its fabric was, the cat-clawing contest was followed with fascination. Mrs. Astor appeared to have won the first round, but Lillie was still warming up. "One would imagine from the tone of writers that I had never been pure and was born degenerate," she said. As for the society ban on her, "Bless me, these estimable ladies quite overlook the fact that I began with society, while they are ending with it." Good jabbing, though not enough to jolt Mrs. Astor.

The tea concert at Sherry's was to benefit the hospital ship *Maine,* a project originated and headed by the widowed Lady Randolph Churchill—a joint Anglo-American effort, although the ship and the funds to sustain it had to come from the United States. As an American, Lady Randoph knew the difficulties involved; sympathy in America tended toward the Boers who were presumed to be fighting for their independence. Lillie sensed this, too. Still, there was a great need for hospital funds, and no self-appointed grande dame like Mrs. Astor would deter her.

Here was a woman with tremendous wealth and unassailable position. What, then, was her weakness? Pride, probably—pride connected with her family. Ward McAllister, pompous and stuffy, had assisted Mrs. Astor in society's rituals. He had died in 1895 and been succeeded by Harry Lehr, "petulant and cynical"—an odd type who suggested to Mrs. Stuyvesant Fish that she have a monkey in evening dress, as guest of honor at a party. Lillie knew the fantastic Harry. He was the harlequin of New York society, loyal to Mrs. A—and disloyal when he chose. She got what she wanted from him and also did some personal research on her adversary—a formidable woman, smug in her fatuous superiority, but an innocent in the ways of the world.

Lillie dispatched a few cables to the right people in England. She received satisfactory answers and, through an intermediary, put her proposition to Mrs. Astor. It revolved on the latter's daughter, the former Mrs. Coleman Drayton, now living in England and using the reflected glory of Mama's position to crash London's society ramparts. She had remarried, and her mother had great hopes for her rehabilitation and success in England.

Mrs. Astor was informed that Lady Randolph Churchill had reported her slight to Mrs. Langtry to the Prince of Wales. The Prince was not amused. In fact, he implied that unless Mrs. Astor favored Mrs. Langtry's benefit tea, her daughter (now Mrs. Ogilvy Haig) would never be acceptable to royalty. Checkmate for Lillie; for Mrs. Haig ostracism; for Mrs. Astor a punch well below her diamond stomacher. It was time to reconsider her edict about never linking her name with that of "an actress."

Her blue blood singing in her veins, Mrs. Astor capitulated.

One day the New York *Journal* was printing an editorial about the tea, under the question "Should good, pure women associate with Mrs. Langtry even for the sake of charity?" The next day it was reporting that *the* Mrs. Astor headed the list of patronesses, followed by such social pillars as Mrs. Ogden Mills, Mrs. Stuyvesant Fish, Mrs. George Gould, etc. The about-face was earth-shaking, enough to crack society's already riddled fortress. In his racy *Town Topics,* Colonel Mann frothed: ". . . for Mrs. Astor's gross violation of the proprieties, the decencies of all social life, there is no palliation." He decried the absolutely impossible association, suggesting that either Mrs. O. H. P. Belmont or Mrs. George Gould be elected to occupy the throne from which Mrs. Astor had tumbled so humiliatingly.

With the arrogant lady over a barrel, Lillie had no trouble lining up performers, sponsors, refined barmaids, and refreshments. The champagne was donated by George Kessler, who represented Moët et Chandon, and by Mannie Chappelle for Mumm's. *Bon vivants* and keenly competitive, they liked to drop in at restaurants, order champagne for everyone in the house, and ask them to compare—compare, for comparisons prove. The happy patrons always obliged. Both salesmen promised to assist in exchange for a little free advertising, and Billy Oliver, an old stockbroker friend, also offered his compelling services.

Ella A. Boole, president of the Woman's Christian Temperance Union, complained to the police about Mrs. Langtry's plans to use debutantes and actresses as barmaids. She threatened to picket Sherry's to prevent drunken orgies. All this made for greater publicity in the newspapers. The *Sunday Telegraph* ran a cartoon showing Lillie and the Prince cakewalking under a huge banner proclaiming "Welcome to New York's 400." Special matinées of *The Degenerates* had to be run at the Garden Theater, with Lillie still finding the time to go down to the Stock Exchange in her landau, just as she had done for her coffee clatch, to sell $1,000 worth of tickets.

The entertainment was long and varied. It featured such singers as Antonio Scotti of the Metropolitan singing the Prologue to *Pagliacci.* The big thing was the pretty actresses. Billed as barmaids but not selling any drinks in deference to Mrs.

367

Boole and the police, they circulated with cigars, candy, cigarettes, programs and favors, accepting only large bills and making no change. Among them were such stars as Anna Held, Edna May, Cissie Loftus, May Robson, and Maxine Elliott. Lillie supervised their efforts, dashing about to talk to this social light and that matron, and collecting $1,158 in her kit bag.

Mrs. Astor was pointedly absent, nursing her grudge on Fifth Avenue; but she was hardly missed, what with the long list of socialites *and* Governor Hogg of Texas. Another old friend of Lillie's, the Earl of Yarmouth, was bartender and, of course, Abe Hummel was there too. Now that Lillie was married, she confessed that these were the only two men with whom she would appear in public. It was a long, frenzied, bang-up affair that raised about $8,000 for the *Maine*.

In the face of the barrage of criticism and in-fighting that had preceded it, the press was rather awed by the success of Lillie's *chantant*. Not so Colonel Mann, who foamed at the mouth for pages in *Town Topics,* cutting the tea and Lillie to shreds in his best astringent style. He saw it as the most demoralizing spectacle that had ever disgraced New York. Belaboring everyone and everything associated with "this vile scheme advertising a notorious actress and her filthy play," Colonel Mann said that the Earl of Yarmouth, Lillie's barkeep, after "his peculiar social experience in Australia and elsewhere," was reluctant to help Lillie, then changed his mind because: "It may make a bit of a stench over here, but, you know, it will do me a lot of good with the Prince."

The circulation of *Town Topics* was mostly of a backdoor nature. Colonel Mann was a busy gadfly raising welts on one patrician rump after the other. Everyone disapproved of his publication, but wouldn't have missed an issue. Newspapers raged at the colonel's ethics only to have him complain that they stole his best material. Edward Michael was furious.

"I'll show this to Mr. Hummel," he raged. "We'll sue the rotter!"

"Oh, don't let's fuss about it. The *chantant* was a success and nothing else matters. Colonel Mann used to be a friend of mine."

twenty-two

ALTHOUGH Lillie could excuse Mann as a twisted personality out to avenge a personal insult, the all-out attack that greeted her in the Philadelphia *North American,* while she played the City of Brotherly Love, was something else again. Identifying her with the degenerate Mrs. Trevelyan (supposedly pronounced Thivvilian by the British cast) she portrayed, the paper set out to demolish her character and spoil her engagement at the Chestnut Street Opera House.

It featured a full page of articles labeled, among others: "What a Pure American Woman Thought," "What a Mother of Innocent Children Thought," "What a Minister of the Gospel Thought," "What a Journalist Thought." To skewer Lillie, the principals ignored the play they had seen. Arthur McEwen, the journalist, was by far the most articulate.

> Mrs. Langtry [he wrote] is ophidian in the temperature of her blood and her heart is a cash register. . . . She has always been her collected, selfish, cynical self in society, the theater, and her own pleasures, resolved to get out of life whatever money could bring her in the way of luxury and freedom. . . . Anybody who has a fortune to spend has been welcome to do it—raw boy, dissipated rounder, dissolute old sport, prince, commoner, gentleman, blackguard, anybody. . . .

America's sacred institutions—virginity, motherhood, religion—were called upon to destroy her. The vilifications, the lies stung. Worse, they could poison the public against her and sabotage her tour. Her loyal cast and friends were indignant, Michael beside himself at the "violent and scurrilous catalogue of slop and slush." He conferred with Abe Hummel about suing for libel, and the situation was so serious that Lillie called for a staff meeting presided over by Frederick Kerr, her leading man. Michael had done some detective work. The minister involved was one Reverend C. L. Seasholes, "a converted cowboy of enormous physical stature," put up to the hatchet work, like the others, by the *North American,* that self-appointed guardian of public morals. Hummel was definitely of the opinion that all these people could be sued. The hitch was that litigation would take time. Lillie would have to stay on in Philadelphia and cancel the tour.

"There must be a better way," she mused. "Some way in which I can be defended publicly by a disinterested person of some importance."

"Well," said Edward Michael, "we ought to find some leading newspaper to print your defense. They love these press wars here."

"Of course! And the New York *Herald* is just the paper. Commodore James Gordon Bennett is an old friend."

Dispatched to New York, Michael talked to Rieck, the *Herald*'s managing editor who liked Mrs. Langtry and liked the idea. It was good controversial copy, but who would man the defense? Why not Clement Scott who was now in America writing dramatic criticism for the *Herald*? suggested Michael.

"Clement Scott!" said Rieck. "Why, you brought me a letter from the Commodore instructing me that Scott was on no account to write a criticism of the play after the way he panned it in England."

"Right, but I know my Scott, Mr. Rieck. He's an incurable sentimentalist, and he'll delight in doing this sort of thing."

In a long article in next day's *Herald,* Scott came through as predicted. As Beerbohm Tree put it, it was the critic at his most "Scotty without being Clement." He effectively defended Lillie while putting the parson, the mother, the spinster, and the rest through his meat grinder. In a fine frenzy of chivalrous vindication, he stressed that criticism had no concern whatever with the private lives of artists, bringing in the scandals and eccentricities of such greats as Edmund Kean, Sarah Bernhardt,

Dickens, Ruskin, Carlyle, Chopin, and Bulwer-Lytton which had no concern with their genius. Lillie was grateful and sent a telegram of thanks "for auld lang syne." And Frederick Kerr also defended her in a bristling letter published in the press.

Lillie was lonely without Hugo and had no news of him until she reached Chicago. There she heard he was ill with fever in the Capetown Hospital. Her composure briefly deserted her. She burst into tears, and the intermissions were prolonged to accommodate her. She made a curtain speech hailing the city as a "haven of refuge" and incidentally denied she had ever slipped a piece of ice down the Prince's back. Apologies of any kind were contrary to her nature, but *The Degenerates* had been banned in Pittsburgh, Cleveland, and Washington. In other cities, she found herself required to put on special trial performances for various mayors, chiefs of police, and other censors before being allowed to play for the public. Rather than submit to this indignity, she canceled those appearances. All this was ridiculous and humiliating.

"I confess," she admitted, "that I have felt wounded at some of the attacks on the play and upon myself, but at nothing so much as the accusation made in some places that mine was a vulgar performance. Whatever people may say about me and my affairs, nobody who knows me could believe I would appear in a performance that was unrefined in spirit and tone. *The Degenerates* is critical and harsh perhaps, but in no sense vulgar."

She was kept from Detroit after its mayor, William C. Marbury, personally went to Toledo to check on the play. He thought it indecent. "The plot is a continuous laisson [*sic*] between men and women. The dialogue has reference to these laissons. The language is unmistakable and points directly to the purpose of the plot." (He also happened to be pro-Boer and head of the Boer Relief Fund.)

Zealous officialdom was doing everything it could to keep the public from seeing a play it was dying to see. Lillie was not going to deny Detroit the privilege. That pompous ass Marbury and his "laissons"!

"Mr. Michael, what's the closest town to Detroit over the Canadian border?"

"Windsor, I believe."

"Then go there, engage any kind of a hall for one performance, and advertise it well in the Detroit papers. And send two tickets to Mayor Marbury with my compliments!"

With the snow deep, the temperature below zero, the Windsor Opera House sold out. A flimsy barn of a building, inadequate even for amateur theatricals, it had an old-fashioned roller curtain. The only source of heat was a big, iron stove in the center of the auditorium, into which six-foot cordwood had to be hand-fed. The stage facilities—lights, sets, and properties —were so limited that the company had to improvise. If it was cold in the orchestra, it was icy backstage where the faint heat could not penetrate.

Before the curtain, Lillie waited in décolleté, her teeth chattering, her breath visible. She was calm and smiling, and the company took its cue from her.

"You're making history, Mrs. Langtry. I don't think any other actress of your stature has played above the Arctic Circle."

"It's a lark, Mr. Michael. For Mayor Marbury's sake, I'll go through with this even if I catch my death of cold."

Stamping their feet and blowing on their hands, the actors laughed with her and set the mood for the play. In one scene, Lillie was supposed to visit a luxurious bachelor's den. Under the circumstances the Windsor Opera House's bare set called for a tremendous leap of imagination. "What a queer place you've got here," was her line. The cast went into fits of laughter; so did the audience. Further on the tense scenes were successively undermined by the janitor, who had no interest in the drama but knew his stove. Clumping down the middle aisle in hobnailed boots, he clanked it open. He thundered about in the woodbox, crashed in several big chunks, banged about with the poker, clanged the stove door, hurled down the poker, slammed the woodbox lid, and galumphed back up the aisle until his next appearance. The loud hilarious interruptions convulsed both actors and audience. *The Degenerates* had its most original performance.

Newark banned the play in what was called a spasm of spring virtue before the coming elections. It was no hasty decision but was arrived at during a solemn meeting of the Chief of Police, the Board of Police Commissioners, the Common Council, the License Committee, the Chief of the Police License Inspectors, and the City Attorney. Lillie wondered who was protecting whom from what. She would have been amused if such stupidity hadn't been costing her money.

In New England, where difficulty might have been expected, especially in Boston, all went smoothly. Wherever there was a protest, it worked to her advantage. Several ministers charged into their pulpits in Worcester to warn against Lillie and her vile play, with the result that a lot of people who hadn't meant to go bought tickets.

"You see," she told her manager triumphantly. "Word of mouth advertising is the best kind. And this was all free."

Reporters' questions always amused Lillie. Back in England in late May, 1900, the routine was dreadfully familiar. She hardly knew what to answer when asked what had been the turning point of her career.

"Life is such a complex thing," she replied. "It has so many turning points. We begin the world with such limited prospects and we surprise ourselves sometimes. Many artists, much greater than I am as an actress, have had their private lives raked over for sensational readers. If I were asked by a stage aspirant when I felt the turning point in my career had come, I think I should say when I discover that land of Utopia where drama critics are to be relied on by the actors and the public. My turning point, as I should like to see it, has not arrived."

The reporters took this down, noting that Hugo's name, once constantly on her lips, was no longer heard. Also that, after for a while having signed and spoken of herself as Lillie de Bathe, she was once again Lillie Langtry. They pondered the significance of this as she embraced her daughter, a lovely, self-possessed young thing who had popped from secluded adolescence into brilliantly sophisticated womanhood with the consummate ease one might expect of a Langtry.

Of course, there was still a lot of mystery about Jeanne Marie. Take that business of her supposed engagement to Arthur Hill which had startled society. Young Hill, the eldest son of Lord Arthur Hill whose uncle was the Marquess of Downshire, was something of a playboy. At one time he'd been quite fond of the American actress Fanny Ward. At a dinner given by the Maharajah of Kurperthala, attended by both Jeanne and young Hill, among others, the Maharajah had pointedly directed his attentions toward Jeanne. Afterward, it was said that he'd taken Mrs. Langtry aside to explain that he was mad about her daughter, wanted to give a dinner just for her, and would adorn her with pearls and diamonds if she so honored him.

The story went that, the picture of outraged motherhood, Lillie turned on him scornfully. "There are no millions in the world that can buy my daughter. There are plenty of women who would be tempted by your offer, but my daughter is not for sale!"

She swept off to Jeanne, told her what had happened, and Jeanne thereupon announced her engagement to Arthur Hill. But then the whole thing seemed to be a fiction.

No denying the girl was a social hit in London this spring. She was a great friend of Constance Edwins-West and was seen a great deal with Mrs. Herbert Asquith, who as Margot Tennant had been the high priestess of a strange coterie of intellectuals known as "The Souls." And it was a fact that the Prince of Wales seemed to be sponsoring Jeanne socially and invariably singled her out for notice when he saw her. This couldn't have been done without embarrassment except that Mrs. Langtry had raised enough money for the war in Africa to receive some kind of royal recognition.

The Prince had asked certain powerful ladies of his smart world to sponsor Jeanne: the Duchess of Manchester, the Countess of Dudley, the Countess of Warwick, the Marchioness of Granby, the Duchess of Devonshire, Lady Paget and, of course, Mrs. Cornwallis-West.

Lately Jeanne had been living with another of the Cornwallis-West girls, the gay Princess of Pless. Only a few weeks ago, while her mother's play had been stirring up such a rumpus in the United States, Jeanne had been presented to Queen Victoria at one of her famous drawing room receptions. She appeared to have the good will of Princess Alexandra, too.

It all went back to the Langtry, however. She had set about with such intense, determined purpose to reflect her glorious self in her daughter. "I must see my daughter placed in the proper position which is hers by birth, education, and blood. It is the dream now of my life." The Jersey Lily had a remarkable way of making dreams come true.

Surely Jeanne's social success was a source of great pleasure to her mother. Though Bertie had kept his word, Jeanne owed little to his prestige. She had beauty, charm, intelligence, and talent. Lillie neither looked nor felt like a middle-aged mother of a grown daughter. There was nothing so unusual about a woman of forty-seven having a husband of twenty-eight. As a matter of fact, this July Lady Randolph Churchill—of all people!—who was Lillie's age or perhaps a year older, had married Mary's son, George Cornwallis-West, aged twenty-six. Lady Randolph had ruled high in London society. No family could touch the aristocratic Marlboroughs of Blenheim, and her late husband had had a government post as Chancellor of the Exchequer.

The brouhaha over *The Degenerates* had made the play a valuable property. The provincial managers were clamoring for Mrs. Langtry, and she asked Michael to arrange a tour. It was necessary to keep the money coming in for Jeanne and the stables and herself. She liked to go to the track often, always putting down large bets. The gamble intrigued her. She was back the next day trying to win back what she'd lost the day before.

As the summer sped by, she took time off to give a special performance in Jersey. The old theater in St. Helier had burned down in March, and the islanders had petitioned her to open their grand new one. Sweet Duchess was infirm now, her mind slipping as she spoke of the dean as if he were still living. But she attended the opening, sniffling at the great tribute given her daughter as a native islander. Lillie delighted her audience with a curtain speech in Jersey patois.

The press had always spoken of Hugo as "fighting in Africa," and he returned to London in December, having been gone barely a year. His crusade had been abortive, and he was loth to speak of his experiences. He had been denied a commission and kept from the front. The African heat and the stories of Boer atrocities had quenched his fastidious valor. He had resigned himself gallantly to limited local duty in Capetown and, having caught a fever, was invalided home.

Lillie was glad to have him back safe. Hugo lacked the sense of humor which might have helped him accept his charming weaknesses, and because his feelings were easily hurt she gave him his head. If her leniency were misinterpreted, what matter so long as it did him good? She shrugged off reports of a coolness between them. If Hugo wanted to escort other women, she had no objection whatever.

It was a bit awkward, however, to dine at the Carlton with friends and catch sight of Hugo at a nearby table with Georgie Reed, a young actress he'd known as a bachelor. Georgie was playing at the Lyric Theater. She had started a fad for painting butterflies on her bare shoulders while wearing low-cut evening dresses. The Duke of Manchester had said she was the only chorus girl with both brains and beauty. She listened raptly to Shuggy's description of his hand-to-hand struggles with the Boers.

"I say, Lillie! Isn't that your husband over there?"

"Think nothing of it," said Lillie, smiling. "I think it's good for husbands to be attentive to other women. And he's been through *so* much. I want dear Shuggy to enjoy himself."

Hugo remained in London while Lillie and Jeanne spent Christmas in Paris. Lillie ordered gowns for her tour and saw all her Parisian friends, who were delighted with Jeanne. *Une beauté comme sa mère!*

Lillie fumbled through the pile of mail that had been brought to her on a silver tray. She glanced at Abe Hummel's letter containing the terms Harry S. Alward had arranged for her scheduled South American tour next year. Interesting. She'd like to see that country. Then she extracted the clipping about

376

Freddie Gebhard which Abe had included. He had left his Waldorf-Astoria apartments and arrived in Sioux Falls, South Dakota (hadn't she played there once?) with eleven trunks, in order to get a divorce. The story said Freddie still had much dash at forty-four—was it possible?—and had taken the gold cure at White Plains. What was wrong with the dear man? she wondered.

"The carriage is waiting, madam, and Mr. Michael attends you."

Lillie thanked her butler. She took her gloves and purse from her maid and tripped downstairs. She was pulling on her spotless gauntlets as her manager came forward.

"I'm so glad to see you, Mr. Michael." She handed him Hummel's letter. "Take care of this matter for me. And remember, don't give my address to anyone under any circumstances whatever. Mr. de Bathe and I want to enjoy the Riviera undisturbed. I don't want you to use it either, except in the case of great and unexpected emergency."

"I trust not, but I hope they keep their word about having the Imperial ready."

"They will have to do as ordered," she said decisively. "And now, Mr. Michael, *au revoir*. Everything is arranged at the bank; try to leave me a little money for my hotel bills. Please keep a full diary. And don't trust the costume or scenery people —make them keep to their delivery dates as we planned. I shall be back in London on March 23 and we will open in April on the date we fixed."

Michael had misgivings as he watched her brougham file through Tedworth Square, pedestrians' heads turning mechanically to follow the Jersey Lily. The Imperial Theater was a headache. Mrs. Langtry had spent enough money on it to ruin herself. But she had wanted a London theater of her own, and this Ritchie had offered her the Imperial at the low rental of twenty-five pounds a week, plus repairs, re-seating, and installing electricity to a total of four thousand pounds. Then she'd got hold of her architect friend, Frank Verity. In her dream of owning the handsomest and most luxurious theater in the world, she had accepted every one of his audaciously costly suggestions and incorporated her own to the tune of fifty-five thousand pounds!

Michael's eyes followed Lillie's brougham out of sight. How serenely she had sailed out of this confusion! Yet she had worked as hard as anyone. The hectic activity, the frantic preparations had wearied him. He went over the long list of things still to be done, eliminating one after another methodically— then bad news, an impasse. The builder said they couldn't get delivery of the vital cantilever girder for two months—so sorry!—and completing the Imperial on schedule would have to be postponed indefinitely. Michael fretted, wrestling with his conscience. Was this a "great and unexpected emergency?" He decided it was.

He sat down and composed a long, exhaustive cablegram giving all the reasons for the inevitable delay. Should he put off the opening? He waited the answer, biting his nails. When it came, he was afraid to open it. The reply was pithy, concise: WE ARRANGED TO OPEN APRIL 27—LANGTRY.

Shown the cable, the builder could only mutter, "Well, I'm damned," with Michael wanting to add he certainly would be if he didn't fulfill his contract. The steel appeared magically; the girder was put in place. The crews worked night and day, and the job was completed on time.

Michael brought up the subject on Lillie's return, but she dismissed it immediately.

"*Of course,* the house had to be ready. Never trust builders, Mr. Michael. They're the most terrible bores, don't you think so?"

Feeling cheap for even having thought the absurd incident worth discussing, he showed her the balance sheet with its 55,000-pound debit.

"Hmm," she said, examining it. "And you have paid this out? We will have to do something about this, but at least London has *one* modern theater it can be proud of."

Together they toured the vast, magnificent theater. Lillie glanced at the stall dado of green satin embroidered in gold with swans and griffins whose eyes were emeralds, amethysts, and

378

topazes; the red plush seats; the eight hangings of royal purple embroidered with the imperial eagle and surrounded with ermine; the richly jeweled yellow satin curtain falling from the dome of the royal boxes and embroidered with fleur de lis. She approved of the great, twinkling chandeliers, the gleaming carpeting, spacious cave of stage, the marble walls specially quarried in Italy, the spring color motif of purple, green, and gold.

"It's rather nice, don't you think?"

Edward Michael opened and shut his mouth.

"Naturally, the play is what counts, but till now the place where the play is shown has always been ignored. I like beautiful surroundings. They can make up for so much."

With rehearsals Lillie had less time for Hugo. He had had his innings on the Riviera as an inept yacht captain and timid gambler. She had let him go sailing with some pretty French actress. Shuggy had tipped over and nearly drowned the poor thing who couldn't swim. He had sweated at the loss of 20,000 francs at Monaco as Lillie casually lost 200,000. Then he plunged on one number and lost 500,000. He made her laugh, and he was such a good dancer.

Jeanne's "engagement" to Ivor Guest put a new complexion on her relationship with her mother, for it brought into uncharitably clear focus Lillie's influence on her life. According to the newspapers, Lord Wimborne, Ivor's father, was a millionaire coal and iron mine owner. Lady Wimborne was one of the late Lord Randolph Churchill's sisters and one of the aristocrats of the artistocrats, as Jennie Cornwallis-West intimated. The public could understand why the Wimbornes regarded their son's match with Jeanne as a *mésalliance* and why it was broken off "through the hostility of Lady Wimborne."

No formal announcement had been made. In fact, Jeanne's feelings about Ivor hadn't crystallized, but there was little doubt that he was enamored of her. Where had the newspapers got the information they published? Someone close to the source inevitably leaked out the latest gossip, and there was always inclination to publish news derogatory to Mrs. Langtry,

379

especially now that her prince was king at last. Jeanne's being hurt in the process was incidental—and only to be expected for the daughter of the notorious actress.

After the young people decided not to see each other any more, Jeanne discussed the matter with Lillie.

"I've always been honest with you, dear," said Lillie, "ever since I thought you were old enough to accept the truth. I'm not going to account for my actions now, nor try to explain why I did all the things I did."

"But, Mother, I didn't think nice people ever acted as the Wimbornes did."

"They do and they always will, Jeanne. I've always accepted things as they are, not as they should or ought to be. The past is the past, and I say bless its finality. There's no point in asking you to put yourself in my place when I first came to London. It happened that way, and it's done. Nor does it help to say that there are others in your position. You know about Ellen Terry. But I will say this: if the Wimbornes thought the marriage a *mésalliance,* I thought it doubly so."

"Oh, Mother!" she sobbed. "Mother!"

"I'm sorry you were hurt, Jeanne, but you're well rid of Ivor. Marry a man who makes up his own mind about what he wants. I don't know what better advice I can give you."

Jeanne brushed away her tears, and they were silent a while.

"Is that why they hate you?"

"Partly." Lillie tapped the cigarette she took from her case. "I have done and lived as I pleased. According to one interpretation, I should look it by now and go down to my physical, moral, social, and financial ruin, as the proverbs predict. Flouters of convention are expected to pay for their sins. Not that I could ever tell you exactly what sin is, but these people know only too well."

"You're wonderful!" Jeanne burst out. "No one can say anything—"

"But they do, and will again."

"Will I have to find a man who approves of you before he'll marry me?" Jeanne asked naïvely.

"Approve of an actress, race horse owner, a woman who consorts with gamblers, bookmakers, track types, a divorcée with a husband years her junior? Ah, that's asking the impossible of a society weaned on Victoria's uprightness and memories of Albert the Good. No, all your man has to do is love you enough. If he's worth anything, how could he help himself?"

"Oh, Mother, if only I were like you!"

"Be glad you're not. You're fine as you are."

Jeanne kissed her mother and went up to change for her party of the evening. Lillie smoked thoughtfully. Then she went to the music room and played the piano for a while. It was almost time to eat. The lonely five o'clock suppers were one of the things she had always disliked most about the theatrical profession. It was a dreary business eating alone before a performance. Any company was preferable—even Shuggy's. She rang for the butler and asked if Mr. de Bathe had come in. He was out somewhere in one of his autocars. Lillie ate alone.

He was all apologies when she came home after the theater.

"Awfully sorry I missed you at supper, Lillie. I was seeing about the engine. Needed tinkering and things, you know."

"Not at all. First things first, by all means."

"I thought you'd see it that way." He tweaked his mustache ends. "I say, have I told you how lovely you look today?"

"Not today, Shuggy, but thanks ever so. By the way, have you considered a monocle?"

"Can't say I have. Nothing wrong with my eyes, you know."

"You could wear a clear glass like the others. It adds such a distinctive touch, and you'd have something to fuss with besides your mustache."

His brow furrowed. He went to the mirror and studied his face. "You really think it would add a certain *je ne sais quoi,* eh? But my features—are they right for a monocle?"

"Oh, definitely!"

"Awfully good of you," he said, registering pleasure. He bent over to kiss her, letting his lips linger on hers to see if she were in a relaxed, receptive mood. "Do you want me to—could we— I mean, would this be a good time?"

Lillie thought it very well might.

"Then let's," he said warmly. "I'd like to stay a while."

"Awfully good of you." Lillie smiled at herself in the mirror.

Lillie found herself involved in Jeanne's affairs when an-other man became interested in her daughter. She whisked Jeanne off to spend the 1901 Christmas holidays in Paris, and both were conspicuous at a great New Year's party at the Ritz. Lillie wore a black-net gown spangled with gold and made up over an apple-green sash, and a very flat wide toque of camellias. Jeanne shone in a blue tulle dress lined with nar-row satin ribbons and set off by a black-and-white tricorne with a wreath of pale roses at the side.

"How lovely she is!" exclaimed Madame Nellie Melba in her throaty voice, watching Jeanne whirl off on a gentleman's arm. "She has everything necessary to make a great success on the stage."

"Everything except the desire," said Lillie.

Jeanne was determined to settle down to children, domestic-ity, and wifehood such as her mother had never known. She was approaching it in a spirit of defiance, much as Hugo had gone to Africa to prove himself, except that Jeanne had the capacity to succeed. Her eagerness to live a normal, conven-tional life in contrast to Lillie's was understandable; it was also a little pathetic, thought her mother, since, for her, such self-expression would involve complete subservience to a husband. Oh, yes, Jeanne would find that kind of man. I want her to be happy and marry well, Lillie told herself, and I must remem-ber she and I are not alike. How could we be? I will not hold her back.

"He *is* serious," said Jeanne joyfully on their return. "He said London was empty without me, and he didn't know what to do with himself."

"One likes to be missed," said Lillie. Odd that Shuggy al-ways said much the same thing, without realizing that it was the frequent separations which made their union bearable. "And how do you feel?"

"I missed him, too. I think he wants to marry me, but I'm not committing myself till I'm sure."

"You're wise, Jeanne."

"You know, Mother, I've had a grander offer from a more important man," she went on breathlessly, "but I'm determined to marry the man I love or not marry at all."

Eventually Jeanne's young man put the question and was accepted. The announcement of their engagement came as a complete surprise to the public. Jeanne had floated like a lovely flower on the brilliant pool of smart London society—a favorite pursued by throngs of men as her mother had been years before—yet she and her fiancé had been so discreet as to outwit the sharpest gossips. Lillie made no comment. According to a society columnist, "Mrs. Langtry (she is never called Mrs. de Bathe any more) like Bre'r Rabbit 'Lies low and says nuffin'.' "

Frankly, there was nothing to say. A determined young man had met a determined young woman, and that was that. Of Scot parentage, impeccable background, wealthy in his own right, due to inherit a greater fortune, vast properties, and certainly a title, he was at thirty-three considered "one of the rising political young men of the year." A Conservative Member of Parliament, he had been in diplomatic service as an attaché to the Berlin and St. Petersburg embassies. He had been assistant private secretary to Lord Salisbury, the present prime minister, and his future was assured. The papers called him the darling of society because of position, wealth, and good looks. He was regarded as a great match for Jeanne and the match as a master stroke for Lillie, although she had had nothing to do with it.

A tall, strongly-built man with classical features handsomely set off by curly blond hair and a small, carefully-twisted mustache, he was, according to some, a "pretty" man. Clever, too. He had once thought of being a playwright and had written an extravaganza for his good friends the Marlboroughs (Ah, there, Lady Wimborne!) which had been put on at Blenheim Palace. Lillie had to respect the man, although she recognized the hard core under the handsome surface. Here was the talented amateur with his contempt for professional players; the frugal, conforming Scotsman with his devotion to the church, decorum, and the Foreign Office; a stout-hearted resourceful man fully capable of looking after his own interests. No need for him to mingle with the Marlborough Set or curry favors from the King when he had the backing of Lord Salisbury and the diplomatic corps.

He was independent. He would never need help from his mother-in-law or her influential friends. Lillie had no trouble sizing him up as they discussed the wedding at a meeting of the families. He was cordial and polite, all the more so beside the ill-concealed antagonism of his relatives. They had made up their minds long ago about the Jersey Lily. Nothing could melt their attitude or condone her obvious transgressions. She had no doubt that he loved Jeanne. Like his family, he was so impressed with her beauty and good nature that he was willing to overlook her mother's faults. Lillie guessed that her close relationship with Jeanne would have to be curtailed unless she changed her ways, her friends, her life. Impossible, of course, but she would pretend to agree for Jeanne's sweet sake.

"He really likes you," said Jeanne. "They all do. It's just that they've heard so much about you they don't know what to think."

"I know what they think, and it couldn't bother me less."

"They're not used to actresses and stage people."

"Ah, we're a race apart—wicked, immoral, sensational—but there's hope for *some* of us. Thank God for Sir Henry Irving and Sir Squire and Lady Bancroft—honored by Queen Victoria herself, mind you."

"Mother, that's not what I—"

"Do you love him, Jeanne? Tell me that."

"Yes, I do," she said in a low voice. "Very much."

"Then you take him." Lillie smiled. "Because they're so willing to make allowances for me on your behalf, I am more than willing to do the same for them on his. Not for him so much as for his love for you."

"Oh, Mother. My Rose! Nothing will ever separate us. You've done so much for me! I love you so, and I'm so proud

384

to be your daughter." Jeanne's tears were wet on Lillie's cheek.

A good man in his own right in every way, Lillie thought. Good-by, Jeanne, good-by. I wanted you to have the best, and you have it. She stroked Jeanne's hair, putting her out of mind as her thoughts turned familiarly to the theater, her play, the trouble over the Imperial, the American tour. If she hadn't had this fulfillment, this dramatic other-life, she would have dried up and died. It was just as she had told an interviewer: "Next to seeing your own horse win a race, the applause of an audience is the best thing in the world. It keeps one young forever."

Pressing Jeanne close, she felt happy for her—and sad over what she would never experience.

Lillie's son-in-law-elect was given to having various matters inferred diplomatically, if irrevocably. It was understood that Hugo, who had met him only briefly, was not to attend the wedding. The fact that Jeanne's amiable stepfather was some four years younger than her fiancé was—now, really—don't you know—yes, indeed! Lillie saw to his banishment, which dear Shuggy accepted in good part. She would have sent him to Regal Lodge, only she didn't trust him around the stables. He would probably bring a good horse up lame, be thrown, or something. Better for him to go down to Nice for sailing lessons or to look up that silly French actress he'd dumped into the Mediterranean. Hugo kissed Jeanne before he left and wished her luck.

"He's really very nice, isn't he?" she said to Lillie. "I wish he could be there only—"

"Let's not go into that. But Shuggy is nice, the most obliging of husbands, don't you think?"

"I wonder if my husband—" Jeanne looked self-conscious. "Will he listen to me the way Hugo does to you?"

"Make no mistake, Jeanne. You've got another dish of porridge there. You will have to conform to the clan."

"I'll be happy to," she said proudly.

Lillie laughed. "You're a most unusual young woman!"

When Her Majesty the Queen sought Jeanne out at the

Duchess of Devonshire's ball a week before the wedding, the gesture was noted by the press. It was the first occasion since the death of Queen Victoria that Alexandra had honored any assemblage with her presence. She and Jeanne were marked as the two most interesting women among the guests at the august duchess's splendid Piccadilly palace.

The wedding took place at noon, June 30, 1902, at St. Margaret's of Westminster in the shadow of the Abbey. Society columnists said it had to be reckoned as one of the most fashionable of the season. King Edward had been invited and would certainly have been present had he not been recovering from the appendectomy which had put off his coronation.

Jeanne's bridal gown was trimmed with silver embroidery and lace which the groom had collected in India. She carried a white vellum prayer book instead of a bouquet. Six bridesmaids attended her, including Mrs. Francis H. Leggett of New York. Lillie gave her daughter away and the ceremony went off like clockwork. The crowded church was fragrant with flowers, many of them lilies, the bride a radiant vision, the bridesmaids becomingly dressed, and purely as a June spectacle it was satisfactory. Jeanne's fiancé had invited a number of notables, but these were matched by distinguished friends of her mother's. The guest roster included the Duke of Argyle, Sir Squire and Lady Bancroft, several rajahs the groom had known in India, Lord Hugh Cecil, John Morley, M.P., George Wyndham, Chief Secretary to Ireland, William Redmond, M.P., P. H. McHugh, M.P., and Lord Belcarries.

Checking the house as she did instinctively, Lillie's eyes stayed briefly on George Wyndham. He smiled sardonically, and she made a connection. Her son-in-law was Parliamentary Secretary to the Chief Secretary to Ireland. George, an old and ardent admirer of hers, must have filled his ears with gossip. He liked to make the Irish obey and had expected notorious actresses to do the same. The more fool he, but what intrigue lay behind the simple ritual being enacted here in St. Margaret's?

There was no public reception, but the two families did meet at a luncheon in Lillie's home, Tedworth Square. Jeanne and her husband were so happy that differences were forgotten in felicitations. The display of four hundred gifts from most of London's aristocracy filled three rooms. The King, the papers reported, sent "a splendid jewel with an autograph letter to the daughter of his old favorite, in whom he has been unusually interested since birth." The bridegroom gave Jeanne a diamond necklace with pendant, his parents a great diamond necklace transformable to a tiara. Lillie, who had already settled 50,000 pounds a year on her daughter, added a rosette of diamonds and pearls set in silver, a complement of house linen, and a big check. The Duchess of Devonshire sent a work table; Alfred Rothschild, a diamond horseshoe.

Lillie watched Jeanne's new family as they registered each dazzling gift and its noted donor. They were impressed, kept their faces tight to conceal it, but their dislike was not abated. The fact that such well-known people would bestow friendship on an actress must prove her taint. They tried hard to look pleased. They spoke of the loveliness of the house, its beautiful appointments, the perfection of the wedding, Jeanne's sunny charm. Lillie shook off their compliments.

"I do wish my husband could have been here. Dear Shuggy is defending his cup in the Monaco yacht races. He was desolated to miss the wedding. But no true sportsman can refuse a challenge, can he?"

With pinched mouths they agreed. The string quartet played on in the minstrel gallery, the butler passed trays of champagne glasses, stars danced in Jeanne's eyes. Lillie winked at George Wyndham.

"It's criminal how young you look, Lillie," he grumbled. "But you'll feel differently when Jeanne makes a grandmother of you."

"I can hardly wait."

After Jeanne and her husband had gone, the last guest departed, Lillie hurried to change. Then she rushed out to the nearest race track taking deep breaths of the rich June air. She plunged heavily on a hunch, won, and felt better than she had all day. She read until late that night. Before turning off the light, she went down the hall to look at Jeanne's room. It had a forbidding emptiness, exactly like a bird's nest fallen out of a tree, neat, perfectly serviceable, never to be used again. I shall sell this barn as soon as I can, she thought. Sweet little Jeanne's wedding night. She remembered her own in Southampton, the memory no more than cold ash. Over the years the picture of her brother Reggie and his horse skylined on the Jersey cliffs had become much more vivid, much more poignant.

It was three weeks before she saw Jeanne again. Her daughter dropped in unexpectedly, looking poised and happy. A new assurance and maturity overshadowed the gay naïveté that had always seemed so winning.

"So married life agrees with you, dear?"

"Oh, so much, Mother! He's wonderful."

"Naturally. Does he know you're calling on me?"

"Well, I did say I was going shopping."

"Then you must tell him."

"Of course." Jeanne looked pained. "We're going to see each other as often as we wish."

"Are we? Nothing could make me happier."

Lillie was much preoccupied the rest of the summer with her play, Regal Lodge, and her horse Smilax. Ridden by the American jockey, Danny Maher, the filly did well in a number of minor races. She was expected to win the big ones soon.

The American tour was all settled. She was disturbed about the Imperial, though. There was trouble with the impossible Ritchie over the lease, and a lot depended on her American reception. She and her staff had discussed ways and means of overcoming the bad publicity over *The Degenerates* two years earlier. She was going to present a play she and J. Hartley Manners had written together, *The Crossways*, along with *Mademoiselle Mars*. If only she could bring in her new play with some special mark of distinction! With Michael she had agreed on trying it out in the English provinces, then going on straight to America without the judgment of the London critics. But she still wasn't satisfied.

She was pondering this when she went to Paris to order her

388

American trousseau from Paquin, which she now patronized in preference to Worth. There on November 21 she received word that Mrs. Le Breton had died in Jersey. She left for the island immediately and helped with the funeral and burial arrangements. Although not unexpected, the loss grieved her dearly. Of course Sweet Duchess had been lost to them for some time because of increasing blindness, deafness, and impaired qualities of thought and speech. In spite of this, she had been her neatly dressed adorable self to the last.

Lillie's heart was full of love and gratitude as she and Clement watched their mother's coffin being lowered into the ground of St. Saviour's churchyard beside the graves of her beloved dean and Reginald. How peaceful it was here in the shadow of the rambling old rectory so filled with memories. Time was remorseless. Out of a family of eight, only Clement and herself survived. I'm far from ready to go, Lillie mused, but when I do I want to be buried here. A mist formed over her eyes as she looked at the big old rectory. I began here and I'll end here, but not yet . . .

Lillie went over her mother's effects, sorting out family remembrances and heirlooms before hurrying back to London.

The Crossways did well enough in the provinces. Still, Lillie hoped to leave for America with some sort of unimpeachable testimonial that could be widely publicized. She was answering Bertie's letter of sympathy over Mrs. Le Breton's death when the thought came to her: what could be better than royal approval? A foolish notion, but Bertie considered himself a patron of the arts. He would be amenable if the suggestion could be made to come from himself spontaneously. Of course, his kingly stamp would be sneered at by American critics, but the public would respond. He would give her the peg on which to hang her tour.

She wrote asking him to pay her his respects before her departure. Bertie replied immediately. He was pleased to be King Edward VII at last, but he was sixty-two now and had aged. Nearly bald, his portliness accentuated by his short stature, his grizzled beard and mustache slashed white, his deep-set, hooded eyes wreathed with wrinkles, it was hard to believe that this jovial, grandfatherly figure had once held her in his arms, breathing ardent, cigar-reeking endearments. Or that she had been frightened of him. As king, he stood erect, his clothes meticulous, his courtly charm and affability unchanged, his manliness apparently undiminished. But much more serious now, and tired.

The bond between them was unshakable. They talked easily of the past, his stables, Smilax's record, and Jeanne's husband.

"A remarkable young woman. Princess Alexandra was quite taken with her. And she's found a good man with a promising future, Lillie. Not the sort I take after—too much the intellectual and prudent Scotsman." He chuckled. "How my mother would have approved of him! And how is your husband?"

"Hugo is—very much Hugo. We get on. You look very well, Bertie. I suffered with you through that long, exhausting coronation ceremony."

"It was far worse for the old Archbishop of Canterbury. I thought he'd collapse and die on the Queen and myself. Spilled the anointing oil all over her. And did you hear about the Duchess of Devonshire wanting to leave the Abbey on the heels of the royal procession? A terrible breach of etiquette, but then she's always considered herself above an empress. Tried to push through the Grenadier Guards, fell down the steps on her back, and sent her coronet flying. A shocking spectacle." He laughed with Lillie. "Several hauled her up, and Mrs. Asquith rescued her coronet. Then off she sailed with a full head of steam. Amazing woman!"

"Do you like being king, Bertie?"

"I find the responsibilities, the work involved, fascinating, but—sixty years the Prince of Wales. That's some kind of record. No, at my age it has come a little too late."

"You're not old."

"How long can I expect to reign?" He sighed. "There's much to put to rights, and I could do so little before. The French as our firm friends, the Russian threat, the wild talk of my nephew in Germany. I wish Her Majesty, my mother,

390

had abdicated long ago and let me rule when time was at my disposal." He smiled at her expression. "But who would have trusted Bertie then, eh? So you're off to America now with a new play. A pity you're not playing in London so the Queen and I could see it."

"I can't risk exposing my work to the critics before America. It's too important, and I have to make up my investment on my theater."

"I'd send the whole crew to the Tower if I could. You lost a lot on the Imperial, did you, Lillie?"

"A great deal. That's why I'm bypassing London." Lillie looked distressed. "But I do wish you and Queen Alexandra could see *The Crossways*. It's most entertaining."

"So do I, so do I. I'd like to send you off with my blessings for old time's sake." He frowned. "Could you arrange a special performance for us?"

Lillie remembered to look startled. "Why, I don't know!"

"Well, think about it and send me a message as soon as you can." She promised she would, and his frown deepened. "I hesitate to bring up this matter, Lillie, because I've always trusted your good judgment. But this is a new reign. It's best that the past be forgotten for all our sakes—that's the only reason I'm mentioning it. You've been asked to write your memoirs, I presume?"

"Many times. By newspaper and magazine editors as well as book publishers. And I have had fantastic offers." She touched her hair. "They seem to think my life consisted only of scandal and gossip."

"Editors' minds seem to run that way. But don't you think memories are better left intact in the minds of those to whom they mean most? Why hurt one's friends and expose intimates to public ridicule? I'm sure you'll be discreet should you ever be tempted to put your life on paper."

Lillie eyed him calmly. "You know I shall."

"Then we understand each other?" She did not flinch from his gaze. "Good! Loyalty is the basis of all true friendship. I have never had the slightest cause to doubt yours."

391

"Nor I yours." She smiled. "I've never ceased to deny that ice story which has always plagued me. I've never been so ashamed of anything."

Bertie grunted. "What we won't do with the proper provocation, eh? Ah, we were young then, Lillie, and life was gay." He looked up, as if the past were a leaf floating to the ground and he could catch it before it fell. "Times have changed—except for your beauty, which never changes."

twenty-three

THE company was packed for the boat. The costumes and sets crated, the Imperial dark and shuttered. Now, with almost no time for adequate preparation, they were scheduled to put on a command performance of *The Crossways*. It meant re-opening the theater, cleaning and airing it, unpacking everything, and producing the play for just one night—an almost superhuman effort.

Lillie drove them hard. She put in hours and hours herself and looked the freshest of them all on December 9, 1902. To London the affair was "both a mystery and surprise." Denials to the contrary, His Majesty had indeed "commanded" Mrs. Langtry to play before the king and queen; a distinction King Edward had accorded to no one else in the realm. It was understood that the stalls and boxes were to be occupied by Their Majesties' friends. Lillie had graciously given pit and gallery tickets to the Queen for distribution to the staff and servants of the royal household. Mr. Ashton, the King's Agent, was in charge of the project, including the apportioning of seats.

No tickets were sold at the box office. The performance was not advertised, yet never in memory had there been such an unusual first night or greater demand for admittance. Because many of the free seats could not be used by the recipients, a lively black market in tickets sprang up. Members of the fashionable audience who simply *had* to be present paid scalpers' prices outside the theater. Some had to be satisfied with standing room.

Not a hitch marred the performance or indicated that it was

a one-night stand. The Imperial glistened so that it might always have been open. Edward Michael's shaky nerves, the cast and stage crew's exhaustion, Lillie's own relentless supervision went unnoticed in the uniquely brilliant pageant. Between the third and fourth acts, the royal party retired to the handsome anteroom off their box, where Michael had cigars, whiskey, and refreshments waiting. The King commanded Mrs. Langtry's presence. He told her how much he liked the play, and Queen Alexandra expressed her pleasure.

So Lillie was off to America with the exclusive seal she had sought for her play.

Royal sponsorship of *The Crossways* had stayed the pens of the critics and protected an inferior play from unfriendly comment. It was not to be wondered that Lillie proposed a toast to King Edward at the last-night party on the *Celtic* off Sandy Hook. While the American public might be expected to be impressed by his espousal of *The Crossways,* columnists, editors, and writers prepared to disabuse Mrs. Langtry's credulous admirers. It was wrong of Mrs. Langtry, "still warm from the embraces of royalty, to expect the bird of freedom to moult his pin feathers into her box office." This time she'd have to stand on her own dimpled toes instead of the gouty pedestals of the Defender of the Faith. Anyway, what did Tumtum know of the theater?

And by the same token, Mrs. Langtry ought to grow up. At fifty sentiment languished, romance got wrinkled. Back in 1882 she had been at "that bewitching period of life, when the charms of youth are mellowed by the ripeness of age, when springtime melts into the bloom of summer." A radiant creature of thirty, a prince knelt at her feet in England, bankers over here thought more of her than the ticker. Just today a venerable magnate of Wall Street, now a double grandfather, said of her: "Gad, sir, I would have bankrupted myself twenty years ago for Mrs. Langtry, but Freddie Gebhard carried her off from me." No more stage-door Johnnies young or old for Langtry, no eager bucks to dissuade. The doorman could sleep peacefully. This year, the New York *Press* argued, Lillie stood on art, not on nature.

394

Lillie stood on nature facing the press on the White Star Line's *Celtic* in New York Harbor. She was beautifully dressed in a brown fur garment trimmed with ermine, and wearing a wonderfully white veil. Noting that she had brought twenty-two trunks and thirty odd pieces of baggage, the reporters fired away. Was she divorcing Hugo?

"I am very well satisfied with my present domestic relations. My husband objects to traveling and, moreover, is afraid of coming to America because of the progressive newspapers. He dislikes being interviewed and doesn't like America, but we are very happy."

The command performance?

"We gave it before such a distinguished audience. You know it was by request of the King, and a king's request is the same as a command, isn't it? We did not want to be criticized in London. Americans are so clever and if they like a play it is sure to be well received in London. That's really the best way to do, isn't it?"

Did Mrs. Langtry know that an autographed letter from the King to her was on sale in a New Street store in New York?

"How extraordinary! The servants, I suppose. You know I received twenty-five or thirty letters from the King, written when he was Prince of Wales. One of them must have escaped."

Harriet Hubbard Ayer, now writing for the *World,* cast a keen feminine eye over Lillie's drawing room, dining room, dressing room, and bedroom in the Imperial Hotel. Superb Oriental embroideries covered the tables and chimney shelf, a riotous lot of tempting cushions transformed the hotel sofa into an artistic couch. American beauty roses swarmed everywhere, and there were photographs of her idolized Jeanne and King Edward and Queen Alexandra. To Mrs. Ayer she looked slender, tall, young, and charming in soft clinging white with a girdle of moss-colored velvet about her waist. Mrs. Ayer observed her smooth, incomparably lovely throat and thought her serenely beautiful face and classic features unharmed by time.

Mrs. Langtry was glad to explain her beauty secret, which had nothing to do with electricity, massage, or a surgical skin-peeling process she was supposed to have undergone. The principal secret was a combination of work, sunshine, soap and water, plain food, fresh air, and a happy spirit. Off stage, she used only fluffy baby powder, no other cosmetic. She believed in physical culture, knee bends, touching the toes, etc. And, oh, yes, going to bed early and taking a cold bath every morning.

The beauty-secrets gambit was an old and tiresome business to Lillie, but the press never seemed to have enough of it. It would never do just to say she was lucky. Calling on her the day after the opening, Michael showed her a newspaper cartoon titled "The Shadow That Draws American Dollars." There she was on a stage strewn with lilies, while King Edward smirked on a throne behind her, crowned and sceptered.

"From the *Evening Journal*, Mrs. Langtry. This doggerel goes with it." He read it to her:

"Sing a song of Lily
Who never seems to fade,
In four and twenty gorgeous gowns
Alternately arrayed.
And hats and fans and feathers,
That cost like anything;
Isn't that a blossom fair
To set before the King?
The King was in his royal box
'Plugging' the applause,
The Queen was there beside him
Applauding, too, because.
When came the dainty Lily
To learn the drama's fate
The good King beamed a beamy beam
And shouted out, 'It's great!'"

Lillie smiled. "To be sung to the tune of *Sing a Song of Sixpence*, I take it. How are the reviews, Mr. Michael?"

"About what you would expect. Quite a few mixed. Some like you and not the play, some dislike both. Mr. Winter is pleased."

396

"Now is the winter of our discontent made glorious summer by this sun of the *Tribune*. May I see it?"

Writing in his guarded, kindly vein, the dean of New York's theatrical reviewers concluded that this appearance of Mrs. Langtry's was superior to all her previous ones. As the Duchess of Keensburg in her own play, she showed "a solid, satisfying maturity, a depth of thought and feeling, and a comprehension of the facts of life she has not shown before." What could Winter possibly have meant by "the facts of life?" She glanced at the vicious reviews, stopping at one sneering that "A fine performance. Mrs. Langtry great—Edward VII" should be emblazoned on a notice outside the Garrick.

Her interviews were impromptu, yet smoothly running productions. There was no one like Mrs. Langtry, exuding charm and good breeding at forty-nine and captivating hardened newsmen as easily as in 1882. A thrill to have her butler answer the door, hear from an inner room the voluble disapprobation of her two French maids discussing the high price of Camembert in America, and await Lillie's breathlessly dazzling entrance. A few lingered to suggest that she do an as-told-to biography for their publication. That came up all the time these days. She shook her head mysteriously, letting them infer that she knew too many secrets about too many people. EMPIRE BREATHES AGAIN AS LILY HOLDS BACK LIFE STORY, the next feature was headed. So-called authoritative sources had it that she had some sort of agreement with the royal family *not* to write anything autobiographical. The nastier gossip implied she was being paid to keep quiet.

New York, Lillie found, was still changing, still moving uptown. Her old 23rd Street house, so hard to rent until the Pasteur Institute took it, was now in a run-down neighborhood. But Adelina Patti was still singing in New York, a good sixty at least, and Freddie hadn't changed, either. He was still on the prowl, and the papers reported that he was a suitor for the hand of Miss Drina de Wolfe of Mrs. Osborn's Playhouse Company. Abe Hummel told her Freddie had teamed with Diamond Jim Brady, who gave big parties at Gilsey House down below Greeley Square. Freddie, always a party man, was now helping Jim entertain railroad executives and other important people.

"How do you mean entertain, Mr. Hummel?"

"Well, Jim provides lots of good food, champagne, and diamond garters, and Freddie supplies the chorus girls. They find hundred-dollar-bills under their plates."

"What delicious food!"

The *Lalee* had burned in a railroad yard fire, and Lillie wouldn't tour without a private car, so Harry S. Alward, taking over for Michael as tour manager, hustled about to find one. Traveling was a high art for Lillie now. Her English butler and two maids set to work as soon as she entered her hotel room in Bloomington, Peoria, or wherever else. Immediately draperies hid the crude outlines of mantlepieces, silk scarves covered ugly table tops, and the maids set out statuettes of horses, autographed photographs of European royalty, bits of color, and decorative bric-à-brac.

One room became a private dining room, complete with lovely china, silver, and Lillie's own table linen with her private crest. The butler then struggled with the crude hotel waiters so that he could supervise the preparation of his mistress' food and serve her in style. Her bed had her own monogrammed linen, her own table was set at the bedside with a special reading light and choice books. Silk and lace draperies and dresser coverings disguised the other rooms. It was worth the trouble to create a home away from home wherever she went—only a traveler could appreciate the squalor of provincial hotels that sickened the soul.

Wherever she was playing, Lillie had a habit of walking to the theater in the late afternoon to see how the advance sale was going. Once in Eau Claire, Wisconsin, Alward accompanied her; and as they passed a laundry they saw standing in front of it a gleaming delivery wagon with a magnificent, dappled gray Percheron hitched to it. Both horse and rig were turned out handsomely enough to enter the National Horse Show. The harness had towering arched hames with great traces bearing the owner's name.

"Oh, what a wonderful horse!" said Lillie. Another horse and wagon similar to the first came and tied up at the laundry. "There's another of those grand horses. This laundryman must be a horseman worth knowing, and I am going to know him."

Alward went into the laundry with her. In a few minutes, Lillie and the owner were deep in the subject of work horses, their best qualities, and their treatment. She was so impressed at his knowledge that she gave him a box for *The Crossways*. The laundryman was overwhelmed. He sent four dozen roses to the theater and must have told all of Eau Claire about his meeting with the Jersey Lily. Throughout the evening he sparked the applause from his box. The audience yelled and clapped at every opportunity. The next morning the whole town was at the railroad station. Gifts of all kinds were thrust on her, everyone wanted to shake her hand, and the crowd almost tore off the side of the train shed to reach her. After shaking every hand held out to her, Lillie made a speech from the rear platform of her car.

"How infectious enthusiasm can be, Mr. Alward," she said, as they pulled out. "If only drama critics were as lovable as that wonderful laundryman."

Edward Michael reminded her of *Mrs. Deering's Divorce* when they reached Providence, Rhode Island. She had commissioned the play from Percy Fendall, had paid two hundred pounds royalty over her brother Clement's objections, and had agreed to produce it in a year's time. Somehow the play had never seemed right for her. Now the year was up, and Michael had cabled asking for a month's grace.

"He's adamant, Mrs. Langtry. Unless you produce it, he'll take it away and sue you on grounds of non-production."

"Oh, dear, not another law suit! And that charge is almost as alarming as race suicide, Teddy Roosevelt's *bête noire*. Don't let's fuss, Mr. Michael. We'll rush it into rehearsal and trust in Providence to save us from too heavy losses."

Because it was a compulsory production expected to be a failure, Lillie and her company romped through *Mrs. Deering's Divorce*, throwing away lines, playing up bits of business, and enjoying themselves lightheartedly.

399

To her amazement, the Rhode Island critics said it was the best thing she'd done in years. Her sense of comedy was complimented, and the play was cited as a typical example of Langtry luck. In one act a man accompanied her to her dressmaker's where she "undressed" behind a screen in sight of the audience. It was "daring" in spite of the fact that she was still clothed in voluminous petticoats. The men enjoyed it and women had the chance to study Lillie's neck, arms, and shoulders—remarkable for a woman rumored to be almost a grandmother.

Then she had to return to England to watch Smilax race at Newmarket and settle the tangled legal situation that had arisen over the Imperial Theater. It was all the fault of that hairy, querulous Mr. Ritchie, manager of the old Aquarium, who had sold that antique to the Wesleyans. That meant they owned the Imperial, of which she was tenant and on which she had spent a fortune. Lillie was determined to buy the theater from these Methodist dissenters; Ritchie had indicated they were amenable, but she had received icy replies to her feelers. It was clear now that Ritchie was a devious go-between and had treated her unfairly.

"I told you, Mr. Michael. It's never safe to have anything to do with a man who has tufts of hair in unexpected places!"

"It's a question of morals," said Michael. "The Wesleyans refuse to have the devil's work in the shape of a playhouse on their property. Their leader, Sir Robert Perks, wants the Imperial razed. But he did say that he'd see no injustice was done to you."

"Injustice." She shuddered. "My poor, beautiful theater. The only real temple of art in London."

"They're the owners, Mrs. Langtry. I'm afraid you're going to lose a lot of money."

"Well, we've hardly exploited the new play. Thanks to you it may be my biggest success since *As in a Looking Glass*. Cable little Hummel that I will go through with the fall tour. Tell

400

him to have Mr. Alward forward me the South American itinerary."

She saw no point in brooding over the fate of the unfortunate Imperial Theater. Where a loss was inevitable she accepted it, pushed hard at the next profitable project—in this
case the Mrs. Deering play—and kept going without slowing
the momentum.

She telephoned Jeanne, guessing from her uneasiness that
her husband had been unable to decide just how to deal with
his irresponsible mother-in-law. Perhaps time would heal the
family relationship. How could the man deny her her daughter's love?

Hugo was another matter. She couldn't imagine how anyone
could keep so busy doing nothing. At least he was active, having a good time, looking sleekly fit. And he was awfully glad
to see her, wasn't he?

"Join me in America later, Shuggy, won't you? I'll keep the
reporters away, and you'll enjoy touring the country."

"Perhaps I will when the weather here turns beastly. Join
you in the Southern states, what?" He curled his mustache, looking very serious. Lillie hid a smile. "Father's been very ill, you
know. Thought he'd go under, and the whole family gathered
at the bedside. Very grim business. Everybody said nasty things
about you, and I had to be quite brutal." He looked pleased
with himself. "Yes, indeed, quite brutal."

"Shame on them. Dear Shuggy, my gallant defender."

On July 18, 1903, she read of Jimmy Whistler's death with
a sense of shock. So many of those she had known were gone.
But Jimmy had had an imperishable quality about him, a dynamic spirit one couldn't imagine being stilled. He had died
famous and so secure in his fame as to forever silence those who
had hooted at his art. He had never finished "Arrangement in
Yellow," the portrait he'd begun of her—whatever had happened to it? Jimmy had left something enduring, not like Oscar. It was three years since Oscar had died in France, and
still no one dared speak of him. Jimmy would be pleased, in
his Satanic way, that he'd accomplished more, been the greater
genius after all.

401

There was no one around London today to match either of them in the vigor of their wit, brilliance, and art. Or was *she* growing old like wretched people who kept praising the past and damning the present? But who else would have said and done the things Oscar and Jimmy had? Made a career of the outrageous? It was Oscar who had said, "The three women I have most admired are Queen Victoria, Sarah Bernhardt, and Lillie Langtry. I would have married any one of them with pleasure."

Lillie went to watch Smilax run in the Whitsuntide Plate at Hurst Park. The weather was clear and lovely. She just had time to bet on her filly before the race began. She sat in her box between Leopold Rothschild and Richard Croker, the American politician long the leader of New York's Tammany Hall. Smilax, ridden by Danny Maher, had drawn sixth position, she announced, and with Hackler's Pride was the favorite. Mr. Jersey's filly got off to a good start. She broke for the front nicely, but was bumped and cut off badly at the rail on the first turn by Halsey on Hackler's Pride. This slowed her, and she fell back. She rallied well, though, still looking a winner as the field thundered into the last quarter.

The crowd was howling, "Smilax wins!" but Lillie was not deceived. "Smilax is beaten," she murmured before the horses passed the finish line. So she was, blood streaming from a gash on the shoulder as she barely hung on to the leaders, then falling back to fourth place, well behind Lord Ellesmere's winning Wild Oats. A bitter unexpected defeat. Lillie congratulated the owner with a smile and no hint of her own disappointment. She seemed not to give a thought to having lost her large bet, as she hurried down to praise Danny Maher and look after Smilax.

"That's part of the fascination of racing," she explained. "In most situations we never know the unpredictable hazards that defeat our purpose. Here it is different. I saw it happen and I knew it when it happened, and there's no one to blame but chance."

New York felt as Providence, Rhode Island, had about *Mrs.*

Deering's Divorce. The critics, with a professional distaste for Lillie and her approving public, picked away at her performance and decried the disrobing scene. She had been booked solidly for this tour. Hugo, who joined her in New Orleans, never more a stranger in a strange land, did not stay with his wife long. The one-night stands, the constant pounding of the railroad train, and the changes in food and environment were so exhausting that Lillie let him go back to New York to buy the yacht he had set his heart on. Business was good. Critics and public approved, and women flocked to gape at her clothes and "her appearance of being thirty years old."

In California, she was tempted to visit her ranch but decided against it. The past ought to stay buried. Ah, the wonderful successes she had envisioned for Langtry Farms! Horse-breeding, wine-making, cattle-raising, wheat, corn . . . The happy time with Freddie. He had sold his adjoining property long before. Now, finally following Abe Hummel's advice, she reluctantly disposed of hers to a family called McCreery for $42,000, half of what she had originally paid for it.

The past did come back in her visit to Joaquin Miller in the hills back of Oakland. He was hardly the grotesque "Westerner" she remembered to have made up a spur-of-the-moment stanza to her or to have scattered rose petals in her path. A thin, shrunken old man dying slowly in a great bed covered with a patchwork quilt and a buffalo robe.

"The same eyes, the same blue eyes," he said sonorously. "Where did you get those big blue eyes?" This was like an echo of what he'd said at their earlier meeting at Lord Houghton's. "You look as lovely as when I first saw you."

"I'd like to believe that. I'm so glad that Mrs. Miller and your daughter let me see you."

"Who would refuse to see Lillie Langtry? When you reach heaven, St. Peter will open the gates wide."

Lillie's thoughts wandered to a song she had heard in New York:

> *Oh, Peter looked so wicked*
> *When I asked him for a ticket,*
> *Climbing up the Golden Stairs.*

> *Go tell the Jersey Lily*
> *That the sights will knock her silly,*
> *Climbing up the Golden Stairs.*

She smiled involuntarily.

"But, tell me," Miller went on, "what happened to all the people I knew in London, the poets and painters, Whistler and Wilde?"

"Dead, I'm afraid."

"I'll join them soon, and then it won't matter whose poems are best and who is the greatest. Nothing will matter but dust, and I am ready. I have built my own funeral pyre high on a precipice over the Pacific." He waved a trembling hand. "The winds shall waft my ashes through the Golden Gate. I shall sail on, sail on toward the unknown like Columbus."

A confusion in booking forced Lillie to be crowded out of the Mason Opera House in Los Angeles by Adelina Patti. As a consequence, Lillie had to switch to a hasty one-night stand in Santa Barbara, playing to a small audience. Poetic justice in a way: it had taken Patti twenty-one years to even the score with her for spoiling her concert at the Academy of Music the night *An Unequal Match* opened at Wallack's.

Most of all Lillie enjoyed finally visiting the town of Langtry, Texas, in the hope of meeting Roy Bean, "the funny old man writing to me all these years." But Judge Bean, who had changed the town's name from Vinegaroon to Langtry in her honor, had died at seventy-eight almost a year ago. Southern Pacific officials arranged a special stop. The passing of the Sunset Express was always a great event; for it to stop in sleepy Langtry was world-shaking. Lillie thought she had come to the end of nowhere. The area was desolate, the ground barren and sandy; not a tree, only sagebrush and tumbleweed, and she could see neither houses or people. But the porter assured her it was only because her private car, being at the end of the train, was out of Langtry proper.

Lillie began walking forward, then saw a delegation advancing the length of the train and kicking up clouds of dust. She first shook hands with Justice of the Peace Dodd, then Postmaster Fielding, and other officials. Then came cowboys in

404

checked shirts and sidearms. Behind them were a number of girls, presented all at once as "the young ladies of Langtry," and finally "our wives." The railroad had granted a half-hour stop, so the reception had to be rushed. The cowboys shot off their revolvers in an official salute and she was escorted into "town."

She stared hard at the shanty in which Roy Bean had dispensed justice and liquor. It had signs across it reading ICE, BEER, THE JERSEY LILLY [*sic*], JUSTICE OF THE PEACE. LAW WEST OF THE PECOS, BILLIARD HALL, and JUDGE ROY BEAN, NOTARY PUBLIC. Inside, a ladder led to a loft; there was a bar at one end of the room, chairs and tables at the "court" end. The tables were chipped and scarred from knives and greasy packs of cards lay on their rough surface. On one wall was tacked an old torn three-sheet of her as Pauline in *The Lady of Lyons*. It was not at all as she had imagined it; yet it was exactly as she had imagined it.

They showed her the schoolhouse and a few other wooden buildings. The cemetery was down the pike a way; only fifteen of its occupants, they told her proudly, had died a natural death. The town had about one hundred people now, and it was growing. Everyone followed her, tried to talk at once, tell her about something Judge Bean had said.

"This is sure a great day for Langtry, you comin' here like this." There was a long pause and the lanky, sun-burned man, who looked naked with his broadbrimmed hat off, shuffled his feet. "Roy'd be real proud, ma'am. *Real proud.*"

The train whistle blew and Lillie barely had time for a little speech. Somebody rushed up with a baby mountain lion in a cage, a boy gave her two horned toads, a burly man tried to kiss her, she signed two autographs, she gave Judge Dodd fifty dollars for the school as the whistle blew again. The last thing she saw was the name LANGTRY in big letters on the ridiculous station. She was so proud she wanted to cry. She'd always love that miserable, darling town and it's wonderful, peculiar people. Perhaps long after she was dead and forgotten, Langtry would thrive and prosper.

The town of Langtry felt she needed a token of her visit, so she was sent Roy Bean's revolver, all polished and gleaming. Engraved on it was: "Presented by W. D. Dodd of Langtry, Texas, to Mrs. Lillie Langtry in honor of her visit to our town. This pistol was formerly the property of Judge Roy Bean. It aided in finding some of his famous decisions and keeping order west of the Pecos. It also kept order in the Jersey Lily Saloon. Kindly accept this as a small token of our regards." The revolver remained one of Lillie's proudest possessions in a conspicuous place on her mantel.

From Langtry the tour led into Canada where she had always been popular. In Toronto she came on May Hallatt, a pretty young English actress, in distress and stranded after an engagement had petered out. As the company was concluding its season and returning to New York, Lillie took Miss Hallatt with her and introduced her to Charles Frohman in the Empire Building, Broadway and 24th Street. The producer put Miss Hallatt in *The Silver Slipper* with Edna Wallace Hopper and Sam Bernard.

Hugo had been having a good time in New York, always making a good impression socially. He was the model English gentleman with a dash of man-about-town, the boulevardier, and a snobbery equal to any of New York's upper crust.

"I say, Lillie, it's been deuced good fun! I've had the jolliest time with the natives. And I've found a marvelous tailor. Wetzel. Almost as good as mine in Savile Row."

He was proud of his yacht and on a trial run down the Bay took Ned Center, George Kessler, Manny Chappelle, the celebrated champagne salesman, Jimmy Hyde, and Center Hitchcock, president of the Brook Club. They were old friends of Lillie's and pleasant company. They got a kick out of Shuggy's mannerisms. He loved the formalities of sport—the proper dress, the approach to it, the rules—more than the sport itself. He ran his yacht in high nautical style.

They were along the Narrows as Shuggy became involved in an altercation with a sailor over the way to display life rings on the rail. Demonstrating how they should be hung, he leaned far over the side and tumbled into the water with an impressive splash. Heaving to, the captain dispatched two sailors in a dinghy to pick up Shuggy.

Treading water in his Wetzel yachting uniform, Shuggy hailed his rescuers indignantly. "Am I or am I not the owner of this boat?"

"Yes, sir," said the confused sailors.

"Then go back, you bloody fools, and get the captain and the steam pinnace and ten men in their best uniforms! Don't you know how to rescue your owner in proper style?"

The dinghy came back and the flustered captain prepared to take out the pinnace. The guests looked at Lillie.

"Shuggy would rather drown than be rescued incorrectly," she said, tongue in cheek. "High style always, you know."

Abe Hummel advised her to get rid of some of her expensive possessions, and she agreed it would be wise. Why these huge establishments when she no longer had to consider Jeanne? Hugo would always fit in anywhere. Regal Lodge and her stables were enough to handle.

She sold her big London home and most of its valuable furnishings. She put up a casket of jewelry at Christie's for auction, receiving 133,700 pounds for a collection of odd pieces which had been in a bank vault most of the time. For her London stops a suite of rooms in the newly modernized Savoy Hotel was exactly what she needed. There she had servants, heat, light, and rent, freedom to come and go without worrying.

Major economies in a woman who had never economized were startling. Aha! said the gossips and feature writers. The Jersey Lily was pictured as ruined, ignored by her daughter, abandoned by her friends, and utterly wretched. The smug articles about her "downfall" and "pitiable plight" made luridly exaggerated reading. One writer, much closer to the truth, maintained the Jersey Lily was as sound as the rock of Gibraltar and had profited enough on her last tour to leave 150,000 pounds with her Chicago broker to invest. As for her daughter cutting her, this was nothing new. From the day Jeanne had married the Scot prig, his family had forced the girl to ignore her mother.

Expected to go into obscurity after Jeanne's marriage, Lillie had continued to ride high, affront convention, disrobe on the stage, consort with racing people, and capitalize on her notorious friendship with King Edward. Many obstacles had stood in the way of the marriage, said the columnists. They told how Jeanne's husband's family had imposed conditions permitting her to see her mother only twice a year, half-hour visits at some agreed-upon place.

In painful situations of this kind, someone has to give. That neither side was so inclined is evident in Lillie's autobiography in which Jeanne is never mentioned, nor her existence even hinted at. After Lillie's death, David Belasco said her later years had been "fraught with sadness" in spite of her earlier adulation and fame. Regarded as the coldest of women, he said, she was really one of the most warm-hearted. Her first great unhappiness, Belasco believed, had been that the acclaim attending her stage début constituted a tribute to the beauty and the fame acquired before her professional career. The second was her estrangement from her daughter, whom she loved dearly.

twenty-four

VAUDEVILLE was the rage in the United States now. There were chains all over the country, and the producers had conceived the idea of bringing culture and great acting to the masses at popular prices. They had been sniffed at, jeered. At first stars like Sarah Bernhardt, Mrs. Cora Brown Potter, and Lillian Russell had not consented to doing a twenty-minute skit before a public used to acrobats and jugglers. But later they were unable to refuse the tremendous salaries offered by B. F. Keith and F. F. Proctor.

"I'll admit it will seem like doing a music-hall turn, Mr. Michael, but the audiences will be people who've never seen me."

"I hate to see you sign with Proctor and Keith."

"It's hard to refuse twelve thousand pounds a week. What else is left? Grundy's written no new play. Ibsen? Pinero? Shaw? I can always get a good play later."

But first there was another adventure for her. She did not much want to speak to the producer who insisted on seeing her, but the instant she heard his proposal she knew she would accept. It couldn't have come at a better time, and the prospect of a hot sun and lush, green vegetation seemed alluring after the London blues.

"Do you want to come to South Africa with me, Shuggy?" she said that night. "I'm going there to open a new theater in Johannesburg, then go on to Capetown, Durban, Pretoria, Pietermaritzburg, and lots of other wonderful places."

409

"South Africa? Capetown?" He nearly gagged. "Why, I almost died there."

"I know, shooting down the Boers, snatching assegais from the Zulus, and vanquishing for Victoria. Well, will you?"

"You don't have to joke. I went through hell."

"Do it again for me, then."

"I'm sorry, Lillie, but, really—well I couldn't go back there."

She had expected him to say no, and she never insisted with Hugo. He was like a pet dog with a roster of three or four tricks he could perform admirably. He had no ambition to learn more, nor Lillie the desire to teach him. Besides, old Sir Henry was still ailing, and Hugo thought he ought to stand by, as he put it.

Several staff meetings were necessary before Lillie was ready to sail on the *Walmer Castle* with her company, scenery, properties, stage paraphernalia, maids, and her secretary, Ina Goldsmith. She decided to appear in her old successes, including *As You Like It,* a personal favorite and trademark, at the request of the South African producer. Fifty-three-year-old Rosalinds were a rarity, but none had looked like Lillie. In March when the announcement came that she was a grandmother—how it must have annoyed *certain* people for the news to be treated as the arrival of the great Jersey Lily's grandchild!—the newspapers said it was hard to believe from her face. And a New York editorial rightly put it that grandmother or no, she was "still young because she keeps a-doing."

The South African tour took six months. To Lillie it was a new, breath-taking experience in an exotic land, where she scored triumph after triumph as one of the first great stars to visit there. She was met by mayors, bands, and reception committees in town after town, entertained in style by all the famous residents, and shown Cecil Rhodes's favorite vista on Table Mountain by Rudyard Kipling. The extremes of heat bothered her, especially on stage when the cast seemed to be moving in a furnace. But the lovely flowers, the mountains, the animals, the friendly audiences and critics made up for the discomforts. The eligible young actresses in her company were

410

given diamonds, offers of marriage. Lillie herself was propositioned by a number of wealthy men, one of whom begged her to stay with him in Durban.

An ardent tourist when she wasn't acting, Lillie saw everything she could. In Pretoria she went out of her way to photograph the wall over which Winston Churchill, Jennie Jerome's impetuous young son, had escaped from the Boers after his capture as correspondent for the London *Morning Post*. Lillie sent Winston the snapshot.

She returned to England in late May, 1906, richer and happier than she'd left. Good entertainment was hard to come by in South Africa, and she had never played to such uncritical, demonstrative houses. She went to Regal Lodge, prepared to enjoy the summer racing before beginning the vaudeville venture. One of her best afternoons on the track was at Folkestone the same day she was to try out her sketch before the public. Mr. Jersey's Aurina won the Kent Handicap; then another turquoise-and-fawn entry took the Hythe Juvenile Maiden Plate. To have two winners, to have bet on both and then paraded them before the cheering crowd, gave her a pleasant sensation. Enthusiasts mobbed her for autographs, and she had to pose for press photographers.

Understandably, she was elated as she prepared for her playlet that night at the Folkestone Pier Pavilion. Piers were an English tradition. Every seaside resort had one. For twopence they provided a place to walk over the waves, games of chance, a shooting gallery, and an entertainment pavilion. This was a tryout for *Between the Daytime and the Night,* a drawing-room sketch about infidelity in which Lillie ran the gamut and was shot dead in the last-scene blackout. It had rough edges, but it played. Lillie may have cut it a little fine. She was aiming at twenty minutes; later the management said it was only seventeen minutes long. At any rate, there was little applause. Lillie thought nothing of that. Two winners in an afternoon, the center of attraction at the track, she was still bubbling as she left the pier, nodding and smiling, to come on a crowd of hostile people.

"You cheat! You call that a show?"

"We paid for nothing!"

About thirty women were booing and calling her "Pussy!" "Bitch!" "Sow!" A policeman broke it up and escorted her to the hotel. She was very much upset. It had been so unexpected —and coming on top of the happy afternoon—a calamity! The newspapers explained that people had expected a whole evening's entertainment and felt they had been robbed.

Lillie was still depressed two weeks later, when she attended a premiere at the Garrick Theater in London with Sidney Grundy. Here she was the subject of another demonstration. People waved and smiled between acts. At the end of the performance, the pit and gallery rose to cheer her in her box, as if called upon to avenge the insult at Folkestone. They followed her to her car "hurrahing lustily."

Lillie dabbed at her eyes with her handkerchief.

"I told you, Lillie," said Grundy. "You can't judge your audience on the basis of a few hooligans. Don't you *dare* cancel that vaudeville contract."

English producers thought the Americans were ruining them. The London stage was in a slump because of high rents and the reckless building of big theaters on land with high ground rents. They also blamed American producers for spoiling actors, actresses, playwrights, and stagehands with high salaries. Vaudeville was a low-class entertainment for a low-class people. Mrs. Langtry was to be condemned for supporting it.

Proctor and Keith, meanwhile, were banging the publicity drum hard for the Jersey Lily. Their officials claimed that her salary "represents the largest pecuniary outlay that has ever been made by Mr. Keith, Mr. Proctor, or any other vaudeville manager to secure the services of an act." The figure wasn't mentioned, but everybody knew it was $2,500 a week plus expenses. There was great interest in Lillie's sketch. The newspapers suggested such stunts as a cakewalk with King Eddie, a hoe down with Father Time, and a screaming comedy with Freddie Gebhard "Coughing Up the Dough." A cartoon showed Lillie holding a high-hatted sport by the ankles and shaking the money from his pockets.

412

Lillie arrived in New York on the *Philadelphia* looking smart, fascinating, and youthful ("about 25"). She was accompanied by two maids, a butler, a private secretary, and two Russian wolfhounds. Lillie was voluble as usual. She didn't like to have her playlet referred to as a sketch; that was too "vaudevillainous," so she called it "a tabloid tragedy."

"What do you think of Freddie Gebhard's marriage to a chorus girl?" asked a reporter.

"De mortuis nil nisi bonum," she said, smiling.

"That means let the dead past bury its dead," a press agent hastily guessed.

"Why not let Mr. Gebhard and his new bride be happy? I am happy, and I don't want to recall any old memories that might make others unhappy."

How were her horses doing?

"On the day I left, my mare Aurina won the ten-thousand-dollar Prince Edward Cup at Manchester. And I had four thousand dollars bet on her at eight to one."

She waved and went off to the Hotel Gregorian.

A tremendous audience attended her vaudeville début at the refurbished Fifth Avenue Theater October 1, 1906. With an effort Lillie recalled that almost twenty-four years before to the month she had appeared for the first time in the United States. The ovations, the bravos, the curtain calls, the messages crammed into the frame of her dressing room mirror! All of that was flattering, but more so the producers who descended on her afterward with all sorts of play offers. She hadn't lost her public. She was a grandmother denied the right to see her grandchild, but thousands of people loved her. Thousands. She was as potent a draw as ever. She would go on and on, with the stage always the main concern of her life and horses her pleasure and relaxation.

Dear old William Winter wrote gallantly for the *Tribune*:

Mrs. Langtry endeavors to express the emotions of a wife who is simultaneously apprised of her husband's infidelity and urged to elope by and with the man whose wife has become her husband's paramour; whereupon she goes out disguised as her hus-

413

band and is shot by her infuriated suitor. This is a charming situation for a charming woman, and everybody is charmed.

Not quite everybody, of course, or it wouldn't be show business. There were critics who gleefully panned her appearance between the trained monkeys and acrobats, but they were in the minority. The public swarmed to see the Jersey Lily in vaudeville. It was the smart thing to do, society attending in box parties and leaving after her act. Famous actors such as Richard Mansfield reserved whole boxes for themselves so as to study her performance. Her mail was heavy. She read all her letters, haughtily handing back all those addressed to Lily Langtry with the tart comment, "There is no such person." Her current photographer was fascinated by this agelessly lovely actress. "I have never met a woman who could smile so steadily for so many seconds as Mrs. Langtry. With the average woman, a smile becomes a grin or fades away. She is a wonder."

Interviewers sought her out for her *real* beauty secrets, the inside story on the memoirs she was supposed to be writing, and they posed such teasers as whether she was happy.

"Why—uh, I suppose so—yes, of course I am happy as happiness goes, for a woman who has so many memories and who lives the lonely life of an actress. It is lonely and restricted, as all artistic life must necessarily be, and often I've put in as many as forty weeks a year on the stage."

Some regarded her with superstitious awe, a living legend, like the heroine of Rider Haggard's *She*. Others could not do enough for her. Mr. Keen, owner of Keen's Chop House, opened his exclusive men's grill to honor her in an unprecedented gesture. Women reporters trailed her to record everything she said, did, and wore. She was overheard saying to a gentleman at Hoffman House, "who looked an awful swell," that it was "a bilious green and yellow day, tinged with touches of immoral magenta color." (How proud Oscar Wilde would have been!) And as if to match the weather "she dazzled her matinée audience at the Fifth Avenue with a new gown of green chiffon with garlands of gold and silver embroidered in the Empire style with a bunch of immoral magenta roses palpitating at her bosom."

Things were going so well with her that she regretted the

414

bad news about little Abe Hummel. Of course, he was crooked and an artful cheat, who had punched holes everywhere in the fabric of the law to help murderers, bank robbers, and abortionists, but he had always loyally represented her interests. District Attorney William Travers Jerome, long a Howe and Hummel nemesis, had at last managed to bring Abe to trial. He had been convicted, but putting him in jail was not easy. He kept turning up legal technicalities to postpone his sentence. Abe was strangely optimistic about his chances.

"I'm sorry I can't be of service to you any more, Mrs. Langtry. I'm far too busy defending myself for a change." He chuckled. "Odd that it should be Leonard Jerome's nephew hounding me like this. The old gentleman never did approve of his puritan streak. You know he raided Dick Canfield's casino on 44th Street? I wonder what his English cousins think of him."

Without being asked, he gave her the gossip about Freddie. Freddie's divorce had backfired. Louise had filed a countersuit and was now Mrs. Henry Clews, Jr. Freddie's new wife was Marie L. Gamble, known on the stage as Marie Wilson of the Floradora Sextette. Hummel said she was the daughter of a Washington businessman and had eloped at sixteen with a Government Printing Office clerk named Urimstatt. A smart girl supposed to have made $750,000 speculating in Wall Street. A good thing for Freddie, because he was nearly broke. He'd had to borrow $75,000 from his sister, the rich Mrs. Frederick Neilson of Newport. A lawyer Abe knew said she had obtained a judgment against him for the money, and Freddie had only just paid it back.

"He sold a lot of his personal effects a while ago. Curios, souvenirs, collector's items, that sort of thing. He did well on the sale. But I heard that at the last minute he took away a lady's handbag before the auctioneer put it up." Hummel paused. "It was one of yours."

"Dear Freddie. How sentimental of him!"

"Aren't you sentimental, Mrs. Langtry?"

"I can't afford to be," she said, thinking of Jeanne.

After touring in plays, it seemed incredible to be sandwiched on the vaudeville circuit between other acts devoted to black-face artists, dancers, rope twirlers, tumblers, jugglers, trained ponies, dancing dogs, and heaven knows what else. But, as she told Boston reporters, "I worship the golden calf and there is money in vaudeville." Many of the houses on the circuit were new and pretentious, far different from the crude barns she had often played in on tour in the *Lalee*. They merited being called palaces, for they were crawling with footmen, thick rugs, rococo decorations, and marble fountains.

She could no longer use a private car, but she always insisted on drawing rooms on the regularly scheduled trains. She carried her red carpet as of old and still gave the order to roll it out. She was treated like a queen; on occasions she had to behave like one. In one city, she arrived to find billboards everywhere advertising the appearance of Lily Langtry. She was furious. She hated the name. In the first place, it was Lillie. Secondly, she had made her reputation as Mrs. Langtry and *that* was what she would be called. Her contract called for her to be billed only as Mrs. Langtry. The management heard her out in consternation.

"Until the name 'Lily' is covered up on every billboard in your city, until every newspaper has eliminated it, until every program in which it appears has been destroyed, I shall *not* appear on your stage or in your theater."

Thousands of dollars in posters, programs, and advertisements had to be painted out. Lillie was greatly criticized for her high-handed hauteur, but the changes were made.

Walking along Broadway, Edward Michael ran into Lillie as she was leaving her hotel.

"How do you like vaudeville?" he asked.

"Well, it's hardly a branch of art I would choose permanently, but there is a lot of humor in the life, and if I were a queen I couldn't be treated with more courtesy or consideration."

"How are you getting on with the press these days?" said Michael warmly.

"Oh, these ghastly women reporters! They are so deadly in earnest, so naïve, and know so little. One of them invited me to a function where I should meet interesting people and then

416

asked me if I was not very much impressed." Lillie gave her delightful laugh. "That was really *too* quaint! 'My good woman,' I said, 'you forget that I'm in the impressing business myself!' "

The long-awaited announcement reached her in Cincinnati on January 6, 1907, after she had drawn three thousand people to two performances. General Sir Henry Percival de Bathe was dead at eighty-four. Shuggy was now Sir Hugo de Bathe, and she had become Lady de Bathe. The newspapers congratulated her sarcastically, speculating on the horror of London society at her new title. The excited management asked her if she wanted her billing changed. Her retirement was predicted, but Lillie maintained that she "had given her plans for the future as a baroness no consideration."

Sir Hugo and Lady de Bathe. Sir Shuggy and Lady Jersey Lily. She had to smile. Hypocrisy and sham, but, oh, what it meant to so many people—and to me too! she thought. Yes! to me. Jeanne would call herself Lady some day, but her notorious mother had beaten her to it. What a gnashing of teeth in her husband's family! Shuggy had his title and nothing else except some impoverished estates in Sussex, Devonshire, and County Meath, according to the newspapers. Old Sir Henry had left $134,770, the interest going to his widow for life, then to his sons, barring Black Sheep Hugo.

The next day the stagehands, the performers, everyone called her everything from your grace, your ladyship, your highness to your majesty. Lillie only smiled. She was guest of honor at a farewell dinner given by David Belasco. Richard Le Gallienne read a poem which he dedicated to her:

> . . . So all I bring,
> As tribute to your feet
> Is that most precious thing
> The joy you gave,
> Indifferently sweet
> As some bright star,
> That shines alike for all,
> And shines for none alone;

Shines but for shining's sake
In the high heavens afar.
Fair star, too soon to sink
Behind the sea,
My little hoard of stardust
Here I bring,
As offering:
You unto you—from me.

Shuggy greeted her gravely, his mustache a little more bristling, his shoulders straighter, a new importance to him. He seemed to think that by coming into his knighthood he had accomplished his life's work. Now he had something to bracket with his wife's fame. He had conferred a title on her; she was Lady de Bathe because of *him.*

"Ah, I see you're wearing mourning, my dear. It's in excellent taste. Rather jolly to have a title at last, what? It makes me feel like somebody, but a fat inheritance would have been more practical. All the same, people do notice 'Sir' before one's name, don't they? Which reminds me. Do you think it appropriate for a baroness to be a vaudeville queen?" He flushed at Lillie's expression. "Well—really—I mean—now, my dear—you mustn't . . ."

Shuggy was still the incomparable weekend guest and extra man, the life of the party who could talk nicely with the old dowagers, dance with the matrons and flatter them, swim, ride, play tennis, and fondle the young things when they let him. Toward Lillie he was courteous and gallant as always, cheerful and companionable to a point. The biggest thing they had together was their titles. As Sir Hugo he relished a distinction all his own, and Lillie had the wherewithal. Her vaudeville tours were necessary business trips on behalf of the corporation.

Lillie was two persons now. Always Mrs. Langtry on stage; at Goodwood, at home, in London society Lady de Bathe; and the snubs could fall where they might. They went to Monaco in the high style that suited Shuggy. As Sir Hugo he reveled in their train of two maids, a valet, a woman secretary, two chauffeurs, and a courier. In Monte Carlo, however, it seemed that the Langtry luck abandoned Lillie. Friends watched her lose a big sum at the *trente et quarante* tables with her charming aplomb. She was annoyed, but she didn't show it. As she left, she had a hunch and put all her chips on the number 32 on two tables. People stopped to watch skeptically. The numbers came up simultaneously, paying off thirty-five to one. It took the croupiers ten minutes to count out her winnings. Lillie stood by calmly, apparently unmoved by the excitement her coup had aroused.

"That number just won a second time on a table," said one. "You must be psychic!"

"My word," said Hugo.

"Lose big, win big, isn't that the ticket, Shuggy? I'll buy you a new set of golf clubs."

Grundy had a new play ready on her return. After two successful seasons in vaudeville, she opened in April, 1908, at the Haymarket, a familiar theater to her, in *A Fearful Joy*. The theater was doing double sessions with a Shaw play. "Today at 2:30," it said on the marquee, "GETTING MARRIED. To-night at 8:30, A FEARFUL JOY." The perfect mordant comment on the married state, thought Lillie.

It closed earlier than she expected. She returned to Regal Lodge and settled down happily to writing, working in her extensive gardens, and being Mr. Jersey. Her new trainer was twenty-one-year-old Fred Darling, who looked sixteen. She had doubts about his ability, but he soon proved himself. Yen-toi, bought just for the purpose, won the 1908 Cesarewitch easily, eleven years after Merman had won the same race. Plunging heavily, as she always did on her favored entries, Lillie collected over forty thousand pounds, highly gratifying after her recent losses. Her stables were now among the best and most consistent in England. King Edward frequently turned to her for advice about his horses, coming down to Regal Lodge for tea and consultation.

While hearing and reading of Jeanne's doings, Lillie knew nothing really about her daughter and grandchildren. Once a society columnist reported that Jeanne was vacationing at Hamburg, a German spa, referring to her as "the sister to Lady de Bathe, formerly Mrs. Langtry."

London was surprised when a book, long reputed to be Lillie's memoirs, appeared in 1909. It turned out to be a light, frothy 75,000-word novel called *All at Sea* and signed Lillie de Bathe, with "Mrs. Langtry" in parentheses. The plot concerned a lovely woman and her husband who agreed to live apart during a trip across the ocean, the wife posing as a widow, the husband as a bachelor. There were quips such as "Love is a soufflé which marriage turns to bread and butter pudding." A typical dialogue exchange was: "Poor Kit's not very well; he's neurasthenic." "That means immoral, doesn't it?"

She'd had fun writing it. Naturally the literary critics and her enemies kicked it around, but it amused readers. Best of all, the novel made 500 pounds for her. "That wasn't so bad, was it, for one little book?"

At the same time the New York *Review* was quoting Lillie's philosophy—"Anyone's life truly lived consists of work, sunshine, exercise, soap, plenty of fresh air, and a happy contented spirit"—the obituary columns carried news of the death of Frederick Gebhard of pleurisy complications at the Garden City Hotel, Garden City, Long Island. The date was September 8, 1910, his age fifty. Freddie had been New York's most elegant wine salesman in his last years. The last time he had figured in the news, said the notice, was last year when Phil Dwyer had bet him $2,000 to $1,000 that he couldn't walk twenty miles at a stretch. Diamond Jim Brady had willingly backed Freddie, but the bet had apparently never been run off.

Just as well, too, thought Lillie, fingering the clipping sent to her by an American friend. She remembered Freddie limping after her in the early morning as she strode around the Sheepshead Bay track in sweat clothes. She remembered . . . so much. They spoke of him as a has-been. His prominent place in the fast life of the metropolis, escapades with Mrs. Langtry, his clothes, his clubs, a man who had devoted his life to spending his income, a rich young man whose affairs had become the public's delight. A gay wastrel, a failure somehow—not the Freddie she had known.

New York without Freddie. New York without Abe Hummel, who had served a year at Blackwell's Island, paid a five hundred dollars fine, and then gone abroad to comfortable oblivion. Everything changed so much, so fast. The past was so many leaves irrevocably turned in a book, and it was a blessing she was busy.

She had *The Right Sort,* a one-act play adapted from *The Degenerates,* ready for the British vaudeville circuit that fall. Her American vaudeville success had created a similar interest for her in England; it pleased her when the managers outdid themselves to get her on the British circuit.

Between tours, she always returned to Regal Lodge, glad to be in her own home and free to work with her hands among the flowers she loved.

"I have just made a new sunken garden at my place in Suffolk," she said to a reporter, "and I am trying to grow rhododendron where they have never grown before. I am dreadfully scientific on soils and so on. My agent, by the way, tells me that I am drawing the largest salary ever paid in the halls of England. Wonderful, isn't it? for a quiet, rural gardener like myself."

At fifty-nine she was still a phenomenon. In New York executives canceled business conferences to attend matinées and experience the old thrill of the moment when the most beautiful woman in the world came on stage. Because, of course, she was that—and they weren't so old either.

The times were more informal now. Lillie was much more approachable backstage. Lady de Bathe liked to sit on the trunks in her dressing room, her wonderful laugh captivating reporters as of old, talking and rambling on. In Boston, reporters remarked that she looked thirty, her neck and throat as soft as seventeen. The question of age bored her.

"How do you keep looking so young?" she was asked.

"But I don't. And you know it, and I know it. There isn't any woman who doesn't look every day and minute of her age. We can't be, nor look, younger than we are, but we can be well preserved."

Back to London, Regal Lodge, racing, Paris for clothes, and a chance meeting with a shrunken Abe Hummel, lost and terribly out of place in the Place de la Concorde. A forlorn, lonely Abe going to the theater every night, eager for news of New York. Then back to America in September, 1912, as Lady Victoria Vandeville in the suffragist sketch *Helping the Cause*, with Pat Rooney on the same bill.

Lillie kept on the circuit to the Coast and back, sometimes bumping into the past in unexpected ways. An oil portrait of hers, once Freddie's possession, was for sale at the ironically named Abingdon Storehouse, 491½ Eighth Avenue, New York, with sixty dollars due in storage rates. An eighteen-year-old claim against her was entered in Oakland, California, allegedly the balance of a well-digging contract for her ranch. It was outlawed by the statute of limitations, but Lillie paid the bill. The same for a bill dating back to 1887, which one Andrew F. Link said he had been trying to collect for some twenty-six years. He had been owner of the Bristol Hotel, Chicago, near which the *Lalee* had been tied up, and he said she owed him for supplies and storage on some trunks.

In February, 1913, "Mrs. Langtry's Own Story," as told to Archie Bell, appeared in *Green Book* magazine—a graceful if innocuous account. She was still subjected to newspaper criticism, still notorious, still vilified but, as she reiterated to a reporter, "No person in the world ever lost anything by being nice to me."

Following the example of Sarah Bernhardt, James Hackett, and others, she let Daniel Frohman talk her into making a motion picture under his direction for Famous Players Film Company headed by Adolph Zukor. The new medium struck her as a cold, mechanical method of dramatic production, jerky and primitive in its way, but modern and novel. It would afford her a relative film immortality. And Dan Frohman was one of the most kindly and persuasive of men.

The film was made that April in New York and considered

422

unusual. Shot entirely inside the studio with "modern effects and a near absence of subtitles," *His Neighbor's Wife* was an elaboration of *Between the Nightfall and the Light*. It opened on Broadway in October, 1913, was praised for Lillie's performance, strong situations, and nice photographic effects.

"It's the first time I've *seen* myself act, and I can't say I'm impressed. But what a paradise for conceited actors! Now they can applaud themselves in an empty theater."

If America was in transition, how unrecognizable England became to Lillie following the death of King Edward VII on Friday, May 6, 1910!

Lillie was alone when the news reached her. She kept to herself all the next day. Her feelings were mixed, but she did not cry. She had never loved Bertie. She had been in awe of him at times, but they had always been close. To the end he had been loyal and thoughtful. How could she bear to lose this best of friends!

Bertie had died at the height of his power and prestige, esteemed for his wisdom in finally allying France firmly with England—the most respected ruler in the world. He was lauded in the press as no other king had been lauded before him. The Empire, the world mourned him, and his death at sixty-nine was a shocking tragedy.

Later the appearance of an acid biography by the scholarly Sir Sidney Lee set up a reaction. He was pictured not only as an idol with clay feet, but as with a clay body, heart and mind. To Lillie, this was not unexpected. It was human nature. So few people understood that there were no real gods, idols, or kings; that there were simply human beings, men born to exalted positions and given responsibilities, with the same hopes, passions and average abilities as their fellows. How ridiculous then to ascribe godlike qualities to them—qualities which they had never pretended to have—and later in hindsight destroy them for not having had these impossible gifts!

With Bertie's son King George V on the throne, there seemed to be a hurried, general house cleaning, a Victoria-like scrubbing of the royal escutcheon, a frantic expunging of the Edwardian taint. No more could Lillie expect palace favors, congratulatory summonses to the royal box. The Marlborough set, the London she had known was dead, and its epitaph gave off a stench. She felt grateful to Shuggy for having made her Lady de Bathe so fortuitously. That honor, such as it was, couldn't be snatched away.

Yet Buckingham Palace couldn't forget Mrs. Langtry, wouldn't for years to come if only because of Jeanne. King George was as morally upright as his grandmother—human enough to use Navy quarterdeck language in anger, but no more. Jeanne was on the right side now. If there were favors to be had she and her morally upright husband would have the royal nod.

Lillie indulged in some memories, of course. Bertie hadn't looked well the last time she had seen him, and Lillie had begged him to take care of himself.

"There's too much to do. I don't trust that sword-rattling nephew of mine in Germany. The Kaiser is a dangerous man."

That day Lillie had confessed she had sold her memoirs to an American magazine.

"They're paying me such a fabulous price I couldn't refuse. It's a chatty thing, but nothing like the gossips expect. No revelations."

"I trust your discretion, Lillie. You have the light touch. I liked *All at Sea*. I'm not one for literary works, but that made me laugh. It was just like listening to you talking. Right from the first you could always make me laugh, you know."

"We didn't do so badly, do you think?"

"I would say we did well. And now you have grandchildren like me."

Lillie played with the notion of retiring, but she was too restless. She had to act. Vaudeville was diverting, and the public still delighted in her appearances. Its applause made the old sweet music. She was glad she kept on when England went to war in 1914. Entertainers were never more valuable than in wartime. Any diversion was an antidote to austerity. Her playlet now was *Ashes* by Percy Fendall, "modern, amusing, and with a touch of Boccaccio." She did this in vaudeville in London and the provinces, and also toured with *Mrs. Thompson,* a Sidney Grundy play.

With the same spirit that had sent him to Africa, Hugo went into the service immediately. So did Lillie's brother Clement and Jeanne's husband. For Lillie herself, it was good to be able to help the Red Cross, give benefits, raise money, anything to feel useful.

The impact of the war came to her early during a Zeppelin raid on London. It was her birthday and she was having dinner in the Savoy Restaurant with friends as the bombs fell close by. No one panicked. They all kept on eating, but the last three minutes of the raid were terrible, for the room shook. It was worse when the wounded were brought in screaming from the blacked-out streets. A little girl with her hands blown off . . . a bellboy helping to bathe away the blood with a bowl of water . . . a doctor in evening clothes doing what he could. The calmness of the patrons was amazing.

When she next arrived in New York—with a London company of twelve, two maids, a secretary, a carload of stage furniture, and forty trunks of new frocks—the Jersey Lily was found to be miraculously the same. She was dressed in the latest fashion, clutching a huge sable muff, her traveling skirt ending at her shoe tops. "I feel like a schoolgirl," she admitted.

She kept commuting tirelessly between England and America, each tour being announced as her farewell, a teaser of the management's. With the Germans pushing back the Allies in France and London under bombardment, hysteria lurked everywhere. Lillie's composure was the best example of British fortitude. At sixty-two she still amazed people who knew her well. Mrs. Gerald Lawrence watched her rehearse on the huge, empty stage of the Drury Lane with the pitiless overhead lights casting grotesque shadows on the actors. "To see her standing there in that ghastly revealing light without a trace of make-up and still not looking a day over thirty-five—it really was unbelievable."

twenty-five

RETURNING from Liverpool to New York in 1916, Lillie met Somerset Maugham on the boat. His major novel *Of Human Bondage* had been published the year before; he was forty-two and perhaps in the first flush of writing success. As the two most important people aboard, they naturally gravitated together. Maugham later said, "She still had a fine figure and a noble carriage, and if you were walking behind her you might have taken her for a young woman. She told me she was sixty-six." (But she was only sixty-three.)

He liked to hear her talk, and Lillie told him of herself and Freddie Gebhard.

"Who was he?" Maugham asked.

Lillie was astonished. "You mean to say you never heard of Freddie Gebhard? Why, he was the most celebrated man in two hemispheres."

"Why?"

"Because I loved him," she said, and the writer thought this "the proudest thing I ever heard a woman say."

Since she was a legend, he had to believe legends. Lillie confessed that she had been deeply in love with Crown Prince Rudolph, and he had given her a huge emerald ring. Then they'd quarreled. Lillie flung it into the fire.

"He cried out," she told Maugham, "threw himself down on his knees, and scrabbled out the hot coals to snatch his precious ring." Her lip curled scornfully. "I couldn't love him after that."

Lillie told Maugham that if he were anything like the other

426

writers she'd known, the minutes of their meeting would all be put down into a book some day—and another legend perpetuated. (They were, in *A Writer's Notebook,*1949.)

Maugham was later shocked to have her admit she loved dancing and for amusement often went to dance halls "where the men danced beautifully and you only had to pay fifty cents." Gigolos and suave dancing partners were common on the Continent. Women often availed themselves of their services when unescorted or accompanied by poor dancers. It was done in America, too. But it gave Maugham a nasty turn. "The notion of this woman who had the world at her feet paying a man half a dollar to dance with her filled me with shame."

Peaceful New York was garish after blacked-out London, but Lillie sensed a feverish pulse underneath. It was only a question of time before the United States would get into the war. Benefits were more and more frequent, patriotic citizens with guilty consciences substituting dollars for blood. She assisted in one for the Permanent Blind War Relief Fund in the ballroom of the Ritz-Carlton. It was under the direction of Miss Elsa Maxwell. Will Rogers, the nasal-talking, rope-twirling comedian, announced the acts.

Lillie continued on the vaudeville circuit with *Ashes,* supported by Lionel Atwill. Saturday, March 10, 1916, she fell on an icy sidewalk on the way to the Majestic Theater, and dislocated her left arm. A painful injury with the bones of her forearm bulging through her elbow. Dr. Max Thorek knew what to do immediately: one quick stab of pain and the arm was back in its socket. Lillie didn't miss a performance.

"You're a real tough cookie, Lady de Bathe," said the Majestic's manager, and she liked both the wording and the sentiment.

In the fall the management asked her to run the Coast Orpheum circuit. Lionel Atwill had left her company, so Lillie decided on Alfred Lunt, the boy Laura Hope Crews brought to her rooms at the Savoy Hotel on Fifth Avenue. Lunt recalls the meeting vividly: "It was late afternoon and I shall never forget her silhouette against the sky, exactly as she looked in her early photographs. It was a beautiful profile. I must admit that in full light some of the aura was dissipated, but she was still a handsome woman, rather big, with the bluest eyes I have ever seen. She used to bead them with blue wax for the stage. Her hair was browny gold but the color, she said, varied with her mood." For a young man serving his stage apprenticeship, acting opposite Mrs. Langtry was a tremendous experience. He learned his part on the way out to San Francisco, and they opened after one rehearsal.

Hollywood was just then being established as *the* film city. As a visiting celebrity, Lillie was one of a number asked to attend the grand opening of the Municipal Dance Hall. She stood next to Anita King, a current film star, in the receiving line to shake hands with some sort of contest winners. One was a waitress, rather excited at the prospect of meeting Lady de Bathe, a member of the British nobility. Afterward she exclaimed, "My gawd, can you beat that? It was some dame from the Orpheum circuit." Lillie enjoyed the story.

She was used to these raw young things, these brash girls with no respect for people older than themselves. Some played with her on the same bill, and it was asking a lot for a performer in the thirty-fifth year of her stage life to put up with their rudeness. At Keith's in Louisville, a pretty tango dancer stood in the wings as Lillie awaited to go on. "Where did they find *her?*" she said to her partner in a loud stage whisper. "This game is getting fierce. There's no chance for real talent any more." Lillie exchanged looks with her supporting players. Then she went out to give a tight, deft performance that put *Ashes* over as it hadn't been done in weeks. Coming off stage to tumultuous applause, she shot a triumphant glance at the dancer as if to say, "Match *that*, kitten, if you can." It was risky to put the Jersey Lily on her mettle.

Alfred Lunt played with her for twenty-six weeks on the whole Orpheum circuit. He noticed how her performance varied with her audiences. For most she put out, but for some who clearly preferred the trained dogs and patter comedians, she let her boredom with *Ashes* show. In a letter home, Lunt said:

428

Mrs. Langtry in the best of sashes
Every evening turns to "ashes."
Many times the house grows chilly
But no one dares to poke the Lily.

In Detroit reporters who associated Lillie with Lillian Russell and Mrs. Leslie Carter thought she looked better than either. And she was always good for a feature story as she talked in her friendly, unaffected way.

"It was so kind of you to mention that I don't wear stays. What's the use? If you squeeze it in at one point, it only comes out at the other."

She took Clement Le Breton's scissor-censored letter from her purse and spoke of the Zeppelin raids, the terrifying darkness of London at night, and the relief at having no blackouts in the United States.

"Will I return to England? I don't know. My husband is a general's chauffeur somewhere in France, one of my brothers-in-law is at the front, another is in charge of the ambulance train running from the trenches to Calais. But there is a play waiting for me, if I decide to return. I'll think it over."

"Is this really your farewell tour, Mrs. Langtry?"

Lillie laughed. "Oh, that's one of Mr. Keith's little jokes."

Best of all were the late sessions after the last performance with old friends, reporters, and actors dropping in on her dressing room. Lillie sat on a trunk, a hostess in her salon, and talked in her low, deep, soft, flowing voice.

"I do not regret one moment of all my life. I have lived. And when one has lived, one does not regret. There is no time. Ah, me! those mad days. A country girl fresh from the Isle of Jersey thrust by a freak of fortune into the heart of London's gayest society. I was beautiful and now, because I am old, I take no shame in so saying. They saw me, those reckless seekers of beauty, and in a night I was famous. How they flocked about then! The titled beaus and the titled ladies, literary, artistic London sought out Lillie Langtry, and I hailed them as friends. On one night of my début the Prince of Wales, the Princess, and the duchesses of London came to see me, and they loved me for what I was and what I gave them."

The lights were dim and there was something haunting about this woman. Noises drifted in from the street, the laughter and shuffling about of other performers changing to go back to their hotels, stagehands moving sets, members of the orchestra putting away instruments. They passed the door, stopped, looked in, and stayed on to listen. At a lull in the spellbinding, very carefully someone asked about Langtry, Texas.

"That is a page out of Bret Harte. A colorful, wonderful page. You wouldn't believe how the town was named for me and how I got the Limited to stop there half an hour years ago. I was met by the whole population, headed by the mayor, who wore revolvers at his belt and wanted to kiss me. He pointed to the town's leading saloon, 'The Jersey Lily,' and the cowboys came and shook hands while they blushed and rode madly away firing pistols. I wanted to give them a drinking fountain, but they told me they didn't drink water. It was a hot, dusty little town, but I loved it and I so wanted it to grow great and wonderful. But even if it didn't, I still love it."

Lillie sighed as she reached for a cigarette. The women murmured as she graciously accepted a light and inhaled deeply.

"What a cry it was from foggy London and the mincing men of fashion to that sun-blazed sky and wild freedom of man and beast. But each little chapter in its place. It has all gone to make my life, and I have lived. Ah, I have lived! I have known great things and wonderful persons, and I have known homage." She looked around the crowded room. "Does it seem boastful? I do not mean it so. I am a grandmother now, and that means age is creeping on, creeping on."

Lillie kept her vaudeville engagements back and forth across the Atlantic through 1917. The passage was increasingly hazardous and she was tired of *Ashes*. There was little to keep her at home. Horses and racing were out of the question with the country at war. The separation from her daughter was final. Jeanne had three sons and a daughter now. Lillie wanted to see them. Time might help, what little there was of it, and, thank God, the young were curious. Some day her grandchildren might come to her. She hoped so. They had good blood and a priceless legacy. Jeanne's husband had a staff job with the British Red Cross that took him to France, Switzerland, Russia, and America. He was now a Conservative M.P. from Croydon, and private secretary to Foreign Minister Arthur Balfour on various diplomatic missions. Indeed, Lillie had barely missed running into him in Washington this year. He would never attend vaudeville. But if they'd met, would he have shaken hands, nodded, or looked the other way?

Lillie finished her life story for the Hearst Syndicate at a record price of $1,000 each for ten installments, supposedly as much as Rudyard Kipling, the highest-paid writer, received per chapter. Ramsey Morris, who managed John Drew, helped her in the writing and editing. It was called *Myself and Others,* the first installment appearing in the *Cosmopolitan* for May, 1917. More personal than the *Green Book* articles she had prepared with Archie Bell, but still discreet.

Writing one's memoirs seemed to put one on the shelf. Perhaps that was another reason she had put it off so long. Lillie had an urge to settle down, but not in America—nor in England. The public still thought of her. It was odd to read that the new beauties—Marion Davies, Justine Johnston, Phoebe Foster, Irene Bordoni, and Olive Thomas—were taking the place of Lillian Russell, Lillie Langtry, and Maxine Elliott. Good heavens, she thought, it's about time.

Crossing the Atlantic in 1914, 1915, and 1916 had always been hazardous, and in late 1917 the German submarines were out in force. Most transport was by convoy and restricted to essential personnel. Lillie was anxious to get home. She managed to book passage on a small Spanish-line boat, which she considered a relic of the Armada. She landed at Vigo, Spain, after a long passage, unnerving because of discomforts, rats, and cockroaches though not submarines. She went on to Madrid by train and spent a week looking at the Goyas in the Prado Gallery, then crossed into France and went on to London.

In December she played at the Coliseum in *Overtones,* an indifferent sketch not too well received. Her last appearance on any stage was again at the Coliseum, early in 1918, in a short piece called *Blame the Cinema.* It was much too soon for anyone to know all that would be blamed on that medium, but Lillie had a chance to show her remarkable composure under fire during that last engagement. She was on stage just as bombs struck nearby buildings. Bits of plaster were dislodged upon the audience. More bombs fell so close that a disturbance in the balcony made the performance inaudible. People stirred in their seats, ready to run in hysteria.

Lillie kept on steadily with her lines, holding the cast together, and urging the actors to increase their volume. The explosions had no effect on her. At the conclusion of the sketch, there was an ovation.

"You were magnificent, Lady de Bathe!" said the stage manager, squeezing her hands. "They were getting ready to bolt for it, and your coolness prevented a panic."

"This is the real danger spot, isn't it?" she said, pointing to the glass roof over the stage.

"I'm afraid so. The auditorium roof is protected with sandbags."

"Then I don't know why the audience felt bothered."

"Not everyone has your nerves, Lady de Bathe. But you may cancel your appearance if you wish. After all, such an upsetting experience—"

Lillie looked the man up and down. "Don't let us fuss, *please*. I shall fulfill my contract, no more nor less."

Lillie was glad to return to the comfort and the quiet of Kentford, where she spent most of the last year of the war raising acres of vegetables with the help of village girls. The armistice was overdue good news. The moment the blacksmith bellowed the news from house to house, she rushed tempestuously to London "to join the celebration." Then came the let-

432

down, the inevitable malaise that follows everything coming to a dead stop after a period of frenzied activity.

As she put it: "After a world-shaking cataclysm such as we had just been through, ideas and plans which before had seemed of such paramount importance now seemed trivial by comparison, and for the time being I found my interest lapse in both acting and racing. I felt weary of the responsibility of owning houses, and was glad enough, when I found eager purchasers, to pass mine on to others."

A combination postwar depression and hangover experienced by many people, but hard somehow to explain to Shuggy. He had been through hell again—getting boils from the general's car cushions or whatever—and he wanted to live.

"You mean you're giving it all up?" He was almost speechless with astonishment. "Good God, Lillie! That's what we fought for—to come back to things as they were."

"Then you're in for disillusion. They're not and we're not."

"But the stage and racing! How can you give *them* up?"

"Like that." She snapped her fingers. "I've loved them both and may again. But I don't want them just now, Shuggy. What are you going to do, now that the war is over and you're your own man again?"

"I don't know. That is, I thought that you—that I—I don't know."

"Let's go to Nice, to Monaco where it's warm and cheerful and the colors are bright."

Southern France had always been an enchanting land to Lillie. She hadn't been in Monaco long before she decided to buy a house there. She had left England determined to shed responsibilities, but in every land she liked she always had to have her own home. The English phase, the American phase, and now Monaco. And the end? Oh, no, surely not yet. She had plenty to do. She might return to the stage. There were still producers after her. If a good part in a good play came along . . .

Then there was Shuggy. Sometimes these things didn't work out so well. She wouldn't say he'd been the best of husbands,

433

nor she the best of wives. But they had been an unusual combination. They'd done fairly well, considering. She didn't think he'd leave her for another woman—not legally. At least she was luckier than Jennie Cornwallis-West. George had left her after thirteen years to marry Mrs. Patrick Campbell, a handsome woman and a good actress.

"The house you've bought." Shuggy was puzzled. "It's rather small, I notice, and you never consulted me. You don't want me to live there?"

"We need separate establishments, you and I, Shuggy, the way we're used to. I'm going to live with my companion, Mrs. Peat. You might say an old lady with an old lady. But I would like you close by. I saw just the house for you in Nice."

"Do you want a divorce, Lillie?" he said with unaccustomed bluntness.

"Don't let's fuss, please. We can talk about it some time. You enjoy sailing, don't you? And having your own motor car and entertaining pretty French actresses and American heiresses?" He had the grace to redden, and she laughed. "You see, I know you, Shuggy, as well as I know myself. We can be the best of friends and remain husband and wife."

"In name only, eh?"

She gave a low, throaty laugh without coyness. "That depends on a lot of things, doesn't it?"

Lillie did not want anything like the conventional, luxuriously styled villas of Monaco. She had chosen a small house that had belonged to one of the casino croupiers. She named it Villa Le Lys and put her own inimitable stamp on the bungalow halfway down the ravine of Sainte Dévoté as she had in Norfolk Street, Pont Street, Tedworth Square, Kentford, 23rd Street, Lake County, and countless hotel rooms across England and the United States. A new bedroom here, a delightful kitchen made over from a spare room there, two small rooms combined for a living room, a view of the ocean, and everything remodeled in her charming good taste.

She had saved her best things and now had them shipped over from England. The exquisite painted dining-room furniture, the Louis XVI fauteuils and settee, a valuable tapestry

434

and cabinet of the same period, a bust of Diana, a Brittany wardrobe, a Boulle linen cupboard, a lovely collection of colored glass, and a Viennese dinner service. These things fitted perfectly into her new home, along with souvenirs, bibelots, and mementoes of all kinds. The oil portrait by Poynter, engravings of her by Millais, sketches by Frank Miles, a silver épergne inscribed to Sir Thomas Le Breton, a Georgian tray inscribed to the dean, paintings of and trophies won by her horses, signed photographs of King Edward, Queen Alexandra, King George, Queen Mary, and many other famous people she had known. From her turquoise-and-gold dressing table set to Roy Bean's revolver, Lillie was surrounded by loved and familiar objects.

She spent most of her time working in the extensive garden she brought to bloom on the side of the ravine. In an impossibly steep place beyond cultivation, flowers and vines came unbidden like guests certain of their welcome. Graceful alpines, stocks, maidenhair ferns, wild orchids, wallflowers, bluebells, snapdragons, and masses of geraniums. Everything grew in the gentle invigorating climate. She planted roses, iris, mimosa, lavender, datura, cyclamen, primula, rosemary, heather, azalea, cineraria, and lemon trees. All bloomed and prospered under her loving hands.

She was never happier than among her flowers. A little thing, such as winning a medal from the Horticultural Society of Nice for having the best garden on the Riviera, gave her pleasure. The Jersey Lily never remained an amateur in anything she engaged in. A ribbon, a citation out of proportion to other triumphs, yet her satisfaction at excelling was intensely real.

Her rock-clinging house with its mountainous background and vista of the blue Mediterranean was all she desired in beauty, combining the best of Jersey and California, while down below was a little Paris. She liked both Monacos, the tinsel excitement of the Casino and Sporting Club for amusement, and the company of interesting permanent residents for conversation and leisure. She belonged to the Sporting Club and, whenever she felt inclined, visited the Casino and indulged her old passion for gambling. She was adroit at the tables, her intuitive sense often paying off as people watched her curiously.

The past mattered so little now. She despised people who lived in the past. They were already dead and didn't know it. To put one's hand in rich soil, to cultivate and work it, then be rewarded by nature was a fulfillment that made age bearable and carried with it a needed sense of accomplishment and continuity. She was out of things, a faithful horse put out to pasture, and she didn't mind it.

Lillie had many friends in Monaco. Reporters still visited her for nostalgic feature stories, professionals dropped in on her, and producers sought her out. Young people to whom she was a legend came to confirm the legend. They were always charmed. Others wanted advice about acting and a stage career, and Lillie enjoyed helping them. Shuggy came from time to time. She was working on her autobiography. And there was always the presence of her companion, the thoughtful, self-effacing Mrs. Mathilde Marie Peat.

Lillie looked forward to the yearly visits of Alfred Lunt and his lovely, talented wife, Lynn Fontanne. Mrs. Langtry was a landmark in his career, so he felt that visiting her was as pleasantly obligatory as calling on a favorite aunt. A great lady, the last of her race, he said, the retired dowager queen of the theater—regal, fascinating, imperishable. Miss Fontanne thought her "like a beautiful, old, portly country squire."

Lillie's serenity gave her a new perspective on her husband. Having his own villa in Nice and bound to Lillie only by name, he behaved like an emancipated gallant tossing his whims like quoits. His genial polish gave him a popularity of his own. He was Sir Hugo de Bathe, the gay knight, the clever, amusing Shuggy who gave a fillip to Riviera house parties. In his fifties now, chipper as ever, he had a passion for pretty girls many years his junior. It was turnabout in a way, and Lillie couldn't blame him, but his escapades made distasteful news copy. The press gave all the details of his love for Meroud Guiness, the young daughter of Mr. and Mrs. Benjamin Guiness, "formerly of Washington Square now of Belgravia."

"Do you want to marry her?" Lillie asked.

"Of course not. She doesn't expect it."

436

"Worry about the parents, never the girl."

"What a mess!" He smoothed his mustache and stroked a rough place under his chin. "They keep starching my shirts when I tell them not to. Do you think you could find me a decent laundry, Lillie? My French just doesn't do the job."

"I'll look next time I'm in Nice. Now come see my garden before lunch. And you are staying, aren't you? I'm sure Miss Guiness won't mind if you eat lunch with your wife."

Their visits were always amicable. If Lillie was faintly aware that her interest in Hugo was on the maternal side, she shrugged that off. As she told a friend, "Somehow, whenever we meet, there's so much to talk about we never get around to discussing divorce." Shuggy was contented as an ageless playboy; he would have to tire of the role before he could seriously consider divorce.

Lillie's autobiography, *The Days I Knew,* appeared in 1925. With a foreword by Richard Le Gallienne, it was a pleasant hodgepodge of recollections and anecdotes, laced with great names. It glossed over her life in skillful evasion, circling the famous episodes (no mention of Freddie, a single vague reference to "A.B."), more important for what it did not say than for what it did. For all that, it had a certain winning quality. Again Bertie would have found no fault at his part in the days Lillie knew.

She was glad her memoirs were done with. Literary narcissism bored her, and she was sick of looking at portraits of herself in younger days. Standards of beauty had changed dramatically, the big, long-haired, voluptuous, full curved woman giving way to the willowy, flat-chested, bobbed-haired. Sorting the photographs had confirmed her ideas about the exaggerated opinions of her looks. In so many she looked a little ridiculous, so did her clothes, so did the past. And so would future years laugh at this present day.

Lillie visited London every year or so. She went to the theater with Mrs. Peat and found that she hadn't been forgotten there. Someone always pointed and she was recognized in her box. People stood up to see her. Soon everyone in the house would be clapping. It brought a flush to her cheeks, and her lips trembled as she acknowledged the tribute. A wonderful, heartwarming thing, but hardly comparable to seeing her grandchildren. The eldest child, then a schoolboy, remembers being "rather overawed" at meeting her. Later on he came to see her in Monaco with his brother and found her "remarkably good company."

They had come to her as she had hoped, these children who were like flowers flourishing in her garden, sweet, colorful, and fresh. She loved them for their innocent youth, unspoiled good nature, and Langtry heritage. Lillie was seventy-four now, and no denying it. Newsmen came on her birthday, gratefully putting down her statement that she'd spent the five happiest years of her life in the 23rd Street house.

The next time she made the news occurred in 1927. It came about because Viscount Herbert John Gladstone, son of the Prime Minister, was sued for libel by a Captain Peter Wright, who had written a debunking book called *Portraits and Memories*. In it, Wright had accused the Grand Old Man of English politics of being a moral hypocrite and having had Lillie Langtry as his mistress among others. Gladstone's seventy-three-year-old son had retaliated by calling Wright "a liar, coward, and foul fellow," resulting in the suit. Indignant at the accusation, Lillie sent off a cable to the present Gladstone, reading, "I strongly repudiate the slanderous accusation of Peter Wright," and this was read into the trial testimony.

The storm set in motion by the case upset her, but it was pleasant to be remembered. She worried about the reaction in Monaco, now that she had made a quiet place for herself in the community. She wondered if she would be ostracized at the Sporting Club. Everyone rallied to her. Women friends kissed her against a background of tables covered with green. Friendly, commendatory cables came from England and America.

"Sympathy is charming," she said to a newsman, "but it does not make up for pain. I have always been willing to take the blame for the things I have done. It is hard to have blame fastened on me for things I never did."

438

She still read a lot, gardened, played at the casino, and danced occasionally with the flattering gigolos in Monte Carlo hotels. Her famous hair was bobbed now, the Langtry knot long forgotten. She'd had it dyed, and it was rather scrubby as a result. She accepted invitations to dinner only if she could wear a hat.

The newspapers, the obituaries, made her feel her lonely eminence. How few of the old ones were left! Modjeska had gone in 1909, dear Tree in 1917, Sarah Bernhardt in 1923 at seventy-nine, and Ellen Terry this year (1928) at an incredible eighty. King George had made Nell a Dame of the British Empire before she died.

Actors were accepted socially now. Irving had showed the way, and they had buried him in Westminster Abbey. Sir Squire Bancroft, Sir Charles Wyndham, Sir Johnston Forbes-Robertson, Sir Beerbohm Tree. Wasn't it an elegant profession now! Dame Madge Kendal, Dame Genevieve Ward, probably Dame Olga Nethersole some day when the *Sapho* scandal became dead enough, but never a Dame Langtry from the king— but, thank God, a Lady de Bathe all on her own. An amusing business, and she was forever grateful to Shuggy.

And Jeanne was a Lady now, too. Both the Langtry women were ladies.

The thought of death had rarely troubled Lillie until the serious illness of her friend the Duc de la Rochefoucauld. She was fond of the Duchesse and brought meals from the Villa Le Lys to the Monaco hospital, where the Duchesse kept vigil. Lillie did all she could after the Duc's death, and before the funeral, his calm, sleeping appearance, his look of effortless serenity soothed her anxiety.

"I didn't believe death was like that—so peaceful," she confessed.

Lillie visited London in the fall of 1928, posing for her seventy-fifth-birthday picture and seeing friends. There she suddenly fell ill of bronchitis and pleurisy. She was put to bed in her rooms at the Cadogan Hotel on Sloane Street, around the corner from Pont Street—by coincidence familiar ground, since in alterations the hotel had incorporated part of her handsome old home there. Lillie failed rapidly. A worried Mrs. Peat called Jeanne. Her lawyer was summoned to draw up another will. Harold Ommanney and Major John Thompson were named co-executors and trustees. The manager of the Cadogan Hotel was one of the witnesses.

The crisis passed, however, and Lillie convalesced slowly. London was cold, gloomy, and fogbound. She was impatient to return to the Villa Le Lys.

"I was lucky," she told friends, "after being so bad I could hear the angels singing. But I must hurry back to my house and flowers in Monaco. The most lasting and pure gladness comes to me from my gardens."

She intended to live on many more years.

Mathilde Peat looked on her with affectionate admiration that had increased over their years of friendship. Lillie was still a-doing, neither looking nor acting as a woman is supposed to in her seventy-sixth year. But then she had never behaved as expected. And how gay she was at the Ambassadeurs! Her friends responded to her good humor and flashing wit, listening appreciatively to the ideas bubbling from her keen mind. Lillie was in charge and they were content that she be. All around the tables people stared and whispered. Who was that? Who? Mrs. Langtry? The Jersey Lily? Not really! No more than her companions, they couldn't take their eyes off her.

"That was a marvelous luncheon, wasn't it, dear?" she said to Mrs. Peat, as they started back to the Villa Le Lys. "But that photographer stopping us to snap our picture. Why in the world should anyone want to photograph an old woman like me?"

She smiled as she asked the question. Knowing it was rhetorical, Mrs. Peat said nothing.

The winter of 1929 was one of the coldest Europe had experienced in many years. The wind never seemed to stop blowing. Colds, influenza, and pneumonia were common all over the Continent. In sunny Monaco people were shivering. Weakened by her severe illness in London, Lillie caught a chill.

440

Mrs. Peat called a doctor. The diagnosis was influenza; rest, medication, and absolute quiet were prescribed.

As good a patient as she had always been a traveler, Lillie did not complain. She stayed calm and cheerful, obeying the doctor's orders, but Mrs. Peat sensed a withdrawal that made her uneasy. She mentioned this to the doctor after his daily examination and did not receive an answer that satisfied her. After seeing him to the door she went back to Lillie. She straightened pillows, then slipped into a familiar pattern of bromidic remarks.

"Well, well," she said overbrightly. "How nice you look today! Even the doctor spoke of your appearance."

"Said I was beautiful, did he? He's being paid for treatment, not flattery."

"He did say you were much better."

Lillie shook her beautiful head. "I know I am at the end. I shall never get better, dear." The fateful words came out casually.

"You mustn't talk like that."

"Doctors are like kind critics letting an actor down easily. Don't you think an actor knows when he gives a bad performance?"

"Just because you're sick now doesn't mean that you won't get—"

"Don't let's fuss, please," Lillie interrupted impatiently, sweetly. "I'm not afraid, and I never liked long last acts. Feed the dogs, won't you? I hate to hear them barking like that."

All that week the weather continued blustery and frigid. Lillie's condition remained unchanged until one night, the coldest thus far, she was much weaker. No one could spend much time with the French poodles now. Their yapping echoed through the villa, mournful and distracting. Outside the wind surged over the Chapelle Sainte Dévoté, up the ravine by the Villa Le Lys, through Monte Carlo bending the trees double and whisking powdery sand along the beaches fronting the heaving Mediterranean. It shook the windows. Blasts of icy air leaked around the sash, making Mathilde Peat shiver in her bathrobe. Goose-pimples rose on her body and her toes curled in her slippers as she bent over Lillie's bed.

"I've called the doctor, but he's been delayed," she said hoarsely, gathering her robe over her thin shoulders with blue, trembling fingers.

"Don't bother the poor man on such a night."

"Is there anything I can do?" She passed her hand over the feverish forehead. "Oh, Lillie!"

"I don't think so."

Mrs. Peat moistened Lillie's forehead with a cologne-dipped cloth.

"It's terrible for you to be alone like this. Don't you want Hugo? I'm sure he'd come if I called him—if he knew."

"Let Shuggy be." Lillie smiled, a thoughtful, inward smile.

"Someone ought to be here besides me. Your own family. Jeanne—"

"No." The voice was unexpectedly firm. "Nobody."

"You're going to get better. Only yesterday the doctor said so."

"He's a fool." The voice was fainter now. "I told you I know I am at the end."

A gust of wind shook the windows. In a back room the poodles set up a frenzied lament. Mrs. Peat's cupped hands joined in prayer.

"No," she insisted. "No."

"I should be able to manage quite nicely," said Lillie weakly. "I did it often enough—practiced, rehearsed, did it over and over before thousands. Now there's just you."

She coughed harshly, the paroxysm racking her body, sending her still-beautiful head lolling. The barking was a doleful chorus now.

Mrs. Peat wrung her hands, listening worriedly for the doctor. "It's only a seizure." She reached for the cologne cloth. "The doctor said it is always worse at night."

Lillie muttered something she couldn't hear. Lillie's eyes dimmed, and her pallor, under the high spots of fever on her wasted cheeks, was more pronounced. Her lips moved as she

442

fought for air, struggled to speak. Mrs. Peat leaned far over the bed to bring her ear close.

"I am going, dear. I am very, very sorry, but I am going. Good-by."

As if at a signal, both of the little dogs barked frantically. The curtains fluttered on cue with the rattling of windows. Gusts of glacial air swept the room, and Mrs. Peat's teeth chattered. With streaming eyes she took Lillie's limp hand and felt her pulse. It was still there, a stuttering beat. She went to the dressing table without thinking and took up an elegant turquoise-and-gold hand mirror. She held this over the blue lips and was encouraged by the misty spot that appeared on the glass. Then she hurried to the telephone in the next room, noticing that the mantel clock was striking two. The dogs were barking louder than ever as she jiggled the hook for the operator.

Three doctors responded to the last summons. But Lillie, as she had known, was beyond medical care. She died around five o'clock on that chill Tuesday morning, February 12, 1929, of a heart attack brought on by influenza and complications.

Even if Lillie had truly thought herself forgotten, the obituaries, articles, and features in newspapers all over the world would have astounded her. In every case, her death made the front pages with her picture and a long story detailing her career and perpetuating every legend. More than that, the newspapers all carried editorials about her.

Lillie left a personal estate with a net value of 47,445 pounds, 18 shillings, and two pence. Outside of bequests to various friends, including a generous one to Mathilde Peat, Lillie left most of her estate in trust for her four grandchildren. Besides, they were each remembered with some treasured personal possession. To Jeanne she gave only her silver and mother-of-pearl dessert service. And her servants were each left a year's wages, in addition to whatever was due them. Lastly, Emilie Charlotte de Bathe wished "not to be cremated but to be buried at St. Saviour's in the Island of Jersey."

Hugo wasn't mentioned in her will, but that didn't mean he hadn't been remembered, did it?

On February 23, 1929, Lillie was buried in the churchyard close to the rectory in which she had been born, on her beloved "quiet island." Her coffin had lain for the night covered with lilies of the valley and amaryllis lilies. Their fragrance filled the church during the ceremony. Everything was as she would have remembered it, except that the big rectory's thatched roof had been replaced by a slate one. Inside, her name, Lillie Le Breton, was still inscribed on the window, just as she had scratched it on the glass with her engagement ring the night before her marriage to Edward Langtry in 1874. (It remains to this day.)

After the service, a small procession of islanders followed the coffin to the site under a large tree, near the stones marking the graves of the dean, Mrs. Le Breton, and Reginald. The sky was a clear blue, the sun warm in spite of the brisk wind—a typical Jersey winter's day. The chief mourners, according to the newspapers, were her daughter and her eldest grandson. Sir Hugo Gerald de Bathe was not present, and Lillie would have seen no need for him to be there either.

The islanders clustered in knots after it was all over. They watched the daughter and grandson leave quietly. One said it was fitting that Mrs. Langtry was back in Jersey, in St. Saviour's where it had all begun, lying close to those she had loved best.

Across the way, old George Merritt limped through the graveyard, a small bouquet of flowers in his hand. He put it on the freshly turned earth, near a spray of lilies, then stood cap to his breast, white gnarled head bent in prayer. George was well known in Jersey. He was eighty-six and never tired of telling people he had been captain of Edward Langtry's *Red Gauntlet*. They waited for him. George began talking about Lillie just as they'd hoped.

"Why, I remember like it was yesterday. They got a special license so they could be married early and catch the tide. Black as pitch it was, then down to the Royal Yacht Hotel in St. Helier for the wedding breakfast with postilions riding in front of the carriage. Oh, she was *beautiful,* merry and gay. Looking

444

like a princess and him looking at her like a knight does his lady fair. The Lily loved to tease. I used to carry her from the yacht to land where there was no pier. How she used to fidget!" He laughed to himself. "She'd pretend she was falling into the water. She'd scream to rattle me, wriggling all the time in my arms." He held them out as if he could still feel his lovely burden. "Then she'd break out laughing and I—and I— Oh, she was a one!"

The men filled their pipes and nodded. On the new grave below them, the lilies fluttered in the breeze like emblems. The show was over. The lights were dimmed, the audience gone. Now the few remaining stragglers turned away, still discussing the star ("the world's sweetheart," "woman of the century") and her farewell performance.

What a woman!

bibliography

Ayer, Margaret Hubbard, *The Three Lives of Harriet Hubbard Ayer*. Philadelphia and New York: J. B. Lippincott Co., 1957.

Baruch, Bernard, *Baruch, My Own Story*. New York: Henry Holt & Co., Inc., 1957.

Beerbohm, Max, *The Works of Max Beerbohm*. New York: Dodd, Mead & Co., 1922.

Bodley, John Edward Courtenay, *Mr. Gladstone Prepares to Meet Mrs. Langtry*. New York: Brooks Brothers, 1925.

Booth, John Bennion, *A "Pink 'Un" Remembers*. London: T. Werner Laurie, Ltd., 1937.

Bulloch, John M., *The Last Baird, Laird of Auchmedden and Strichen—The Case of Mr. Abington*. Aberdeen: privately printed, 1934.

Clunn, Harold P., *The Face of London*. London: Spring Books, n. d.

Corbett, James J., *The Roar of the Crowd*. Garden City, New York: Garden City Publishing Co., 1926.

Cornwallis-West, George, *Edwardian Hey-Days*. New York: G. P. Putnam's and Sons, 1931.

Cornwallis-West, Mrs. George, *The Reminiscences of Lady Randolph Churchill*. New York: The Century Company, 1908.

Cowles, Virginia, *Gay Monarch—The Life and Pleasures of Edward VII*. New York: Harper and Brothers, 1956.

Croffut, William A., *An American Procession* (1855-1914). Boston: Little, Brown & Co., 1931.

Dale, Alan, *Familiar Chats With Queens of the Stage*. New York: G. W. Dillingham, 1890.

Forbes-Robertson, Johnston, *A Player Under Three Reigns*. London: T. Fisher Unwin, Ltd., 1925.

Frewen, Moreton, *Melton Mowbray and Other Memories*. London: Herbert Jenkins, Ltd., 1924.

Frohman, Daniel, *Encore*. New York: Lee Furman, Inc., 1937.
———, *Daniel Frohman Presents*. New York: Kendall & Sharp, 1935.
Gagey, Edmond, *The San Francisco Stage*. New York: Columbia University Press, 1950.
History of the Providence Stage 1762-1891. Providence, Rhode Island: 1891.
Hughes, Glenn, *A History of the American Theatre 1700-1950*. New York: Samuel French, 1951.
James, Henry, *The Scenic Art*. New Brunswick, New Jersey: Rutgers University Press, 1948.
Kouwenhoven, John A., *The Columbia Historical Portrait of New York*. Garden City, New York: Doubleday & Co., 1953.
Kraus, Rene, *Young Lady Randolph*. New York: G. P. Putnam's Sons, 1943.
Langtry, Lillie (Lady de Bathe), *The Days I Knew*. New York: George H. Doran Co., 1925.
Lawton, Mary, *Queen of Cooks—And Some Kings (The Story of Rosa Lewis)*. New York: Boni & Liveright, 1925.
Leslie, Amy, *Some Players—Personal Sketches*. Chicago: Herbert S. Stone & Co., 1899.
Leslie, Anita, *The Remarkable Mr. Jerome*. New York: Henry Holt & Co., 1954.
Leslie, Shane, *Sketches in Sublime Failure*. London: Ernest Benn Ltd., 1932.
Leverton, W. H., *Through the Box Office Window—Memories of 50 Years at the Haymarket Theatre*. London: T. Werner Laurie, Ltd., 1932.
Lloyd, Everett, *The Law West of the Pecos*. San Antonio, Texas: The University Press, 1931.
Macqueen-Pope, W., *The Gaiety—Theatre of Enchantment*. London: W. H. Allen, 1949.
Maugham, W. Somerset, *A Writer's Notebook*. Garden City, New York: Doubleday & Co., 1949.
Maurois, André, *Edward VII and His Times*. London: Cassell & Co., Ltd., 1933.
Michael, Edward (in collaboration with J. B. Booth), *Tramps of a Scamp*. London: T. Werner Laurie, Ltd., 1928.
Modjeska, Helena, *Memories and Impressions of Helena Modjeska*. New York: The Macmillan Company, 1910.

447

Morrell, Parker, *Diamond Jim—The Life and Times of James Buchanan Brady*. New York: Simon and Schuster, 1934.

————, *Lillian Russell—The Era of Plush*. New York: Random House, 1940.

Pearl, Cyril, *The Girl With the Swansdown Seat*. Indianapolis and New York: Bobbs-Merrill Co., 1956.

Pearson, Hesketh, *Labby—The Life and Character of Henry Labouchère*. New York: Harper and Brothers, 1937.

————, *The Last Actor Managers*. London: Methuen & Co., 1950.

————, *The Man Whistler*. New York: Harper and Brothers, 1952.

————, *Oscar Wilde, His Life and Wit*. New York and London: Harper and Brothers, 1946.

Private Life of Edward VII, by a Member of the Royal Household. New York: D. Appleton, 1901.

Robertson, William Graham, *Life Was Worth Living—The Reminiscences of William Graham Robertson*. New York: Harper and Brothers, 1931.

Rogers, Agnes and Frederick Lewis Allen, *The American Procession*. New York and London: Harper and Brothers, 1933.

Rovere, Richard H., *Howe & Hummel*. New York: Farrar, Straus & Co., 1947.

Ruggles, Eleanor, *Prince of Players*. New York: W. W. Norton, 1953.

Sonnichsen, C. L., *Roy Bean: The Law West of the Pecos*. New York: The Macmillan Company, 1943.

Stanley, Louis T., *The London Season*. Boston: Houghton Mifflin Co., 1956.

Terry, Ellen, *The Story of My Life*. New York: The McClure Company, 1908.

Tharp, Louise Hall, *Three Saints and a Sinner*. Boston: Little, Brown & Co., 1956.

Winter, William, *The Wallet of Time*. New York: Moffat, Yard & Co., 1913.

Worth, Jean Philippe, *A Century of Fashion*. Boston: Little, Brown & Co., 1928.

MAGAZINES AND PERIODICALS

Bolce, Harold, "The Passing of the Jersey Lily." *Theatre Magazine,* April, 1929.

Golden, Sylvia B., "The Romance of the Jersey Lily." *Theatre Magazine,* November and December, 1930.

Goss, Helen Rocca, "Lily Langtry and Her California Ranch."

Quarterly of the Historical Society of Southern California,
June, 1955.

Hughes, C., "Lily Langtry: The Passion Flower." *Coronet,* January,
1950.

Kropotkin, Princess Alexandra, "The Jersey Lily—The Life Story
of the Lovely Langtry." *Liberty Magazine,* five parts beginning
December 14, 1929.

Lake, S. N., "Vinegaroon and the Jersey Lily." *The Saturday Evening Post,* February 7, 1931.

O'Connor, T. P., "The London of Lillie Langtry." *Living Age,*
April 18, 1925.

Weiss, David, "I Am the Law." *Sports Illustrated,* January 27, 1958.

"Beauty as a Career." *The Nation,* February 27, 1929.

"How the Jersey Lily Doted on the Gee-Gees." *The Literary Digest,*
April 24, 1926.

"The Jersey Lily as a Later Helen of Troy." *The Literary Digest,*
March 2, 1929.

Also other books and periodicals; microfilms of the *New York
Times*; letters of Mrs. Langtry, and the Townsend Walsh and
Robinson Locke scrapbooks in the Theatre Collection of the New
York Public Library; hundreds upon hundreds of newspaper and
magazine clippings from England and the United States in that
same collection; and many news clippings in the Theatre Collection
of the Museum of the City of New York.

index

451

452